IRONS OF THE SOUTH

West Ham United in the Southern League 1900/01 to 1914/15

John Powles

A SoccerData Publication

Published in Great Britain by Tony Brown,
4 Adrian Close, Beeston, Nottingham NG9 6FL.
Telephone 0115 973 6086. E-mail soccer@innotts.co.uk
www.soccerdata.com

First published July 2008

The cover design is by Bob Budd.

John Powles was born and bred in West Ham and attended the local Plaistow Grammar School. He saw his first match at Upton Park at the age of eight in 1943 and has been a season-ticket holder at West Ham United for many years.

He wishes to thank John Northcutt and Stuart Allen for their statistical confirmation and assistance, Per Netzell, a Swedish 'Hammer', for some early sporting images, Steve Marsh for several photographs, David Twitchett for Memorial Grounds photos and the letters of the late Jimmy Kaine, the staff of the Newspaper Library at Colindale, and the Newham Local Studies Archives, particularly Jenny Moore-Collins.

SoccerData publications cover the historical and statistical aspects of the national game. The "Definitive" series of club histories include one on West Ham United. The "Match by Match" series will eventually list results, scorers and line-ups of every League and Cup game from 1888 to 1970. Historical texts include "The Lads of '23", an account of West Ham and Bolton's visit to Wembley for the 1923 FA Cup Final. Please write to the publisher for a catalogue.

Printed and bound by 4Edge, Hockley, Essex
www.4edge.co.uk

ISBN: 978-1-905891-08-5

CONTENTS

The original Hammers. A Thames Ironworks XI at the Memorial Grounds in September 1899. The Iron joined the Southern League Division Two in 1898-99 and won promotion to the First Division that season. In 1900-01 they were 14th out of 15 clubs. They resigned from the Southern League and were wound up in June 1900. On July 5th 1900, West Ham United FC was registered as a company and took the Irons' place in the Southern League. Herein is the first part of West Ham United's history, to 1915.

1900/01 A NEW DAWN

There is no doubt that Arnold Hills, the Managing Director and owner of the Thames Ironworks & Shipbuilding Company, was the man responsible for the founding of West Ham United FC. Without his initial funding, the club, originally known as Thames Ironworks FC, would not have existed. His original involvement began back in 1895, when he granted permission for a football section to be implemented at the Works as part of his Sports and Social club. Affiliation to the Football Association was acquired and over the next five years the club went from strength to strength. Although the club was originally strictly amateur, Arnold Hills, under pressure and strangely against his principles, agreed that the club should turn professional in 1898. Two years later, regretting his earlier decision, he decided that he could no longer continue with his involvement. This was partly due to a mixture of moral apprehension, and the realisation that being solely responsible for financing a professional football organisation could indeed become an economic disaster. In 1899 he had already spent heavily on acquiring an engineering company (John Penn & Sons) to add to the Shipbuilding title, and this could also have had an influence.

Arnold Hills

It became obvious that meetings had taken place regarding the choice of directors and how the project of setting up a new club was to be financed. As early as March 7th 1900, which was almost two months before the end of the 1899/1900 season a notice appeared in the 'West Ham Guardian': "...*it is announced that the committee of Thames Ironworks F C are to consider some sort of reorganisation. A proposal is evidently on the table. For one who has it on authority says 'it will, if adopted, undoubtedly be to the club's advantage.' This is good news. Supporters are tired of seeing the club so low down as fourth from the bottom*". (A reference to the standing of the Ironworks in the Southern League table at the time).

This was followed by a further notice in the same newspaper some six weeks later. *'The Ironworks' supporters......have for some weeks past been in low spirits. Ill-luck and bad results account for the depression, and there is a big balance on the wrong side of the treasurer's account to be faced at the end of the present season. This, however, will in all probability be wiped off by their generous president, Mr A.F. Hills. With regard to next season however, a meeting will be called, and the Mayor of West Ham will be asked to preside, at which gathering the locals will be asked to take up 500 £1 shares. If this amount be raised Mr A.F. Hills will add to it another £500, and, in addition, grant the use of the Memorial Grounds. Another condition is that all members of the team must be teetotallers. It is probable too, that the name of the club will be changed to Canning Town.'*

On Wednesday 18th April 1900 the 'West Ham Guardian' reported that the meeting was held *'at the Public Hall Canning Town, for the purpose of forming a limited liability company to carry on a professional football club in the borough. The Mayor presided during the first portion of the meeting. He said that he understood that they had met for the purpose of considering the desirability to form a football club for the borough of West Ham, into which the present Thames Ironworks club would be merged. Mr Hills's proposal was, he thought, to have a capital of £1,000, which he (the Mayor) thought would be sufficient for the purpose. Mr Hills had offered to take £500 worth of shares, and had also agreed to give the club the free use of the Memorial Grounds, and that would give them a capital start. Mr Hills had suggested a directorate of ten gentlemen, five to be appointed by himself. Personally he thought there was no doubt that the thing would be a great success.*

Mr Hills, the chairman of the Ironworks Football Club, said they had done very well until they branched out as a big professional team. Many of the teams of the Southern League were in low water, and the year altogether had been bad for football enthusiasts in Canning Town, and hoped there would be no difficulty in getting the money required. If they were to do well they must have a first-class professional team.

It was decided to form the company with a minimum capital of £1,000 in 2,000 ten shilling shares, and to call the new club the West Ham club, if the Association would allow it, but if not, to call it the Borough of West Ham club.

Mr Davis asked whether the proviso of Mr Hills that members of the team should be teetotallers was still binding.

Mr Osborne: Quite.

Many propositions and amendments followed as to what privileges shareholders should be entitled to in the shape of season tickets etc, but the matter was left to the general meeting of shareholders. A provisional committee of 12 gentlemen was then elected and at the conclusion of the meeting several applications were made for shares.'

When the prospectus was announced, it included a change that the directors had proposed to make regarding the cost of season tickets for shareholders for the 1900/01 season. It was that the admission to the ground, and open stand would be seven shillings and sixpence, and admission to ground, enclosure and grandstand, 10 shillings; to non-shareholders 10 shillings and sixpence and twelve shillings and sixpence respectively.

The 'West Ham Guardian', remarking on the decision to accept players who would be taken on providing they were teetotal stated:- *'There must be something remarkably timid, however, in the constitution of a football management that has to seek a remedy of this kind, and we shall watch the movements of the West Ham recruiting sergeant with great interest.'*

After a number of meetings there were ten directors elected to the club. They were all businessmen and tradesmen from the local area and the first chairman was Lazzeluer Johnson who was employed as a clerk at Thames Ironworks. All in all, considering the organisation that was involved, the founding of the new club had proved to be a smooth transition.

Undoubtedly the new professional club would not have come to fruition without Arnold Hills' generosity. He could merely have wound up the original club and walked away from it. He should never be forgotten in the sporting annals of the East End.

For what was effectively a new club, the directors had the task of recruiting a new playing staff. A number of the existing players from the Thames Ironworks club were taken on, with most still employed in various work at the shipyard. There were no less than eleven former Ironworks' players who would play a part over the coming season at some time or other. They were goalkeeper Tommy Moore, defenders Syd King, Charlie Craig, Charlie Dove and George Neil, half-backs Bob Allan and Roddy McEachrane, and forwards Fred Corbett, Frankie Taylor and Len Walker. The eleventh was Walter Tranter, who appeared for the Ironworks from 1896 until 1899, but then spent one season with Chatham, and then returned to sign for the new club of West Ham United.

Billy Grassam

Players of experience with other clubs of longer standing were also needed, and there was much transfer activity between the club's founding date of July 5th 1900 and the opening game on September 1st. The seven new additions included a strong Scottish flavour of four signings, with goalkeeper Hugh Monteith probably the most well known. He had seen experience with Celtic, Loughborough and latterly Bristol City and was to prove an outstanding acquisition. Both Billy Grassam, and Jimmy Reid who were forwards, came from Burslem Port Vale, and the fourth Scot was Luke Raisbeck, a centre half signed from Middlesbrough.

The most experienced addition was 24-year-old Fergus Hunt, who had appeared for Middlesbrough, Darwen and latterly Woolwich Arsenal. For those three clubs he had scored an overall total of 61 goals in 137 appearances. Another two forwards arrived – Fred Fenton, signed from Gainsborough Trinity, and Albert Kaye from Chatham, and formerly Sheffield Wednesday, with a record of 22 goals in 64 outings.

When the team that was now under the brand new title of West Ham United took the field for their opening match of the 1900/01 season, those spectators that were present noticed that the line-up included only four players that were familiar to them from the club's former banner of Thames Ironworks FC. They were Tranter, Craig, Dove and McEachrane, all competent players and included in the side on merit. The local reporter was able to get a few words with the captain, Roddy McEachrane in the dressing room before the match against Gravesend United. Asking the Scotsman what he thought the team's prospects were the conversation proceeded:-

'Yes, we have got a splendid team together, and we hope to do better than we did last year–we mean to have a good try, at any rate.'

'You think the prospects good then?'

'Yes; there is plenty of material in the team for excellent work during the coming season.'

'What do you think is the weakest spot in the team?'

'There is none as far as I can see. Of course, the men haven't been tried yet, but I think I can safely say the forwards will do well. In fact, all the players should do well.'

'Now, what about your own self?'

'Oh – what? Where I was born? Well, if you must have it, Inverness, up in Scotland. When I was yet in my teens I was to be found playing for the Inverness team as inside left forward. Then I came south, and played for the old Ironworks club. This my third season in this district, and I hope I shall have as successful a time as in the past.'

The reporter then collected up his pen and paper, and managed to get an interview with Welshman Lew Bowen, the secretary of the new club, although he was still employed by Thames Ironworks. After asking similar questions about team prospects, he was asked about the club itself. He replied:-

'We have been successful in getting a larger number of people to take up season tickets this year. As to the shares, we have about three hundred not taken up. As these are to be obtained at 10s. each, there ought to be no difficulty in disposing of the whole lot in a sport loving district like this. We trust we shall be well supported during the season.'

The attendance for the opening match was something of a disappointment when just 2,000 followers came through the gates. For what was effectively a 'new beginning' a little more interest was expected to have been shown. Admittedly the weather was not at all good for the time of the year, with drizzling rain at the start.

Gravesend United took the field first, and then came the 'Irons', as they had originally been known, and for many still would be (and still are). The committee had made a slight change to the team's colours. Instead of the light blue shirts, white shorts and claret stockings, a claret stripe went down the white shorts, and the stockings were all black. The light blue shirts remained.

The contest itself turned out to be very much a one-sided affair, with Fergus Hunt and Fred Fenton's blistering pace on the flanks being too much for the Kent side's rearguard, and in all honesty it could have been more than the 7-0 scoreline as Kaye was guilty of some glaring misses. As it was Billy Grassam notched four goals, and his haul and the margin of victory, was never to be bettered in the whole of the club's time in the Southern League.

One incident epitomized how the game differs to the present day with respect to the treatment of goalkeepers. Although players had at one time been allowed to charge 'keepers, even when they were <u>not</u> in possession of the ball, this was not now the case, but they could still attempt to attack the ball at the goalkeeper's grasp, and it was up to him to keep a firm grip on it, or lose the ball. In the Gravesend game Monteith, in a rare attack from the visitors, made a save and it was said that he *'sat on the ground and held the ball tight until half the visiting team rolled over him, and then he threw it away.'*

It would not be until the following season that the maximum wage of £4 would be imposed, but it is interesting to note that Ernest Needham, the Sheffield United and England International wing half, wrote at the time regarding the transfer of professional players to the South:

'But the end of this is in view. Attempts are being made in the most influential quarters to restrict the temptations offered by higher salaries, and it is quite possible that changes of locality will be rarer in future. We must not forget also that the speculative payment of large sums to the members of a team cannot go on for long without remunerative returns in the form of gate money; and this, in my opinion, puts another limit on first-class Southern football .... It may be seen already in the teams for 1900/01 that fewer changes in personnel have been made. This I regard as conclusive evidence of a standpoint being reached in salaries, in purchase and change of players, and in the advance of football south of, say, Derby. Certainly some few teams, such as Thames Ironworks and Tottenham Hotspur, will probably always be in a position to attract first–class men......'

Perhaps Needham was not aware when the above was written that Thames Ironworks FC had become West Ham United, and the club was certainly not now in a financial position to risk large amounts of money on new players. The Ironworks' organisation certainly had some financial 'clout', but Arnold Hills had not been prepared any longer to put his money into what had become basically a professional club in 1898/99, and that is why he passed it on, after generously giving the new club some initial financial assistance to start up. After all, he was against professionalism per se, and he was not prepared to invest any further money in it.

After such a good start, the team came down to earth when they met Millwall at East Ferry

Charlie Craig

Road. Bob Allan came in for Hunt on the right wing and Tommy Moore came in for Hugh Monteith in goal. It was Tommy's mistake however, that gave the 'Dockers' their opening goal when he let the ball slip through his fingers. Charlie Craig was a tower of strength at the back, but the result was a 1-3 defeat. It was generally considered that the home side were flattered by the score, and the local scribe reported that:- *'I came away from the ground feeling that the ill-luck that persistently followed the old Thames Ironworks team had made its reappearance with the new named eleven. I could not make much encouraging noise, but when I did I'm afraid I shouted 'Go ahead Ironworks!' more often than I did the new name. Several friends have expressed the difficulty they have also experienced in 'tumbling to' the registered name.'*

The fixture with Southampton was a big attraction. The South Coast club had won the Southern League title in 1897, '98 and '99 seasons, and had been beaten finalists in the FA Cup in 1899/1900. The attendance was a good one for the Irons as 7,500 came through the gate. All were more or less expecting the Saints to record a victory, but after withstanding some early pressure West Ham gave a good account of themselves and got on top, eventually scoring when Jimmy Reid converted a cross from Hunt. Although the game was pretty rough in the second half, with one or two injuries hindering the play, the Irons played well and Hunt scored the second after the opposing 'keeper had came out too far from his goal.

The halves were probably the best of the home side, with Dove prominent at centre half, and all in all it was a very unexpected but well-earned two points. The most disappointing aspect of the afternoon came at half-time when a considerable number of boys and youths climbed over the picket style fence and swarmed on to the pitch, took possession of the ball and created havoc for about twenty minutes. There were just two police constables on duty, who seemed incapable of clearing the field, and the referee stated that he would not re-start the game. Roddy McEachrane, the West Ham captain, stepped into the breach and talking persuasively to the mob, got them to leave the field. The club directorate was criticised for the lack of a larger police presence, also with the prospect of Bristol City as the next visiting opponents.

Prior to the club's next away fixture at Chatham the 'Football Sun' called West Ham United the 'Water Drinkers'. Other alternative nicknames arose such as the 'Syphons' and 'Ginger Pops', but these died a fairly quick death. This was a reference to the condition that Arnold Hills had imposed when he handed the club over to the new board of directors, whereby alcohol should not be consumed by the players at any time, and all team members must always be teetotallers. It was obvious that this was a condition that would be very difficult to manage, and it was often not adhered to. In fact, the club had to devise a system of fines, and players were placed 'on probation' if they were found guilty of imbibing.

A small contingent of supporters had travelled down to Chatham from Holborn at mid-day. Trains at the time could be just as unreliable as they are now, and it was said, with sarcasm, that:- 'We journeyed down......in one of the best trains the railway company could give us. Result, we arrived only half an hour late.'

There was an attendance of around 2,000 for the match, but the home support was described as 'a leather lunged lot......if Chatham could only lend West Ham a few of its par excellence shouters, who with foghorn eloquence could inspire our fellows to do brave and doughty things, they would be conferring a great benefit, and would be the indirect means of securing a dividend for the shareholders of West Ham Football Company Limited.' In the club's time as Thames Ironworks, there had always been criticism over the lack of vocal support. Maybe this was due, in part, to the wide-open spaces of the Memorial Grounds, and the distance between the terraces and across the cycle and running tracks to the field of play.

Although the Irons beat the Kent side by the only goal to gain a further two useful points, Chatham eventually resigned from the Southern League due to financial difficulties, and those two points were to be deducted.

Bristol City, another team with a good pedigree, came to town and showed their class after going away with a 2-1 victory. Hugh Monteith was in goal against his former City colleagues, and was in no way at fault for the two goals conceded, and with Charlie Craig and Roddy McEachrane were the best of the home side. The attendance was 5,000, which was reasonable, but it could have been better.

Syd King

On a very windy day at Swindon, Syd King came in at right back in place of Tranter, and alongside Charlie Craig made a formidable full-back partnership. The encounter was quite even with both sides having an equal amount of forward play, but the Irons picked up both points through the persistence of Fred Corbett. Hovering about amongst the Swindon defence, two or three of the home players left one another to kick the ball clear, and whilst they dithered, Freddie nipped and tapped the ball into the net. It was said that it was a 'soft goal', but Corbett should have been given more credit for his intervention.

On yet another day of fierce winds, Watford visited the Memorial Grounds. The Hertfordshire club had been promoted from the Southern League Second Division, and had surprisingly defeated 'Spurs the previous week. Tommy Moore came into the side in goal, and George Neil who had played for Thames Ironworks from 1896 on, took the place of the injured Bob Allan at right half. George took over as the club Secretary between 1898 and 1900, and this was to be his one and only first team appearance under the banner of West Ham United. He sadly died of consumption at the age of 30 in 1905.

As for the game, the Hammers proved to be too good for the visitors and won by two clear goals, both being scored before half time by Corbett and Fenton. This win put the club in a heady 3rd position in the Southern League table.

There was always the thorny issue of the differences between the professional and the amateur around this period, and to declare oneself an amateur, meant adhering strictly to the rules regarding any payment. A meeting of the Football Association at the time included the following item:- "In answer to a question by the London FA as to whether the status of amateur players would be affected if they accepted prizes for taking part in a six a side football tournament, the Committee were of the opinion that unless prizes are in money, the status of amateurs would not be affected."

A victory was expected at Luton, and West Ham had arguably the best of the play, being certainly the most cohesive unit with their combination play. Goals are the object of the exercise however, and Luton, although their play was of more of a disjointed nature, scored twice in the second half for the victory. It was possibly the Hammers' attitude that cost them the game, for their passing movements had the air of 'cock-suredness', without any end product about them, which was something to guard against in future. Craig had his usual steady game, and Fenton on the left wing was very speedy and proved a handful. The local scribe was at it again in his praise for the opposition's vocal support:-

'......the three thousand persons who assembled there made more encouraging noise than I have heard come from the whole of the thousands which have gathered together on the Memorial Grounds for a season. There is one thing about the Lutonians, and that is, they know how to cheer, and part of the form shown by the homesters on Saturday was due to the incessant promptings of the crowd. Did the home men show up, then the leather-lunged supporter was ready with the cry 'Play up Lu-u-t-on.' West Ham must take the hint. Perhaps I have been inconsiderate in this direction in the past, and have forgotten that the crowd might feel afraid of waking the dead in the adjoining cemetery.'

The visit to White Hart Lane to play Tottenham was expected to be tough and it was. Although 'Spurs had most of the game they were constantly thwarted by Monteith in goal, and Roddy McEachrane was splendid at half-back, first in defence and then helping out the attack. West Ham also had their moments and earned their point in a scoreless draw. One member of the Press, confidently reckoned that 'Tottenham are a shade of what they were, their former greatness is passing, and although there are occasional glimpses of past glory, yet the general trend of events indicate a lost supremacy.' Like many a Press prediction, this one backfired as Tottenham became FA Cup winners at the end of the season!

Before the match a correspondent of the 'Football Star' interviewed Roddy McEachrane and asked him about Southern League football:-

Its better now than it was last year, on the whole. The clubs are better balanced and more equal.

And as far as you are personally concerned?

You mean West Ham? Oh, there's no doubt we have improved. I honestly think we have one of the best teams in the South.

And it's all down to mineral water?

You mustn't chaff. I don't know that the temperance stipulation has made much difference except to keep us together. We are a very clannish lot, and I don't believe there is a better spirit – -?

Eh?

Oh, I see. I mustn't use that word. That is to say that we are all for each other. And the social success of a team encourages combination on the field.

You don't think you've quite the best team in the Southern League?

No. Our defence is strong enough, but our forwards are not quite of the essential experience. One or two of them are young and not fully developed. Forwards require to be thoroughly seasoned, and I think we should be improved by the presence of a good second forward with a personality. A team is the better for an old stager in the front rank, but he must not be too old......I don't know that I have a right to call them the ideal team, but certainly the best lot we have met this year has been Bristol City when they beat us at Canning Town by 2 goals to one. They played a First League game.

Then you don't think Southern League football generally is First League football?

No. Some of the Southern League clubs play up to the best standard, but it isn't the class of all the clubs. I don't know why it should not be so, but I think steadiness is more pronounced among the Northern and Midland cubs than in the South. The cooler the team, the better its football, of course.

Have the referees anything to do with this?

Perhaps. We get some queer referees, and we get some very good ones. Probably we expect too much. If players fail occasionally, it is reasonable that referees should do so too.

You have plenty of work at half-back?

Yes, it's a lively position. I began as a forward and drifted into the middle line. My friends tell me it suits me, and I don't dislike the task. Still, there's not much credit, and there's a good deal of blame attached to half-back play.

You must have played a good game to dispose of Southampton?

I don't think the Saints are as good as they were last year, though we beat them more easily then. Curiously, we do as well as most teams at home, though at the Memorial grounds we don't get the support we feel entitled to. A good roaring crowd means much to the home side, as we know from experience away from home.'

(When the conversation ended, McEachrane smiled harder than ever as the team were preparing to take the field against Tottenham. When he got on the field he was smiling no more, but there was no doubt at the finish, when the result was 0-0, his face had widened considerably).

The Hammers had to compete in the 3rd Qualifying round of the FA Cup competition, and were drawn against a local amateur side by the name of Olympic FC. This was not a particularly attractive tie for the locals and the attendance was just 3,000. Cup ties where one side is undeniably the underdog are never ones where a lot of quality is evident, and so this proved. It was a scrappy affair, producing high kicking and indiscriminate action, and the amateurs' play was distinctly nervous. The game was really settled after just ten minutes by something of a fluke when Fenton, flying down the left wing, hit what was an obvious cross into the centre, and the ball floated under the crossbar and into the far corner of the net. (Something like Konchesky's goal in the FA Cup final against Liverpool in 2006, to be perfectly honest). The remainder of the game was West Ham versus Meates in the Olympic goal, who performed heroics to keep it at 1-0.

When West Ham travelled to Fratton Park, they were not given much chance against a Portsmouth team that were on top form. After just twelve minutes the Hammers were two goals to the good from Kaye and Reid, and the home crowd were nothing less than flabbergasted. It was no fluke as Portsmouth struggled to find their way. Had the score remained so at the break, two points might have come to the East End club, but almost on half time a penalty was conceded which was converted. The second half had Pompey back in their stride with two further goals, and the Hammers left empty handed at 2-3.

FA Cup time came round again, and the Irons were drawn away to New Brompton. It was within the rules at the time for a club that was drawn away to tempt their opponents with a cash offer to reverse the venue. This was nothing less than a bribe, but it was not uncommon. The West Ham directors tried hard to get the Kentish team to come to the Memorial Grounds, and offered a substantial sum in addition to halving the gate money. The club were very eager to reach the next round and go further, but the offer was not accepted. They should not have worried, as the result was a 1-1 draw, which meant a replay at home, and a double benefit in receipts. Craig came into the centre half position because of an injury to Dove, and Tranter made a rare appearance at right back. The Hammers scored twice in the opening half, firstly when Corbett headed through Syd King's free kick, and then from a goal by Hunt. Tranter was strong in defence, and he also took time to provide a pass for Kaye to net the third after the break. Both sides scored from a penalty before the end, and West Ham were through at 4-1.

George Neil

With Dove still out through injury, the club acquired Willie Kelly from Hamilton Academicals and he made his debut at Bristol Rovers. It was a poor display where the forwards were the main culprits in a two-goal defeat, but defensively King, Craig and McEachrane were a credit to the club. There was more newspaper comment about being a Temperance Eleven, because the team were now slipping down the league table. Conversely, when the club began well, it was supposedly for the same reason. Far too much was being made of it by the Press.

Two points were gained in a single goal victory against Reading. George Ratcliffe had been signed from Grimsby Town where he scored 19 goals in 57 appearances for the Football League Second Division club. He promptly scored for the Hammers on his debut playing at inside left. It was a fortunate victory in awful weather against a side that were unlucky to lose, but it meant a lift up to 6th place in the table.

Local enthusiasm was at its peak for the 5th Qualifying Round of the FA Cup. The Hammers had drawn amateur side Clapton, domiciled just a few miles down the road at Forest Gate. They were an old established club that enjoyed a fair amount of support, which went some way to realising the best gate of the season at the Memorial Grounds of 10,000. Arnold Hills, the former chairman of Thames Ironworks FC and founder of West Ham United paid a visit, and was in the stand for the match. With a strong wind blowing against them Clapton were the first to attack, and Monteith was forced to save, but the Irons went ahead after just five minutes when Kaye scored from the spot. The visitors fought back and equalised before half time. It was 'end to end' stuff after the interval, but there was no further score, which meant a replay at the Spotted Dog ground.

Hugh Monteith, the Hammers' goalkeeper, was interviewed by the 'Football Sun' and stated that the difference between Celtic, the Scottish club for whom he played one season, and West Ham, was that the Celts simply worked like a machine. The half-backs and backs passed to each other as much times as some of the Southern forwards. He then went on to say:- *'There is more force in our game, I don't mean that it is rough between man and man; but there is a lot of energy used up in getting a game through that is not required in the game played by the Celtic and English First League teams. They check and checkmate; we bustle and break up - that's it.*

How do I like Southern crowds? Well, much better than some I met up North. For one thing there is no 'chipping', and chipping a man does a lot to put him off his game'

Whom do I fancy for the Southern League Championship? Bristol City or Southampton. West Ham are only striving for a fair position, but I really think Bristol City are the best team in the South this year. It will be a rare fight between these two.

Portsmouth? No, I don't fancy them, nor Millwall either. In fact, those have so fallen away in defence since last year that anything might happen to them if they chance to go crocky.

Yes, I am a stay-at-home goalkeeper. I don't believe in touring up among the half-backs. They can mind their own game, and I like them to let me mind mine. But, of course, one has sometimes to go out a bit to save. As a rule, the penalty line is as far as I care to venture, and the less I have to go there the better I am pleased. The success of a penalty goal is more a matter of the man kicking than the man saving. Every penalty kick should mean goal.'

There are some interesting comments there. Monteith's opinion appeared to be that Southern League football did not have the quality of play that existed in the English League First Division, or that of the Scottish sides. Goalkeepers were also allowed to handle (but not carry) the ball right up to the halfway line at the time, and indeed, right up to 1912, and his views regarding leaving his goal to 'tour up among the half-backs' explains that.

For a goalkeeper to leave his goal at any time is a risky business, and Monteith's comments were in some way justified when the Hammers went to the Spotted Dog ground for the FA Cup replay against Clapton. With West Ham already one goal up by virtue of Grassam's opener, Earle, the home 'keeper, ran out and left his goal unguarded, and Grassam pounced on the ball and drove it into the empty net right on half time. The amateurs made a tremendous fight back in the second half, but there was a steadiness and level headedness about the West Ham side in the closing stages against Clapton's determination and spirit, that won the day at 3-2, with Billy Grassam achieving a hat-trick.

After the opening day's demolition of Gravesend by 7-0, a comfortable victory was expected in the return, as the Kent side were struggling at the bottom, but the Irons disappointed in a 0-0 draw.

Just three days before Christmas the home game with Millwall was abandoned with twenty minutes remaining, due to fog, and there were no fixtures scheduled over the Christmas holiday period. The club travelled down to the South Coast on the 29th December 1900 to meet Southampton, riding high in the table, and favourites to win the title. After surviving some early pressure the Hammers settled down, and as they did at Portsmouth, shocked the home crowd by going ahead when Hunt easily beat the famous CB Fry down the flank and scored. This was followed by a goal from a corner when Fenton netted for the second. Unfortunately the Pompey scenario was repeated when the Saints attacked continuously after the break, and it was their refusal to accept defeat that powered them to a 3-2 victory.

West Ham got a home cup-tie they were hoping for when the first round of the FA Cup (more popularly known at the time as the English Cup) was announced, when the draw paired them with Liverpool. Prior to the match a dinner and concert was arranged at the Public Hall, Canning Town. Before proceedings began Mr Cearns proposed a toast to 'West Ham United Football Club'. He thought the club had achieved very satisfactory results, and hoped to see them climb to the top of the Southern League. The toast was enthusiastically drunk, and with a cry 'May they beat Liverpool!'

Councillor Aitken Brown, who by trade was a brass founder, and one of the directors of the club, responded to the toast, and gave a very impassioned speech about the club, its difficulties and hopes for the future. He felt certain that many in the room could reply better to it than he could. Probably they were aware of the first meeting they had in that hall to inaugurate the West Ham United Football Company. They had the Mayor of that day down with a great flourish of trumpets to start the founding of the club and he should have liked to have the late Mayor with them that night for several reasons. He should like to ask him if he had fulfilled his promise to take up shares in the club. They were probably aware of the struggles they had had. It had not been all honey in the starting of the company.... he might say that the capital was spent before a match was played, but with the assistance of Mr Hills, who was the first to pay up the whole of his shares as far as he was required to, they had gone on. He felt proud of the gentlemen Mr Hills nominated as directors; he felt more proud of them than he did of the directors the shareholders themselves chose, for the simple reason that he happened to be one of the directors that the members themselves chose, and he knew very well that he had not anything like the ability of the gentlemen that Mr Hills chose for his representatives on the directorate.

When they found that they had not the money to run the club, they paid their own shares right up to the hilt, and they went to the bank and became security for £400, so that the club might continue. That day they were not yet out of debt, but he hoped that with the result of Saturday's match, and a big win at that, they would not only be out of debt, but have a balance on the right side. He was sorry their team were not there, but they were preparing for one of the greatest contests there had been in London for some years past. Liverpool were second to none in the First League. It would be one of the greatest victories that could take place if West Ham could only beat Liverpool on Saturday.

Their team themselves as well as the directors felt sanguine that Saturday would see them victorious at the Memorial Grounds. Should West Ham win the match he had not very much doubt then where the English Cup would land. He hoped that when that anticipation was fulfilled that the hall would be crowded to crown the success of the West Ham team. They had confidence. They were told that they would never succeed, and in a certain direction they were boycotted, but let them boycott them as much as they liked, they would succeed. Their team consisted not only of Englishmen but Scotchmen and Irishmen. He felt certain that with the rose, shamrock and thistle united, they would yet bring victory to West Ham, and he hoped they would support them to the utmost of their ability.

At this point the speaker pointed out that Mr Hills had been kind and generous enough to grant the free use of the Memorial Grounds to the club for the next three years. As there were 400 shares unapplied for in the West Ham United Football Company there was no reason why, and no objection to, anyone taking that balance of shares. Previous to Mr Hills's generosity, of course, none of them knew how long they would have use of the ground, but now it was assured for three years, there was a certain success for the club and company, and he himself sincerely hoped that those who had not applied for shares would take the balance.

The above indicates what a precarious financial position the club were in, and it is fair to say that without the assistance of Arnold Hills, the club may well have gone to the wall within a very short time.

There were great expectations of a large gate for the Liverpool match, and the club arranged for extra entrances and exits, and extra staff to man the turnstiles. However, due to their decision to obtain additional income by doubling the prices, all these arrangements were for nothing as a relatively poor crowd of just 6,000 came through the gates.

As for the match itself, the Hammers entered the field with their usual (for this season) light  blue shirts, white shorts with a claret stripe, and black socks. Liverpool followed on, clad in salmon pink! The contest was a titanic struggle in which Monteith, Craig, McEachrane and Dove played exceptionally well in their defensive duties, but the visitors had the class up front. Liverpool won by the only goal, which was hotly disputed. Liverpool's Cox, receiving the ball in an offside position, beat one defender, but Craig with a fair charge knocked him off the ball, but fell himself into the net. Reybould, following up smashed the ball into the net. Several defenders protested, but the referee allowed the goal, and West Ham were out.

It was back to the 'bread and butter' of the league, and a visit to a very good Bristol City side. Monteith made some excellent saves, although the game was territorially equal, and could have gone either way, but it was City who broke the deadlock and won by a single goal.

Weather wise it was another miserable afternoon at the Memorial Grounds when Swindon Town were the visitors. The rain, which had been falling all morning, continued, making the ground very heavy and impossible for good play. The 'Railwaymen' took the lead, but Corbett, who struck the bar after some aggressive play, then equalised after taking a pass from Fergus Hunt, who had run almost the length of the field. Billy Grassam hit the second and Corbett, who was the star on the day, added the third. Dick Pudan, who was standing in for Craig had a torrid time of it, but was covered well by his captain, Roddy McEachrane.

Roddy McEachrane

At Watford, in a game that saw both Hunt and Taylor hit the bar in the first half, King and Craig stood firm in defence, and Grassam got the winner after the interval.

With the travel facilities in the area being totally inadequate, it was a great relief that the London, Southend and Tilbury Railway Company at last opened their new station - West Ham - adjoining the ground and on a direct route to Fenchurch Street station. It was expected that this would bring the extra support to the club that was desperately needed. It was ironic then that the attendance for the visit of Luton Town was the equal worst of the season at 1,000! In a 2-0 victory young Frankie Taylor, on his third appearance, was the Irons' best player. It was he and Corbett who were the scorers. Frankie had appeared at outside left for Thames Ironworks on 14 occasions in 1899/1900 and had now worked his way back into the first eleven.

It was now three wins 'on the trot' with the next opponents being Tottenham Hotspur, a fixture which was eagerly awaited. The attendance of 5,500, which was the second best of the campaign in the league, was still lower than expected, being a local derby. It could have been due to the weather, of course, for the rain came down in torrents before the match and for some time afterwards. From the Irons' point of view this was a contest best forgotten as 'Spurs ran out winners by four goals to one. Sadly, most of the blame went to Tommy Moore, in goal for Monteith, who was suffering from lumbago. On the field, Tommy was suffering from a nightmare, as he was directly responsible for three of the visitors' goals. After having given good service to the club, especially under the banner of Thames Ironworks, he never played for the first team again and left at the end of the campaign. Mention of goalkeepers; very often, when under close pressure, they would decide to kick the ball clear rather than attempt to hold it, from fear of having it knocked away from them by a hefty charge, something forwards were allowed to do at the time.

Another London derby, this time against QPR at Kensal Rise saw two points gained when the Irons took a two goal lead in the first half through Grassam and Taylor, and maintained it. Monteith had a superb game, and the Rangers' supporters showed their frustration by taking their feelings out on the referee and linesmen. There was some cause for amusement at the start of the match when Rangers were waiting for Alf Hitch (formerly of Thames Ironworks) to take the field. His delay was caused by the apparent loss of his boots and socks. The contest began without him, but after about three minutes he came on in his boots but minus his socks, to much laughter from the crowd.

When Portsmouth came to town, there had been heavy morning rain, which created muddy conditions, but then a gale force wind picked up from the South West and the visitors enjoyed the benefit of it in their favour in the first half. Billy Joyce, who had played for the Ironworks the previous season, scored for them after 43 minutes. There was an amusing incident after the break, when the referee was accidentally knocked over, and whilst he was on the ground he blew his whistle to stop the game. The Irons kept plugging away for an equaliser and McEachrane got it in the 83rd minute. The crowd were delirious with delight and continued cheering until the final whistle. It had been said that there was not enough vocal encouragement from the crowd at the Memorial Grounds. When a goal was achieved, they were keen to do so. Like the modern chant 'You only sing when you're winning!!'

Tommy Moore

A useful away point was picked up in a 1-1 draw at New Brompton, which kept the club in 6th position in the table.

For most of the campaign the inclement weather appeared to be a regular feature at the Memorial Grounds. When it was not heavy rain, it was cold, with strong winds that blew across the wide-open spaces of an arena that often appeared dismal enough during the winter months. When Bristol Rovers came to Canning Town, it was another morning of rain, indeed right up until kick off, which would have deterred a number of people from travelling, and the extra support that was lost meant less money through the gate. The Hammers mainly had Monteith to thank for the victory, as he saved many a goal bound shot in the second half as the Rovers were chasing a two goal deficit, after Corbett had scored the first in the 18th minute, and Grassam had put a penalty away after the speedy Taylor had been brought down in the box, just before half time.

It was reported in the local press at this time that:- *'The idea of an amalgamation with West Ham and Millwall clubs at the end of this season has caught on rapidly, and is being freely discussed as an almost accomplished fact. It would doubtless be the making of the Memorial Grounds.'* Club finances might well have been in a poor state, but someone, thankfully, with the right influence must have persuaded whoever made the proposal, that this was an idea, especially for both sets of supporters, that was not, to put it politely, welcome.

Coincidentally, the 'Dockers' were the next visitors. This was the fixture that was originally abandoned in December due to fog. As it had to be rescheduled for a Thursday, more revenue was lost as only 2,500 were able to get to the match. Usually the attendance for a match against the club's nearest neighbour would have been more than double that figure. The weather was at its worst again, and there was a strong wind blowing, and it was a bitterly cold day. As could have been expected the play was littered with fouls, made worse by a number of offsides, and the visitors left in a bad mood when the Irons scored in the last 5 minutes after the referee had consulted a linesmen to confirm whether it was offside or not.

After having beaten Kettering away from home (1-0), a draw just a week later against the same club was a disappointment. Yet another appalling day's weather saw the pitch well soaked due to heavy rain, and any chance of even reasonable football was ruined by a strong gale. With the team having gone six matches unbeaten, a gate that would probably have numbered 4,000, was reduced to 1,000 due to the weather. The team retained their unbeaten run, but after an average performance, they had to come from behind to gain a point when they equalised with just two minutes left, for a 1-1 draw.

There was an improved display on Good Friday when QPR were the visitors. Frankie Taylor was in top form again, and it was his run that gave Ratcliffe the opportunity to open the scoring, and Ratcliffe increased the lead before half time. The Irons were deserved winners on a day that saw some bright and sunny weather for a change, even though it was cold.

Although gates had been disappointing, due in part to the bad weather all season, the club enjoyed a hard core of support, and always had a number of followers at away matches. A Mr L. Batchelor was one of those who organised various horse-drawn brake parties (the modern equivalent of a mini-bus) that he had been running all season, and he signified his intention of taking up shares in the club. It was hoped that others would follow his lead.

There was no brake party for the final away encounter of the season at Reading, (1) due to the distance and (2) because the fixture was arranged for Wednesday afternoon. Reading followers themselves were apathetic as the attendance was barely 1,000. Unfortunately West Ham's good run of 8 games without defeat came to an end. Grassam had scored with a long dipping shot in the first half, but the home side scored three goals inside ten minutes in the second.

A week before the final match of the campaign the local press advertised the following:- *'...please bear in mind that West Ham take their benefit at the Royal Albert Music Hall, Canning Town on Thursday. All who propose visiting the 'Albert' on that night have a treat in store, for Mr Relf always provides something good on benefit nights, or any other time for that matter.'*

That final fixture was against New Brompton, and played in ideal weather, which was the only time that it had occurred throughout the season. It was a very one-sided affair that ended in a 2-0 victory, and sadly it was to be Charlie Dove's final appearance. Charlie was the only player left at the club who had figured in the first season of the club's history as Thames Ironworks FC back in 1895/96.

The victory meant that West Ham United finished in a respectable 6th position in the Southern League, although the financial situation of the club was still quite weak. Further capital had recently been put into the club, however, and directors and shareholders alike hoped it would put the club on a sounder footing.

Players only. Back: Tranter, Monteith, Craig. Centre: Allan, Dove, McEachrane.
Front: Hunt, Corbett, Reid, Kaye, Fenton.

1900/01

6th in Southern League Division One

#	Date		Opponent	Score	Scorers	Att	Allan R	Corbett F	Craig C	Dove C	Fenton F	Grassam W	Hunt F	Kaye A	Kelly W	King S	McEachrane R	Monteith H	Moore T	Neill G	Pinder	Pudan R	Raisbeck L	Ratcliffe G	Reid J	Taylor F	Tranter W	Walker L
1	Sep	1	GRAVESEND UNITED	7-0	Grassam 4, Reid 2, Hunt	2000			3	4	11	8	7	10			6	1					5		9		2	
2		8	Millwall Athletic	1-3	Reid	10000	7		3	4	11	8		10			6		1				5		9		2	
3		15	SOUTHAMPTON	2-0	Grassam, Reid	7500	4		3	5	11	8	7	10			6	1							9		2	
4		29	BRISTOL CITY	1-2	Kaye	5000	4	8	3	5	11		7	10			6	1							9			
5	Oct	6	Swindon Town	1-0	Corbett	2000	4	8	3	5	11		7	10		2	6	1							9			
6		13	WATFORD	2-0	Corbett, Fenton	4000		8	3	5	11		7	10		2	6		1	4					9			
7		20	Luton Town	0-2		4000	4	8	3	5	11		7	10		2	6	1							9			
8		27	Tottenham Hotspur	0-0		6000	4	8	3	5	11		7	10		2	6	1							9			
9	Nov	10	Portsmouth	2-3	Kaye, Reid	5000	4	8	3	5	11		7	10		2	6	1										10
10		24	Bristol Rovers	0-2		3000	4		3			11	8	7	5	2	6	1						10	9			
11	Dec	1	READING	1-0	Ratcliffe	4000			3		11	8	7	10	5	2	6	1							9			
12		15	Gravesend United	0-0		1000			3	4	11		7	10	5	2	6	1						9	8			
13		29	Southampton	2-3	Fenton, Hunt	4000			3	4	11		7	10	5	2	6	1					3	10	9			
14	Jan	12	Bristol City	0-1		2500	4					8	7	11	5	2	6	1					3	10		11	
15		19	SWINDON TOWN	3-1	Corbett 2, Grassam	4000	4	9				8	7		5	2	6	1						10		11	
16		26	Watford	1-0	Grassam	2000	4	9	3			8	7		5	2	6	1						10		11	
17	Feb	9	LUTON TOWN	2-0	Corbett, Taylor	1000	4	9	3			8	7		5	2	6		1					10		11	
18		16	TOTTENHAM HOTSPUR	1-4	Grassam	5500	4	9	3			8	7		5	2	6	1						10		11	
19		23	Queen's Park Rangers	2-0	Grassam, Taylor	6000	4	9				8	7		5	2	6	1			3			10		11	
20	Mar	2	PORTSMOUTH	1-1	McEachrane	3000	4	9	3			8	7		5	2	6	1						10		11	
21		9	New Brompton	1-1	Hunt	2000	4	9	3			8	7		5	2	6	1						10		11	
22		16	BRISTOL ROVERS	2-0	Corbett, Grassam	4000	4	9	3			8	7		5	2	6	1						10			
23		21	MILLWALL ATHLETIC	1-0	Corbett	2500	4	9	3		11	8	7		5	2	6	1						10			
24		23	Kettering Town	1-0	Grassam	1000	4	9	3			8	7	11	5	2	6	1						10			
25		30	KETTERING TOWN	1-1	Taylor	1000	4	9	3			8	7		5	2	6	1						10		11	
26	Apr	5	QUEEN'S PARK RANGERS	2-1	Ratcliffe 2	4000	4	9	3			8	7		5	2	6	1						10		11	
27		10	Reading	1-3	Grassam	1000	4	9	2	3		8	7		5		6	1						10		11	
28		20	NEW BROMPTON	2-0	Ratcliffe, Taylor	2000	4	9	2	3		8	7		5		6	1						10		11	
			Apps				24	21	25	13	14	20	27	14	19	22	28	24	4	1	1	2	2	17	13	12	4	1
			Goals					7			2	12	3	2			1								4	5	4	

F.A. Cup

Rd	Date		Opponent	Score	Scorers	Att	Allan R	Corbett F	Craig C	Dove C	Fenton F	Grassam W	Hunt F	Kaye A	Kelly W	King S	McEachrane R	Monteith H	Moore T	Neill G	Pinder	Pudan R	Raisbeck L	Ratcliffe G	Reid J	Taylor F	Tranter W	Walker L
Q3	Nov	3	OLYMPIC	1-0	Fenton	3000	7		3	5	11			9	10		2	6	1					4	8			
Q4	Nov	17	New Brompton	1-1	Corbett	1200	4	9	5		11		7	10			3	6	1						8		2	
rep		21	NEW BROMPTON	4-1	Kaye 2, Corbett, Hunt	4000		9	5		11		7	10			3	6	1					4	8		2	
Q5	Dec	8	CLAPTON	1-1	Kaye	10000	4		3		11	8	7	10	5	2	6	1							9			
rep		12	Clapton	3-2	Grassam 3	5000			3	5	11	8	7	10	4	2	6	1							9			
IR	Jan	5	LIVERPOOL	0-1		6000			3	5		8	7	11	4	2	6	1						10	9			

		P	W	D	L	F	A	W	D	L	F	A	Pts
1	Southampton	28	13	1	0	44	12	5	4	5	14	14	41
2	Bristol City	28	12	2	0	40	6	5	3	6	14	21	39
3	Portsmouth	28	12	2	0	33	6	5	2	7	23	26	38
4	Millwall	28	11	1	2	36	10	6	1	7	19	22	36
5	Tottenham Hotspur	28	12	1	1	35	8	4	3	7	20	25	36
6	WEST HAM UNITED	28	10	2	2	28	10	4	3	7	12	18	33
7	Bristol Rovers	28	10	3	1	29	8	4	1	9	17	27	32
8	Queen's Park Rangers	28	9	1	4	28	17	2	3	9	15	31	26
9	Reading	28	7	2	5	16	10	1	6	7	8	15	24
10	Luton Town	28	9	1	4	32	20	2	1	11	11	29	24
11	Kettering	28	7	4	3	21	12	2	1	11	9	34	23
12	New Brompton	28	5	4	5	20	19	2	1	11	14	32	19
13	Gravesend United	28	5	5	4	23	27	1	2	11	9	58	19
14	Watford	28	6	3	5	17	16	0	1	13	7	36	16
15	Swindon Town	28	3	6	5	15	18	0	2	12	4	29	14

1901/02   ON AN EVEN KEEL

The club's first season under the new banner of West Ham United had been a reasonable success on the field. Sixth place in the Southern League First Division was as good as could be expected. Off the field was a different matter. Attendances at the Memorial Grounds could have been better, and it had been hoped that with the opening of West Ham railway station in the previous February, easier access to the ground would have attracted new followers to the club. It was early days in that respect however, and the Board of Directors, all local businessmen, new to the running of a professional football organisation, were thankful at least to Arnold Hills, the founder of the club, who had very generously put the Memorial Grounds at the disposal of the club for a further three years, and rent free into the bargain.

Syd King, right full-back, and captain of the club was given the job of secretary of West Ham United in addition to his playing duties, taking over from Lew Bowen, a clerk from Thames Ironworks. Bowen moved to the position of financial secretary, and later in the season in 1902, King was made secretary/manager.

Several players left the club in the close season. Fred Fenton went back to Gainsborough, and thence on to Preston, WBA, Bristol City and Swindon. Albert Kaye crossed the Irish Sea to play for Distillery (later returning to England to play for Stockport County), Luke Raisbeck was released, and Jimmy Reid moved briefly to Fulham before signing for Gainsborough Trinity. Also moving on were three players who were with the club in their days as Thames Ironworks FC. Goalkeeper Tommy Moore

Jimmy Bigden

went to Grays United, Walter Tranter tried his luck in Belfast, and saddest of all Charlie Dove, who made at least 18 known appearances in that very first season of 1895/96. Charlie signed for Millwall, playing on 23 occasions in the Southern League in 1901/02, but after just 3 outings the following season he retired from playing due to injury problems.

On the way in to the club came James Bigden. He was no stranger to the Memorial Grounds as he had played for Thames Ironworks in 1899/1900, but then threw in his lot with Gravesend United the following season making 26 appearances for them. At 5ft 8in and of stocky build he was to prove a more than useful addition to the half-back line.

Bill Jenkinson, a forward from Burnley was taken on, and Bill Linward, a very useful left winger from Doncaster Rovers also signed. A couple of local lads signed for the club, Aubrey Fair and J. Hitchens.

The opening fixture of the season was scheduled for Monday 2nd September with a kick off at 6.30 pm. Unfortunately due to the late arrival of visitors Wellingborough, the match did not get under way until ten minutes to seven. Due to the bad light later on the referee had to abandon the game with twelve minutes left to play. Fortunately neither team held an advantage at the time, as the score was 1-1. There was some relief for two of the players when the whistle blew, as both goals were of the 'own goal' variety. The match did have one unhappy outcome however, as Fergus Hunt received a serious knee injury in the second half which put the ex-Woolwich Arsenal man out of action for a couple of months.

This meant that Bob Allan switched to outside right and Jimmy Bigden came in at right half for the trip to Bristol to play the Rovers at their Stapleton Road ground. The home side had been beaten only once in the previous season on their own ground, and it came as a surprise and a disappointment to their followers that West Ham inflicted defeat so early in the campaign. Grassam and Corbett scored in a 2-0 result where the visitors were smarter in front of goal. One excuse offered by the West Country men was that the team played in jerseys that were too hot for them!

The club had already had a reserve team as members of both the South Essex League and the London League Division One in 1900/01, but it was now decided to enter the first eleven for the Western League and the London League Premier Division in addition to their Southern league fixtures. This would mean further fixtures in midweek, but then some players excluded from the main competition would probably get a run out against reasonable opposition. The most important reason of course, was that extra revenue would come into the club's coffers and improve the financial situation.

Any competition that brought local rivals Millwall to the Memorial Grounds was met with enthusiasm by the home supporters, and so it proved. This meeting was the first in the London League Premier Division and considering the match was played on a Monday with a 5pm kick off it was well attended, with more than 3,000 lined up on the terraces at that time. The game was fought out quite rigorously by both teams, but the visitors often overstepped the mark with some rough play, and it was as early as the 10th minute when they conceded a penalty which Billy Grassam easily slid home. Millwall were prominent for the rest of the half, but after the break Grassam added two more, and his hat-trick was greeted with 'deafening applause' – such was the enthusiasm of the locals for a victory over the 'Dockers', whatever the competition. Ratcliffe completed the rout scoring the fourth, and the crowd went home clearly satisfied with result. In addition to Grassam's goalscoring feat, Jimmy Bigden, at right half received much praise for his confident display.

When Brentford came to Canning Town for a Southern League fixture the weather was warm and sunny: ideal for the assembled crowd, but possibly too warm for the players. When West Ham took the field they were wearing their new colours for the first time - *light blue jerseys, with a claret band, and white knickers with a red stripe,* and it was said they looked very conspicuous in the new outfits. The attendance was 4,500, with the visitors bringing a large contingent of 800 supporters with them. They were to go home disappointed as the 'Irons' were certainly too hot for the 'Bees', winning a one-sided game by two goals to nil, with Grassam responsible for both goals yet again. The victory was achieved despite the period of absence of centre half Bill Kelly, who received a head injury and was off the field for some time in the second half. He needed 5 stitches to the back of his head.

Two days later came the club's first ever match in the Western League. Saturday's weather had changed to one of heavy rain for the journey across London to meet Queens Park Rangers on their latest ground at Latimer Road, Notting Hill. Rangers had financial problems at the time and had lost their previous ground at Kensal Rise. The West London club had not had the necessary time to bring their new abode 'up to scratch' and the place was in an awful condition. The surface of the pitch was very rough and uneven, and there was absolutely no covered accommodation at all for the spectators. When West Ham arrived there was no dressing room available and the team had to make use of a public house

Fred Corbett

nearby. Rather ironic, considering the club's dubious misnomer of the 'Teetotallers'.

The young reserve, Hitchens came into the side in place of the unwell Ratcliffe, but Bill Kelly, usually good in the air, turned out despite the stitches to his head, and he defended very well with his feet. The constant rain meant everyone, spectators and players alike were soaked, but the Hammers were much the better side, and were superb in defence, with Charlie Craig at his best. It resulted in a resounding 4-1 victory with Linward, Hitchens (2) and Corbett scoring. The local correspondent summed up with the following comments:- *'The Rangers took their defeat badly, and I understand that several of them will be reported for 'baiting' the referee. He was very shabbily treated by players and spectators...... and he was hooted and shouted at on the ground and as I came away, a large crowd were 'waiting for' him at the gate. I hope that the Rangers and their supporters will learn how to take a defeat better than this in future.'*

Shades of the future and of the past were in evidence at this time when a 'scratch' team, calling themselves Boleyn Castle, assisted by a number of guest players, were playing on the same site that West Ham United would be occupying three years hence. Included in the Castle side were two ex-Thames Ironworks players from the years of 1895 to 1897, William Chapman and Fred Chalkley.

A very even Southern League game at New Brompton resulted in a scoreless draw with the Hammers' forwards continually being caught offside, and just one goal was enough to inflict defeat on Kettering when they came to town. The visitors were criticised for some rough and vicious play after they had gone behind in the final fifteen minutes of the game. The referee went so far as to call the whole 'Ketts' side together to warn them about their behaviour. Aside from the two points gained the West Ham executive were more than pleased with the 'gate' of 6,000 on the day.

Bill Jenkinson, acquired from Burnley in close season, had not been chosen in a Southern or Western League fixture at this time and decided that he was not going to fulfil his engagements with the club. Leaving them 'thin on the ground' in the forward positions the directors decided to act quickly, by signing on Peter Kyle, a beefy 6ft forward from Scotland. He played in a reserve match and the West Ham faithful were expecting him to make an appearance in the next first team encounter, but he did not appear in the replayed fixture against Wellingborough on the following Monday. It was said, that this was due to insufficient training, something that would sooner, rather than later, come to a head. To avoid any possibility of a further abandonment the match began at a little after 3.30pm, and consequently the attendance was only 2,000.

Freddie Corbett had not been performing well in the previous two Southern League matches and quite probably would have been replaced by Peter Kyle. Maybe with that thought in mind, Fred was at his best, scoring a hat-trick in a 4-2 victory. The 'Irons' were now undefeated in five matches and went to the top of the table. The position was maintained in an exciting tussle at Northampton where the Hammers overcame the home side by 4 goals to 3.

West Ham v Luton Town at the Memorial Grounds; Linward is about to score for the Hammers.

Peter Kyle made his first start, with a less than adequate performance, appearing in a Western League fixture against Reading at home which resulted in a 1-1 draw. There were no changes to the Southern League line-up for the visit of Luton Town to the East End, which meant that the same eleven had contested the first seven matches in the main competition. West Ham had a comfortable two goal lead at half time, but it was all Luton after the break. Monteith in goal, and King and Craig, the full-back pair, were outstanding, and continually repulsed the visiting forwards, with just one goal conceded after continuous attacks. On the other hand, the 'Irons' had little forward play, but netted twice for a flattering 4-1 triumph. Corbett's brace meant he had scored six goals in seven Southern League appearances. Rather strangely, the team discarded the light blue shirts with the red band, and used the all white shirts (occasionally used in 1900/01) for this game, which was confusing, especially for the referee as Luton's attire was somewhat similar.

There were no less than 7,000 spectators at White Hart Lane on the following Monday for the Hammers first clash of the season with 'Spurs for a Western League fixture, but it was pretty much one-way traffic with the home side dominant, although the Hammers' defence, particularly Monteith was outstanding in a 1-2 defeat.

The first changes to the Southern League line-up came for the trip to Watford. Yenson and Hitchens came into the side, with Bigden moving across to centre half. A satisfactory display in a 0-0 draw kept the club on top of the table.

The next two Southern League encounters were both at home and eagerly anticipated, for the opponents were Millwall followed by Tottenham Hotspur. Arrangements had now been made for the standing spectators to be allowed to cross the cycle and running tracks and stand close to the touch line in order for a better view. This was quite an astonishing decision, bearing in mind the problems that were caused at one particular match during the previous season when spectators climbed over the fence, onto the cycle track, and caused mayhem on the playing pitch for twenty minutes, before order was restored. The club also spent some money on erecting a small stand to accommodate the press. This was a raised structure capable of holding around 14 reporters and erected in front of the grandstand directly opposite the centre of the field.

Bill Jenkinson reversed his decision to leave the club after all, and was included in the side to meet Millwall, instead of Peter Kyle, who was to have been his replacement. Kyle's presence, or more to the point, his lack of it, was something of a mystery. As it was, the Hammers lost for the first time in the Southern League by two goals to nil, with the forwards being particularly ineffective. Millwall brought their local band with them and rather cheekily played 'See the Conquering Heroes Come' when the match was over. When they had collected the few pennies that had been thrown on the pitch they then played 'Break the News to Mother', and left the ground.

Dates for the FA Cup rounds are set before the season begins, and club administrators have to re-arrange their respective league fixtures accordingly. With West Ham coming into the competition at the 3rd Qualifying Round the club were drawn against Leyton away from home on Saturday 3rd November 1901. The Southern League fixture already scheduled for that date was against Tottenham

Hotspur at home. This was a meeting that was always certain to bring in one of the largest crowds of the season. Moving the fixture to midweek would considerably reduce the attendance and the consequent drop in gate money. The club took a very risky decision by playing the 'Spurs' game on the original date, and sending the reserve eleven to Leyton for the FA Cup tie, having faith in the 'stiffs' to take the club through into the next round.

This decision, luckily, was vindicated as the second eleven triumphed by the narrow margin of one goal scored by Frank Taylor, and the Southern League game brought in 17,000 through the gate, which proved to be the best of the season. Unfortunately the result went in favour of Tottenham (0-1), but it could have gone either way in a very intense match. Bigden was probably the 'Irons' best player, but the forwards could not find a way through, and there was much criticism of Corbett at centre-forward. It was the third league game in succession that the club had not scored. 'Spurs had won the FA Cup in the previous season of 1900/01 and took the opportunity to charter a special cab to bring the trophy along to the Memorial Grounds to put it on display in a blatant show of one-upmanship. One of their officials stood by to guard it.

It was at this match that, due to the large attendance, the directors of the club decided to allow spectators across the cycle track for a view closer to the side of the pitch. This event makes the claim that the Memorial Grounds had a crowd limit of 100,000 wide open to question. There is no doubt that it was a vast arena; the cycle track, recognized to be the fastest in the country, was one-third of a mile round and a running track also encircled the football pitch. The accommodation for spectators around the outside perimeter was limited, however. The main stand and adjacent paddock together held around 1,500 and a pavilion opposite on the back straight could hold another 1,200. Extending right around the complex was a raised area, banked up by 2 feet with a width of 26 feet. With such a shallow draft this was only capable of holding rows of people five deep. Also, the raised area was interrupted by a long building around the whole of the first bend, which was used as a covered cycle storage stand. It is difficult to estimate the real capacity, but the expectation that the venue was capable of holding a semi-final was rebuffed when an FA Committee viewed the ground and dismissed the idea.

WEST HAM UNITED v QUEENS PARK RANGERS

When making the decision to permit spectators to advance nearer to the pitch, the club directors had obviously forgotten the mayhem that was caused during the Southampton fixture the previous season, when a crowd crossed the cycle track and invaded the field of play for twenty minutes. As it was, at the 'Spurs match a mob set upon and occupied the newly raised structure built for the use of 14 members of the Press. The box was in danger of caving in until the police arrived and cleared the offenders off. Further misdemeanours took place alongside the pitch, which meant that the directors had to consider alternatives for future matches when a large attendance was a strong possibility. When that situation arose, the problem was overcome by allowing spectators to stand directly behind the goal (at both ends if necessary) in rows 4 or 5 deep, and allowing crowds to stand on the banking of the cycle track behind the level of the goal line.

It must be remembered that Arnold Hills established the arena first and foremost for the benefit of his workers, in order for them to seek a healthy and athletic lifestyle by their own participation in the sporting pursuits on offer. It was not initially constructed for any substantial commercial gain, although the proceeds from cycling, motorcycling, athletics and other events certainly helped with the costs of the upkeep of the arena.

Sending the reserve team to fulfil the FA Cup fixture did have one drawback in that the second eleven should have been playing Tottenham reserves in a London League (First Division) match. The club had to scramble together a side of virtual 'unknowns' to meet their obligations and were soundly beaten by eight clear goals. It was not so much the result, but the London League committee imposed a fine of £10 on the club for fielding a weak side, a very heavy forfeit at the time.

Although Kyle played in the Leyton FA Cup tie, the players were basically the reserve side, so his debut in the first eleven came when the Hammers visited Queens Park Rangers. His inclusion did not improve the team's luck, and a defeat meant their third consecutive league loss as Rangers won by 2 goals to 1.

The Hammers were drawn against Grays United in the next round of the FA Cup, and had met them in the same competition under the banner of Thames Ironworks FC in 1899/1900. The result then was a 4-0 victory, and there was no reason to think that the outcome would be any different. In the one hundred years plus since that game, followers of the East End club have often suffered through cup defeats against clubs from lower leagues, and their Essex village opponents began that malaise with an odd goal victory (1-2), although to be fair West Ham were not beaten by another lower league side in the cup in the pre-Great War period of 1900-1915. Nevertheless it was a financial setback to be out of the competition, and the crowd for the game just about reached 2,000. This was possibly due to early fog in outlying districts, deterring people from travelling. The fog became more dense in the latter part of the game in which goalkeeper Tommy Moore, a great favourite in his Thames Ironworks days at the Memorial Grounds, put on a splendid display for Grays and denied his old team an equaliser.

It had become obvious to Syd King, secretary and manager, and especially Abe Norris the club's trainer, that as good a player as Peter Kyle potentially appeared, he would have to be 'on his way', and out of the club. As far as Kyle was concerned, his view of training was that it was something that every other player did, and it was of no interest to him. The club then very swiftly moved by arranging a 'swap' deal with Kettering in which Billy Jones, a centre half who had already been capped for Wales, came to West Ham, with Kyle going in the opposite direction.

Maybe Kyle would have been keen to practice more with the ball, because very little of that was done at the time, as there was more emphasis on making a player physically fit. Weight training with heavy clubs and dumb bells to provide body strength, ball punching and 20 minutes continuous skipping for co-ordination, and sprinting followed by an eight or nine miles walk at a brisk pace for stamina were the required elements.

There was no doubt at all that Kyle had the skill and ability to succeed as a goalscoring forward. His subsequent record of goals with Kettering, Tottenham, Woolwich Arsenal, Aston Villa, Sheffield United and Watford was 55 goals in 145 appearances, a reasonable haul in a period when goals were not easy to come by. His training 'misdemeanours' with his various clubs meant his eventual departure from most of them. He could surely have achieved much more with the right attitude.

The Hammers had now fallen to fourth place in the table with their recent form, and the run of poor results continued. There were forced changes to the team for the visit to Reading but both Southern League points were lost in a 0-3 defeat. This was followed by three consecutive Western League encounters. West Ham faced Portsmouth, who would become eventual champions of the competition, home and away, and lost them both 2-4 at home and 2-3 away, but a brief respite from the continual defeats in all competitions came with a victory over a depleted Bristol Rovers side by 3-0.

When the team journeyed to the Dell to play Southampton they suffered their fifth straight defeat in the Southern League. The 0-4 scoreline meant that just one goal had gone into their opponents net in five matches, and there was much local criticism of the Selection Committee of Directors that was responsible for picking the team. Syd King, even after taking over as secretary/manager, would not be involved in actual team selection, and it was not until 1911 that he began to have some say in that procedure. It must not be forgotten too, that Syd was still a full member of the first team and would not retire from playing until the end of the 1902/03 season.

Only in a few respects could managers then, be compared to those of today. It was not unusual at all for directors of clubs to undertake the role of team selection, for they considered that they were responsible for the overall control of the club, with the manager taking on the role of a 'go-between' with the trainer and players, and being involved in their welfare in a paternal-like manner. Syd King was one of the rare breed of professional footballers at the time who had a sound educational background, having attended grammar school in Watford, but despite the directors overall control, they all had businesses to run, and Syd was given the day to day running of the club. He was responsible for carrying out certain organizational and administrative procedures at the requirements of those directors, even to the task of ticket arrangements and for contacts and communications with the press, something like a marketing man today. There was an example of King's press duties as secretary at this point in the campaign, when there had been rumours that West Ham were amalgamating with a local amateur club. He issued the following statement:-

'The West Ham United FC enjoys an existence which is in no way dependent upon, nor has it any affinity with any other team, professional or otherwise. I understand that certain sections of the staff and workmen of the Thames Ironworks are identified with amateur organisations of their own, but intended, I believe, only to satisfy a taste for this particular class of football, and does not, so far as I know, aspire to meet the requirements of supporters such as those of West Ham United. In short, I have no doubt that in the opinion of the promoters of the amateur teams, there is room for all and no collision of interests is intended. I may add that any use of the Memorial Grounds by these minor teams will always be subordinated to the requirements of the premier and professional club. Signed E.S. King.'

A postscript was added:- 'It is quite wrong to suppose that the existence of the WHUFC Company is in any way threatened financially or otherwise.'

When Arnold Hills initially granted West Ham United use of the Memorial Grounds until 1904 (at least) rent free, it was agreed that when the club did not have a fixture at the ground, it would be at the disposal of certain amateur clubs. It is probable that some individuals were of the opinion that one, or more, of the clubs that used the ground were affiliated to West Ham in some way or other because they believed that the club itself was in financial difficulties. King's statement in respect of Thames Ironworks appears overly critical considering that the chairman of the shipyard was solely responsible for the formation of West Ham United, and that many of the Thames Ironworks were supporters of the club.

After the Southern League defeat at Southampton the club were desperate to sign a forward player capable of scoring goals, and they signed Alex McDonald from their recent opponents. Alex had also had experience in the Football League with Everton, so much was expected of him. To fund this move, Fred Corbett was sacrificed, and he signed for Bristol Rovers. Fred later played for Bristol City and Brentford, scoring over one hundred goals, (considerably more than McDonald) during a career that lasted until 1913.

Swindon Town were languishing at the bottom of the table when they came to the East End, and the game resulted in a welcome two points by the not too convincing score of 2-1. Billy Jones, the Welsh International centre half signed from Kettering, made his debut and showed up well. The victory brought some confidence back into the side and several good results followed. Deadly rivals Tottenham were beaten in the London League Premier Division by three goals to one, despite the loss of Ratcliffe though a head injury after just three minutes.

Alex McDonald scored both goals, one a superb header, in a 2-0 home triumph over Bristol Rovers in the Southern League, and there then followed three victories over three days of Christmas (25-27 December) in three different league competitions. Southampton were defeated on Christmas Day 1-0 in the Western League, Millwall were beaten on Boxing Day by no less than five goals to one at Greenwich in the London League Premier Division, much to the delight of the travelling support, and a well-earned two nil victory at Wellingborough brought two points in the Southern League.

On New Years Day the Hammers completed their run of good results with a London League Premier Division victory over Queens Park Rangers by 2-1. A total of seven consecutive wins! A great pity they were not all in the Southern League competition. The run came to an end when the team failed to score in three matches – one a 0-0 draw with New Brompton when the Memorial Grounds pitch was in a dreadful state, and two narrow 0-1 defeats, Kettering (away) and Northampton (home).

To be able to regularly field an unchanged side in any league competition, providing the majority of the team are of a reasonable standard, is something of a bonus. Players develop a sense of understanding with one another and are often able to anticipate their colleagues' movements during vital parts of the action on the field of play. So it was with the final eleven matches of the Southern League campaign.

With the exception of Yenson, with three appearances, Pudan with two and Allan with just one over that run-in of fixtures, it was the same side of Monteith in goal, King and Craig at full-back, Bigden, Jones and McEachrane at half-back, Grassam, Ratcliffe, Hunt, Jenkinson and Linward as the forwards. It was good to see Fergus Hunt back in the side after missing so many games through injury, and Bill Jenkinson, who was on the verge of leaving the club earlier in the campaign, giving steady regular performances.

Luton Town were brushed aside by three clear goals on their own ground, and Watford were beaten 3-2 on a cold and blustery February day at the Memorial Grounds. With the strong wind in the Hammers' favour there was laughter from the spectators when Hugh Monteith, in goal, was seen to be crouching down behind the boards at the back of his net in order to shield himself from the elements. On the other hand, there were howls of derision from the home crowd when the scores were level, as the visitors, with the aid of the strong wind, continually kicked the ball out of the field, wasting considerable time into the bargain.

A useful point picked up at Millwall, was followed with a victory over bitter rivals 'Spurs at White Hart Lane. Monteith was the star of the side, saving difficult shots as if his life depended upon it, in a 2-1 triumph.

Queens Park Rangers were on the end of a 4-0 pasting with Fergus Hunt scoring two superb goals, although both Jones and Craig had to be in top form in defence, and Brentford, the fourth London opposition in succession, were defeated at their Boston Park ground by two clear goals.

It was at this point in the season when the club realised that the hasty decision to take on Alex McDonald from Southampton in December, and let Fred Corbett go had proved to be a mistake. After scoring twice in his first game, McDonald appeared in three further Southern League fixtures, without scoring, and then picked up an injury. He returned to play in two Western League matches, one of which was at centre half, then appeared in what was basically a reserve friendly against United Hospitals, and did not score in a 4-1 victory. He was suddenly released, and he returned to the South Coast with its clean air and signed for Portsmouth. Perhaps the polluted factory fumes of Canning Town did not bring out the best in him! Whatever the reason, it shows how a panic buy during a spell of poor results does not always bring a change of fortune.

The excellent run of results continued when Reading came to the East End and left pointless after a home win by 2-1, with Fergus Hunt scoring his fourth goal in three Southern League matches, and the Hammers were up to third place in the table.

The visit to Portsmouth to play the league leaders resulted in a stalemate, but to come away with a point and not concede against a very good side was a great achievement. There was an abundance of rough play and Yenson, standing in for Bill Jones who was on International duty with Wales, came in for some criticism after throwing his considerable weight about.

Now occupying second place in the Southern League there was just a faint chance of the title, but only if Portsmouth lost their final three fixtures, and other results went their way. There was a great deal of praise from the West Ham faithful at the recent run of results and the sports journalist of the local paper reported that:-

'I have received a card from Mr W. Hall, hon. Treasurer to the movement which is on foot to show the appreciation which the supporters of the West Ham United FC feel towards the team for the gallant show they have made in their recent matches. It will depend largely upon the amount raised as to what form the testimonial will take, and donations will thankfully be received by the above named gentleman at 152 Milton Avenue, East Ham.'

This devoted and sincere appeal by a group of followers shows early involvement and loyalty to the club. Down the years, despite setbacks, this has remained solid. It's a case of 'keeping the faith'.

When Southampton came to the Memorial Grounds they were looking forward to their second FA Cup Final in three years, and were tucked in just behind the Hammers in the table. Coincidentally the 'Saints' had been the visitors against Thames Ironworks two years previously, when the South Coast club had also just reached the final. On that occasion the 'Irons' were victorious and history repeated itself as the visitors were beaten again, Grassam and Ratcliffe scoring in a 2-1 victory. Critics, of course, pointed out that Southampton had their thoughts on the Cup Final, but it was a hard fought game, which resulted in West Ham sitting on top of the table. Portsmouth, Tottenham and Southampton however, had games in hand.

Swindon Town were struggling at the foot of the table and well adrift when the Hammers visited for their final away fixture in the Southern League. It was supposed to be an easy victory but the team were lucky to win by a single goal, and the extra matches of the London Premier League and the Western League were beginning to take their toll. Two defeats in the former competition meant that the team had to avoid defeat against 'Spurs in their final game to win that league, which fortunately they did with a 2-2 draw. In and out form in the Western League meant a poor finish of 7th position out of a league composed of nine teams.

Portsmouth had already lifted the Southern League title when they came to Canning Town for the final match of the campaign, but it was a fine match. West Ham had the upper hand throughout, and should have won comfortably but for some woeful shooting. The result of 1-1, and the 'games in hand' victories by 'Spurs and Southampton over their rivals, meant a final finish of fourth in the table, but it could have been even better.

It would not be an exaggeration to say that it had been another campaign in which the weather had been horrendous, with many mud-spattered encounters due to heavy rains, and this was not conducive to good quality football. Although the Memorial Grounds had been laid with adequate drainage, the area was set out on the original wetlands of the Abbey Marsh with obvious consequences in rainy weather. To make matters worse, the low-pressure climate was accompanied on many occasions by high winds, which made accurate passing and control very difficult. Such conditions reduced the value of home advantage.

Competing seriously in three league competitions in a season with a relatively small squad of players, and attempting on almost every occasion to put out the strongest eleven, was optimistic to say the least. There was no doubt that the club executive had problems in keeping the club finances on an 'even keel', and income depended upon gate receipts alone. At this time the Southern League consisted of 16 teams, which meant only thirty matches per season. Participating in the Western League and London Premier League meant an additional twenty-four fixtures, which would provide additional finance. Avoiding failure in any of those leagues relied on a decent size squad of players of reasonable ability, and so it was something of a gamble with the small number of professional men available. Very fortunately, it was a gamble that paid off to a certain extent, as the club suffered no substantial injuries throughout the season. This also had the effect of being able to field an almost unchanged side especially at the start, and again in the final third of the campaign, which resulted in two unbeaten runs.

As soon as the campaign ended the club lost the first of its truly 'home grown' players when Dick Pudan, born in Canning Town and a scholar at Denmark Street School, left to join Bristol Rovers where he was a regular up until 1907 when Newcastle United came in for him. Two years later he signed for Leicester Fosse, where he eventually became a director of the club and a successful businessman. There is a tale that when with the Irons, he was ill and was ruled out of playing. He produced a doctor's certificate, and a month later the situation arose again, but later five other players had their wages docked through unauthorised absence.

The club had been well served by four Scots throughout the season, and it was significant that all four were selected in a Scottish players v English players representative match to help raise funds for the Southern League. There was no doubt at all that they were the backbone of the West Ham team. Monteith, in goal, made 29 out of a possible 30 Southern League appearances, Craig at full-back 28, McEachrane at half-back 25, and Grassam up front, made 29.

It would be important for the club to retain the Scots, and bring in players of quality to add to the existing squad, in order to have a good chance of honours in 1902/03.

Standing: F King, ES King, H Monteith, C Craig, F Hunt, A Norris (trainer). Centre: J Bigden, P Kyle, W Kelly, R McEachrane. Front: R Allen, W Grassam, F Corbett, G Ratcliffe, W Linward.

The team colours above are light blue shirts with a claret band across the chest, white shorts and claret socks. They were worn for seasons 1901/02 and 1902/03 before the conventional claret and blue were established in 1903/04.

1901/02

4th in Southern League Division One

League Matches

#	Date	Opponent	Score	Scorers	Att
1	Sep 7	Bristol Rovers	2-0	Corbett, Grassam	5000
2	14	BRENTFORD	2-0	Grassam 2	4500
3	21	New Brompton	0-0		4000
4	28	KETTERING TOWN	1-0	Grassam	6000
5	30	WELLINGBOROUGH T	4-2	Corbett 3, Grassam	2000
6	Oct 5	Northampton Town	4-3	Grassam 2, McEachrane, Bennett(og)	2000
7	12	LUTON TOWN	4-1	Corbett 2, Linward, Ratcliffe	6000
8	19	Watford	0-0		4000
9	26	MILLWALL ATHLETIC	0-2		9000
10	Nov 2	TOTTENHAM HOTSPUR	0-1		17000
11	9	Queen's Park Rangers	1-2	Linward	4000
12	23	Reading	0-3		5000
13	Dec 7	Southampton	0-4		4000
14	14	SWINDON TOWN	2-1	Linward, McEachrane	2000
15	21	BRISTOL ROVERS	2-0	McDonald 2	2000
16	27	Wellingborough T	2-0	Allan, McEachrane	2500
17	Jan 4	NEW BROMPTON	0-0		2000
18	11	Kettering Town	0-1		2000
19	18	NORTHAMPTON T	0-1		5000
20	25	Luton Town	3-0	Hunt 2, Grassam	5000
21	Feb 1	WATFORD	3-2	Ratcliffe 2, Grassam	2000
22	8	Millwall Athletic	1-1	Ratcliffe	3000
23	15	Tottenham Hotspur	2-1	Jenkinson, McEachrane	8000
24	22	QUEEN'S PARK RANGERS	4-0	Hunt 2, Ratcliffe 2	4000
25	Mar 3	Brentford	2-0	Hunt, Jenkinson	500
26	8	READING	2-1	Hunt, Ratcliffe	6000
27	15	Portsmouth	0-0		6000
28	22	SOUTHAMPTON	2-1	Grassam, Ratcliffe	7000
29	29	Swindon Town	1-0	Ratcliffe	1000
30	Apr 12	PORTSMOUTH	1-1	Ratcliffe	6000

Appearances (shirt number per match)

#	Allan R	Ambler C	Bigden J	Corbett F	Craig C	Fair A	Grassam W	Hitchens J	Hunt F	Jenkinson W	Jones W	Kelly W	King S	Kyle P	Linward W	McDonald A	McEachrane R	McGeorge R	Monteith H	Pinder	Pudan R	Ratcliffe G	Taylor F	Wallace L	Ward T	Yenson W
1	7		4	9	3		8					5	2		11		6		1			10				
2	7		4	9	3		8					5	2		11		6		1			10				
3	7		4	9	3		8					5	2		11		6		1			10				
4	7		4	9	3		8					5	2		11		6		1			10				
5	7		4	9	3		8					5	2		11		6		1			10				
6	7		4	9	3		8					5	2		11		6		1			10				
7	7		4	9	3		8					5	2		11		6		1			10				
8	7		4	9	3		8					5	2		11		6		1			10				
9	7		5	9	3		8	10					2		11		6		1							4
10	7		4	9	3		8				10	5	2		11		6		1							
11	4	1		7	3		8					5	2	9	11		6					10				
12					3		7			9		5	2		11		6		1			10				
13	7		4	9	3		8			6		5	2		11				1			10				
14	7		4		3		8			9	5				11		6		1		2	10				
15	7		4		3		8				5				11	9	6		1		2	10				
16	7		4		3		8		9	10	5				11	9	6		1							
17	7		4		3		8		9	6	5		2		11				1							
18	4		6		3		8		7	10	5		2		11	10			1							
19	7		4				8		9	10	5		2		11	9	6		1							
20			4		3		7		9	10	5				11		6		1		2	10				
21			4		3		7		9	10	5		2		11				1			8				
22			4		3		7		9	10	5		2		11				1			8				
23			4		3		7		9	10	5		2		11		6		1			8				
24			4		3		7		9	10	5		2		11		6		1			8				
25			4		3		7		9	10			2		11		6		1			8				
26			4		3		7		9	10			2		11		6		1			8				5
27	7		4		3				9	10	5		2		11		6		1			8				
28			4		3		7		9	10			2		11		6		1			8				5
29			4				7		9	10	5		2		11		6		1			8				
30			4		3		7		9	10	5		2		11		6		1			8				3
Apps	18	1	28	12	28	0	29	1	15	19	15	12	28	1	30	4	25	0	29	0	5	24	0	1	0	5
Goals	1			6			10		6	2					3	2	4					10				

One own goal

F.A. Cup

#	Date	Opponent	Score	Scorer	Att
Q3	Nov 2	Leyton	1-0	Taylor	2000
Q4	Nov 16	GRAYS UNITED	1-2	Linward	2000

#	Allan R	Ambler C	Bigden J	Corbett F	Craig C	Fair A	Grassam W	Hitchens J	Hunt F	Jenkinson W	Jones W	Kelly W	King S	Kyle P	Linward W	McDonald A	McEachrane R	McGeorge R	Monteith H	Pinder	Pudan R	Ratcliffe G	Taylor F	Wallace L	Ward T	Yenson W
Q3	7	1		2			10		9							4	6		3				11	8		5
Q4			5	8									2	9	11		6	4	1		3	10				7

League Table

		P	W	D	L	F	A	W	D	L	F	A	Pts
1	Portsmouth	30	11	4	0	35	5	9	3	3	32	19	47
2	Tottenham Hotspur	30	11	2	2	42	11	7	4	4	19	11	42
3	Southampton	30	12	2	1	54	10	6	4	5	17	18	42
4	WEST HAM UNITED	30	10	2	3	27	13	7	4	4	18	15	40
5	Reading	30	10	4	1	38	9	6	3	6	19	15	39
6	Millwall	30	9	3	3	33	13	4	3	8	13	18	32
7	Luton Town	30	8	5	2	16	10	3	5	7	15	26	32
8	Kettering	30	9	4	2	31	12	3	1	11	13	27	29
9	Bristol Rovers	30	11	1	3	37	10	1	4	10	6	29	29
10	New Brompton	30	10	2	3	27	8	0	5	10	12	30	27
11	Northampton Town	30	7	4	4	40	28	4	1	10	13	37	27
12	Queen's Park Rangers	30	7	4	4	22	16	2	2	11	12	39	24
13	Watford	30	7	2	6	21	19	2	2	11	15	39	22
14	Wellingborough	30	8	2	5	23	18	1	1	13	11	54	21
15	Brentford	30	7	2	6	23	21	0	4	11	11	40	20
16	Swindon Town	30	2	3	10	13	27	0	0	15	4	65	7

1902/03 AN AVERAGE CAMPAIGN

The shareholders' meeting had revealed that the club had managed to keep its head above water from a financial viewpoint when a small profit was realised at the end of 1901/02, and another 500 shares were taken up. With expectations high, season ticket sales doubled to 110, but disappointment came before the campaign began, as three of the four Scottish players were enticed away to Football League clubs. Hugh Monteith, who had been with the club under its new name for two seasons, left for First Division Bury, where he was to gain an FA Cup winners medal in 1903. During those two campaigns with the Hammers, Hugh had conceded just 57 goals in 60 Southern League and FA Cup matches, a remarkable record.

Sadder perhaps, were the departures of Charlie Craig and Roddy McEachrane. Both players had played for the club when it was under the banner of Thames Ironworks FC; Roddy from 1898/99, and Charlie one season later. McEachrane joined Woolwich Arsenal where he had a long and distinguished career making 313 appearances for them until 1913/14. Craig was snapped up by Nottingham Forest and after 4 seasons there, played for Bradford Park Avenue, Norwich City, Southend United and Merthyr Town.

Thankfully Billy Grassam stayed. Billy had been equal top scorer along with George Ratcliffe with ten goals each, but George also left before the campaign began, signing for Second Division Doncaster Rovers.

There were further departures as Bill Jones, the Welsh International centre half, went back to Wales to play for Aberaman Athletic, and the reliable Fergus Hunt returned to Woolwich Arsenal. Later on Bill Jenkinson was to return to his former club Burnley without making any further additions to his Southern League appearances from the previous season. In addition to the playing staff, trainer Abe Norris had already been sacked in January 1902, and was replaced by Jack Ratcliffe.

The exodus of so many key players must have come as a big disappointment to the club's followers. They were all regular first team players in the three league competitions entered for, and had showed a degree of understanding which was proved with their fourth place finish in the Southern League and their winning of the London League Premier Division. From the viewpoint of the players themselves the moves were attractive to them, with the lure of appearing in the Football League, and for some, an increase in wages up to the maximum of £4 per week. The only player not to progress to the Football League was Bill Jones, who could not resist the call to return to the country of his birth.

It was a pity that the club executive could not persuade those men to stay with the club. Most of the Board members were basically businessmen who at this stage had no real experience or grasp of the importance of a player's worth to the club on the field of play. It is probable that Syd King in his roles of secretary/manager and player could have had little say in the departures.

Syd, of course, was involved in their replacements. Nine were signed of varying pedigree and experience. Two goalkeepers were added, William Biggar from Sheffield United and the huge framed Fred Griffiths from Preston North End. Defensively the acquisitions were George Eccles, a full-back who could operate on either flank and had considerable experience with Burslem Port Vale, Wolves and Everton, having made a total of 142 appearances over the three clubs. John Dow with a similar total of 138 with Newton Heath, Luton Town and Middlesbrough, was equally at home at home at right and left back. From Everton came a wing half by the name of Joe Blythe, who excelled more in defensive duties than an attacking role. Much was expected of Tommy McAteer, a huge bear of a player who was signed to occupy the centre-half berth and had three years experience and 59 games with Bolton Wanderers.

Billy Barnes

Up front, John Campbell, a tricky Scottish winger at only 5ft 5 inches and ten stone, was signed from Glasgow Rangers, with whom he had gained four Scottish League winners medals, having also played 55 matches for Blackburn Rovers. A well-known centre-forward by the name of Jack Farrell arrived. He had been a member of Southampton's very accomplished Southern League side, and had an FA Cup runners-up medal to his name. He also had two spells at Stoke City.

Without doubt, the signing of left-winger Billy Barnes from Sheffield United was a real coup. He had scored the winning goal in the previous season's FA Cup Final replay, but had been unable to command a regular first team place at Bramall Lane. This was a player that had really slipped through West Ham's net, as he had begun his career at South West Ham, and had a spell at Thames Ironworks FC as a 16 year old during which time he had scored the winning goal in the club's first ever cup final (the West Ham Charity Cup in 1896). Two years later he was picked up by Leyton and signed professional forms for them. After a string of outstanding performances, he came to the attention of Sheffield United and played in their First Division side over three seasons.

Biggar, Griffiths, Eccles, Dow, McAteer, Campbell and Farrell all had good experience at what was considered a higher level, but were not now 'in the first flush of youth', and were prepared to move to the Southern League, although the gap in quality as opposed to the Football League at this time was not as wide as supposed. As for the signings of Billy Barnes and Joe Blythe, they were both young players, with Barnes wishing to return to the South and his roots in the East End, and Blythe looking to establish himself on a regular basis and further his experience.

Just before the campaign got under way an announcement was made that after the occasional 'scratch' games in 1901/02 at the Boleyn Castle, a new club had now been officially been formed under the name of the Boleyn Castle FC, composed of well-known amateur players. It went on to say:-

'The committee have been fortunate in securing an excellent pitch, situated in the Boleyn Castle School grounds, Green Street, which is easily approachable from all parts of the Borough. They have also received support and co-operation of all the leading tradesmen in the district. Two teams will take the field each week, the first team having to meet their engagements in the English Cup, Essex Senior Cup, and South Essex League Division One, while the reserves will make great efforts to secure the Essex Junior and Leyton and District Alliance Cups. The first team have also been honoured with an invitation from the West Ham Hospital Charity Cup authorities.' The announcement went on to include all the names of the tradesmen involved from the president and vice-presidents down to the patrons. One of those named was Sam Heliar, a printer, who was the grandfather of Jack Heliar, who for a large part of the 20th century was the editor and compiler of the West Ham United matchday programme.

George Eccles

It would be just two years after this announcement of course, that the Boleyn Ground would become the official residence of West Ham United Football Club Ltd.

The first match of the season at the Memorial Grounds was a London League Premier Division fixture and full first teams played. The club were reigning champions but lost the opening game to Woolwich Arsenal 1-3, with ex-Hammer Roddy McEachrane having an outstanding match against his old club. As for the new boys, Billy Barnes shone, and both Blythe and Dow had good games. Eccles and Farrell were disappointing, and Biggar in goal, was at fault for one, possibly two of the goals. But new players need time to acclimatize.

The attendance for the Monday evening encounter was 3,000, but on the previous Saturday West Ham United held a Sports Meeting at the Memorial Grounds. This consisted of foot racing, with various Athletic clubs participating, and both cycling and motorcycle races. The latter had become quite popular since its inception two years earlier, and resulted in a crowd reported as 16,000! After all expenses were taken into consideration net profits went to the club.

The opening Southern League fixture was a home clash with Reading. The talking point was a converted penalty given against Eccles for handball, which was accidental, but gave Reading, who were mostly under siege, a point.

An amusing incident took place in connection with the club's visit to Kensal Rise for the Southern League match with Queens Park Rangers. During the first half the West Ham side gave a blistering performance going forward, but failed to score (this continued in the second half, hence a 0-0 scoreline.) At the same time the club had combined another Sports Meeting with a London League reserve match at home. The half time score of the match at Kensal Rise had been relayed via Syd King to the crowd as 0-0, and even at this early part of the 20th Century, Saturday evening newspapers, when possible, announced the local scores in their early evening editions. To the joy and delight of their followers, the newspaper showed the final score as 4-1 to the Hammers, and the paper was almost a sell-out. It was later revealed that a 'practical joker' had taken the trouble to stamp up between five and six hundred copies with the bogus scoreline in order for a quick sale. It is not known what happened to the culprit with the 'East End enterprise' when he was discovered!

The London League reserve encounter that took place as part of the Sports Meeting was only a 'bit player' in the entertainment. It began with an attempt by A.A. Chase, a motorcycling ace of the time, to break his own speed record over ten miles from a standing start, which failed. Tandem cycling followed on, then the first half of the football. At half time cycling races took place, followed by the second half of the match, and finally motorcycle racing ended the proceedings.

For many people, a football pitch surrounded by a track, be it for athletics, cycling or greyhound racing, is not something that is entirely satisfactory from a spectator viewpoint. For home supporters there is feeling of a lack of contact with the players, and vocal support seems to be dissipated by the distance between the spectators and the action on the field, especially in a wide open arena. This could have been the reason that, at times, there was criticism that there was not enough vocal encouragement of the team whilst resident at the Memorial Grounds, and why some spectators preferred to stand, when allowed to, on the cycle banking or directly behind the goal.

Billy Barnes was the pick of the forwards supplying ammunition from the left wing after several tricky runs, in a 3-0 victory over Brentford in the London Premier League. He also managed time to score himself with a bullet-like header. The other stars of the team were Eccles in defence, and Bigden at half-back, although the crowd were particularly impressed with Tommy McAteer's rocket like shooting, with one effort pole-axing a Brentford defender. What Tommy lacked in speed he made up for with some powerful shooting and his strength in the tackle.

The start of a two mile race at the Memorial Grounds: the total width of the cycle track, the cinder athletics track and a grass verge between them came to almost 55 ft right around the ground, too far away from the spectators for any sense of close involvement.

With a blank Saturday on 20th September the club entertained the Southampton first team in a Western League fixture. The 'Saints' were one of the strongest teams in the South outside of the Football League and were always an attraction. With it being early season and fine weather into the bargain, no less than 9,000 spectators came through the turnstiles, an excellent attendance for this competition. It was a battling contest, perhaps too much so for the 'Irons', as with less than five minutes on the clock, McAteer received some of his own medicine and was off the field for a full twenty minutes. Worse was to come in the second half however. After Bill Linward had opened the scoring, Campbell twisted his ankle and had to be carried off, and just three minutes later Eccles, after receiving a bad kick in the stomach had to retire, looking the worse for wear. So the remaining time was played with just nine men with Southampton equalising in that period.

At half time in the above match there was an on-field presentation by the Directors and friends of Mr J. Grisdale, the popular vice-chairman, with a handsome silver breakfast salver, with cruet etc, as a memento of their esteem with the thoughts of his wedding which was to come off on the following Monday.

On that same Monday there was not a lot of good cheer for the lads in the team, much changed due to injuries, when they travelled to the West Country to meet Bristol Rovers in another Western League match, and were 'lead up the aisle' and defeated by five goals to two.

A visit to Wellingborough followed and against a team that were not considered to be one of great potential, West Ham took a further drubbing with another five goals conceded (1-5). Barnes was the only player to come out with any credit, for his play on the left gave enough chances, particularly to Farrell, for goals to be scored, but the latter was either too slow, or laid off too many unnecessary passes to other colleagues. The final result was due to a second half collapse, as the scores were level at 1-1 at lemon time.

Tommy McAteer

At this point, in all first team competitions there had been just one victory from eight played. Already there were grumblings about comparisons between the players who had left and the new boys. Craig, McEachrane and Monteith, who were all badly missed, had gone to Football League clubs and West Ham were getting poor value for their replacements. The club was not alone, as a number of Southern League clubs were losing good quality players to the Midlands and North. What were coming in the opposite direction were players that were often 'on the way down' in their careers, although this could be tempered somewhat by the amount of valuable experience they brought.

It was suggested in some quarters that local lads of good potential would be of greater benefit in the long run, and less costly. That was certainly the case in the days of Thames Ironworks FC's existence even when the club turned professional, and of course, West Ham United had already included local men. Charlie Dove, George Neil, James Bigden, Fred Corbett, Dick Pudan and Aubrey Fair come to mind. There is, quite plainly, a downside. For a variety of reasons, young men like to spread their wings, and move on to pastures new. It is often soul-destroying when players that have been nurtured through a junior system 'take their boots' elsewhere. Over the years West Ham United have suffered more than most in this respect, particularly in the early 21st century with Rio Ferdinand, Frank Lampard, Joe Cole, Michael Carrick and Glen Johnson leaving for other clubs (and fatter salaries).

After the early season setbacks and criticism from their followers, the team responded by gaining their first Southern League victory when they defeated Bristol Rovers by a solitary goal. It was sweet revenge for the Western League thumping 12 days earlier. It could have been greater as Farrell missed more chances from Barnes hard work.

In a reserve team friendly against Leytonstone, Wallace and right-winger Charlie Paynter were described as the 'pick of the forwards' in a 4-2 victory. In one of those strange coincidences, (although it was not at the time), George Neil, who was still on West Ham's books, but playing for the 'Stones', was at left back in opposition to Paynter. The latter would become the Hammers' manager in 1932, whilst George had held what could be described as a similar position for the club (as Thames Ironworks FC) in 1899/1900. Paynter would go on to have a long career in football, training and managing until 1950, and living into his nineties. Poor George, who had also played for both Thames Ironworks and West Ham United, died of consumption in 1905 at the age of 30.

After another defeat in the Southern League against Northampton by two clear goals, there were rumours of signing a centre-forward as Farrell was still not putting the ball in the back of the net, but it was just that - a rumour. Maybe Farrell 'got wind of it', as he did get on the score sheet in a London League match, scoring twice in a 4-0 victory over QPR.

'Giving him Wat-for (d)'

Little Query__ "Say Hammers! Wot have you been and gorn and done wiv poor Watford?"

Hammers [grim] "Made armour plates of him!"

Points in the Southern League were more important and a poor start had meant a lowly position in the table. It was fortunate that the next two fixtures were against the two clubs that were far and away the worst in the competition. Grassam scored two and Barnes the other in a 3-1 win against Watford at home. This was followed by the team's first away success with a 3-0 triumph over Brentford. Grassam once again hit a brace, and Fred Griffiths played his part by saving a twice taken penalty. Whilst Watford finished the season second from bottom with 16 points, nine points adrift of the team above, Brentford gained just 5 points from 30 matches played.

The Irons were still being referred to in the press as 'the red, white and blues', sporting the same outfits as in the previous season of 1901/02, namely light blue shirts with a claret band across the middle and white shorts. In fact one wag called them the 'Union Jacks'. It was not until the following season of 1903/04 the West Ham United carried the well-known claret and blue in its familiar form.

On the Monday after the Brentford match the team had to travel to Southampton to play in the Southern Charity Cup. They ran out winners by two goals to one, but it was notable that the already famous figure of the great C.B. Fry appeared for the 'Saints' at centre-forward instead of his usual position of full-back.

A valuable Southern League point was gained at 'Spurs in a 1-1 draw, with large numbers of supporters filling special trains from Custom House and Stratford. Sadly, further progress was halted when Millwall came over from North Greenwich and ran out winners by three clear goals on a pitch that can only be described as a mud-heap. With the same team as the previous week everybody had an off-day, especially Griffiths in goal, who was at fault for the second and third goals, when Hulse of Millwall

Fred Griffiths

sent in a low shot which 'Griff' came out to and completely missed his kick, and later, when dashing out to collect the ball, he was beaten to it by an opposing forward, and the ball was quickly put into the back of the net.

Two matches followed, one in the Western League at Portsmouth, and a London League fixture at Kensal Rise against Queens Park Rangers. In the former, in a two-nil defeat, the Portsmouth local correspondent pointed out something that has long since been a tradition of the West Ham character, which generally means plenty of good technical football, especially in midfield, without the lethal finish that such quality deserves. One of the chief culprits in the Pompey game was Jack Farrell who in the opinion of the Portsmouth press 'couldn't shoot for toffee'. Possibly stung by the criticism he redeemed himself by scoring both goals in the 2-0 defeat of QPR!

That same evening club staff, supporters and players - mainly supporters, 'tripped the light fantastic' at the club's third annual Cinderella dance held at Stratford Town Hall, and the total number of people present was more than 300. Amongst those in attendance were directors of the club George Fundell and A.C.Davis, and manager Syd

King, ably assisted by the ever-enthusiastic George Neil who was still socially involved with the club. The event showed that the club and its followers enjoyed a remarkably good relationship with one another at this time.

Included in the evening's entertainment was a programme of 18 dances to the music of Benson Ansley's band, and one of the highlights of the night was a solo turn by tricky right-winger, Johnnie Campbell, who gave an excellent exhibition of step dancing. His colleagues agreed that he was as accomplished on the dance floor as he was on the football pitch.

The players of West Ham and Millwall must have been sick of the sight of one another by the end of November. After their Southern League meeting on the 8th of the month, the two teams met twice more before the month was out. In the Western League there was a 1-2 defeat for the Hammers at North Greenwich where rain fell in sheets throughout the game. It was said that both the players and spectators could have been 'wrung out' at the finish. Five days later a London League Premier Division encounter took place at the same venue, with a 2-2 result. With the three league competitions all basically first team fixtures, most players of those clubs in the London area were likely to meet each other on six occasions.

It was a disappointment that West Ham were dumped out of the FA Cup at the first attempt by football league second division Lincoln City, especially from a financial viewpoint. Bill Kelly, making a rare appearance at centre half was responsible for the mistake that allowed Proudfoot to score the first of City's two goals before half time. In the second half it was the Irons' shooting that let them down once again.

Worse was to follow with a crushing Southern League defeat at the hands (or more likely the feet) of Reading when the home side banged in six goals without reply. At the time this was the worst defeat the club had suffered.

The Christmas holiday period was a busy one for all clubs. Up until the late nineteen fifties matches were always played on Christmas Day and Boxing Day (providing either did not fall on a Sunday). In 1902 there was an added fixture because 25th and 26th December fell on Thursday and Friday, hence there was the usual Saturday game to follow. Players of the modern era have nothing to complain about.

The Hammers lost 1-2 at home to the eventual champions Southampton at home after holding an early lead up to the 83rd minute, and followed this on Boxing Day with a two goal defeat at Portsmouth. Compared to 1901/02 results were disappointing, and the club were in the lower half of the table. Less goals had been scored and more conceded after a similar amount of games in the Southern League. This had an effect on support and just 2,500 went through the gate for the subsequent fixture against Queens Park Rangers. Fortunately it resulted in a welcome two goal victory. The scorers were Grassam and Barnes, who had both been the most consistent forwards since early season; the former for his goals, the latter for his assists.

In an attempt to obtain some more fire-power, the club brought in Alex Davidson, a centre-forward from Reading, and in order to fund the move allowed Bill Linward to move to Woolwich Arsenal. Davidson however, was not the answer and before long he was on his way to Luton, and subsequently Fulham in 1903/04. Linward by contrast, did reasonably well for the Gunners making 47 appearances for them and scoring on ten occasions in the two or so seasons he spent there before moving on to Norwich City.

James Wallace came into the first team after impressing in the reserves and Billy Barnes moved out to the left flank, which in truth was Billy's best position. John Campbell, on the opposite wing, had begun well and was undoubtedly a skilful player, but he consistently took on more of the opposition than was necessary, and his forward colleagues suffered accordingly. He was not retained at the end of the season, and moved on to Hibernian in his native Scotland.

In the New Year revenge was exacted on Wellingborough with a 3-0 victory. Five local lads appeared in that game. Talent from the surrounding area finding their way into the first team at West Ham has become an enduring feature of the club in the century that has followed.

Young Aubrey Fair was beginning to establish himself at full-back. James Bigden at 22 years old had already played for Thames Ironworks in 1899/1900 before spending one season with Gravesend, and was now a first team regular at half-back in his second season at the Memorial Grounds. Bill Yenson, a strong beefy centre half, had also played for Thames Ironworks in 1899/1900 as a 19 year old, and was blending into the first team. Billy Barnes, was also a Thames Ironworks player at the tender age of sixteen, three years before his spell and FA Cup fame at Sheffield United. Finally, the fifth local that lined up against Wellingborough was James Wallace, who had been scoring regularly in the reserve eleven. From this match all five played their part in the side until the end of the campaign.

A useful Southern League point was picked up at Bristol in a 1-1 draw with the Rovers, with Wallace proving his inclusion in the side by scoring. The January weather played a part in the game, as the Hammers, helped by the snowstorm at their backs, consistently pushed forwards. The snow turned to sleet, and the second half gave way to rain. Typical of our changeable weather, a Western League fixture against Tottenham at the Memorial Grounds had to be postponed just two days later when 'King Fog' took over.

An excellent performance at Northampton in what was described as 'one of the best matches of the season' resulted in a 3-2 victory, with Wallace on the scoresheet again. The team's run of three wins and a draw gave hope of moving up to a respectable Southern League position, but the run came to an end at lowly Watford, when Eccles had to leave the field due to an injury early in the second half, and the home team gained the points somewhat luckily by two goals to one.

The offside rule throughout this period stipulated that when a player passed the ball forward in the opposing half to a colleague, there had to be three opponents between him and the goal-line, at the time he released the ball. As this rule was reduced to two players in 1925 (and remains so), it is understandable that goals prior to that date were not easy to come by. When a team were reduced to ten men, for whatever reason, it was common practice to re-arrange the team, and play with just one full-back. By pushing players into a more forward position it was simpler to catch opponents offside, and deny them the opportunity to be in a position to score. Being reduced to ten men was not always a liability.

Two matches against Brentford were next up in two different competitions, one London League Premier and one Southern League. Both were won, 1-0 in the former, and 2-0 in the latter.

Meetings against Tottenham Hotspur were just as keenly anticipated as they are today, and they were just as bitterly fought out. So it was at the Memorial Grounds when 'Spurs were the next visitors. Bigden, Yenson and Blythe were outstanding and with Wallace scoring the only goal, his third since he'd been given his chance, a 1-0 scoreline sealed the victory and sent the Irons' fans home in a happy mood. The result meant that in a sequence of seven Southern League matches five had been won, one drawn and only one lost; an excellent mid-term run towards a respectable position.

Despite using the same squad of players, the Western League, as far as the team's performances were concerned, had become something of a farce. On the other hand, in the London League Premier, also a first team affair, the Hammers headed the table at this stage after beating Woolwich Arsenal by a single goal, with young Robert Bush making his debut at outside right. Maybe the London competition with local sides in opposition gave games a bit more 'edge'.

It was around this time that local amateur club Leytonstone lost two trophies in one day. Sadly, not on the field of play, but at their headquarters, the Elm Hotel. Burglars had broken in during the small hours and stolen the South Essex League Cup and the Wathamstow Charity Cup, both old and much cherished items, which were fortunately insured. They were made of solid silver and would have eventually been melted down, much the same fate as the original FA Cup stolen from a shop window in Birmingham in 1895.

Leytonstone may have lost trophies off the field, but the Irons, for this season, were not about to win any on it. That was not the biggest worry for the club however. Most disconcerting was the financial situation. It was approaching three years since the transition from Thames Ironworks FC to West Ham United had come about, and adequate funds for the day to day running of the club were becoming difficult to maintain. Match day gates were less than had been anticipated, which was highlighted during March when three consecutive home fixtures realised an aggregate total of 5,800. But the greatest dip in finances was due to a larger wage bill, with a number of players receiving the maximum wage of £4 per week. There was of course, no 'fairy godmother' in the form of Arnold Hills to help the club out, and relations with him had become strained as it was. Consequently the club attempted to supplement their finances by organising special events at the Memorial Grounds.

On Easter Monday 1903, with a Western League fixture already arranged at the Memorial Grounds (hardly an attraction given the club's bottom of the table position in that competition), the directors set up a meeting advertised as 'The Great Easter Monday Football, Cycling and Motor Carnival, and free distribution of prizes.' It was estimated that the whole undertaking would realise between £900 and £1000 for the club after expenses. Those directly responsible for launching and publishing the scheme were A.C. Davis, a West Ham United director, and Sam Heliar, a local printer. On the posters printed it stated that '...150 prizes varying in value from £100 to £2.10s would be distributed free of cost among those who purchased tickets. The football match '...will be followed by a shooting competition (archery). The numbers corresponding with the tickets sold will be placed on a target, and a number of persons will shoot as many arrows as prizes given, the number struck by the first arrow being the first prize, the second, the second prize and so on' It was also announced that the person who sold the winning ticket would receive a gold watch, and, as it was expected that between 100,000 and 150,000 would be sold, it was purely a matter of chance who would sell the particular ticket. The archery target was to be about 16ft square, and would have upon it the number of every ticket sold, even if it totalled 150,000!! Each number would be represented by about 7/8 by 3/8 of an inch.

All of the above appears to be somewhat of a convoluted exercise, and it would surely have been difficult to control, but before it could take place it fell foul of the local Commissioner of Police, and both Mr Davis and Mr Heliar were summoned to appear in court for 'unlawfully publishing certain proposals or schemes for the sale of tickets in a lottery'. It was argued that the proposals were something other than a lottery as '...it had been laid down by the Court of Appeal that a lottery must depend on a game of chance, but the object of the present scheme did not in the least involve that the prizes should be given by lottery. Take the shooting for example. Each competitor would naturally aim at his own *ticket on the target, and the smaller the ticket the greater was the skill required. The fact that the person was not in the habit of shooting with bows and arrows did not make it a game of chance. No matter how small was the element of skill introduced into a competition, it made it other than a lottery.'*

After the case was over and a court fine had been paid, Mr Davis told the press that the prize distribution would take place on the Easter Monday, but under a scheme that would be legal. It was a pity for the club that their original idea was to come to nothing. It showed that the club directors were at least showing some enterprise in attempting to add to the club's coffers. As it was, the eventual meeting turned out to be something of a success with between twenty and thirty thousand members of the public attending the event. An exciting programme of cycling and motor-cycling races together with a legal prize lottery resulted in a degree of financial profitability, despite the unseasonable intermittent snowstorms.

After the team's run of seven undefeated games in the Southern League the subsequent results were unexpected. Of the ten remaining matches in the competition only one was a victory, there were five draws and four defeats. Included in those were a 0-6 reverse at Southampton and a 0-4 defeat at Luton. Maybe there were redeeming factors in the latter game as goalkeeper Fred Griffiths struck his fist against a post whilst trying to stop the opening goal, which came after just two minutes. He left the field for half an hour with Eccles going into goal, then returned with his hand strapped to carry on at full-back. It is a pity that the 'powers that be' did not officially agree to introduce substitutes until 1965, but there had been small number of exceptions on the odd unimportant occasion. Strangely enough, one such occurred just a week before the above Luton game. In a 'nothing at stake' fixture in the Western League, young Aubrey Fair fell awkwardly and was badly injured. Syd King, who had become Secretary/Manager, and was in his last season as a player, was allowed to deputise.

There was no doubt that the 1902/03 campaign was a setback on the field of play. Good players had been allowed to leave in the close season and most of their replacements had been inadequate. The final position of 10th in the Southern League table was well down on 1901/02, with goal scoring being a particular problem with only 35 goals scored in 30 matches. Billy Grassam was the exception, for his record was 19 scored from 29 starts, an excellent contribution.

The defence as a whole was not beyond criticism. Their total of 49 conceded, with the exception of the bottom three clubs, was the worst in the Southern League. The Western League proved to be a disaster with a bottom place finish, and the London League Premier Championship was taken from the club by Tottenham. A big improvement was needed on the pitch, but as has already been mentioned, the state of the club off the field was also declining. Come the end of the following campaign an important decision would have to be made.

1902/03

#		Date	Opponent	Score	Scorers	Att	Allan R	Barnes W	Bigden J	Biggar W	Blythe J	Bush R	Campbell J	Davidson W	Dow J	Eccles G	Evans	Fair A	Farrell J	Grassam W	Griffiths F	Kelly W	King S	Linward W	McAteer T	Miecznikowski W	Parkinson H	Sugden S	Wallace L	Yenson W
1	Sep	6	READING	1-1	Barnes	7000		10	4	1	6		7		3	2			9	8				11	5					
2		13	Queen's Park Rangers	0-0		7000		10	4	1	6		7		3	2			9	8				11	5					
3		27	Wellingborough	1-5	Grassam	4000	7	10	4	1	6		7		3	2			9	8				11	5					
4	Oct	4	BRISTOL ROVERS	1-0	Grassam	6500	7	10	4		6					3			9	8	1		2	11	5					
5		11	Northampton Town	0-2		3000	7	10	4		6					3			9	8	1		2	11	5					
6		18	WATFORD	3-1	Grassam 2, Barnes	4000		10	4		6		7		2	3				8	1			11	5				9	
7		25	Brentford	3-0	Grassam 2, Bigden	3000		10			6		7		2	3			9	8	1	4		11	5					
8	Nov	1	Tottenham Hotspur	1-1	Grassam	7000		10	4		6		7		2	3			9	8	1			11	5					
9		8	MILLWALL	0-3		10000		10	4		6		7		2	3			9	8	1			11	5					
10	Dec	6	KETTERING	1-1	Grassam	2500	7	10	4		6		8					3		9	1		2	11	5					
11		20	Reading	0-6		4000		11	8	1	6		10			3				9	7		2		5					4
12		25	SOUTHAMPTON	1-2	Grassam	6000		11	4		6		7	9		3			10	8	1		2							5
13		26	Portsmouth	0-2		18000		11	4		6		7	9		3			10	8	1		2							5
14		27	QUEEN'S PARK RANGERS	2-0	Barnes, Grassam	2500		11	4		6		7	10		3		2	9	8	1									5
15	Jan	10	WELLINGBOROUGH	3-0	Barnes, Davidson, Grassam	4000		11	4		6		7	9		3		2		8	1								10	5
16		17	Bristol Rovers	1-1	Wallace	4000		11	4		6		7	9		3				8	1		2						10	5
17		24	NORTHAMPTON T	3-2	Davidson, Grassam, Wallace	4000		11	4		6		7	9		3		2		8	1								10	5
18		31	Watford	1-2	Campbell	5000		11	4		6		7	9		3		2		8	1								10	5
19	Feb	7	BRENTFORD	2-0	Grassam 2	3000		11	4		6		7	9	3			2		8	1								10	5
20		14	TOTTENHAM HOTSPUR	1-0	Wallace	8000		11	4		6		7	9	3			2		8	1								10	5
21	Mar	7	New Brompton	0-2		7000		11	4		6					3		2	9	8	1					7			10	5
22		14	SWINDON TOWN	1-1	Farrell	4000	7	11	4		6					3		2	9	8	1								10	5
23		23	NEW BROMPTON	1-1	Farrell	1000	7	11	4		6				2	3			9	8	1								10	5
24		28	LUTON TOWN	4-1	Grassam 2, Bigden, Farrell	800	7	11	4		6					3		2	9	8	1								10	5
25	Apr	4	Swindon Town	1-1	Grassam	2500	7	11	4	1	6					3		2	9	8									10	5
26		10	PORTSMOUTH	1-1	Grassam	10000	7	11	4		6					3		2	9	8	1								10	5
27		13	Southampton	0-6		6000			4	1	6		11		3	2			9	8						7			10	5
28		15	Kettering	1-1	Bush	2000			4	1		8	7			2			9			5	3			11	6		10	
29		18	Luton Town	0-4		2000		11	4		6	8			2	3				9	1				5	7			10	
30		25	Millwall	1-2	Grassam	3000	7	11	8	1	6				2	3				9	4								10	5
			Apps				10	27	30	8	29	2	18	9	13	25	1	12	20	29	22	2	9	10	13	3	2	1	16	19
			Goals					4	2			1	1	2					3	19									3	

F.A. Cup

		Date	Opponent	Score		Att	Allan R	Barnes W	Bigden J	Biggar W	Blythe J	Bush R	Campbell J	Davidson W	Dow J	Eccles G	Evans	Fair A	Farrell J	Grassam W	Griffiths F	Kelly W	King S	Linward W	McAteer T
1R	Dec	13	Lincoln City	0-2		3000	7	10	4		6				2	3			9	8	1		5	11	

		P	W	D	L	F	A	W	D	L	F	A	Pts
1	Southampton	30	12	2	1	53	7	8	6	1	30	13	48
2	Reading	30	12	2	1	47	14	7	5	3	25	16	45
3	Portsmouth	30	11	2	2	36	13	6	5	4	33	19	41
4	Tottenham Hotspur	30	10	5	0	34	9	4	2	9	13	22	35
5	Bristol Rovers	30	9	5	1	33	12	4	3	8	13	22	34
6	New Brompton	30	9	4	2	24	9	2	7	6	13	26	33
7	Millwall	30	9	2	4	33	16	5	1	9	19	21	31
8	Northampton Town	30	7	3	5	23	19	5	3	7	16	29	30
9	Queen's Park Rangers	30	8	3	4	25	16	3	3	9	9	26	28
10	WEST HAM UNITED	30	8	5	2	25	14	1	5	9	10	35	28
11	Luton Town	30	8	3	4	28	14	2	4	9	15	30	27
12	Swindon Town	30	8	5	2	24	13	2	2	11	14	33	27
13	Kettering	30	5	8	2	19	12	3	3	9	14	28	27
14	Wellingborough	30	9	2	4	27	15	2	1	12	9	41	25
15	Watford	30	5	1	9	22	33	1	3	11	13	54	16
16	Brentford	30	2	1	12	10	36	0	0	15	6	48	5

1903/04 CLOSE TO DISASTER

The struggle to keep the club solvent intensified. A loss of £151 on the previous season was announced, and the expected revenue from the sale of season tickets at the Memorial Grounds took a downturn when a significant number of supporters failed to renew. The reason may have been due to the previous campaign's poor league position or the failure to strengthen the club with top class signings that were needed to bolster the current squad of players, or just a lack of money in the pockets of the working class men in the area. Whatever the reason, if the deficit was not turned around it would make it almost impossible for the club to carry on.

The awful wet weather of the previous winter and spring continued right throughout the summer and many County Cricket Championship matches were badly affected. The West Ham United board of Directors were certainly not relishing any prospects of further disruption by the weather during the new campaign.

A number of players left the club in the close season. Outside right Robert Allan, who had been with club since Thames Ironwork's days was released, and John Farrell retired from playing. Goalkeeper William Biggar, who had not really impressed, went on to Fulham and appeared on just 6 occasions there, but subsequently moved to Watford in 1904/05. He was obviously a great success there making 217 appearances over 6 seasons rarely missing a match. John Dow, who could play in either full-back position, but never fully established himself overall, signed for Luton Town. John Campbell, who returned to Scotland to play for Hibernian, had a good pedigree when he arrived from Glasgow Rangers, having been part of the club's four consecutive Scottish title wins. He was a tricky winger with good ball skills, but he was inclined to hang on to the ball for too long, and his forward colleagues often suffered from a lack of service.

West Ham decided to part company with all three centre halves on the club's books. Bill Kelly, a regular for the first half of 1901/02, until he received a long-term injury, left for Notts County. Big Tommy McAteer, a regular for the first half of 1902/03, was signed by Brighton & Hove Albion, and Bolton Wanderers came in for local boy Billy Yenson who had displaced Tommy. Bill had begun his career when the club was known as Thames Ironworks FC, and he was to make the Wanderers' FA Cup final side in 1904 when they were defeated by Manchester City.

As replacements the club signed no less than eleven players, in addition to three local lads. Four of the professionals came from Reading. They were goalkeeper Charlie Cotton who had also played for Sheppey United. Herbert Lyon, who was an inside forward with a reputation as an expert at the short passing game, and had experience with Leicester Fosse in the Football League First Division in 1898/99, and later Watford. Tommy Allison, a well respected wing half, who had made 66 appearances for New Brighton Tower in the Football League Second Division, and burly Ernie Watts at 13 stone and 6 ft tall came to fill the vacant centre half position. He had also played for Notts County in the First Division in 1898/99.

To take the position of outside right, Bill Kirby was signed from Swindon Town. Bill, in addition to his flank duties, also had capabilities as a goalscorer. As a direct replacement for Bill Grassam, the experienced Charlie Satterthwaite came from New Brompton. He had also played for First Division Bury and Liverpool, and Second Division Burton Swifts.

Ernie Watts

The remaining five professionals did not 'cut the mustard'. Tommy Duckworth a right wing player from Blackpool, did not directly get a first team chance and took the return journey by mid-October. 'Micky' Earl, an outside left who had experience with Chesterfield and Walsall, appeared just once, and left the club at the same time as Duckworth. Alec Kay a full-back from Sheffield United, played early on in the Western League, but was not considered good enough for the Southern League. Billy Ingham, a forward from Welsh club Aberdare Athletic, failed to impress in his two outings. He moved on to Bristol City and Gainsborough Trinity in the Football League and then Plymouth Argyle in the Southern. Finally, James Butchart was signed from Greenock Morton, played three early season matches in the forward rank, but was not a success.

The club had far better fortune with the three local players. Percy Mapley at left back made thirteen appearances in the Southern League and four in the FA Cup by the end of January 1904, before moving to Tottenham. Billy Bridgeman, a 19 year old forward, and a former a pupil of local Marner Road School, was signed and was to prove an exceptional player, and Len Jarvis a half-back, also at 19, spotted whilst playing at amateur level in Essex. He was to become a long-term favourite with Hammers' fans.

The season opened with a home encounter against Plymouth Argyle in the Western League. Although this competition did not carry the importance of the Southern League it was basically a first team fixture and the local enthusiasts were eager to see the team with some of its added newcomers. The game was scheduled to kick off early evening at 5.30pm, and despite the weather's continuing dampness on this first day of September, it was still summer and quite warm. With the Memorial Grounds being built on what was the original Abbey Marsh it was said that whilst there was a comparatively good attendance of 3,500 it was quite definite that there were just as many mosquitoes!

Although it was the first display of what was a newly constructed forward line, the match ended in a disappointing defeat by a single goal, with some spectators literally itching to leave before time.

More important of course, was the opener in the Southern League against Millwall at North Greenwich. With better understanding up front, two goals were put away. Four goals however, went in at the wrong end.

This was followed by an evening fixture at home against Kettering Town which resulted in the club's first win of the season. It has to be mentioned that three of the 'Ketts' team arrived on the field over five minutes late due to transport problems (after an already late kick-off of ten minutes). During that time Jimmy Bigden netted the Hammers' first goal. This gave the required confidence for the remainder of the game, and a 4-1 victory resulted with Herbert Lyon netting two and Tommy Allison the other.

The result gave the impetus to defeat a very good QPR side at home by 1-0 on the following Saturday with a 6,000 crowd in attendance (5,000 more than for the Kettering game).

The club's opening match in the London League Premier Division was at Plumstead against Woolwich Arsenal. With ex-Thames Ironworks and West Ham favourite Roddy McEachrane on the opposing side and virtually running the show, the home team ran out easy winners by 4 goals to 1. To continue with the story of the club's performance at this point in the London Premier and Western League would be irrelevant as, by the end of the season, bottom place in both competitions was the outcome, with the inevitable 'wooden spoons' to go with them.

When the team faced Reading, after two disappointing displays against Plymouth and Luton, 10,000 spectators turned up at the Memorial Grounds. This figure was boosted by the attraction of a series of Championship Cycle events taking place, before, at half time, and after the match. The game itself turned out to be an excellent battle with little to choose between the sides. Charlie Satterthwaite, renowned for possessing a rocket like shot, scored with a superb twenty-yard strike before the visitors equalised with a similar effort. There were many cries of 'Play up Irons' during the game, something which continues to be heard in the form of 'Come on you Irons' over 100 years later.

Due to an injury picked up in a friendly match against Clapton, Satterthwaite, or 'Satters', as he became known, was unfit for the Bristol Rovers match which followed, and with the other forwards woeful in their shooting a 1-4 defeat resulted. It was early days of course, but Billy Barnes was not producing his usual good form, 'Sunny Jim' Kirby was inconsistent, and Herbert Lyon was not the goalscorer he had been at Reading and Watford previously. As a point of interest, Lyon was known as 'Bertie', but he possessed probably football's longest name at the time, his full name being Herbert Ernest Saxon Bertie Cordey Lyon!

After suffering a 2-3 defeat at Brighton, the tables were turned when the Irons met same club in their next outing - an FA Cup 3rd Qualifying round match. Satterthwaite and centre half Ernie Watts got on the score sheet, and finally Lyon, with his 'share' notched two in a 4-0 victory. With the score just one-nil in the first half, 3 goals in a five-minute spell in the second half confirmed the home side's dominance, despite the over-robust display of Tommy McAteer, anxious to impress his ex-team mates and supporters.

West Ham suffered two odd goal defeats in November against Brentford and 'Spurs, but sandwiched between those two matches came the next round of the FA Cup, when the club was drawn away to local Forest Gate side Clapton at the 'Spotted Dog'. Supporters of the amateur team were alarmed that the price at the gate had been increased to one shilling. A petition was lodged with the club, but it was pointed out that it was a ground that could only hold 5,000 or so in comfort and safety, whereas perhaps three times that many would want to obtain entry at the normal price. The Clapton committee, in all fairness, and seeking to prove that this was not a money-making exercise, chose to give the extra profits to charity, and after the event listed those as:- London Hospital £10, West Ham Hospital £9, East Ham Hospital £9, and St. Mary's Hospital Plaistow £5 15 shillings. The total amount would have meant a great deal for the finances of the amateur club, and they were praised for their honesty.

As for the game itself, it was played in a very tough and fully committed manner. Like many a cup-tie the underdogs threw everything at the team from a higher level, and for the first fifteen minutes the visitors were very close to conceding. Not being used to the size of the pitch, as opposed to the wide open spaces of the Memorial Grounds, and feeling 'hemmed in' on all sides, clearances from the defence were quickly returned. The home side were described as *a troop of warhorses charging over broken ground* and any scientific superiority that was expected from the professionals was soon dispelled. The 'Hammers', realising that playing any type of combination football would not pay off, began to play the 'Doggies' at their own game, and gradually gained the upper hand, opening the scoring just before the break.

In the second half the professional side began more positively and on one occasion Earl, in the Clapton goal, 'went walkabout', as goalkeepers could use their hands outside their own area (up until 1912). In doing so, he was surrounded by West Ham players and could not get back, but the resulting effort was cleared off the line. During this period, with the visitors attacking, there were scuffles between players under the Clapton bar at free-kicks and corners, and no quarter was asked or given. Eventually the Irons added two more goals, and the 'Battle Royal' came to a conclusion, but it was a good deal closer than the 3-0 scoreline suggested.

The 1-2 defeat to 'Spurs at White Hart Lane was a disappointment, but not only did the forwards shooting (or lack of it) leave a lot to be desired, the defence was directly at fault for both goals. Fred Griffiths let the ball slip through his hands for the first, and Eccles and Mapley allowed Jones to easily push his way between them for the second.

Back in 1895 when the club was in its first season under the banner of Thames Ironworks, the very first opponents in the FA Cup were Chatham. Now in the 4th Qualifying round the clubs were to meet again. It was satisfying to reverse that first season's defeat of 0-5 by the same score eight years later. Charlie Satterthwaite scored a hat-trick, with Kirby and Lyon netting the others in a comfortable victory.

Supporters travelled by train to the above tie with club Secretary/Manager Syd King providing train tickets from Cannon Street station at 2/6d each, but not everyone could afford such luxuries. It must not be forgotten that in the district of Canning Town where the West Ham club was situated, there were many working men on poor wages and others who were seeking work daily. The nearby Victoria Docks and Royal Albert Docks provided employment for local workers but there were large numbers who were 'casual labour'. Seeking work at Victoria Docks for those 'casuals' as in all docks in the area, meant firstly being present at a 'list call' at the entrance. A 'list call' meant that the various firms in the docks had a number of men's names on their list as 'good labourers', and when the list was read out, if a man's name was called and he answered it, he was given a metal disc with a number and could start work for the day. If there was no reply to a call by the foreman, men gathered at the front literally pleading for work. 'Wife and three kids here, foreman!' Or 'Sick wife and six, guv'nor!' Quite a pitiful sight. Train tickets to a football match were never on their list of priorities.

Fortunately, although there was much poverty and hardship, there were, within the district many factories where men were fully employed. One of the biggest of course, was Thames Ironworks with its shipbuilding business, but within seven years that would collapse due mainly to the Government preferring to hand contracts to the Northern shipyards.

The club's hope of further progress in the FA Cup came to a halt in the next round when Fulham were the visitors. In a below par display, in front of what was to be the biggest home attendance of the season (12,000), and with just one change to the team when ex-Fairburn House boy Alex Birnie took the place of Bill Kirby who reported lame, Fulham unexpectedly won by the only goal.

An excellent victory on Christmas Day against eventual champions Southampton by two goals to one was some compensation, but on the following day at Fratton Park, the Hammers lost to high-flying Portsmouth by the same score. Revenge for the cup defeat came two days later with a 2-0 success over Fulham. Kirby and Satterthwaite scored and all the forwards were in good form, but Fryer, the opposing 'keeper, saved the visitors from a real drubbing.

This Jekyll-and-Hyde form continued when Millwall came to the Memorial Grounds. Their solitary goal was enough to take the points back to North Greenwich and perform the double, but on this occasion the home forwards reverted to a poor display, and took a great deal of criticism. As Barnes was unfit young Fred Mercer came in from the reserves and was poor, Billy Bridgeman was 'not up to it' on the day, Satterthwaite was too selfish, Kirby was too fond of 'dallying' on the ball, and Bigden was well below his best. On the credit side Watts and Blythe were in good form in the middle of the park.

A 1-2 reverse against Queens Park Rangers at Kensal Rise brought the club nearer to the foot of the table, and after the visit of Plymouth Argyle when just one point was gained in a 1-1 draw the inaccurate finishing of the forwards was again highlighted in the local press when it was stated that:- 'Given a good thirty feet in width and twenty feet in height it is just possible that the Hammers' front rank would score a goal a game, but under normal conditions it is too much to expect.' The comments continued '...in the second half......Lyon evidently thought the posts were located somewhere near the phonograph inflictor'.

The phonograph, with its wax cylinder was one of the earliest forms of music recording machines. 80% of the British record sales were on cylinder and the largest were five inches in diameter. Their heyday was in the period 1900-1904, and they were capable of reproducing a sound recording of up to two minutes. The phonograph itself was probably situated near the corner of the ground with a loudspeaker to provide some music at half time.

The following week the players had seven days off to recharge their batteries simply because everywhere was shrouded in fog, but one week later the weather took another turn when torrential rain fell for the whole day. Perhaps the deplorable state of the pitch favoured the Irons as the team had an easy victory over Wellingborough by four goals to one. (Satterthwaite broke the net for one of his goals with a powerful drive!) As a result of the unceasing downpour the size of the crowd amounted to just 250 spectators. It was to be the club's lowest-ever Southern League attendance.

Perhaps the local pub or tavern was a greater attraction on such a miserable January day. Sinking a pint and staring at the barmaid must have been a better option, but there was a proposal afoot at the time to limit the employment of barmaids on licensed premises. The appeal was made by the British Women's Temperance Association who put several points to the Mayor of West Ham:- '...*many were too young, several were only 15 years of age at a recent survey, 96 hours a week was the average working time, that no matter how bad the language, the barmaid had to remain at her post. Should the purveyors of alcohol be allowed to employ such bright-minded girls for the sake of giving additional attractiveness to the drink they sold? In a very short time the once bright, innocent and pure-minded girls become familiarized with things they ought to know nothing.*' There you have it, 1904 style. Their 21st century descendants in the Boleyn, the Queens, the Central and the Denmark Arms will give as good as they get on matchdays!

Three matches went strictly to form. A 0-4 reverse against a strong Bristol Rovers side was followed by a 5-0 thrashing of a poor Brighton & Hove team with Satterthwaite banging in four goals, with Billy Barnes supplying every one of them. A 2-0 victory over lowly Northampton side made the league position look more comfortable.

In March the Hammers had a disastrous run of five consecutive league defeats without scoring (unequalled until 2006/07) with the forwards misfiring yet again. It was significant that four of those five fixtures were away from home, and that was perhaps the reason why it had turned out to be such a poor campaign. As that away record stood at the end of March the team had not managed one success on 'foreign' soil, with just one draw and eleven defeats in the Southern League.

In the same month the Board of Directors of West Ham United began discussing the possibility of a move away from the Memorial Grounds. The club's relationship with Arnold Hills had become somewhat strained over the previous couple of years, one point being his difference of opinion over the matter of the appointment of possible directors, but the main issue was that the current agreement for the rental of the ground which was due to end at the close of the 1903/04 season. The club directors attempted to obtain a further lease of the ground for a period of seven, fourteen or even 21 years at a good rental, but no agreement could be reached. Arnold Hills's letter stated that he required the use of the ground for his own amateur Thames Ironworks team, and in addition he also required the professional club to quit the offices that it had been using at the Ironworks. The West Ham board decided that they would publish Mr Hills's letter to the local press if any other team besides the Ironworks used the Memorial Grounds.

At such a late stage it was critical that the club found a new ground without delay. The Corporation offered them a piece of waste ground but it was inappropriate. The answer to the problem came as a matter of pure chance. Whilst a football match was taking place between the boys of two Home Office schools at the Memorial Grounds, one of the Brothers of the Boleyn Castle School (a Roman Catholic Reformatory school), was present and was shown Mr Hills's letter. Understanding the problem, he offered to show the club's officials round the Boleyn Castle playing field on that same day, and it was decided to take up the offer after the proper negotiations. Initially the Home Office refused permission, but through the intervention of Ernest Gray M.P., and providing certain conditions were adhered to, acceptance was granted. One of those conditions involved the amalgamation of the Boleyn Castle FC, who were members of the South Essex League. The club had some promising young amateur players in the side, and the best of those were to be included in the reserve team. In addition, an opportunity was given to four Boleyn Castle directors to purchase stock in West Ham United on the understanding that one or more of them would be recommended by the West Ham directors to be elected to their board. Over the two years of the Boleyn club's existence they had enjoyed the support of a small but enthusiastic band of local fans, and it was to be hoped that they would now follow the Hammers with just as much devotion.

On the field of play in April came a hectic period of no less than 5 games in nine days. It began on Good Friday when the net was found at last against a Portsmouth side that was expected to finish at least in the runners-up position. An 8,000 crowd at the Memorial Grounds went home happy after witnessing a 3-0 triumph with Satterthwaite scoring two and Bridgeman the other, but a goalless draw against New Brompton followed the very next day.

With such a dreadful record on their travels the club faced a run of no less than five consecutive away fixtures before their final game at the Memorial Grounds. The position appeared irretrievable, because at least six points would be needed to make absolutely sure of Southern League First Division survival depending on the results of those in the bottom six places. The team, made up mostly of the same players, pulled out all the stops, and fought out two wins and two draws and suffered just the one defeat over those five matches. A battling 1-1 result against the champions-elect Southampton at the Dell was the highlight, but the two victories against relegation rivals Northampton and Kettering were the most vital. (As it transpired there was to be no automatic relegation in the Southern League until 1909/10).

The final match of the season at home to Swindon Town did not now have that urgency as the necessary points for safety had been secured. The talking point of the game was that the referee allowed both teams to play in identical outfits, and such was the confusion, it was a miracle that it remained goalless at the break. The home side were obliged to change colours for the second half, but it was the Wiltshire club who changed the game with a solitary winning goal.

It would have been gratifying for the Hammers had they achieved victory on their very last appearance at the Memorial Grounds, but it was not to be, and so ended the club's tenure at the Canning Town arena. Its stay, which included the period as Thames Ironworks FC, was seven years. In the club's four year period as West Ham United, the results at home were not in the least impressive. If we take the three leagues of the Southern, Western and London Premier competitions and the FA Cup together (as they were all basically first team fixtures) exactly 107 matches took place. Of those, 52 were won and 173 goals were scored. In other words, less than 49% were victories with an average of just 1.61 home goals scored per match. This very modest record can only be put down to woeful fire-power or lack of the 'killer instinct'.

The front view of the main stand at the Memorial Grounds

Some said bad luck haunted the whole arena, and a well-known football journal stated, with heavy sarcasm, that *'The Hammers have never been really happy at the Memorial Grounds. Ill luck has followed the club every inch of the way, and it has not been for want of horse-shoes in the dressing room. Perhaps the players committed the fatal error of nailing them up inside the door. They might have tried one of the goal posts, and, with the exception of one good year, when they reached fourth position in the table, their forwards have invariably failed in front of the mark......'*

Whether ill-fortune played a part is arguable, but the ground itself had a pretty much depressing aura about it. Maybe the large marshy area that it was built upon had a haunting effect that defied description - it was a miserable place during the winter months, and despite the drainage system that had originally been installed, the pitch soon became a mud heap after a period of rainfall. The arena was not well served from the angle of its accessibility, and the opening of West Ham station in Manor Road in 1901 did not improve attendances as much as was expected. That is not to say that the stadium did not have some success, particularly in the summer months, for it was considered one of the finest in respect of its athletic and cycling tracks.

Built in 1897, many sporting meetings were held there including motorcycle races, and often Arnold Hills (the Thames Ironworks managing director) arranged various events such as military tournaments and Wild West shows to augment the sporting meetings. However, the attendances were sometimes disappointing from a financial aspect. It must also be remembered that the whole idea of this sporting complex was the intention to give members of Hills's Federated Clubs within the Works free use of its facilities. So from the competitors and participants' point of view, especially the cyclists,

The boarded-up stand after the grounds had closed

it was considered very favourably. The diagram of the inside of the grandstand drawn by Jimmy Kaine (following) gives an indication of the facilities for the competitors. The General Room and the Rented Room acted as dressing rooms for West Ham United and their opponents, and the large room to the rear was specifically for the cyclists. This room had a high ceiling that allowed cycles to be hung by their frames, and gave enough headroom underneath. Showers and baths were installed, though not shown on Jimmy's diagram. The General Room was also used by the West Ham trainer and Jack Pratt, the masseur.

If the arena did have a 'heyday' it was probably from its inception until 1908, but that year was the year of the London Olympics and White City then became the favoured venue for athletics. Equally upsetting was the fact that the cycling events were held at Herne Hill, which, although in constant use since its construction in 1892, did not have the capacity or facilities of the Memorial Grounds, but it was probably because of the logistical problems that the Canning Town arena was not considered. In addition, the East End was not considered in the early twentieth century as the flavour of the month, year or any other time, as it is today by the 'powers that be', with the 2012 Olympics in vogue.

In August 1912, just a few short months before the sad closure of Thames Ironworks, Hills sold the Memorial Grounds and adjacent land for £12,000, and in May 1914 West Ham Council bought the Grounds alone for £10,000. In early 1918, during the final months of the Great War, the borough engineer reported that the War Office Authorities had entered the Grounds without notice and proceeded with the erection of permanent buildings, making foundations into the concrete track. Basically, an earlier agreement to use buildings on the ground on the condition that the cycle track and football ground would not be interfered with, had been totally ignored. Despite a protest, the War Office quoted a 'Defence of the Realm' regulation and the official 'vandalism' remained, with the War almost over. The Memorial Grounds as a stadium was finished and now the tracks and buildings have gone including the grandstand, which disappeared in the 1980's. Local football and rugby is still played on the flat and windswept landscape, and just the calls and shouts of the players echo those from over one hundred years ago.

(Jimmy Kaine, who was a competitive cyclist at the Memorial Grounds and was also a firm supporter of both Thames Ironworks FC and its successor West Ham United, was, in his old age, in regular communication with eminent cycling historian David Twitchett, and included in his papers were sketched diagrams of the Memorial Grounds tracks and stands, and copies are included here, with the permission of Mr Twitchett.)

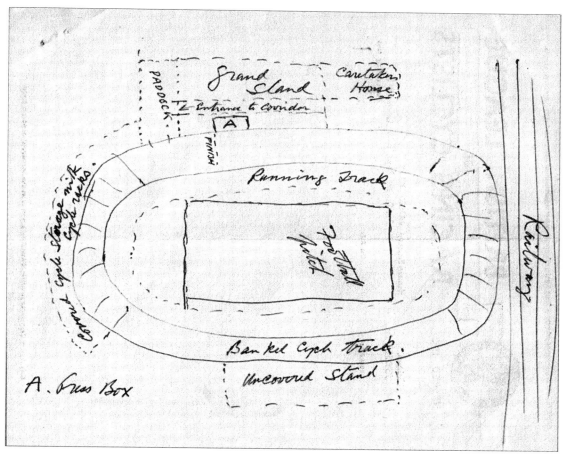

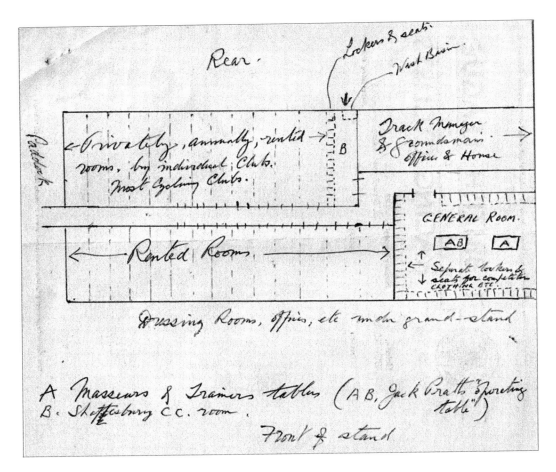

Back row (behind players): J Cearns, G Fundell, J Moss, G Handley, T Williamson. Next to back: G Eccles, A Kaye, F Griffiths, C Cotton, A Fair. Centre: G Hone, ES King (secretary), J Bigden, E Watts, J Blythe, T Allison, W Johnson (trainer), T Tappin, AC Davies. Seated: J Grisdale (chairman), T Duckworth, H Lyon, J Butchart, W Kirby, C Satterthwaite, W Barnes, W White. At front: C Paynter, J Johnson, W Ingham, G Davis, H Simms.

1903/04

12th in Southern League Division One

No	Date	Opponent	Score	Scorers	Att	Allison T	Barnes W	Bigden J	Birnie A	Blythe J	Bridgeman W	Butchart J	Church W	Cotton C	Earl	Eccles G	Fair A	Griffiths F	Hilsdon J	Ingham W	Jarvis L	Kirby W	Lyon H	Mapley P	Mercer F	Oakes W	Satterthwaite C	Thompson A	Watts E
1	Sep 5	Millwall	2-4	Kirby, Satterthwaite	10000		11	4		6		1				3	2			9		7	8				10		5
2	Sep 7	KETTERING	4-1	Lyon 2, Allison, Bigden	1000	6	11	4					8	1		3	2					7	9				10		5
3	Sep 12	QUEEN'S PARK RANGERS	1-0	Satterthwaite	6000	6	11	4					8	1		3	2					7	9				10		5
4	Sep 19	Plymouth Argyle	0-2		5000	6	11	4					8	1		3	2					7	9				10		5
5	Sep 24	LUTON TOWN	0-0		3000	6	11	4						1		2			8			7	9	3			10		5
6	Sep 26	READING	1-1	Satterthwaite	10000	6	11	4						1		2	3				9	7	8				10		5
7	Oct 10	BRISTOL ROVERS	1-4	Watts	5000	6	10	4		8				1	11	2						7	9	3					5
8	Oct 17	Brighton & Hove Albion	2-3	Fair, Satterthwaite	4000	4	11	8		6				1		2	9					7		3			10		5
9	Nov 7	BRENTFORD	0-1		2000	4	11	5	8	6						2		1				7	9	3			10		
10	Nov 21	Tottenham Hotspur	1-2	Kirby	8000	4	11	8		6						2		1				7	9	3			10		
11	Dec 5	New Brompton	0-0		4000	4	11	8		6						2		1				7	9	3			10		5
12	Dec 25	SOUTHAMPTON	2-1	Kirby, Satterthwaite	10000	4	11	8		6	9					2		1				7		3			10		5
13	Dec 26	Portsmouth	1-2	Barnes	14000	4	11	8		6	7					2		1					9	3			10		5
14	Dec 28	FULHAM	2-0	Kirby, Satterthwaite	2000	4	11	8		6	7					2		1					9	3			10		5
15	Jan 2	MILLWALL	0-1		10000	4		8		6	7					2		1					9	3			10		5
16	Jan 9	Queen's Park Rangers	1-2	Kirby	7000		11	4		6						2		1				7	8	3			10	9	5
17	Jan 16	PLYMOUTH ARGYLE	1-1	Kirby	8000		11	4		6						2		1				7	8	3			10	9	5
18	Jan 30	WELLINGBOROUGH	4-1	Kirby 2, Thompson, Satterthwaite	250	5	11	4		6						2		1				7	8	3			10	9	
19	Feb 6	Bristol Rovers	0-4		2000	5	11	4		6						2	3	1				7	8				10	9	
20	Feb 13	BRIGHTON & HOVE ALB.	5-0	Satterthwaite 4, Lyon	3000	5	11	4		6						2	3	1				7	8				10	9	
21	Feb 27	NORTHAMPTON T	2-0	Kirby, Lyon	4000	5		4		6	11					2		1				7	8			3	10	9	
22	Mar 2	Reading	0-1		1000	5		4		6	11					2		1				7	8			3	10	9	
23	Mar 5	Brentford	0-2		4000	5		4		6	11					2		1				7	8			3	10	9	
24	Mar 12	Swindon Town	0-1		3000	5		4		6	9	11				2		1				7	8			3	10		
25	Mar 19	TOTTENHAM HOTSPUR	0-2		9500	5		4		6	9	11				2		1				7	8			3	10		
26	Mar 26	Luton Town	0-1		5000	5		4		6	9					2		1				7	8			3	10		
27	Apr 1	PORTSMOUTH	3-0	Satterthwaite 2, Bridgeman	8000	6		4			9					2		1				7	8		11	3	10		
28	Apr 2	NEW BROMPTON	0-0		5000			4			9					2		1				7	8		11	3	10		5
29	Apr 4	Southampton	1-1	Bridgeman	10000			4			9					2		1			6	7	8		11	3	10		5
30	Apr 7	Northampton Town	3-1	Allison, Kirby, Mercer	1000	6		4			9					2		1				7	8		11	3	10		5
31	Apr 9	Kettering	1-0	Bridgeman	1000	6		4			9					2		1				7	8		11	3	10		5
32	Apr 20	Wellingborough	0-3		3000	4	11			6	9					2		1				7	8			3	10		5
33	Apr 23	Fulham	1-1	Bridgeman	4000		11	4		6	9					2		1				7	8			3	10		5
34	Apr 30	SWINDON TOWN	0-1		4000	4	11	7		6	9					2		1					8			3		10	5
Apps						28	22	33	1	23	19	3	2	8	1	34	7	26	1	2	2	33	29	13	7	14	32	9	25
Goals						2	1	1			4						1					10	4		1		13	1	1

F.A. Cup

Rd	Date	Opponent	Score	Scorers	Att	Allison T	Barnes W	Bigden J	Birnie A	Blythe J	Bridgeman W	Butchart J	Church W	Cotton C	Earl	Eccles G	Fair A	Griffiths F	Hilsdon J	Ingham W	Jarvis L	Kirby W	Lyon H	Mapley P	Mercer F	Oakes W	Satterthwaite C	Thompson A	Watts E
Q3	Oct 31	BRIGHTON & HOVE ALB.	4-0	Lyon 2, Satterthwaite, Watts	5000	4	11	8		6		1				2						7	9	3			10		5
Q4	Nov 14	Clapton	3-0	Lyon 2, Satterthwaite	4500	4	11	8		6						2		1				7	9	3			10		5
Q5	Nov 28	Chatham	5-0	Satterthwaite 3, Kirby, Lyon	5000	4	11	8		6						2		1				7	9	3			10		5
1R	Dec 12	FULHAM	0-1		12000	4	11	8	7	6						2		1					9	3			10		5

Action from the match v Plymouth Argyle at the Memorial Grounds. Note the spectators on the banked cycle track and behind the goal.

		P	W	D	L	F	A	W	D	L	F	A	Pts
1	Southampton	34	12	3	2	43	15	10	3	4	32	15	50
2	Tottenham Hotspur	34	10	5	2	34	19	6	6	5	20	18	43
3	Bristol Rovers	34	11	4	2	38	12	6	4	7	26	30	42
4	Portsmouth	34	11	4	2	24	11	6	4	7	17	27	42
5	Queen's Park Rangers	34	13	3	1	34	12	2	8	7	19	25	41
6	Reading	34	8	6	3	27	15	6	7	4	21	20	41
7	Millwall	34	10	2	5	41	20	6	6	5	23	22	40
8	Luton Town	34	12	4	1	23	9	2	8	7	15	24	40
9	Plymouth Argyle	34	8	5	4	27	16	5	5	7	17	18	36
10	Swindon Town	34	7	7	3	18	14	3	4	10	12	28	31
11	Fulham	34	7	6	4	23	15	2	6	9	11	21	30
12	WEST HAM UNITED	34	8	4	5	26	14	2	3	12	13	30	27
13	Brentford	34	8	4	5	25	18	1	5	11	9	30	27
14	Wellingborough	34	7	4	6	34	25	4	1	12	10	38	27
15	Northampton Town	34	8	4	5	22	20	2	3	12	14	40	27
16	New Brompton	34	4	10	3	18	15	2	3	12	8	28	25
17	Brighton & Hove Alb.	34	5	6	6	27	29	1	6	10	19	40	24
18	Kettering	34	6	4	7	23	23	0	3	14	16	53	19

1904/05   A NEW HOME

The club had suffered a huge operating loss by the end of the 1903/04 season of £793, and would have been very close to disaster had the directors not taken the decision to move to the Boleyn Ground at Upton Park, where the club had high hopes of a greater degree of financial stability. Playing adjacent to the main road in Green Street, which in the previous February had seen the advent of the electric tram system, and having the advantage of Upton Park station less than five minutes from the door appeared to be an attractive proposition. These lines of communication served an area that was more residential and populous, with shops in the north end of Green Street and adjoining Barking Road, which was already a busy east to west artery.

Joseph Grisdale, a coppersmith by occupation, had now been elevated to Chairman of the club succeeding Edwin Smith, a timber converter, and the remaining directors were all local business men and members of a professional class that were willing to invest their time and money. Being local also established their credentials as members of the existing community. Moreover they were not beholden to Arnold Hills and his ideas regarding professional sport and temperance. In fact the Board had one scheme, besides others, to obtain help by contacting advertisement contractors regarding the placing of new hoardings around the ground, and to also 'ask the brewers for their personal assistance.' The directors also put their faith in the future by obtaining loans to a total of £3,000.

With a logistical improvement and a possible financial one too, Syd King, secretary and manager, was interviewed by the press just before the season began as to the progress of the work on the new ground. Whilst the area around the pitch was full of bustling activity with carpenters, joiners and other labourers, tenaciously slogging away at their work to get everything completed for the opening game of the season, Syd explained that £3,000 was being spent but the management felt that it would be a sound investment. Excellent seating accommodation was to be provided with a covered grandstand for 2,000 people, whilst on the opposite of the ground was an already completed covered terrace capable of holding another 3,000. (Later known to all Irons' fans as 'the Chicken Run').

The Boleyn Castle from Green Street

He went on to say that in all, twenty thousand people could be accommodated with entrances in Castle Street, served by twenty turnstiles and two 20-feet sliding gates for exits. An arrangement had also been made with West Ham Corporation to provide extra tramcars both before and after matches. Refreshment rooms would be provided at the ground, one at the Priory Road end of the North Bank, another at the Castle Street entrance, and others at each end of the grandstand, making four in all. As for the players, their dressing rooms were being erected with hot and cold water fittings. Mr King went on further to say that the tenancy on the ground was held on a 14-year lease which was renewable.

After such a very poor season in 1903/04, the directors decided that heads would roll at the Boleyn. Only 5 of 24 players survived the close season purge. This was, and still is, the largest 'clear out' at any one time. The five players that remained were Tommy Allison, Billy Bridgeman, Charlie Cotton, Aubrey Fair and Len Jarvis.

This meant a large influx of new blood. Possibly the most well-known of those was 28-year old goalkeeper Matt Kingsley who had made one appearance for England, and whose previous two clubs had been Darwen and Newcastle United, where he made 72 and 180 outings respectively in the Football League. Tommy Bamlett, a right back, also came from Newcastle, and to bolster the defence on the other flank at left back 31-year-old Dave Gardner arrived. He had captained Newcastle United (76 apps), but came to West Ham from Grimsby Town (51 apps), where he had also been captain of the side. He was to become a great favourite at the Boleyn. Half-back John Russell was signed from Everton, and 24-year-old Frank Piercy arrived from Middlesbrough. Frank was destined to have a long and distinguished career at his new club, including that of assistant trainer for no less than twenty years after his playing days were over. Another from Middlesbrough was Chris Carrick a clever wing forward, who had scored 6 goals in 26 appearances. Bill McCartney, a winger, was signed from Manchester United, and Charlie 'Chippy' Simmons came from West Bromwich Albion. 'Chippy' was a ball playing inside forward who had scored 57 goals in 142 appearances for the Midland club.

Every one of these men was an experienced Football League player, and they were joined by two ex-Reading Southern League forwards in Jack Fletcher and Jack Flynn. Would all this know-how gel into a successful team?

There were also changes on the training side when Bill Johnson was sacked. He had been in the job for just one season succeeding Jack Ratcliffe, who in turn was trainer in the 1902/03 season only. Jack's predecessor had been Abe Norris.

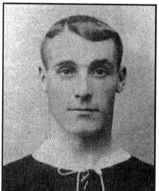

Billy Bridgeman

None other than Tom Robinson returned and took over. He had been trainer from 1895/96 to 1897/98 during the time when the club were in the guise of Thames Ironworks FC. For some years he had also been lessee of the Bow running grounds and had been trainer of a number of successful long distance walkers, along with sprinting, hurdling and long distance runners. Tom, now well into his fifties, was interviewed for the local press at the time and it is of interest to reproduce his comments here:-

'My system? Yes. To start with I am and have been a teetotaller for 40 years. I believe in it, but I do not let my belief interfere with my methods of training. I take a man and deal with him according to his habits. If he is a drinker I deal with him as such, restrict one where necessary, but allow another to indulge in his habits to a limited extent until I have made him 'fit'. So long as a man does not go to extremes I allow a man to follow his own fitness for his work. I don't prohibit a smoker from smoking, but I restrict him when I think it is necessary. I don't generally interfere with a man's diet, but some days before a match I keep him as far as possible off a vegetable diet. No two men can be trained alike. One man is fit as regards weight, whilst another needs reducing, but I don't believe in pulling the latter down too much. I am a great advocate of the outward application of cold water, baths are essential both before and after a game, and I see that they have them. I have my own remedy for strains, stiffness of limbs, soreness of the body, and I apply it my own way. My aim is to get and keep a man 'fit'. I seek to know something about his capacities. If he has the ability for his particular task, then if he is kept in condition I know he can acquit himself to his own credit, and the credit of his trainer. My aim, therefore, as a professional trainer, is to keep a man in condition.'

Tom's statement gives just a glimpse of some of the methods of training in Edwardian times, but there is a lot of straightforward common sense in his account. We do now of course, have the likes of sports scientists and modern methods, and perhaps, a more strenuous approach to fitness. Tom also had Charlie Paynter as his assistant trainer, but note that in this period Syd King, the manager, did not fully become involved, apart from a little 'advice' to the players at certain times, whilst the trainer had his specific tasks, but the modern idea of a 'coach' was a position not yet defined.

One of a trainer's duties was certainly not to use underhand methods to gain inside knowledge about the opposition, which happened in the previous season in the Football League. The trainer of Stoke City, one Jack Eccles, brother of ex-West Ham United's George, before a match against Sheffield Wednesday, examined all the contents of the visiting players' bags, arguing later that he had a perfect right to do so in order to see how their boots were studded. This was reported to the FA with the result that Eccles was fined £1, and the Stoke club were ordered to make a formal apology to the Wednesday club.

Everybody connected with West Ham United was eagerly anticipating the new season with a brand new ground and almost a brand new team to go with it. It was a pity that the opening match had been scheduled for a Thursday with an early evening kick off, as the attendance, although a creditable 10,000, would have been more had the fixture been on a Saturday. Those that were there saw a storming performance against the 'old enemy' Millwall. For the past three Southern League campaigns the visitors had been victorious but the Hammers were due for a victory, and they did not disappoint. Inside four minutes local boy Billy Bridgeman scored the opening goal, and the home crowd cheered and hats were waved in the air in delight. West Ham continued to press forward with crisp passing, but the visitors made a quick break, but new 'keeper Matt Kingsley fisted the ball clear. Allison then moved the ball swiftly to Flynn, and from his centre Bridgeman struck the bar with a stinging effort. Such strong attacks continued with Bridgeman and Flynn both going close before half time. It was much the same story in the second half with Kingsley capably dealing with the few efforts that Millwall managed to muster, and the Hammers having the majority of the attacking play. The home side were rewarded when Bridgeman scored again, followed by a third put away by Flynn. It was said that 'Tiny' Joyce the Millwall goalkeeper, kicked in the dressing room door after the game in anger at conceding three goals.

After the match many agreed that the new ground with its compact arena and its closeness both to the pitch and the players, created a more intense and exciting atmosphere as opposed to the vastness of the Memorial Grounds with its athletic and cycling tracks surrounding the playing area.

Despite Arnold Hills's statement that no team other than his own Thames Ironworks amateur side would be using the Memorial Grounds after West Ham had left, he arranged for Woodford Town, who had won the South Essex League in 1903/04 to also have use of the ground. Woodford had financial problems and withdrew from their league, but how they expected to have followers when they were so far from home is anyone's guess. The club arranged a friendly on the first day of the new season against Hampstead, but the grass on the pitch was far too long, and it was said that, *'failing the use of a scythe it would not have been a bad idea to board and lodge a flock of sheep for a week or so.'* Apparently passes became useless along the ground as the ball *'stopped dead in the standing hay and refused to budge unless kicked very hard.'* Although the Woodford club played several matches at the enclosure their arrangement did not last more than a few weeks and they returned to Snakes Lane, Woodford.

The Hammers' first away match was at Griffin Park, and in a game where there was nothing to choose between the sides, Brentford and West Ham fought out a goalless draw. The visitors were encouraged by the sight and sounds of a fair sprinkling of their supporters in the 7,000 crowd.

On the following Monday it was back to the Boleyn for a Western League fixture against Fulham. There was certainly room for improvement in this competition, having been the holders of the 'wooden spoon' in 1903/04. In a 2-2 draw Billy Bridgeman grabbed another brace of goals in what was described as *'the finest display of scientific football.'* This applied to both teams, but the Irons had very much the best of it. Fryer however, in the Fulham goal, was outstanding and more than earned his team a point.

The promising start to the season was soon disrupted when Queens Park Rangers arrived, and handed out a 1-3 Southern League beating in an impressive display. Before an excellent crowd of 14,000 it was Kingsley and his defence who bore the brunt of the work with the goalkeeper being the busiest. West Ham were three goals down before Allison converted a penalty, but it was Ranger's Alf Hitch who was the star of the match scoring with an excellent bullet header in the second half. The Irons' supporters would no doubt have remembered him from his time at the Memorial Grounds playing for Thames Ironworks FC in 1898/99.

In the return fixture with Millwall the final score of 1-1 came about due to skirmishes around both goal areas where incidents involving the respective goalkeepers would not have been allowed in the game today. For West Ham's goal, Joyce stopped a stinging shot from Flynn, but could not hold it, and when the ball hit the ground followed by the goalkeeper, a rough scramble ensued with Millwall defenders using their weight to protect their colleague and the goal, but Bill McCartney, affectionately known as 'Tubby', outweighed them all and banged the ball home. Similarly, at the other end, Matt Kingsley, who had already had an excellent game, was knocked to the ground in a struggle, and the ball was forced over the line for the equaliser.

As for 29-year-old Matt, he was a vastly experienced goalkeeper. Lancashire born, he first played for Darwen in 1895/96 making 72 Football League appearances for them. He once recollected a match between Darwen and Newton Heath (now Manchester United) when only eight men turned up for Darwen. He had an extremely hectic time performing acrobatics to keep the opposition out, and conceded just two goals. Matt was a specialist at fisting the ball out on most occasions, as goalkeepers of the day were liable to be bundled into the net should they hold onto the ball for too long. He also recalled a game when Darwen visited Woolwich Arsenal. The team left Bolton at 11.00 pm, reaching London in the early morning. The team spent between 7.00 am and 3.00 pm exploring the City, seeing the Monument, riding on 'buses and 'seeing the sights', then arriving just on time to beat Arsenal 3-1. Matt went on to play for Newcastle United, making 100 league appearances and gaining an England cap. He was not in favour of Saturday *and* Monday fixtures, as they came too close together, making the point that players had to be 'doctored' on a Sunday when they could be resting.

The Irons had another local derby to follow, and the club directors were rubbing their hands at the attendance of 16,000 at the Boleyn. As 'Spurs, their opponents, had beaten QPR in their previous match, many supporters expected a defeat but in a very even contest a goalless draw resulted. Two good performances followed, the first at Luton and then the home fixture against Swindon Town. Both resulted in 2-0 victories with Fletcher scoring in both games. This lifted the club to third position in the Southern League with just one defeat in the first seven.

The game against the 'Railwaymen' saw the debut of Chris Carrick, who gave a splendid display throughout, laying on both goals. Although a defeat came in the next encounter at New Brompton by 0-3, Carrick was the outstanding player in the side. His tremendous shot that hit White, the home defender, full in the chest in front of goal at 0-0, might well have seen a different outcome.

Before the introduction of club youth teams after the Second World War, (with West Ham being one of the pioneers in this respect) the club were always on the look-out for young and promising local talent, Billy Bridgeman being amongst the few already discovered. In late September 1904 West Ham approached Harold Halse, a youngster who was born in Stratford and at the time was playing for amateur side Wanstead FC. Why he never agreed to sign for the Irons is not known, but he was probably the first local who could be described as 'the one who got away', as he went on to eventually have a glittering career. Moving on to Clapton Orient and then Southend United, he came to the notice of Manchester United, joining them in March 1908 where he scored 41 goals in 109 appearances. He was a small and rather slight figure, but he had a superb eye for goal often scoring from apparently impossible angles. He played in three FA Cup finals, for Manchester United in 1909, Aston Villa in 1913 and Chelsea in 1915, and was on the winning side for his first two. When Manchester United beat Swindon Town in the FA Charity Shield in 1911 he scored 6 goals in succession and almost repeated that for Aston Villa scoring 5 in succession in a First Division match against Derby County. He surprisingly played only once for England, but then scored twice against Austria in England's 8-1 win. How West Ham would have progressed with him in the side is a matter of conjecture.

It was back to winning ways when Wellingborough came to Upton Park. The visitors were in something of a sorry state both on and off the pitch. The team appeared without six first team members who had all been suspended (!), with reserves taking their places, and the club itself was struggling financially. The outcome was a 4-0 victory for the Hammers, but in all truth it should have been double figures, as the forwards wasted several chances, although Jack Fletcher scored a hat-trick.

The result meant a fourth place position in the Southern League, and with a single goal success over 'Spurs, there was already a vast improvement in the Western League.

A great performance at the Dell against Southampton saw a point gained in a 2-2 draw with Bridgeman and McCartney both scoring superb goals. In the goalless draw with Fulham Dave Gardner at full-back, injured his leg, but Kingsley was at his best in goal, and as ever, so was Fryer, his opposite number in the Fulham team. The referee came in for some severe criticism over some of his decisions, and when one spectator loudly booed him he stopped the action and cautioned the man. Referees in the modern era would not have the time or the inclination.

Despite Gardner's absence in defence, full points were picked up against Plymouth at home with Simmons scoring two goals in quick succession, and the attendance was a healthy 10,000. Everything was pretty much satisfactory, up to third position in both the Southern League and the Western League. Perhaps with something of a good 'run' a possible top two finish in either or both.

Deciding not to participate in the London League Premier Division must have brought some benefits to the first eleven. It did not now have the interest it had initially and resulted in too many fixtures. Sadly, when all is going well there is often a sequence of poor displays after a couple of confidence sapping results, and the seeds were sown after two matches in the Western League, one at Bristol Rovers which resulted in a 1-5 defeat, and a record breaking disaster of 0-8 at Southampton. Admittedly the Western League did not carry the prestige of the Southern, but it was a first team competition nevertheless and such defeats do absolutely nothing for morale.

On the 26th November 1904, West Ham played Bristol Rovers in the Southern League and lost by two clear goals. By the time the team had suffered a single goal defeat to Tottenham on 21st January 1905 the Irons had lost eight consecutive matches in that competition and scored only one goal in the process! Six of those defeats were 0-1, so it was plain to see where the problem lay. The defence of Kingsley, Bamlett and Gardner, and the halves of Allison, Piercy and Jarvis were not the main culprits, but the forwards were continually off target, despite a number of easy chances.

The question of who should be picked for the first team, and their position on the field is strictly the decision of the manager and coaches today, but in most cases over this period, and certainly at West Ham, this was decided by members of the board. This brought criticism in the local press, and Mr Grisdale, the club chairman, made a statement to the effect that it was untrue that Syd King, the manager/secretary, did not have a 'voice' in team selection. (If he did, it is evident that he did not have full control until 1912, but even then members of the board had their say in selection.)

Whatever changes to the team were made during this very poor run resulted in no positive outcome to what is now labelled in common football parlance as 'tinkering'. In the forward line Simmons and Fletcher were switched about and Blackwood and Hamilton (both signed from QPR) had been introduced to no good effect whatsoever, whilst players such as Bridgeman and Carrick had been sidelined.

In the early part of January a shareholders meeting was held at the Boleyn Ground when members were expected to discuss, amongst other topics, the subject of the poor form of the team. Such was the good report of the club's financial position that shareholders conveniently overlooked what the ordinary fan in the street hoped would be discussed. Mr Grisdale reported that in the first four months of the season income had been £3,226, and after expenses had been deducted there was a profit of £712. He also stated that at one reserve match a gate of £40 was taken, whilst at the Memorial Grounds it was not unusual to have a gate of only £4 at a similar game. The directors congratulated Dave Gardner, club captain, on his splendid work, and gave a vote of confidence in the management.

The return of Bridgeman and Carrick to the forward line saw a distinct improvement in the team's fortunes. QPR were thrashed 5-0 in the Western League and more importantly a Southern League success was recorded when Luton came to the Boleyn and were heavily beaten 6-2, with Carrick scoring a hat-trick and Bridgeman two. Things were looking up. Including the Luton victory there came just one defeat in six, and during that period the club introduced a player that would become a legend - George Hilsdon. Unfortunately, 'Gatling Gun', as he became known, spent only his early pro' years and the latter part of his career at the Boleyn ground as we shall see later, because the most productive and prolific years, in terms of goalscoring, were with Chelsea where he scored 98 football league goals in 150 outings. George, a local lad, already had amateur experience with Clapton Orient and Luton Town before he appeared for West Ham. At 19 years old, he made his debut for the club against Bristol Rovers, banging in 4 goals in a Western League fixture. When he appeared in his first Southern League match, against New Brompton, who had ex-Hammers' Fred Griffiths in goal and Ernie Watts at centre half, he sailed past both of them in an impressive solo run and promptly scored. Hilsdon followed up with another against Southampton, who were favourites for the title and still in the FA Cup. The 'Saints' totally dominated, but it was the home defence who took the honours with Gardner, and half-backs Allison, Piercy and Jarvis outstanding.

One of the advantages of the move to the Boleyn ground was the transport links, especially the advent of the electric tram, which now covered the local area and meant easy access to matches for the followers of the team, some of whom were new to the club. Certain problems had arisen that had not been anticipated, such as the lack of width between the tracks and the pavement, which meant that trade vehicles, both motor and horse drawn, when stopping to unload their goods, blocked the tramway, and caused great inconvenience to passengers.

At a West Ham Town Council meeting the borough engineer had made a proposal to allow a margin of eight feet between the tramway rail and kerb. This was up for debate and councillor Thorne considered that had the widening took place when the track was laid, a considerable amount of money would have been saved. Other councillors were concerned about the prospect of a much narrower pavement for pedestrians, and the fact that many shops displayed their wares out on to the thoroughfare. This was evident in Green Street along to Queens Road and Upton Park station where there were a variety of shops and businesses. If the problem became serious it would ruin the neighbourhood. After a vote against, the matter was referred back for further consideration.

It is worth remembering that our forefathers, perhaps unavoidably leaving it late to get to the game and having to use the tram, might have had to contend with the problem of the tramway being blocked, until the whole problem was eventually resolved.

After the team's improved run of one defeat in six games, there was a spell of three consecutive

Matt Kingsley

defeats, one of which was against Brighton & Hove Albion away from home, giving the Sussex club the double over the Irons. As Brighton had also won the FA Cup meeting back in December, they had more than gained revenge for the previous season's drubbings handed out by the East End club. Sadly, an incident occurred in the 1-3 defeat where Matt Kingsley was sent off for kicking Lyon, the ex-Hammers' forward. This must have been somewhat violent, as some of the crowd ventured on to the pitch to get to him, and Kingsley had to be escorted from the field by two policemen, being quickly bundled into a cab and driven away. The goalkeeper played in the two following fixtures before serving his suspension, but he played no further part in the club, and left, joining Queens Park Rangers for 1905/06.

After a home defeat by Reading, when the Hammers had more than dozen shots at goal and Simmons missed a penalty, the league position was now of great concern, for the club had fallen to third from bottom, and the humiliation and repercussions of the 'wooden spoon' looked a distinct possibility. With the next fixture being Bristol Rovers, who were top of the league at the time (and eventual champions), the outlook was bleak, but to the team's credit they pulled out all the stops, and after being two goals down at the break forced many corners in the second half, and were awarded a penalty which McCartney converted. Continuing to push forward George Hilsdon proved his worth by scoring the equaliser with a powerful shot.

7,000 spectators turned up at the Boleyn Castle ground after this display, and were rewarded as the Irons fired on all cylinders, slamming Northampton to the tune of 5-1. All thoughts of bottom place in the Southern League First Division began to disappear when the team went to Fulham just two days later and achieved a 3-0 victory. This was another fine performance, and with the home side fielding Clutterbuck in goal, the Hammers did not have to contend once again with Fryer, one of the best 'keepers in the Southern League.

On Good Friday Portsmouth were the visitors, and eager to perform their good form of late, the West Ham front rank tore into the opposition right from the start and Bridgeman scored inside 4 minutes from a McCartney corner. Pompey had the edge in the second half and Cotton, in his third match in goal since the Kingsley suspension, kept them at bay until the final few minutes when the equaliser came. To round up the season, a comfortable conquest of Watford by three clear goals completed a five match unbeaten run.

In the Southern League the campaign had been a disappointing one with an improvement of just one place from 12th to 11th in the table. Had it not been for the run in the final five matches, 'disappointing' would have read 'disastrous'. As it was, 11th position realised 32 points, whereas Swindon in 17th (3rd from bottom) had just three points less on 29! In the less important Western League, 5th place was attained with eleven clubs competing, and the reserve eleven finished 7th in the twelve club Southern League second division.

It was off the field where there had been success, as the move to the Boleyn ground had proved to be a great advantage. The club was now becoming a financially viable proposition with another operating profit on the season, and average attendances were well up on the previous four seasons at the Memorial Grounds.

Back: H Bamlett, A Fair, M Kingsley, D Gardner, ES King (secretary). Centre: T Robinson (trainer), F Branston, T Allison, F Piercy, J Russell, L Jarvis, C Messer, C Paynter (assistant trainer). Front: W McCartney, C Simmons, W Bridgeman, J Fletcher, C Carrick, J Flynn.

The new Boleyn Ground, 1904

1904/05

11th in Southern League Division One

No	Date	Opponent	Score	Scorers	Att	Allison T	Bamlett H	Blackwood J	Bridgeman W	Brunton F	Carrick C	Cotton C	Fair A	Fletcher J	Flynn J	Gardner D	Hamilton	Hammond S	Hilsdon G	Jarvis L	Kingsley M	McCartney W	Milnes F	Piercy F	Russell J	Simmons C	Smith S
1	Sep 1	MILLWALL	3-0	Bridgeman 2, Flynn	10000	4	2		9					8	11	3					1	7		5	6	10	
2	3	Brentford	0-0		7000	4	2		9					8	11	3					1	7		5	6	10	
3	10	QUEEN'S PARK RANGERS	1-3	Allison	14000	4	2		9					8	11	3					1	7		5	6	10	
4	17	Millwall	1-1	Fletcher	10000	4	2		9					8	11	3					1	7		5	6	10	
5	24	TOTTENHAM HOTSPUR	0-0		16000	4	2		9					8	11	3					1	7		5	6	10	
7	Oct 1	Luton Town	2-0	Bridgeman, Fletcher	4000	4	2		9					8	11	3					1	7		5	6	10	
8	8	SWINDON TOWN	2-0	Fletcher, Flynn	6000	4	2		9		7			8	11	3					5	1			6	10	
9	15	New Brompton	0-3		7000	4			9		7		2	8	11	3					1			5	6	10	
10	22	WELLINGBOROUGH	4-0	Fletcher 3, Flynn	5000	4			9					8	11	3					1	7	2	5	6	10	
18	29	Southampton	2-2	Bridgeman, McCartney	4000	4			9					8	11	3					1	7	2	5	6	10	
11	Nov 5	FULHAM	0-0		8000		2		9					8	11	3				4	1	7		5	6	10	
12	19	PLYMOUTH ARGYLE	2-1	Simmons 2	10000		2		9		10	3			11					4	1	7		5	6	8	
13	26	BRISTOL ROVERS	0-2		7000	4	2		9		10	3			11						1	7		5	6	8	
14	Dec 3	Reading	0-1		5000	4	2		9			3		10	11						1	7		5	6	8	
15	17	Northampton Town	0-1		4000	4	2		9			3		10	11						1	7		5	6	8	
16	26	Portsmouth	1-4	Blackwood	16000	4	2	9				3		8	11			7		6	1			5		10	
17	27	BRIGHTON & HOVE ALB.	0-1		12000			9		4			2	8	11	3		7		6	1			5		10	
19	31	BRENTFORD	0-1		8000		2	9					1		11	3		8		6		7		5		10	
20	Jan 7	Queen's Park Rangers	0-1		8000	4	2	9						8	11	3		7		6	1			5		10	
21	21	Tottenham Hotspur	0-1		12000	4			9		11			8		3		2		6	1	7		5		10	
6	28	LUTON TOWN	6-2	Carrick 3, Bridgeman 2, Simmons	5000	4			9		11			8		3		2		6	1	7		5		10	
22	Feb 4	Swindon Town	3-3	Bridgeman, Fletcher, Piercy	3000	4	2		9					8	11	3				6	1	7		5		10	
23	11	NEW BROMPTON	2-0	Hilsdon, Simmons	6000	4	2				11			8		3			9	6	1	7		5		10	
24	18	Wellingborough	0-3		1500	4	2				11			8		3			9	6	1	7		5		10	
25	25	SOUTHAMPTON	2-1	Hilsdon, McCartney	1500	4					11			8		3		2	9	6	1	7		5		10	
26	Mar 11	WATFORD	2-0	Bridgeman, Carrick	3000	4			9		11			8		3		2		6	1	7		5		10	
27	18	Plymouth Argyle	0-2		7000	4			9		11			8		3		2		6	1	7		5		10	
28	25	Brighton & Hove Albion	1-3	Bridgeman	5000	4			9		11		2			3			8	6	1	7		5		10	
29	Apr 1	READING	0-2		5000	4			9		11			8		3		2		6	1	7		5		10	
30	8	Bristol Rovers	2-2	Carrick, Hilsdon	5000	4			9		11					3		2	8	6	1	7		5		10	
31	15	NORTHAMPTON T	5-1	Simmons 2, Bridgeman, Carrick, McCartney	7000	4			9		11	1				3		2	8	6		7		5		10	
32	17	Fulham	3-0	Allison, Hilsdon, Simmons	1000	4			9		11	1	2			3			8	6		7		5		10	
33	21	PORTSMOUTH	1-1	Bridgeman	6000	4			9		11	1				3		2		6		7		5		10	8
34	25	Watford	3-0	Piercy, Simmons, Smith	1000				9		11	1				3	7	2		4				5	6	10	8
		Apps				30	18	4	27	1	18	5	9	25	20	29	5	10	7	22	29	28	2	33	16	34	2
		Goals				2		1	11		6			7	3				4			3		2		8	1

F.A. Cup

No	Date	Opponent	Score	Scorers	Att	Allison T	Bamlett H	Blackwood J	Bridgeman W	Brunton F	Carrick C	Cotton C	Fair A	Fletcher J	Flynn J	Gardner D	Hamilton	Hammond S	Hilsdon G	Jarvis L	Kingsley M	McCartney W	Milnes F	Piercy F	Russell J	Simmons C	Smith S
Q6	Dec 10	BRIGHTON & HOVE ALB.	1-2	Flynn	6000	4	2		9			3		8	11						1	7		5	6	10	

Upton Park Station as it was when the Hammers moved to the Boleyn Ground in 1904

		P	W	D	L	F	A	W	D	L	F	A	Pts
1	Bristol Rovers	34	13	4	0	51	11	7	4	6	23	25	48
2	Reading	34	13	3	1	36	12	5	4	8	21	26	43
3	Southampton	34	9	4	4	29	21	9	3	5	25	19	43
4	Plymouth Argyle	34	14	3	0	38	11	4	2	11	19	28	41
5	Tottenham Hotspur	34	10	3	4	34	15	5	5	7	19	19	38
6	Fulham	34	10	5	2	32	9	4	5	8	14	25	38
7	Queen's Park Rangers	34	10	2	5	36	19	4	6	7	15	27	36
8	Portsmouth	34	12	1	4	39	19	4	3	10	22	37	36
9	New Brompton	34	8	7	2	25	13	3	4	10	15	27	33
10	Watford	34	12	0	5	30	19	3	3	11	14	26	33
11	WEST HAM UNITED	34	9	3	5	30	15	3	5	9	18	27	32
12	Brighton & Hove Alb.	34	9	2	6	25	15	4	4	9	19	30	32
13	Northampton Town	34	8	4	5	26	17	4	4	9	17	37	32
14	Brentford	34	5	7	5	17	14	5	2	10	16	24	29
15	Millwall	34	7	6	4	26	17	4	1	12	12	30	29
16	Swindon Town	34	11	2	4	30	17	1	3	13	11	42	29
17	Luton Town	34	11	1	5	35	18	1	2	14	10	36	27
18	Wellingborough	34	4	3	10	16	37	1	0	16	9	70	13

1905/06 CONSOLIDATION

In his pre-season interview secretary/manager Syd King confirmed that the previous campaign had been the club's best ever from a financial point of view. He agreed that their present home was smaller than the Memorial Grounds, but with the capacity now at 18,000 he would be quite satisfied with attendances around that figure at the majority of matches. Already the accommodation had been improved. The grandstand now incorporated an uncovered terraced area, and behind the goals the terracing had been enlarged creating greater capacity, with the banking altered for improved viewing of the game. Lavatories had also been installed, and for the players, the dressing rooms at this time were situated between the north Bank and the west side of the ground. On the pitch itself, thirty bushels of grass seed had been sown with good results, and with the playing field now coated with a splendid crop the ground would wear better than the previous season.

Mr King was asked about the team now that the influx of new players had arrived. He replied that he had '..*a rattling good one, and no doubt they will do a lot better than our men of last year.'* A cinder track had been prepared for them at the ground in order for them to practice their sprinting, and the players were already making use of it, tearing up and down the cinder path as if they hadn't a minute to spare.

There was an exodus of players in the close season, as those signed in 1904/05 to strengthen the forward line had not brought the required success. 'Chippy' Simmons went back to West Bromwich Albion where he ironically returned to form, scoring 18 goals in 36 outings. Jack Fletcher signed for QPR, Chris Carrick joined Tottenham, Bill McCartney returned to his native Scotland to play for Lochgelly United, and Jack Flynn was released along with the former QPR pair John Blackwood and John Hamilton. In defence, Tommy Bamlett returned to his native North East to play for non-league side West Stanley.

Lionel Watson

Those forwards who were signed on were Scotsman Bill Ford from Portsmouth, fellow countryman Charles Mackie from Manchester United, who had previously been top scorer for Aberdeen, right winger Herbert Winterhalder from Wellingborough (the club having folded after finishing bottom of the Southern League), and Henry Wilkinson, at 5ft 7in a stocky built and very speedy left winger. He joined the club from Hull City, but was actually a Manchester United player who had been appearing for Hull in 1904/05, but when that club joined the Football League they could not afford the £150 fee. As the West Ham club was a member of the Southern League and not bound by Football League rules he was able to sign for them. The acquisition of the left wing pair of Lionel Watson and Fred Blackburn from Blackburn Rovers was considered something of a coup. At 26 year old, the 5ft 6in and 11 stone Blackburn was a very experienced and clever player. Not only had he made 192 First Division appearances for Rovers, he had been capped for England on 3 occasions. Along with local lads Billy Bridgeman and George Hilsdon who were retained, young Arthur Winterhalder (no relation to the above Herbert) was signed from Wanstead, and the club appeared to be well served up front.

Now that Matt Kingsley had gone, the club replaced him with the experienced George Kitchen who had made 87 appearances for Everton. George was 27 years old and at 6ft 1in and 13 stone cut an imposing figure in goal. Irishman Alex McCartney, a full-back, also joined from Everton, and had six Ireland caps to his name. Goalkeeper Charlie Cotton returned after his eighteen-month spell with Liverpool, and the final capture was Harry Hindle formerly of Nelson, Lancashire, at half-back. With the new men and a blend of youth and experience, expectations were high for the new campaign together with the hopes of a higher league position than the previous two seasons.

The opening Southern League match was against Swindon Town at the Boleyn ground. The Hammers took the field in white shirts and shorts as the visitors wore their usual red jerseys, and there were a fair number of Swindon supporters present who stood directly in front of the press box and made themselves heard throughout the game. The match was very much 'give and take' for the first half, but after half time the action became somewhat frantic. Herbert Lyon, who was now with the Wiltshire side, and had been directly involved in the 'fracas' with Matt Kingsley the previous season, was accidentally kicked in the head and had to leave the field. The 'Railwaymen' then began to get rough, and Bridgeman responded by kicking out at an opponent and was lucky not to be cautioned. Fouls came thick and fast from both sides, and at one time there were no less than five players limping about the field, whilst a spectator suggested that *'the St John Ambulance Corps should be asked to attend future matches.'* Lyon then returned to the field with his head bandaged, but immediately Hindle of Swindon, whose namesake was on the Hammers' side, was completely laid out and had to be carried off. Rather strangely, it was not the visiting players who did the carrying, but West Ham's Gardner, McCartney, Jarvis and Piercy!

With the contest reaching a stalemate, captain Dave Gardner, amidst loud cheers, rearranged the forward line. A captain then would be a player of experience, who could command respect and possess some tactical intelligence in an age when formations and positions on the field of play remained constant. His task was not so much to devise a complicated system, but to decide whether certain players could perform better in another role. There were no substitutes then, who could undoubtedly change the game. Once a team were selected and sent out on the field, they were the eleven men who sank or swam together. Step forward a real captain and do the necessary. With managers, assistant managers and coaches in the modern game, prowling along the touchline, the captain's role is now much reduced apart from 'leading by example' or urging colleagues to 'up their game'.

Gardner's decision led to a more aggressive approach and increased pressure, and after a number of near things, the Irons were awarded a penalty for handball. A new rule had now come into existence that restricted goalkeepers to staying on their line when a penalty kick was taken where they previously had freedom to come well off their line. Before the season began George Kitchen had been asked his opinion whether goalkeepers would find the new rule a disadvantage. *'It won't make it easier for the 'keeper; I should say that there would not be many penalty kicks stopped,'* he replied. This was a double-edged sword as far as George was concerned, for not only was he renowned for saving penalties, he had something of a reputation for scoring them too.

So it was, that all eyed were on him as he prepared to take the kick. Bending down, he gave the ball a pat, stood upright and sent the ball along the ground past Ling, the opposing 'keeper, into the net.

Old rivals Millwall were the club's first away opponents, and once again a solitary goal decided the game. Within the first five minutes in the pouring rain, Kitchen, the hero of the Swindon encounter, saved a powerful shot, but let the greasy ball slip from his hands and Milsom, a Dockers' forward put the ball in the net. The West Ham 'keeper went on to perform heroics from then on in a game that saw a poor performance from his half-backs, especially Jarvis and Hindle, as they failed to provide any service to their forwards.

West Ham had so much superiority in the Western League opener at home to Fulham that the

Dave Gardner

West London side resorted to the 'one back' game. As explained in a previous chapter, the offside rule, as it stood at this time, could be used to advantage when a side were down to ten men, by employing this method. Using one full-back, and pushing up often caught opponents offside if played with correct timing. Fine, if the club are desperate for points, and do not have a full team on the pitch, but to use from the start with eleven players, had as much entertainment value for the spectators as a dose of chloroform. As for the game in question, the Hammers managed to get through for a single goal victory, with the speedy Henry Wilkinson, in his first game, figuring as the best forward on show. Henry was dubbed 'Snowball' on account of his ash-blond locks, a nickname he had already acquired in his days at Manchester United.

A Southern League defeat at home followed when Luton came to town. With ex-Hammer Billy Barnes in their side, the visitors had the best of the first half and led by a goal at the interval, and increased it to two before the Hammers woke up and played much better towards the end of the game, getting a goal back via Fred Blackburn, but it finished 1-2. Freddie stated that he was used to playing at First Division grounds when he was with Blackburn Rovers, where spectators were further away from the pitch. There was a vast difference between those grounds and the one at Upton Park. *'We were at least fifteen yards from the spectators, but here they are almost on top of us. I don't care for that, but it may only be because I am not used to it,'* he said.

A 0-2 reverse at Tottenham meant a third successive defeat in the Southern League, but that was redeemed when Brentford came to the Boleyn and the Blackburn/Wilkinson partnership on the left produced the speed, the power, and the goals when both players scored in a 2-0 victory. Wilkinson's was a beauty when after a fist-out by the opposing goalkeeper, he trapped the ball and slammed it into the net in one swift movement.

Two days later the two teams met again, this time in the Western League at Griffin Park, and the result was the same. Ex-Hammers' goalscorer Fred Corbett was in the Bees' line-up, but it was Charles Mackie who scored both goals for the visitors, although George Kitchen was the busier of the two goalkeepers. Frank Piercy and Watson of Brentford had an argument after a skirmish when Piercy fouled his opponent, but luckily Watson did not react to the Brentford supporters' cries of 'Give 'im one Jock!'

The Hammers then lost two matches – one to Norwich City, 0-1 in the Southern League, which turned out to be Herbert Winterhalder's final first team outing, due to injury, and the other to Woolwich Arsenal 2-3 (Wilkinson and Mackie the scorers) in the Southern Charity Cup. Plymouth Argyle then came to Upton Park. They were top of the Southern League, unbeaten with five wins from six played, but the home side went at their opponents from the first kick, so much so that George Kitchen was marching up and down on his goal line with nothing to do except blow on his hands to keep them warm! As so often happens in such a situation, the opposition breaks away and scores, which is exactly what Argyle did. One down at half time, the Hammers continued to press after the interval, and Fred Blackburn equalised after the visiting goalkeeper punched the ball straight up in the air, and from the resulting scramble Freddie forced it home. Mackie then scored the winner to take both points.

Cheap excursions were offered to supporters wanting to see the game with Southampton at the Dell; three shillings before the day, and 3/6d on the day of the match. It must have been a disappointing journey home after a 0-1 defeat, but loyal fans still made the trip across London for a late Monday afternoon kick off against QPR for a Western League meeting. Despite scoring through Mackie and Bridgeman it finished in a 2-4 defeat, with ex-Hammer Bill Yenson getting on the score sheet for the home side.

The Southern League campaign was already beginning to falter as the next two fixtures brought another two defeats. Before an attendance of 7,000 Reading came away from Upton Park with a 3-2 victory. This was a real 'ding dong' battle with the visitors going in at half time at 2-1. Allison equalised in the second half with a rasping shot that had the crowd wild with excitement, with some shouting 'Bravo, Tommy!' After that goal Reading began to use some rough tactics especially on Bridgeman, Blackburn and Wilkinson. The latter decided to 'get his own back' in answer to the treatment he was getting, and as so often happens with retaliation 'Snowball' came off worse and received a caution. Billy Bridgeman also in frustration, was pulled up for allegedly 'diving' (something unusual at the time), but it was a pity because it was an excellent game overall despite the visitors getting the winning goal, although the Hammers felt aggrieved at not getting a point from it. Every player put his full effort into the game, but at the back Gardner and McCartney were not at their best.

Maximum effort however, was not in evidence for the whole 90 minutes with the visit to Watford. The Irons had cause to complain when the home side were awarded a goal when the ball bounced straight down from the bar. The referee gave it as over the line after consulting a linesman, but such cases are open to dispute even today. After Bridgeman had equalised it was all to play for, but when Watford added two goals in the second half every West Ham player appeared to 'give up the ghost', much to the anger of the visiting support.

Following on in the Western League, which was the lesser competition, it was a different story. Perhaps it was because the opposition was 'Spurs, as the team were always 'up for it' for their meetings. On this occasion the Hammers handed out a 4-1 thrashing, but it was a pity it had not come in the more important Southern League. Billy Bridgeman scored a hat trick, but this was in part due to the perfect service he received from young Arthur Featherstone playing on the right wing. He had been signed on as an amateur from Wanstead FC, and there were calls for him to be given a regular run in the Southern League side.

Despite such a result the club directors were more concerned about the team's position in the major league competition. Overall the side had been playing reasonably well without a great deal of success, but the right back position in particular was becoming something of a problem. Alex McCartney had been signed from Everton, and although he had not appeared in the Merseyside's football league side he was nevertheless an Irish International with six caps to his credit. His displays for the Hammers however, were becoming a little erratic. He had a tendency to rush in 'where others would fear to tread', and did not always come out with the ball in a tackle. His understudy, Syd Hammond, was an amateur and inexperienced at this level, and was not yet the finished article. It was fortunate for the club that at

Jemmy Jackson

this time James (Jemmy) Jackson became available. He was an experienced full-back who had spent two years with Newcastle United and six years at Woolwich Arsenal, and had made something approaching 300 league and cup appearances with those two clubs overall. He had left the Gunners to become player/manager of Leyton but after just a few months he resigned, and it was considered a 'good bit of business' when he signed for West Ham, and he was quickly drafted into the team for the visit of Brighton & Hove to the East End.

There is an amusing sideline to his debut at the Boleyn ground. Jackson had been summoned to appear at the Shire Hall Chelmsford on the day of the match, to give evidence in a case of alleged burglary. It was decided that he should travel to Chelmsford 'in a motor car', accompanied by club officials. Choosing to travel by this mode of transport from East London to Chelmsford and back, and be in time for kick off was certainly risky, due to the road system at the time and the unreliability and lack of speed of motor vehicles, compared to those today. Travel by motor car was still very much in its infancy, and it was not until five years later, in 1910, that the number of car vehicle licences issued in the London area reached even a total 7,000.

On the party's arrival, after waiting for an hour for the case to open, it was decided to make application for it to be postponed until the following Monday. Prosecuting Counsel made the request to the judge who fortunately agreed, remarking that *'I have had many strange reasons given me for the postponement of cases, but never before have I been asked to adjourn a case in order that a man might take part in a game of football.'*

Jemmy made it back to the Boleyn ground with just ten minutes to spare and took part in a 2-0 victory. His display was described as *'cool as a cucumber under pressure'* and one who *'cleared and defended in great style, with an ability to move forward when necessary.'* Young Arthur Featherstone, now in the first eleven on a regular basis, was outstanding along with Mackie who scored one of the goals. Jarvis at half-back, performed well in the first half, but received a nasty injury to his cheek when he was accidentally kicked. He resumed after the break with a sticking plaster over his face.

The victory was an isolated one as another loss came when the team travelled to Northampton. The Midland side were in the middle of a good run, and their 2-1 victory meant that they had gained 11 points from a possible twelve. It was unfortunate that the Irons had met them at this stage, because come the end of the season the home side were destined to finish at the bottom of the table. As a footnote a press report carried what would now be an entertaining headline:- *'Hammers Cannot Hold Cobblers.'*

Defeats began to have an effect on Western League gates, and only a few hundred turned up to witness the encounter with Reading a few days later. Although there was a satisfactory result with a 2-1 victory, the quality of the football was poor. Watson, and George Hilsdon with a penalty were the scorers. Before the match, one of the ground staff had nailed what was described as red, white and blue flags to the corner posts. It is interesting to note that the official club colours, which were always printed in official sporting literature at the time as 'claret and light blue shirts with white knickers', the press always referred to the team as the 'red, white and blues.'

A poor run is often accompanied by the odd injury or two, and so it was when the Hammers visited Craven Cottage to play Fulham in the Southern League followed by an away fixture at Plymouth in the Western League. In the former, Fred Blackburn was injured in the first few minutes, but despite this setback the team gave it all they had for the remainder of the game. The extra man made the difference however, and eventually the home side scored the only goal ten minutes from time. Kitchen had been in inspired form throughout the match, and one incident typified his performance. He had saved a thunderbolt shot that brought him down, and he was unable to hold the ball. When an opponent was just on the point of scoring, he scrambled along the ground and managed to fist the ball away from danger.

An injury also affected the Western League meeting with Plymouth. Arthur Featherstone had scored a marvellous goal by dribbling past two defenders before beating the goalkeeper, and Watson had added another two minutes later. Towards the end of the first half, with West Ham coasting, Dave

Arthur Featherstone

Gardner suffered an injury to his arm and could not continue. After the interval the home side took full advantage, drawing level with two goals, and scoring the winner six minutes from time.

Having dropped to third from bottom in the Southern League, it was a welcome two points gained when QPR came to Upton Park and were beaten 2-0. It was a thoroughly deserved victory for the Irons who were superior to the Rangers in all departments. Jackson was superb at the back, with no 'dilly-dallying' when he cleared the ball, and Allison and Bush were steady in midfield. The forwards were on top form with Featherstone crossing superbly from the wing, and Wilkinson showing a turn of speed on the other flank.

The team's miserable record on their travels continued however, with defeat at Bristol against the Rovers by two goals to one. It meant eight consecutive away defeats in the main competition. A 1-0 home win over New Brompton followed to keep the club away from any danger, but the turning point in the season came with the introduction of two players; one a promising amateur by the name of Harry Stapley, and the other, who was already a familiar face to Hammers' fans, none other than Billy Grassam. When Billy left at the end of the 1902/03 campaign, he had a short spell at Celtic before signing for Manchester United where he was top scorer in 1903/04. At the end of the following season, he joined Leyton, but after just three months there the Hammers were able to sign him again.

Both players appeared together in the forward line when Portsmouth were the visitors on the Saturday before Christmas. Stapley made his presence felt when he scored the only goal of the game.

The introduction of fresh faces into a side often gives team members a 'lift', and the victory over Pompey proved to be a confidence booster, paving the way for the first success 'on the road' when Swindon Town were defeated at the County Ground by 3-2. The team had a 'never say die' attitude in this encounter, as the Berkshire side were 2-1 up with just a few minutes left when Jarvis and Blackburn scored two late goals to take both points. Just as a sideline, the reserve eleven were disposing of Swindon's reserve team by a 5-0 scoreline at the same time, with young Arthur Winterhalder scoring all five goals. More of him later.

In the less important Western League, Plymouth were the visitors on New Years Day. On a frost bound pitch the team felt the benefit of Stapley's skills when he banged home two goals from long range in a 3-2 win.

When Millwall came to the Boleyn they brought a large number of followers with them in a crowd that numbered 15,000. The Blackburn/Wilkinson partnership on the left wing had now become the Blackburn/Watson pairing, as it had been when they appeared together at Blackburn Rovers. Watson scored the only goal of the match, being well fed by Piercy at half-back, with the two defenders, Gardner and Jackson playing superbly at the back.

West Ham were drawn away to First Division Woolwich Arsenal at Plumstead in the first round of the FA Cup, but were unable to include cup-tied Jackson, Stapley and Grassam, which was a disappointment after the team's recent good run. They were not given much hope, but that did not deter a vast travelling support, for cup-ties are not always being foregone conclusions. In the first half the visitors were very much on the defensive with Kitchen performing heroics in goal, making saves and double saves to keep a clean sheet. Allison, Piercy and Jarvis were also prominent in their defensive play, but the Hammers did break away on occasions, and were awarded a penalty for handball before the half ended. After his display between the sticks Kitchen rushed to the other end of the field to take the kick - and scored. Surprisingly West Ham did more attacking than they had managed in the first period, but it was the home side that were given a penalty when Arsenal's Coleman was brought down in the area and the kick was converted. It was 'nip and tuck' until the finish, but a draw was the outcome, and it was all to play for in the replay at the Boleyn on the following Thursday.

Sadly, before a crowd of 12,000, and on a pitch in a wretched state, with patches of mud and pools of water everywhere, the Hammers did not proceed any further in the competition when the Gunners won the replay by 3-2. There were three former West Ham players in the visitor's side – Roddy McEachrane, James Bigden and Charlie Satterthwaite and Arsenal went on to reach the semi-final before being knocked out.

There were several changes in the side for the encounter with Luton at Kenilworth Road when amongst others Grassam and Stapley were included. Also making his debut was Arthur Winterhalder, a young local player who had appeared for West Ham Schools as a fourteen year old in 1899. Arthur had been signed from Wanstead FC, the club that had won the South Essex League the previous season. He had been in the same forward line as Harold Halse, a future star at Manchester United. The Wanstead club had also been innovative enough during their successful campaign to take the side to France where they beat the Football Club de Paris by two clear goals with Winterhalder laying on one goal for Halse. Arthur has often been confused with his namesake Henry, who was also at West Ham in 1905/06, but Henry played just four games on the right wing for the Hammers early in the campaign before injury ended his career.

As for the match at Luton, Stapley scored again in a 1-1 draw, which after the recent run of positive results in the Southern league meant that having reached the 'dizzy' heights of 11th place in the table the threat of any possible relegation/re-election had receded.

Arthur Winterhalder

Two days later in a Western league fixture Arthur Winterhalder showed what a good prospect he was when QPR were defeated by 3-0, as he scored one and laid on the other two for Billy Grassam.

The Hammers' record against 'Spurs in the Southern League was not a good one. From the eleven previous meetings, West Ham had won two and 'Spurs six, and so it continued when the teams met at Upton Park when the visitors went away with a single goal victory in a match which everyone agreed was a treat to watch. The only goal of the game was scored by Peter Kyle who, it was said, had a 'storming match'. He was the forward who left West Ham in controversial circumstances after appearing in just one game in 1901. Training was low down on his list of priorities, which appeared to be at the heart of his problems with several clubs. With such a prevailing attitude he was sacked by 'Spurs just a couple of months later in April 1906, but he still managed a degree of success with later clubs Arsenal, Aston Villa, Sheffield United and Watford.

With West Ham's record in the main competition against 'Spurs now standing at two wins in twelve meetings, it could be said that the odds of another defeat in future would be fairly short. Betting in the early 20th Century on all forms of sporting activity was common despite the fact that there were no betting shops, and bookmakers were not even licensed. At a meeting in the church hall in Meeson Street near West Ham Park, the proposal was 'Should Bookmakers be Licensed?' Those that were against included a Mr Davis, a school attendance officer who in a statement said that '...*on the corner of Beckton Road they could see hundreds of men standing there all day long doing nothing else but betting. He had seen children eight and nine years of age, scores of them, go to the bookmaker in the dinner-time and give him money. The bookmakers did not seem to care for the policeman at all; the only time they cleared away was when the inspector came along. He believed that 75% at least of the poverty in Canning Town was caused by betting and drink.'*

A Mr Harbott said that *'...what they saw in Canning Town and other poor neighbourhoods was the result of horse racing, football betting and gambling in high quarters. He thought that those who ought to know better, and were supposed in years past to have formed public opinion, were responsible for much of the evil habits that prevailed today.'*

A Mr Crabb, police court missionary, thought that *'It would be a retrograde step to issue licences to bookmakers, because it would be countenancing an indisputable evil. The police did do something to stop it, for in one division alone £1500 was paid by bookmakers in fines. One man paid £20 as a fine for taking bets from children in Walthamstow.'*

A Mr East who was in favour, stated that *'he did not see why there should be one law for the rich and another for the poor. In his opinion bookmakers should be licensed and be placed under supervision.'*

Another, a Mr Minett, stated that *'he was of the opinion that the working man should have his bet, whether it was on football or anything else. It was a great evil, but the only way to control it was to licence the bookmakers.'*

Today, every body is free to bet as much as they like, when and where they like, but in the long run it is always the 'bookie' that wins.

Due to cup-ties elsewhere West Ham had a free Saturday on the first weekend in February, and the club arranged a friendly with Leicester Fosse who were in the Second Division of the Football League at the time. The Irons did their reputation no harm with a 2-0 victory with Billy Grassam and Arthur Winterhalder getting on the score sheet. This gave some impetus to the side when Norwich City were the visitors at the Boleyn the following week. With the score 1-1 at half time there was no indication that a rout would follow in the second period. Kitchen began it by scoring from a penalty, and he did a unique 'double' by saving a spot kick later in the game. Maybe the 'Canaries' were more bothered by the conditions than the home side as it drizzled of rain the whole match, and the pitch became something of a ploughed field. Whatever the reason, Blackburn and Watson on the left flank ran riot and the Hammers ran out winners by 6-1. Prior to the game, the crowd who were usually entertained by the Boleyn Castle Band, enjoyed the pre-match entertainment provided by the New Brompton Boys School Band, and the youngsters received a good reception, especially the lad with the drum major staff.

Plymouth Argyle had mustered just three wins in their previous fifteen games in the Southern League, but it was typical West Ham when the team visited the Devon club and were on the wrong end of a 4-2 reverse. Kitchen once again scored a penalty, but on this occasion he also conceded one. There was not one player in the side who could match the goalkeeper's enthusiasm and commitment, as his behaviour in the Western League fixture at Bristol Rovers exemplified. Despite being behind by no less than six goals to one, he ventured right up to the halfway line to urge his men forward in an attempt to reduce the arrears. As far as he was concerned it was irrelevant that the chances of any respectable position in this particular competition were low, it was a matter of pride in your club, in the style of a Billy Bonds or a Julian Dicks, years into the future.

Another blank Saturday gave the chance for the club to show off their potential and for the Boleyn faithful to see Football League opposition in the shape of Bolton Wanderers from the First Division. In front of a crowd of 3,000 the Northerners did pretty much as they liked in the first half to take a three goal lead, but when one of their team received an injury, which left him little more than a passenger, the course of the game changed. Perhaps the visitors thought it was all wrapped up, but the Hammers, with the Blackburn/Watson partnership to the fore yet again, scored an incredible five goals after the break for a 5-3 triumph.

On this same Saturday the West Ham Schools Association team played East Northumberland in the Quarter Finals of the English Schools Championship at Ashington, twenty-five miles from Newcastle. After meeting at Wanstead Park, the team travelled by train with five teachers on the Friday afternoon arriving at Ashington at 10.00pm. They were accommodated at the Grand Hotel, three boys in each bed, with six boys to a room.

Included in the side were two future West Ham United players in Jack Tresadern and Albert Denyer. The latter scored a magnificent goal after outpacing the opposing full-back down the right wing, beating another two defenders and then the goalkeeper, paving the way for the final outcome of a 2-1 victory. After the game was over the party had a meal and caught an early train to Newcastle where they had reserved seats in front of the grandstand to see the Newcastle United versus Blackpool FA Cup tie. Then came a tea, followed by a visit to the theatre till 11.00pm. Finally, there was a walk through Newcastle and over the swing bridge across the Tyne, until they caught the Scots Express train to Kings Cross arriving at 7.15am on Sunday. Truly, one amazing adventure for those young East End lads in the early years of the 20th Century.

When Southampton were the visitors to the Boleyn enclosure they brought a much changed side to that which had just beaten Middlesbrough in the FA Cup, and they paid the price when Stapley scored twice in the home side's three-nil victory. Harry was now beginning to make himself known, and his goal tally was now six in seven Southern League outings.

With an identical line-up the team travelled to Berkshire to meet Reading. The 'Biscuitmen', like their opponents, were not exactly having a great season, distinctly average in fact, but there was no doubt that the Reading club at this particular time was the Hammers' bogy team. Since 1900/01 West Ham had won twice whilst Reading had been victorious on eight occasions in the Southern League, with two draws. The latest defeat of those eight was a 1-6 debacle in which both Gardner and Jackson had experienced poor games at the back. There was a partial excuse in that Bridgeman was injured in the first half and he did not appear for the second. Being in this position the Hammers resorted to the 'one back' game in order to catch the Reading forwards offside, but it had to be played to perfection, and when it didn't it backfired as the final score proved.

Just prior to the above encounter, three players were suspended by the club, due to what was described as 'a little kicking over the traces.' The expression was most likely to have related to alcoholic demeanours, something that a number of players, some at the top of their profession, but lacking in experience and responsibility, become involved in even today. All three of the players in question had been 'frozen out' of regular first team football for a number of weeks, and with the suspension period being two months, it meant that two of those players, Alex McCartney and Henry Wilkinson, would not play for the club again. The third player was Harry Hindle, who was suspended for just two weeks. He later played in a Western League match in a 1-1 draw against Southampton, but gave such an awful performance that he did not play another game for the club.

It is significant that the directors dealt with first team players offences, whilst Syd King was responsible for any punishment handed out to reserve team men.

With goalkeepers still given the right to handle (but not carry) the ball anywhere in their own half, incidents that that would appear unusual in the game today were not uncommon. In the Western League match against Brentford at Upton Park, which resulted in a 2-1 victory, the Bees outside left raced down the wing and caused Kitchen to leave his goal in order to attempt a save. Taking the ball off the winger's toes, he ran with the ball at his feet almost to the halfway line, and passed it to young Arthur Winterhalder, who took it towards Brentford's goal where Whittaker, the Bees' keeper, rushed way out and fell on the ball. According to the local correspondent *'An exciting tussle ensued...'* and it can only be imagined what that meant, but finally *'Whittaker, whilst on the ground, threw the ball backwards over his head, and the ball was cleared.'*

Although the Western League was the secondary competition clubs were still expected to field first team players whenever possible in order to give the league credibility and maintain the interest of the paying public. Over the years this ruling was often abused, but in defence of the West Ham United club, first team players were always fielded excepting under mitigating circumstances. With this in mind the club directors sent a letter to all member clubs to obtain support to alter, at the next annual meeting, the right of clubs to field players in the Western League who were in receipt of £3 per week. (The maximum wage was £4 per week)

> *'Dear Sirs,*
>
> *My Directors have had under discussion that part of Rule 5 of the Western which reads as follows: 'Any player in receipt of £3 per week cannot be objected to on the ground that he does not form part of the best team.'*
>
> *It would appear to us that when this rule was framed it was not meant to allow clubs to play a recognised reserve team in Western League matches, and we feel that this rule is suicidal to the interests of the league, as eventually, if the rule still continues to operate, the Western League will degenerate into a minor competition for reserve teams, with a consequent loss of interest and gate money. If the prestige of the Western League is to be upheld and the competition to be kept up to a first class standard, it can only be done by altering this rule so as to prevent a repetition of the fiascos which have been witnessed this season in many matches, much to the disgust of the public, agitated, as they are by the general adverse, but justly merited, criticism in the Press. We shall be glad to have the opinion of your club on the matter, with a view to amending this rule at the next annual general meeting of the Western League,*
> *E.S.King, Secretary*

There was much controversy over this rule, and clubs continued to field weak teams. All the Southern League clubs that were also members of the Western League resigned en bloc within three years at the end of the 1908/09 season.

Arthur Winterhalder was given a chance in the Southern League game against Watford, but both he and Featherstone on the opposite flank hung on to the ball too long after promising runs, and lost the ball. Stapley was now proving a handful in every game and he very often had three or four opponents trying to stop him, such was his skill, but despite that the match finished without any goals at either end. Both Biggar, ex-West Ham and the visitors' 'keeper, and Kitchen were unbeatable. The latter, yet again, showed his passion, by wandering upfield, with anxiety written all over his face, to urge his colleagues on.

After another goalless draw at Brighton, the Hammers met Northampton at the Boleyn ground. When the clubs played one another in November, the 'Cobblers' were on a good run and in a high position in the table, but since then their form had dipped alarmingly, and they were struggling at the bottom (and remained there). There was not a weak link in the West Ham side, and the result was a 4-1 success with Bridgeman and Stapley both getting a brace.

A blinding snowstorm prior to the Western League fixture at White Hart Lane against 'Spurs did not stop the game being played. In 0-1 defeat, Piercy and Allison both had good games, but Jackson at full-back was in poor form. Maybe the constant heckling that the former Arsenal player received from the Tottenham crowd upset his performance.

A 12,000 attendance gathered for the visit of Fulham who were top of the Southern League (and would finish in that coveted position). A 0-0 draw saw both defences prominent, with the Irons half-back line also outstanding, but the short passing of the Blackburn/Watson partnership, although pleasing to watch, did not produce any goals. After Fulham's Ross had badly fouled Blackburn, the visiting defender was 'hooted at from all parts of the ground when ever he kicked the ball', but even the crowd had to laugh when an opposition player made a high tackle on Jackson and accidentally tore the West Ham's defender's seat of his shorts, exposing his backside. Tom Robinson rushed onto the pitch with an overcoat to hide the player's embarrassment, and he retired to the dressing room to change.

There was no chance of obtaining a respectable position in the Western League after a visit to the Dell where Southampton inflicted a 2-5 defeat. The most consoling aspect of the game was the all-round display of Arthur Winterhalder who scored both goals for the Hammers, and would lead him to secure a place in the remaining four matches of the Southern League campaign.

A single goal victory over QPR at their Agricultural Society Ground at Park Royal preceded the busy Easter programme, and this time of the year also saw the local West Ham Charity Cup being contested at the Spotted Dog ground, the home of Clapton FC. This competition, strictly for amateurs, and also known as the West Ham Hospital Cup, was initiated in 1888. The Cup was won by Thames Ironworks FC in the club's very first season of 1895/96, and locally was still much prized and firmly fought over. The final this year was between Wanstead and Clapton, with the former coming out on top by 2-0. It was a tradition to precede the final with guest teams competing, or a schools encounter, and on this occasion West Ham Boys defeated East Ham Boys by six clear goals. Jack Tresadern, a future West Ham United player, who would appear in the FA Cup final side of 1923, was amongst the scorers.

On Good Friday Portsmouth were the visitors in Western League fixture and in a match devoid of goals George Kitchen missed a penalty, but the following day Bristol Rovers came to the East End and with the home side fielding no less than five locals (Bridgeman, Featherstone, George Hilsdon, Jarvis and Arthur Winterhalder), the Hammers claimed both points by two goals to nil.

Despite it being a Western League match, Millwall's visit was the main attraction of the weekend on Easter Monday. Although this was the third home fixture of the holiday, and one that carried no real importance other than some pride, the attendance was 6,000. The atmosphere, whatever the competition, between the two sets of supporters, was often reflected on the field of play, and the local press made the point that '...if the crowd had its way there would have been trouble. Because a player forgets himself and commits indiscretions on the field, there is no need for the spectator in the grandstand to forget his manners. If players had lost their tempers it would have been the fault of a certain section of the crowd.' The home crowd were not exactly happy to witness a 1-2 defeat either.

The final three matches of the Southern League campaign were all away from home. At New Brompton, Charlie Cotton, in goal for Kitchen, was the man responsible for the gaining of a point in a goalless draw, but at Brentford where the Bees finished up winners by three goals to one, the forward line could have done with Harry Stapley, who was on holiday, touring on the continent. For Harry, being an amateur had its compensations.

West Ham had never beaten Portsmouth at Fratton Park in any competition, and the last match of the season was to be no different. When Pompey scored in the first minute of the game that was to be the final score, although Arthur Winterhalder had two tremendous shots before half time, one of which the opposing 'keeper tipped round the post, and the other which was scrambled clear after a deflection.

The campaign of 1905/06 did not come up to expectation. The club's final position in the Southern League was exactly the same as the previous season–11th place. Goalscoring was low, worse in fact, than 1904/05. This was something of a mystery considering that the forwards were technically better, and their combination play had often been a joy to watch. The left wing pairing of Blackburn and Watson, and prior to that of Blackburn and Wilkinson, had been skilful and impressive. Bridgeman and the experienced Grassam were capable goalscorers, and the introduction of the amateur Harry Stapley augured well for the future. The defence had been fairly consistent with George Kitchen in goal outstanding, Dave Gardner and Jemmy Jackson proficient at full-back. The half-back line, which was mainly the trio of Allison, Piercy and Jarvis had had their second season together, and by now had a good understanding of each other's play. With young players such as George Hilsdon, Arthur Featherstone and Arthur Winterhalder coming to the fore, the club could only move forward positively.

Back: S Hammond, A McCartney, G Kitchen, C Cotton, D Gardner. Centre: W White, ES King (secretary), T Allison, H Hindle, F Piercy, L Jarvis, T Robinson (trainer). Front: W Ford, H Winterhalder, S McAllister, C Mackie, G Hilsdon, W Bridgeman, H Wilkinson, L Watson, F Blackburn, A Winterhalder.

11th in Southern League Division One

No		Date	Opponent	Score	Scorers	Att	Allison T	Blackburn F	Bridgeman W	Bush R	Cotton C	Featherstone A	Ford W	Gardner D	Grassam W	Hammond S	Hilsdon G	Hindle H	Jackson J	Jarvis L	Kitchen G	Mackie C	McCartney A	Piercy F	Stapley H	Watson L	Wilkinson H	Winterhalder A	Winterhalder H
1	Sep	2	SWINDON TOWN	1-0	Kitchen	10000		11	7				8	3					4	6	1	9	2	5		10			
2		9	Millwall	0-1		6500		11	9				7	3					4	6	1	8	2	5		10			
3		16	LUTON TOWN	1-2	Blackburn	10000		11	9	4				3	2					6	1	8		5				10	7
4		23	Tottenham Hotspur	0-2		12000		11	9					3	2					6	1	8		5				10	7
5		30	BRENTFORD	2-0	Blackburn, Wilkinson	8000	4	10	8	6				3	2	9					1			5			11		7
6	Oct	7	Norwich City	0-1		6000	4	10	8	6				3	2	9					1			5			11		7
7		14	PLYMOUTH ARGYLE	2-1	Blackburn, Mackie	5000	4	10	8	6			7	3							1	9	2	5			11		
8		21	Southampton	0-1		6000	4	10	8	6			7	3							1	9	2	5			11		
9		28	READING	2-3	Allison, Ford	7000	4	10	8	6			7	3			5				1	9	2				11		
10	Nov	4	Watford	1-3	Bridgeman	4000	4	10	8			7		3						6	1	9	2	5			11		
11		11	BRIGHTON & HOVE ALB.	2-0	Mackie, Wilkinson	8000	4	10	8	6		7		3					2	5	1	9					11		
12		18	Northampton Town	1-2	Mackie	5000	4	10	8	6		7		3					2	5	1	9					11		
13		25	Fulham	0-1		12000	4	11	8	6		7		3		9			2	5	1					10			
14	Dec	2	QUEEN'S PARK RANGERS	2-0	Hilsdon, Watson	7500	4		8	6		7		3			9		2	5	1					10	11		
15		9	Bristol Rovers	1-2	Hilsdon	5000	4		8	6		7		3			9		2	5	1					10	11		
16		16	NEW BROMPTON	1-0	Jarvis	6000	4	11		6		7		3			9		2	5	1					10	8		
17		23	PORTSMOUTH	1-0	Stapley	8000	4	11		6		7		3	8				2	5	1				9	10			
18		30	Swindon Town	3-2	Blackburn, Jarvis, Watson	4000	4	11				7		3	8				2	5	1			6	9	10			
19	Jan	6	MILLWALL	1-0	Watson	15000	4	11				7		3	8				2	5	1			6	9	10			
20		20	Luton Town	1-1	Stapley	5000				4		7		3	8				2	5	1			6	9	10		11	
21		27	TOTTENHAM HOTSPUR	0-1		16500		11		4		7		3	8				2	5	1			6	9	10			
22	Feb	10	NORWICH CITY	6-1	Stapley 2, Watson 2, Grassam, Kitchen	6000	4	11	7					3	8				2	5	1			6	9	10			
23		17	Plymouth Argyle	2-4	Grassam, Kitchen	3000	4	11	8			7		3	9				2	5	1			6		10			
24		26	SOUTHAMPTON	3-0	Stapley 2, Bridgeman	5000	4	11	8	6		7		3					2	5	1				9	10			
25	Mar	3	Reading	1-6	Watson	5000	4	11	8	6		7		3					2	5	1				9	10			
26		10	WATFORD	0-0		7000	4	10				7		3			5		2		1			6	9	8		11	
27		17	Brighton & Hove Albion	0-0		5000		11		6			7	3	8			4	2		1			5	9	10			
28		24	NORTHAMPTON T	4-1	Bridgeman 2, Stapley 2	4000	4	11	7					3	8				2	6	1			5	9	10			
29		31	FULHAM	0-0		12000	4	11	7		1			3	8				2	6				5	9	10			
30	Apr	7	Queen's Park Rangers	1-0	Stapley	10000	4	11	7					3	8				2	6	1			5	9	10			
31		14	BRISTOL ROVERS	2-0	Blackburn, Hilsdon	9000	4	10	8		1	7		3			9		2	6				5				11	
32		21	New Brompton	0-0		3000	4	11	7		1			3	8				2	6				5		10		9	
33		23	Brentford	1-3	Grassam	2000	4	11	7		1			3	8				2	6				5		10		11	
34		28	Portsmouth	0-1		5000	4	11	7		1			3	8				2	6				5		10		9	
			Apps				28	31	26	18	5	17	7	34	14	4	9	3	24	27	29	10	6	24	13	22	13	6	4
			Goals				1	5	4				1		3		3			2	3	3			9	6	2		

F.A. Cup

		Date	Opponent	Score	Scorers	Att	Allison T	Blackburn F	Bridgeman W	Bush R	Cotton C	Featherstone A	Ford W	Gardner D	Grassam W	Hammond S	Hilsdon G	Hindle H	Jackson J	Jarvis L	Kitchen G	Mackie C	McCartney A	Piercy F	Stapley H	Watson L	Wilkinson H	Winterhalder A	Winterhalder H
R1	Jan	13	Woolwich Arsenal	1-1	Kitchen	18000	4	11	7	8				3			9			5	1			6		10			
rep		18	WOOLWICH ARSENAL	2-3	Bridgeman, Watson	12000	4	11	8					3			9			5	1			6		10		7	

F Milnes played at 2 in both games

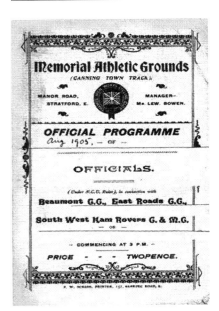

The programme for a cycle meeting at the Memorial Grounds, August 1905

		P	W	D	L	F	A	W	D	L	F	A	Pts
1	Fulham	34	10	7	0	22	6	9	5	3	22	9	50
2	Southampton	34	13	2	2	32	11	6	5	5	26	28	45
3	Portsmouth	34	13	3	1	39	11	4	6	7	22	24	43
4	Luton Town	34	13	2	2	45	13	4	5	8	19	27	41
5	Tottenham Hotspur	34	13	2	2	36	11	3	5	9	10	18	39
6	Plymouth Argyle	34	11	3	3	32	13	5	4	8	20	20	39
7	Norwich City	34	8	8	1	30	12	5	2	10	16	26	36
8	Bristol Rovers	34	11	1	5	37	23	4	4	9	19	33	35
9	Brentford	34	11	3	3	28	19	3	4	10	15	33	35
10	Reading	34	9	7	1	34	15	3	2	12	19	31	33
11	WEST HAM UNITED	34	12	2	3	30	9	2	3	12	12	30	33
12	Millwall	34	9	4	4	26	16	2	7	8	12	25	33
13	Queen's Park Rangers	34	9	3	5	39	14	3	4	10	19	30	31
14	Watford	34	7	6	4	28	20	1	4	12	10	37	26
15	Swindon Town	34	6	4	7	21	23	2	5	10	10	29	25
16	Brighton & Hove Alb.	34	8	5	4	24	24	1	2	14	6	31	25
17	New Brompton	34	5	5	7	10	20	2	3	12	10	42	22
18	Northampton Town	34	5	4	8	17	22	3	1	13	15	57	21

1906/07 TWO STEPS FORWARD......

West Ham in action at White Hart Lane at the start of the 1906/07 season

Despite under achieving in 1905/06, manager Syd King and the directors of the club did not make wholesale changes to the playing staff during the close season. Apart from the three players who had been suspended at the back end of the previous campaign and not retained there were only four others who departed. Robert Bush signed for Chelsea, Charlie Cotton was picked up by newly formed Southend United, and William Ford was not retained. The biggest loss to the club, although it was not realised at the time was George Hilsdon. This young, local centre-forward had played only nine Southern League games for the Hammers, but whilst playing in a reserve match late in the season he was spotted by the Chelsea manager, George Robertson. The West London club had absolutely no history, being formed in 1905 but they were accepted into the Second Division of the Football League straight away in 1905/06. Backed by substantial finances, (sounds familiar) the management were looking to add to their squad of players, and Robertson was impressed by Hilsdon's display, and he obtained his signature for the coming season. Whilst West Ham were reasonably covered in the forward ranks at this time, with the benefit of hindsight this turned out to be a big mistake. George Hilsdon went on to have a successful

David Lindsay

career at Chelsea hitting no less than 98 goals in 150 football league appearances, and gaining 8 England caps, scoring 13 goals in the process. He did return to the club in 1912, but his best days were over by that time.

Only two of West Ham's new signings were men of experience. David Lindsay, a right wing forward and a Scottish International arrived from Hearts, and David Clark, a goalkeeper, who was signed as backup to George Kitchen. He came from Bristol Rovers and had previously made 67 appearances for Glossop in the Football League. The remaining additions were Fred Kemp, a forward from Woolwich Arsenal, and Bill Wildman a full-back from Everton. Both had made just two appearances for their previous clubs. Bill Taylor another full-back, was signed from Gainsborough Trinity, where he had started on four occasions in their Football League side, and James Blyth a defender, from Middlesbrough.

Between the two practice matches at the Boleyn, which both attracted gates of up to 4,000 in late August, some of the players showed their cricketing abilities at Little Ilford Rectory Field where West Ham United met Manor Park Constitutional Cricket Club. The footballers had already defeated their opponents on the Bank Holiday (in those days the first Monday in August), and in this return match the Boleyn lads were victorious again. Batting first, the Hammers made a total of 84 runs with Bridgeman (20), Kitchen (14) and Piercy (12) showing their batting prowess. The Manor Park club managed 47 runs in their innings with Frank Piercy and Harry Stapley both claiming 4 wickets each, with 2 run outs. It was a pleasant way to warm up for the rigours of another football season.

It was not necessary to 'warm up' however, for the opening Southern league match as the temperature reached 92 degrees Fahrenheit in the shade when the Irons visited the 'old enemy' Tottenham at White Hart Lane. The home supporters were taken aback at the manner in which the visitors went about their task despite the considerable heat of the day. Interplay combined with pace and determination went right throughout the team. The Blackburn/Watson wing carried on their good work from the previous campaign, and David Lindsay on the opposite wing was a revelation on his debut. The man of the match however, was Harry Stapley, who scored one and made the other for Watson, and was a constant menace to the 'Spurs defence in a 2-1 triumph.

On the same day, the reserves were demolishing their Brentford counterparts by no less than 8 clear goals at the Boleyn. Billy Bridgeman scored a hat-trick, but despite having been part of the first team set-up for two years he was to continue to be left out of the senior eleven.

With dwindling attendances in the Western League the competition was split into two sections to reduce costs. This condensed the number of fixtures to ten instead of the previous campaign's twenty, and the winners of each section would meet in the final at the end of the season. It was anticipated that this would give the competition more 'edge' and maintain interest for the whole season, in addition to alleviating travelling expenses. The Hammers were placed in Section 1B which consisted of six clubs.

In the opening match Portsmouth came to the East End, and the encounter was fought out in a very competitive manner, with both teams being a credit to their respective clubs. It could have been called a 'game of two goalkeepers' as they both played a significant part in the result. The visitors began very well and scored two early goals from Kirby the ex-West Ham forward, but both of them were efforts that Kitchen should have saved. After the Hammers had pulled one back, the spotlight fell on the visiting 'keeper who had caught a shot from Lindsay, but before he could clear the ball away, Watson, who was following up, rushed up and charged him into the net, ball and all, and West Ham were level. As far as today's rules apply, this action would be considered as nothing less than GBH, and would result in a caution or dismissal for the offending player, but at this time it was commonplace. Goalkeepers were well aware that if they did not get rid of the ball pretty smartly such an event would occur. This was the main reason for punching or pushing the ball out rather than catching or holding it, especially near to the goal line. Before the first half was over, both 'keepers were involved in the next goal when Warner of Portsmouth fouled Stapley in the box. Kitchen ran the length of the field to take the kick and beat Phillips in the Pompey goal quite easily to put the Hammers ahead, but the visitors equalised after the break to make the score in an eventful game 3-3.

Goalkeepers, of course, have always been a special breed, but at this time it was advisable to possess a 'keeper who carried some weight and had a physical presence, but was also agile enough into the bargain. When having to handle the ball it meant keeping hold of it, in order to repel some hefty charging. Willie Foulke, the Chelsea and Sheffield United goalkeeper, in his earlier career was something like 12 stone, but he ballooned to twenty, and there was absolutely no opposing forward who would attempt to knock him off the ball. Another 'keeper was the Notts County man Mordecai Sherwin who must have cut an unusual figure at 5ft 9in and a rotund 17 stone!

Len (Dick) Jarvis

The first home fixture in the Southern League followed when Swindon Town were the visitors. To avoid any colour clash it was the Irons who changed their shirts, turning out in Cambridge blue as against the usual red of their Wiltshire visitors. It was said by those that were superstitious that turning out in the University colours was a good omen, as Cambridge had recently won a famous victory in an eight-oared boat race against Harvard University over the Putney to Mortlake course on the Thames.

The Boleyn boys won by two clear goals, but it really should have been by a bigger margin, especially in the first period, as the ball was mainly in the Railwaymen's half of the field. Stapley came in for some criticism for playing purely for himself rather than for his colleagues, whereas Lindsay and Grassam played a fine short passing game that was a pleasure to watch whilst putting pressure on the Swindon defence. Unfortunately Grassam fell ill at half time, and did not reappear until the final ten minutes or so, which affected the team for a while, but the now familiar half-back line, of Allison, Piercy and Jarvis, was the rock of the side and remained steady throughout. Kitchen, when called upon was reliable, and to emphasize the point regarding ball handling, he collected an opposition shot and was heavily charged, but using his experience, he rode the challenge and turned a somersault before throwing the ball clear.

A good start to the season always sends the crowd home happy, and one of the favourite pastimes of the locals in the area was the Saturday evening visit to Queens Road, off Green Street and along by Upton Park railway station. A street market had existed there for some years, and it was said that it would be difficult to discover anything that could not be purchased there. Everybody went there both to buy and sell or to pick up bargains or to get rid of those that weren't, and those with very little money would find items for a penny or two. In voices loud enough to 'raise the dead' stallholders shouted out their wares – *'Children's patent shoes, only 9d a pair!'* and *'E're yer are, stockings at 6d a pair, pick where you like.'* Youths with their girlfriends could be seen striding up to the sweetstuff stall responding to the call of *'E're yer are, the biggest penn'orth in London.'* In return for their coins came a lump of chocolate or a hardbake. Once it became dark, the scene was lit by the flare of oil lamps, and children gathered round a huge wind-up gramophone listening to the music whilst disregarding the attendant's appeal to buy penny copies of popular ditties. To add to the general noise of the stallholders' cries and the hubbub of the buying and selling, came the occasional song and dance of the local boys and girls with their combination of noise and disturbance. This continued until around eleven o'clock at night and the atmosphere was difficult to equal in any part of London. It was an alternative way for some to spend and enjoy Saturday night, especially for the football fans, knowing that their favourite team had played well and won the points, rather than drowning their sorrows in the Queens pub or the Boleyn Tavern when they hadn't.

There was no cause for celebration after the trip to Norwich when the home side gained a 3-2 victory after two controversial penalty decisions, neither of which went in favour of the Hammers. The first occurred in the opening minute when Frank Piercy was penalised for handling the ball when it clearly hit him on the chest, and the home side converted. The other came in the last few minutes when, with West Ham pressing for an equaliser, Harry Stapley was brought down in the area and the referee waved play on. The point is often made that such decisions are equalled out over a season and it probably true, but at the time it goes against you it is very frustrating.

Despite the loss, there was the visit of Millwall to look forward to on the Monday following, even if it was in the less important Western League. In whatever competition the two clubs met there had always been keen rivalry as in any local derby, and this encounter would be remembered more for the violence than for any skilful football, as any attempt to play it was entirely ignored. The referee came in for most of the criticism as he could, and should, have stopped the game entirely. From the start trouble was brewing, but it came to a head when Dean of Millwall was seen to be leaning heavily on Jarvis. The latter seized Dean by the waist, and literally threw him against the iron advertising hoardings around the ground. Dean was unable to get up and several players carried him to the dressing room. A doctor's examination revealed that the muscles in Dean's back had been badly injured and he took no further part in the game.

The bad feeling spread to the terraces and there were a number of fights. The Press did not care much for the behaviour of the crowd in the grandstand 'who consistently yelled out their biased opinions.' It was stated that those that frequented that area were usually conceived to be better behaved, and should have set an example to the others, and, it was snobbishly reported that 'one can expect such things, and even worse, to come from other parts of the ground.'

Fortunately some relief and amusement came when a black dog ran on to the field and chased the ball. The game was stopped and all the players at some time, attempted, without success, to catch it. Eventually it ran off, and the kicking resumed, without the referee gaining any vestige of control. Just for the record, George Kitchen scored a penalty against his Millwall counterpart to settle the match.

Due to the circumstances and the many misdemeanours that took place during the match an FA enquiry was carried out a few weeks later, as we shall see.

In contrast to the behaviour at the Millwall game, Luton Town came to the Boleyn in a Southern League fixture and there were very few fouls to speak of, with the game being played out in an exemplary manner, and skilful football from both sides. When the visitors went into a 1-0 lead inside seven minutes, and by playing the neat passing game, West Ham looked in for a difficult afternoon, but the Blackburn/ Watson partnership was on top form, and Lionel Watson grabbed a hat-trick, to make a personal total of five goals in four Southern League matches. The Hammers finished up 5-1 winners.

It was a disappointment then, that just two days later on a visit to Bristol Rovers, a 0-3 defeat was suffered. There were no excuses. Their opponents were the better team.

On the 29th September 1906 West Ham visited Selhurst Park to play Crystal Palace for the very first time in any competition. Throughout the game the football was of a very high standard, but it was Palace who had the majority of the forward play and led by a single goal at the break. The home crowd had a surprise in the second half when Needham, one of their forwards, hit a screamer that looked to have gone in the net. The Palace supporters cheered, but the ball was sandwiched between the net and the guide rope, and looked to all intents inside the goal, but was wedged on the outside to their great disappointment. Just to rub it in, with only a few minutes remaining, Arthur Winterhalder equalised from close range for the Irons, who were grateful for a point from the game.

The reserve team, with no less than eight local lads in the side met Southampton reserves at the Boleyn on the following Monday, and demolished their opponents by a record score at the ground by 11 goals to one. The 'Saints' were giving a trial to a young goalkeeper from the Birmingham area, so maybe there was some excuse for the visitors.

On the Thursday of the same week the Boleyn Social Sports Club was opened. The club was situated adjacent to West Ham United's ground in the estate of the old castle grounds, and occupied one of the buildings there. Amongst several events on its opening night an exhibition game of billiards was played between a Mr Lock and George Kitchen, the West Ham goalkeeper. Although George was quite a 'dab hand' at the game he was beaten. Whilst his opponent's highest break was 49, George's best was 44. Many of the members of the Social club were also keen Hammers' followers, and a couple of weeks later the players were the guests of a Mr Taylorson. He had promised the players, before the season started, that if they beat Tottenham on the opening day of the season, he would treat them with a leg of mutton supper, and now the Social club was officially opened, he kept his promise.

Kitchen had to be at his best against Brentford in a Southern League fixture. Going in at half time three goals to the good, the team was deprived of David Gardner in defence for the whole of the second half as he suffered a calf strain. Added to this, Lionel Watson was injured when he received a cut above the eye that necessitated three stitches, but he played on. So it was a pretty much a defensive display in a second period that saw Kitchen concede just the one goal, which was a penalty. George, the 'penalty king' himself, missed from the spot for the first time of the season at the other end.

It was very satisfying for the home crowd for the team to follow this up with a 5-0 thrashing of the 'old enemy' Tottenham in the Western League, with Grassam, Kemp (2) and Arhur Winterhalder (2) being the scorers. This victory put the club at the top of their section in this competition.

There were rumours of an impending riot should matters get out of hand when the Hammers visited North Greenwich to meet Millwall, but with a very strong referee in charge, the contest was played out in a much better spirit, and controversy took a back seat. Jarvis made a conciliatory gesture by shaking hands with the now recovered Dean before the start, and he and his half-back colleagues Allison and Piercy were the pick of the team that gathered a Southern League point in a 1-1 draw.

It is well to mention here the responsibilities of the half-backs. Teams were set out in a strictly 2-3-5 formation, with the three half-backs having a dual role of feeding the forwards in attack and assisting the defence when necessary. A wing half would combine with his relative inside forward and winger, and if successful an eventual cross or centre would find its way into the opposing area, or that winger would attempt to cut in and score himself. There was also an understanding that each wing would compete on their side of the field, and not wander to the opposite flank. Play, of course, was switched from one wing to the other by way of a pass, when necessary. The defensive roles of the half-backs was to block the opposing forwards and halves from carrying out the same principles, and also to assist the full-backs when they were able. The centre half, who had not yet been converted to a 'stopper' until the change in the offside rule came about in 1925, was a busy player, floating more than any other player between defence and attack. All is fine in theory, but once a match is under way, with all its continuous ebb and flow, all theories can deviate, but that was the basic premise.

Up to this time the Hammers were unbeaten at home in both senior competitions, but this record fell when Bristol Rovers paid a visit on the following Monday for the return Southern League encounter. In fact, the Boleyn boys could have been beaten by a bigger margin than the single goal that secured the points as the performance was in direct contrast to recent displays. The half-back line of Allison, Piercy and Jarvis were the main culprits, dismaying those who witnessed their collective display against Millwall. William Taylor, previously with Gainsborough Trinity, was drafted in at full-back, but was out of his depth. He went on to make a further 3 Southern League appearances later on, before being released at the end of the season. George Kitchen was the only player in the team exonerated from any criticism for his display against the Rovers, also adding another penalty save to his record.

In typical West Ham fashion the Irons redeemed themselves when Leyton made their first ever visit to the Boleyn enclosure. The visitors had joined the second division of the Southern League in 1905/06 and were promoted at the end of that season, but they had turned professional as early as 1898. The new recruits at this level were no match for the Hammers however, and the 3-0 result did not flatter the home side, who now found themselves in third spot in the table.

A Billy Grassam hat-trick against Portsmouth at Fratton Park meant 5 goals in two games for this skilful Scottish forward, but unfortunately Pompey triumphed by 4-3 in a most exciting contest that knocked the Irons from third place in the league. There was a different form of excitement, more anticipation, to follow when a bigger crowd than usual turned up for a Western League clash with Southampton at the Boleyn ground. This was due to the FA Commission being present to announce the results of their report into the West Ham United v Millwall fiasco in September.

Their findings resulted in the referee being suspended until the end of the season for his total lack of control of the game, which caused play that was far too vigorous, and was compounded by numerous fouls that went unchecked. Dick Jarvis was suspended for fourteen days, (which the London Press thought far too lenient) and the players of both teams were warned as to their future conduct. With regard to the behaviour of the spectators the West Ham club was requested to post special notices on their ground warning spectators of the consequences that may result from such behaviour. As for the ground itself, the commission recommended that there should be a distance of 10 feet between the touchline and the wooden railings and supports, as currently that space was too narrow. Iron advertisement hoardings were not to be attached to the fencing without the edging being properly protected, and there was to be a clear space of 15 feet between the goal posts and the spectators. The work was to be carried out in the close season.

Fred Blackburn

For the record, the Hammers won that Western League fixture, defeating the 'Saints' by three clear goals, with Billy Bridgeman, who had yet to make an appearance in the more important Southern League during this campaign, grabbing two goals.

The Boleyn lads then went on to record no less than six consecutive draws in the major competition. The team had performed consistently throughout, but captain Dave Gardner was not the player he once was, and his place, in the main went to Syd Hammond in the left back position, as the second half of the season progressed. Bill Wildman however, after a shaky start was now firmly established on the other flank. Allison, Piercy and Jarvis, now in their third season as the half-back trio, were playing as well as ever, and the forwards of Lindsay, Grassam, Stapley, Watson and Blackburn, ably backed up on occasions by Kemp and Arthur Winterhalder were arguably the most skilful in the division.

Over the period of November and early December 1906, West Ham reserves were mostly on the winning trail in both competitions entered, namely the Southern League Second Division and the London League.

The return Western League fixture against Southampton at the Dell resulted in a single goal victory which kept the club at the top of the table, helped by George Kitchen adding a further notch to his penalty record when he saved yet another spot kick.

On the 12th November 1906 the West Ham directors showed their appreciation to a member of the club who was to become one of the legends at the Boleyn ground, namely Charlie Paynter, by granting him a benefit match. Charlie was originally a player with South West Ham, signing on for West Ham United in 1901 when the club occupied the Memorial Grounds. Charlie never did play in the Southern League, but made appearances for the club in reserve competitions, and also turned out for the West Norwood club in the FA Cup. He was appointed assistant trainer in 1902, and in the current season was training the reserves, and it was in part due to him that the side were doing so well at this time. The benefit match was arranged with Arsenal reserves and 'Charlie's boys' ran out winners. Tommy Randall, the young lad with the balding head, scored both Hammers' goals. More on him later.

One young player in the reserves at the time was 22-year old Billy Bridgeman. Always remembered as the first ever player to score for West Ham at the Boleyn ground in 1904, Billy was now unable to win a place back in the first team. As a consequence, Chelsea, who had no history whatsoever, having been created in 1905/06 by the wealthy Mears family, came after the undoubtedly talented Billy and secured his transfer. He had a long career at the West London club making 147 appearances in their Football League side until 1914 when he left to sign for Southend United.

Over the Christmas period the Irons had some real success. Meeting Fulham at Craven Cottage, a defeat would not have been unexpected, but a 4-1 triumph over the eventual champions was recorded. This proved to be the only occasion that Fulham's colours would be lowered on their own ground in the Southern League in 1906/07. Everyone 'worked their socks off', especially Lionel Watson who scored a hat-trick, his second of the season.

On Christmas Day itself Southampton were the visitors. Always a strong attraction, no less than 20,000 attended the match, and a rousing reception greeted the Irons after the victory over Fulham. Another victory resulted on a frost bound pitch with Harry Stapley scoring the all-important goal in a 1-0 victory, bringing his total to eleven at this stage. This slightly built amateur, who was a schoolteacher by trade, was not the stereotypical centre-forward with the power and weight usually associated with players in that position. With a slightly built, wiry frame and a languid style he was occasionally criticised for his slow approach, but he was an entertaining player who used his brain as well as his feet. He was as capable as any other forward for hitting the conventional goal, but he was more renowned for his remarkable dribbling skills, rather than that of the goalpoacher. His goal against Watford some four weeks or so previously would be talked about for some time amongst those that witnessed it. Dribbling the ball past four or five opponents, and placing the ball in the corner of the net was worth coming a long way to see.

The third, and for Hammers' fans, the most satisfying victory, came four days later when 'Spurs came to Upton Park. In an entertaining match a 4-2 scoreline was just about right, with Arthur Winterhalder scoring a hat-trick, with all three being strong 'all along the ground' shots. Remarkably, young Arthur had also scored a hat-trick on Boxing Day in a 6-2 drubbing of Plymouth Argyle in a Western league match.

The spotlight next fell on the FA Cup, more popularly known then as the 'English Cup', and West Ham were drawn away to Blackpool. In the game today, criticism is often made when a lower or non-league club decides to give up the right to play a home tie by transferring the game to their opponent's venue, especially if they are drawn against a Premier League club. This is sad for the regular home support, but the decision is made purely for economic reasons as this amounts to a guaranteed subsidy, allowing the 'minnow' to look forward to some financial security. This arrangement, of course, is quite within the regulations. In Edwardian times, another rule existed whereby a club, at any level, if drawn away from home in the FA Cup, could offer money to the home side to switch venues. Although quite legal this was nothing less than a bribe to obtain an advantage. Such 'offers' were occasionally taken up. During the previous season Blackpool, had been persuaded by Sheffield United, to switch a home tie to Bramall Lane for the sum of £250. This backfired on the 'Blades' as Blackpool won the tie.

The West Ham directors risked, some would say, £250 to induce the Blackpool club to play the match at Upton Park. The Lancashire club, obviously recalling the similar situation that occurred the previous year, and expecting the same outcome readily agreed, as they were a Football League Division Two side at the time, and obviously underestimated the opposition. Despite the difference in status, the Hammers, playing in pale blue shirts to their opponent's red, were well on top for most of the match. Allison never put a foot wrong, and was the star of the side, in which Lindsay and Arthur Winterhalder were prominent up front. West Ham won by two clear goals, scoring through Stapley and Winterhalder, and also had the luxury of missing a penalty when the Blackpool goalkeeper saved Watson's kick.

A week prior to the cup victory the Irons had suffered a 0-2 setback at the hands of Swindon Town, but after their display against Blackpool, the team returned to Southern League winning form when they outplayed Norwich at the Boleyn by 3 goals to one with Stapley grabbing a brace.

When the draw was made for the second round of the FA Cup Everton came out as the opposition to travel to Upton Park. Mirroring the West Ham directors offer to Blackpool, the Merseyside club offered the Hammers a 'big cheque' to switch the tie to Goodison Park, but this was declined, much to the delight of the East End 'faithful'. One of the Everton directors, possibly taking offence at West Ham's decision, came to the Boleyn before the tie was played and measured the pitch to ensure it complied with regulations! Unfortunately the club increased the general admission charge to one shilling, which reduced what would have been a bumper gate to 14,000. Nevertheless there was much excitement at the ground, and prior to the start of the game the New Brompton Boys' Band entertained the crowd with a selection of music. With 'I'm Forever Blowing Bubbles' some years off into the future, the favourite for the Boleyn crowd was 'Three Cheers for the Red, White and Blue', which was greeted with roars of approval.

As for the match itself, the home side played well enough in the first half with Grassam and Lindsay on the right flank reaching their best form. Winterhalder was strangely ignored on the left wing, and he had to wander off to become involved, which was a pity because it was through his brilliant run and cross from the wing that Stapley obtained his goal. Everton, despite being a goal down at half time, showed their class throughout and eventually overcame the Hammers territorially, scoring twice in the second period. Dave Gardner at the back, was directly at fault for both goals and had a poor game. He was dropped, and as a result played just one Western League fixture later, before being released at the end of the season. It was sad, because Dave had been an excellent servant and club captain over two campaigns, but his form had dipped alarmingly during the current season, something that was not helped by injuries. He joined Croydon Common for 1907/08.

With a 0-0 draw against Brentford at Griffin Park there was more interest at the half yearly meeting of the shareholders of West Ham United at East Ham Town Hall. Mr Grisdale, the chairman of the directors, congratulated the shareholders on the report. For the 4 months ending December 1906 total receipts were £3,796 while expenses were £2,834, leaving a profit balance of £962. In the *whole season* of 1901/02 at the Memorial Grounds the total receipts were only £2,702. He stated that it was evident therefore, that the move to the Boleyn ground had been a most successful change. There was a question from those attending about strengthening the defence, but the chairman stated that they had approached both Aston Villa and Everton, but clubs did not want to part with players at cup-tie time. In answer to another question, no application had been made to the Second Division of the Football League for acceptance. (Fulham FC's application at the end of the season was accepted. Their case was strengthened by their second consecutive Southern League championship.)

The usual large crowd, 16,000 on this occasion, turned up for the visit of Millwall, who having had the majority of the play, came away with both points, which dropped the Hammers down to 6th place in the table, and the forwards were much criticised when the team visited Leyton and failed to score for the third week running in a poor 0-0 draw.

Billy Wildman

The sequence was broken when QPR were beaten 2-1 at home thanks to two penalties, both taken by Watson, the first converted and the second saved, but only parried, and Grassam was on hand to hit the rebound into the net.

One of the best performances of the season followed when Portsmouth came to Upton Park. The Hammers reached something of their true form and came out 3-0 winners. Owing to injuries Piercy was unable to play, and Watson was moved from his usual inside forward position and handed the centre half spot, and he performed with credit in a position unfamiliar to him. Of the forwards Stapley added another two goals to his record, and Grassam, once again the most selfless player in the team with his usual 'assists', played at his best. Tommy Allison was a born leader at half-back, and full-backs Wildman and Hammond dealt efficiently with any Pompey attacks.

Northampton (away) 0-0, Plymouth (home) 0-0, Brighton (away) 0-2. These three results put any thoughts of a Southern League title right out of the minds of those associated with the club. With the Argyle in 15th position and the 'Cobblers' eventually finishing in bottom place, full points should have been taken from both sides which would have given the East End club a third spot finish in the division come the end of the campaign.

At this time West Ham Schools were drawn to meet Northampton Schools at home, at the 'Spotted Dog', in the Quarter Finals of the English Schools Shield. The matter of a 'bribe', even at this level of football, arose when the Northampton Association officials offered a guaranteed gate of £25 if the game was transferred to their home venue. This was refused and the young Hammers went on to win 5-2 to win a place in the semi-final.

Between the Northampton and Plymouth league games the club arranged a friendly with First Division Middlesbrough at the Boleyn. The North East side treated the game as somewhat of an exhibition, but did not reckon on the Irons' eagerness to gain a victory, which they did, to the tune of 4 goals to one. Fred Kemp was included in the line-up and banged in a hat-trick, which gave him a place for the Plymouth and Brighton encounters but he failed to make any impression at all. Prior to the fixture at Brighton, Syd King and Tom Robinson took the team to Eastbourne, just along the coast from the Goldstone ground for a week, but the benefit from it was nil, matching their goal tally.

As part of the transfer agreement regarding Billy Bridgeman, a friendly was arranged with Chelsea. Not much interest was taken and only a few hundred turned up on a late Monday afternoon. To many people at the time, Chelsea appear to have acquired the nickname of the 'Buns', something that would be 'difficult to swallow' and not go down too well at Stamford Bridge today. The Hammers fielded almost a reserve side, but it was a bit ironic that both Hilsdon and Bridgeman scored for the West London side in a 2-1 victory for them.

When Crystal Palace came to Upton Park much was expected, as the visitors had experienced a good run in the FA Cup, but it was a disappointing 1-1 draw. Young Arthur Winterhalder scored, and was the best player on the pitch, but this was yet another point dropped to a lowly side that would eventually finish in next to bottom position. Dropping points to lowly teams had become something of a habit.

There was better news on the junior front as the West Ham Schools team won its way through to the Final of the English Schools Shield when they convincingly defeated Swindon Schools 4-1 in the Semi Final at the 'Spotted Dog'. Young Albert Denyer, a future West Ham United player, laid on two of the goals, and the young Hammers went on triumphantly to lift the trophy after defeating Sunderland Schools by no less than 6-2 in the final (after a 1-1 draw).

With two very good wins over Easter against Reading at home by 2-0, and by 3-2 at the Dell against Southampton, the Irons now gave themselves a chance to gain the third spot in the Southern League table, and although the final two matches in the Western League had been lost, the team had finished top of Division 1B and could look forward to the play-off final at Stamford Bridge against Fulham, winners of Division 1A.

Fulham had already won the Southern League title by the time West Ham met their West London opponents in that final and were considered favourites. Maybe they took the opposition for granted, but they were definitely knocked out of their stride when the Hammers tore into them right from the kick-off. The Fulham full-backs panicked every time Blackburn (who was the most outstanding player on the field) and Watson bore down on them, and it was fortunate for them that Fryer, who was rated as the best goalkeeper in the division, was in top form. Ross, the Cottager's right back, who was an experienced defender, seemed to lose confidence, and on one occasion passed the ball back to his 'keeper from the halfway line, something almost unheard of at the time. With so much pressure it was surprising that it was still scoreless at 87 minutes, but Lindsay, at last, receiving the ball from Blackburn found the target for a 1-0 triumph. It was the first piece of silverware for the club since the London League Premier Division was won in 1901/02.

The third spot in the Southern League was unobtainable after two matches out of three were defeats, but one final game remained, and it was against Fulham (again) who had already wrapped up the Southern League championship. Could the Hammers do the double on the West Londoners who were unbeaten on their own ground in the league?

On the Tuesday before that final encounter a 'Cinderella' dance was held at the East Ham Town Hall for all connected to West Ham United. This was the idea of the management to bring together the officials, players and a number of supporters for a social gathering and entertainment. A good programme was arranged with Weston's Quadrille Band playing a lively selection of music. Several directors acted as stewards (extremely unlikely to happen today!) along with Syd King, the manager, and Tom Robinson and Charlie Paynter, the trainers. Players that attended with their wives included Kitchen, Piercy, Jarvis, Allison, Horn, Bourne, Blackburn, Winterhalder and Watson.

With the team's attention now turned to the last match of the season it was the Hammers who led champions Fulham a 'merry dance' when a convincing 4-1 victory was achieved. This was typical West Ham, dropping points to lowly teams and scoring a double over the champions, and conquering them in the play off for the Western League into the bargain.

In that final game Blackburn and Watson were on the scoresheet, but also finding the net was young Tommy Randall, making his initial appearance in the first eleven at inside forward, but who would figure at half-back in the latter part of 1908/09 and serve the club consistently well until 1914/15. The remaining scorer was Arthur Winterhalder, who was surprisingly allowed to leave after Everton came in for him. He appeared for them on only four occasions, but went on to Preston, who were also a First Division club at the time, and spent three seasons there making 56 appearances and scoring 6 goals. Arthur was just one of a number of above average local players nurtured by the club and allowed to leave in the period up to 1915.

So ended another campaign. It was one however, where perhaps the club had played its best football since coming under the banner of West Ham United. It was worthy of a higher position than that of fifth in the table.

Back: (Directors) H Iggulden, H Mattocks, G Davis, T Williamson, Halmeroth, J Johnson, G Fundell, G Handley, H Sutton, J Cearns. Next to back: J Campbell, S Hammond, W Wildman, D Clark, G Kitchen, A Taylor, D Gardner, S Bourne. Centre: D Woodards, T Allison, F Piercy, T Blyth, L Jarvis, G Horn, Frewin, T Robinson (trainer). Seated: W Bridgeman, D Lindsay, W Grassam, J Grisdale (chairman), W Davidson, L Watson, F Blackburn. On ground: A Featherstone, H Winterhalder

1906/07

5th in Southern League Division One

No.	Date		Opponents	Score	Scorers	Att	Allison T	Blackburn F	Blythe J	Bourne S	Clarke D	Fair A	Featherstone A	Gardner D	Grassam W	Hammond S	Horn G	Jarvis L	Kemp F	Kitchen G	Lindsay D	Piercy F	Randall T	Stapley H	Taylor W	Watson L	Wildman W	Winterhalder A	Woodards D
1	Sep	1	Tottenham Hotspur	2-1	Stapley, Watson	17000	4	11						3	8			6		1	7	5		9		10	2		
2		8	SWINDON TOWN	2-0	Stapley, Watson	10000	4	11						3	8			6		1	7	5		9		10	2		
3		15	Norwich City	2-3	Blackburn, Stapley	10000	4	11	2					3	8			6		1	7	5		9		10			
4		22	LUTON TOWN	5-1	Watson 3, Lindsay, Stapley	13000	4	11						3	8			6		1	7	5		9		10			
5		24	Bristol Rovers	0-3		3000	4	11						3	8			6		1	7	5				10	2	9	
6		29	Crystal Palace	1-1	A Winterhalder	10000	6	11		4				3	8					1	7	5				10	2	9	
7	Oct	6	BRENTFORD	3-1	Allison, Grassam, Stapley	12000	4	11						3	8			6	11	1	7	5		9		10	2		
8		13	Millwall	1-1	Stapley	15000	4								8	3		6	11	1	7	5		9		10	2		
9		15	BRISTOL ROVERS	0-1		4000	4								8			6	11	1	7	5		9	3	10	2		
10		20	LEYTON	3-0	Grassam 2, Stapley	12000	4	11							8	3		6		1	7	5		9		10	2		
11		27	Portsmouth	3-4	Grassam 3	12000	4	11						3	8			6		1	7	5		9		10	2		
12	Nov	3	GILLINGHAM	1-1	Stapley	7000	4	11	6					3	8		10			1	7	5		9			2		
13		10	Plymouth Argyle	0-0		10000	4	11						3	8		6			1	7	5		9			2		
14		17	BRIGHTON & HOVE ALB.	0-0		5000	4	11						3	8		6			1	7	5		9		10	2		
15		27	Reading	2-2	Grassam, Lindsay	4000	4	11							8	3	6	10		1	7	5		9			2		
16	Dec	1	WATFORD	1-1	Stapley	7000	4	11	6						8	3		10		1	7	5		9			2		
17		8	Gillingham	2-2	Stapley, Watson	5000	4	11						3	8			6		1	7	5		9		10	2		
18		22	Fulham	4-1	Watson 3, Blackburn	10000	4	11							8	3		6		1	7	5		9		10	2		
19		25	SOUTHAMPTON	1-0	Stapley	20000	4	11							8	3		6		1	7	5		9		10	2		
20		29	TOTTENHAM HOTSPUR	4-2	A Winterhalder 3, Stapley	14000	4				1				8	3		6			7	5		9		10	2	11	
21	Jan	5	Swindon Town	0-2		5000	4						7		9	3		6			8	5				10	2	11	
22		19	NORWICH CITY	3-1	Stapley 2, Lindsay	7000	4						7		9	3		6		1	8	5				10	2	11	
23		26	Luton Town	1-1	Stapley	4000	4							3	8			6		1	7	5		9		10	2	11	
24	Feb	9	Brentford	0-0		6000	4	6							8					1	7	5		9	3	10	2	11	
25		16	MILLWALL	0-1		16000	4					3			8			6		1	7	5		9		10	2	11	
26		23	Leyton	0-0		10000	4					3	7		8			6		1	7	5		9		10	2	11	
27		25	QUEEN'S PARK RANGERS	2-1	Grassam, Watson	4000	4	11				3	7		8			6		1		5		9		10	2		
28	Mar	2	PORTSMOUTH	3-0	Stapley 2, Lindsay	11000	4	10							8	3		6		1	7	5		9			2	11	
29		7	Northampton Town	0-0		2000	4	10							8			6		1	7	3		9	5		2	11	
30		16	PLYMOUTH ARGYLE	0-0		6000	4	11							8			6		1	7	3		9			2		
31		23	Brighton & Hove Albion	0-2		6000		11							8	3		6	10	1	7	5		9			2		
32		25	CRYSTAL PALACE	1-1	A Winterhalder	3000		10							8	3		6		1	7	5		9			2	11	4
33		30	READING	2-0	Allison, Blackburn	6000	4	11							8	3		6		1	7	5		9			2	11	4
34	Apr	1	Southampton	3-2	Jarvis, Stapley, Watson	8000	4	11							8			6		1	7	5		9		10	2		
35		6	Watford	0-2		4000	4	11							8			6		1	7	5		9	3	10	2		
36		13	NORTHAMPTON T	4-0	Grassam 2, Stapley 2	2500	4	11							8			6		1	7	5		9	3	10	2		
37		20	Queen's Park Rangers	0-2		5000	4	11							8	3		6		1	7	5		9		10	2		
38		27	FULHAM	4-1	Blackburn, Randall, Watson, A Winterhalder	10000	4	10						3	6					1	7	5	8			9	2	11	
			Apps				36	29	3	1	1	3	2	14	37	16	4	30	8	37	37	37	1	35	4	32	37	12	2
			Goals				2	4							10			1			4		1	20		12		6	

F.A. Cup

No.	Date		Opponents	Score	Scorers	Att	Allison T	Gardner D	Grassam W	Hammond S	Jarvis L	Kitchen G	Lindsay D	Piercy F	Stapley H	Watson L	Wildman W	Winterhalder A
R1	Jan	12	BLACKPOOL	2-1	Stapley, A Winterhalder	13000	4		8	3	6	1	7	5	9	10	2	11
R2	Feb	2	EVERTON	1-2	Stapley	14000	4	3	8		6	1	7	5	9	10	2	11

Another group fron 1906/07. Back: W Wildman, G Kitchen, S Hammond. Centre: Tom Robinson (trainer), T Allison, F Piercy, L Jarvis, ES King (secretary). Front: D Lindsay, W Grassam, H Stapley, L Watson, F Blackburn

		P	W	D	L	F	A	W	D	L	F	A	Pts
1	Fulham	38	13	5	1	34	12	7	8	4	24	20	53
2	Portsmouth	38	15	3	1	45	11	7	4	8	19	25	51
3	Brighton & Hove Alb.	38	12	4	3	33	16	6	5	8	20	27	45
4	Luton Town	38	12	4	3	37	22	6	5	8	15	30	45
5	WEST HAM UNITED	38	12	5	2	39	12	3	9	7	21	29	44
6	Tottenham Hotspur	38	13	4	2	46	12	4	5	10	17	33	43
7	Millwall	38	14	3	2	53	12	4	3	12	18	38	42
8	Norwich City	38	9	6	4	34	21	6	6	7	23	27	42
9	Watford	38	9	7	3	31	18	4	9	6	15	25	42
10	Brentford	38	14	3	2	39	16	3	5	11	18	40	42
11	Southampton	38	9	6	4	31	18	4	3	12	18	38	35
12	Reading	38	12	3	4	42	11	2	3	14	15	36	34
13	Leyton	38	9	6	4	26	23	2	6	11	12	37	34
14	Bristol Rovers	38	10	4	5	41	21	2	5	12	14	33	33
15	Plymouth Argyle	38	7	9	3	26	14	3	4	12	17	36	33
16	New Brompton	38	9	4	6	30	21	3	5	11	17	38	33
17	Swindon Town	38	11	7	1	28	8	0	4	15	15	46	33
18	Queen's Park Rangers	38	9	5	5	32	16	2	5	12	15	39	32
19	Crystal Palace	38	7	4	8	29	28	1	5	13	17	38	25
20	Northampton Town	38	5	8	6	22	25	0	1	18	7	63	19

1907/08 ...... ONE STEP BACK

By 1907 all first team players earned between £3 and £4 per week. New players almost always received higher wages than existing players who had not reached the maximum of £4 per week, and they also received a signing on fee of £10. Another advantage came in the close season when there was a difference. During the summer of 1907 three players were on £4 and another 3 were on £3 per week. Some players took outside jobs, but if they earned more than £2 10s per week they were barred from taking another job.

When the first public practice match took place in late August it would be seen that some players had moved on. Aubrey Fair and James Blyth had not been retained, Arthur Winterhalder had signed for Everton, and Dave Gardner and William Taylor had been picked up by Croydon Common. Amongst those that came into the club were three Scots, namely William Brown, a forward from Scottish side Vale of Leven, James Gault, a full-back from Aberdeen and Robert Young, a defender from St Mirren. Other signings were Alf Harwood, a forward from Leeds City, Tommy Lee, a forward from Woolwich Arsenal, and Archie Taylor, a gutsy full-back from Brentford. Apart from the latter, none of these signings, at the time, appeared to be of any significance, which must have been something of a disappointment to the assembled crowd of 3,500, who would have noticed the ground alterations that had been implemented due to the previous season's FA Commission recommendations.

The club arranged a second public practice match which attracted over 5,500 to the Boleyn ground, and all the players appeared in the peak of fitness, which augured well for the opening Southern League fixture against Swindon Town at home in the late afternoon on Monday September 2nd. Unfortunately they needed to be fit, but for all the wrong reasons.

The weather was unusually cold for the time of the year, and raining for most of the match which made it miserable enough, but the amount of violent charging and rough play from both sides could not have been worse. It was noticed that there was a considerable amount of sly tripping off the ball, mainly by the visitors and out of sight of the referee. That apart, the Hammers overall gave a poor display with the exception of new boy Archie Taylor at full-back who was a revelation, sliding in with last-minute tackles, but Dick Jarvis received a cut eye early in the first half, and took no further part in the game. With Swindon a goal up, West Ham fought back in the second half, and were awarded a penalty that the visitors hotly disputed. Then came a moment that epitomized the whole affair. After Billy Grassam had converted the spot kick, the players were walking back to the halfway line, when Bannister, who had handled the ball for the penalty, came behind Frank Piercy and kicked him in the leg. Frank immediately retaliated by turning round and giving Bannister a right-hander that knocked his opponent out cold. Although Piercy was guilty of an offence there were many present who sympathized, but it meant a suspension for Frank. As for the final result, a 1-2 reversal meant it was the first time that the Hammers had lost their opening league match since 1903/04.

Frank Piercy

Another home game in the Southern League quickly followed when the 'old enemy' Spurs came to Upton Park. Robert Young took the place of Jarvis who had not recovered from his cut eye, but that was the only change in the side. It would not be more than five minutes however, before the home team would be depleted again when Bill Wildman, after sustaining a knee injury, and appearing for a few minutes after treatment, hobbled off in obvious pain. Piercy moved to back, but 'Spurs took the lead through Reid, and to make matters worse, Taylor received a cut lip, with two teeth being knocked out in an accidental collision just before the half ended, and he also took no further part in the match. After the interval the Hammers lined up with four forwards, three halves, one back and a goalkeeper. With an obvious advantage the visitors pressed hard, but due to West Ham playing the 'one back' game 'Spurs were caught offside time after time. This was a very dangerous game to play, but the Boleyn boys played it to perfection, so much so that they had the determination to move forward themselves, and this resulted in Fred Blackburn sending in a dropping shot from the wing which went into the net off a post, much to the jubilation of the home crowd. Everyone in the side played their part especially Watson who fell back to the centre half position, and Robert Young whose tackling and distribution were outstanding on his debut. With only nine men for a long period, 1-1 was a fine result.

As a consequence of the injuries and exertions on the Saturday, West Ham did not field a full strength side for the opening match in the Western League campaign at Millwall and lost 0-3. There is nothing to add.

The return fixture with Swindon at the County Ground was not, thankfully, the heated affair that took place at Upton Park, and although three penalties were awarded each one was for handball. The Hammers converted their one through Billy Grassam, but Swindon scored one, and missed the other when George Kitchen added one more spot kick save to his record, and the team came away with a point.

It was at this time that Swindon's Bannister thought fit to write to the editor of the 'East Ham Echo' regarding the fracas with Frank Piercy in the opening game of the season.

Sir,

In you paper of September 6th appears a statement very injurious to me, and absolutely untrue. It says that 'Bannister went up behind Piercy and kicked him on the leg.' I emphatically deny I did anything of the kind. I made a remark to Piercy with reference to something in the game we did not like, and was struck in return unexpectedly. The remainder of the remarks I pass over at present.

Yours Truly etc..

At the disciplinary hearing the above statement cut no ice at all, and Bannister as well as Piercy received a four-match ban.

Whatever the competition, there was always a good attendance for any clash with old rivals Millwall. So it was for the return match in the 'not so important' Western League, when 5,000 turned up for a late Monday afternoon kick-off at the Boleyn. The 'Dockers' had assembled a strong eleven for the campaign and did not intend to pick up the 'wooden spoon' in this competition as they had done in 1906/07, whereas the Hammers, being the Western League holders appeared to more concerned with obtaining Southern League honours. As for the match, the visitors 'went like blazes' for a victory, but it ended all square at one goal each. Alf Harwood made his debut at centre-forward and scored the Irons' goal, but the former Fulham and Leeds City forward was later converted to a left back, but his first team appearances were to be few.

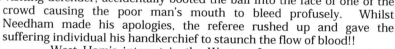

Although the Hammers gained a Southern League victory by a single goal over Crystal Palace at the Boleyn, the display was very disappointing, and the visitors must have felt very hard done by. The 'less than average' performance was not the fault of the defence, as it was quite solid, but the forward line, which at this stage was more or less the same as the previous campaign, was far from its best. Harry Stapley in particular, came in for some heavy criticism – *'slow, dithering and too slight in stature for a centre-forward'* was one observer's harsh opinion.

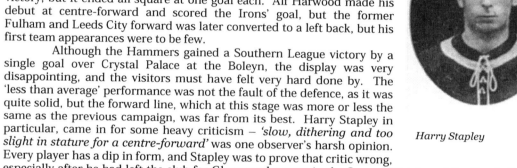

Harry Stapley

Every player has a dip in form, and Stapley was to prove that critic wrong, especially after he had left the club for Glossop who were in the Second Division of the Football League when he joined them. He scored no less than 86 goals in 189 appearances for them between 1908 and 1913. He never entered the professional ranks, being a schoolmaster by occupation, but he was capped for England as an amateur on 10 occasions before World War One.

There was an incident that occurred in the Palace match that a section of the crowd found cruelly amusing. Needham, a visiting defender, accidentally booted the ball into the face of one of the crowd causing the poor man's mouth to bleed profusely. Whilst Needham made his apologies, the referee rushed up and gave the suffering individual his handkerchief to staunch the flow of blood!!

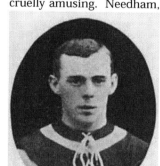

Tommy Lee

West Ham's interest in the Western League, even at such an early stage, appeared to be on the wane already as they were defeated at Luton by a single goal. This was emphasized by the fact that the home side had just nine men for some of the first and the whole of the second period.

A Southern League fixture followed against the same team, again at Kenilworth Road. Fred Kemp came in for his first game of the season alongside Fred Blackburn, and Lionel Watson took up the centre half position in place of the suspended Frank Piercy. Lionel had twice 'stood in' for Frank in that position during the previous season. Tommy Lee deputised again for David Lindsay on the right wing. The Hammers gave a much-improved display and achieved a three goal victory. After Grassam had scored in the first half, Tommy Lee made a sensational start to the second by bursting down the right and crossing for Stapley to put the ball in the net. Late in the game it was Stapley again, when he scored a 'cracker' from twenty yards.

Brighton & Hove Albion were scheduled to be the next opponents at the Boleyn, and it is of interest to quote the previous notes from the Brighton official programme, the language of which is indicative of the Edwardian period:-

'We shall wait on the 'tip-toe of expectation' the news from West Ham on Saturday, and our scoring board 'telegraphist' will endeavour to make his arrangements so that the half-time score and result will be got through in record time. We quite expect a good contingent to make the journey, and we trust they will bear in mind the good advice tendered them in our programme on Saturday, viz: Cheer your pets on to doughty deeds, and accept the official rulings like good sportsmen. You have the opportunity to show the good people of West Ham that you can appreciate good play and appreciate their hospitality.'

Unfortunately the 'telegraphist' at Brighton would not have needed to get too excited as the encounter ended in a 0-0 draw, but for those that did travel it was a thrilling one, and the scoreline could well have read 4-4, as it was 'end to end' stuff with numerous chances for both sides.

The Hammers remained without a victory in the Western League after losing to 'Spurs 1-2 at White Hart Lane, with the only point of interest being that the proceeds of £116 from the match were to be set aside for John Watson, a long-serving full-back, who had been with Tottenham for six years.

The situation in the Southern League was certainly looking a lot better. The visit to Fratton Park to meet Portsmouth resulted in a 2-0 victory. Although former West Ham forward Bill Kirby struck the woodwork twice for Pompey, the Hammers defence was outstanding. It was the fourth clean sheet in succession in this competition.

It was the 'same old story' however, in the Western League when Luton came to the Boleyn and recorded a 2-1 victory. The one consolation of the match was the display of Robert Young at centre half, who ventured as much up in attack in addition to performing his defensive duties, and capped his display with a real stinger of a goal smashed in from 30 yards.

It was at this time that Tommy Robinson, a goalkeeper who had played for several local clubs, and was the son of West Ham United's trainer, signed amateur forms for the Hammers, although he never actually appeared for the first team. This was a surprise, as he was to be regularly praised for his abilities as we shall see.

In May 1907 Bradford Park Avenue, a brand new club, sought permission to join the Football League, but the application was rejected. Fulham however, had left the Southern League at the same time, and the Yorkshire club applied to fill the vacancy, and were accepted. Being situated in the north of the country must have been a logistical problem for the new club together with the extra expense involved. Bradford PA finished the season in 13th place, but then resigned. The club's application to join the Football League Second Division in 1908/09 was then accepted. For a club of just one season's experience, without the large financial backing that Chelsea had when they joined the League, it seems a little strange considering there were a number of larger and more experienced clubs in the Southern League that would have qualified to be members. Had West Ham United applied it is possible that the club would have been accepted.

When the Yorkshire club visited the Boleyn enclosure for the first time the crowd of 12,000 gave them a warm welcome. Their team had a number of experienced players signed from other clubs, and one such was Charlie Craig, once of Thames Ironworks and West Ham United fame, playing as well as ever in his defensive role at the back. A situation arose in the game that typified Charlie. He came into collision with Harry Stapley, both receiving cuts to the head. Whilst Harry went off for a while and later returned with his head adorned with sticking plaster, Charlie took the sponge from his trainer, and whenever he felt it necessary he busily sponged the blood from his face.

The match finished as a scoreless draw, but once again it was an encounter where both side sides had enough chances to have found the net. What it did mean was that the Hammers had now conceded just four goals in eight Southern League games.

A large number of supporters made their way across to Greenwich to cheer their favourites on against Millwall, but there was nothing to celebrate in a 0-1 defeat. Ex-Hammer Joe Blythe had a sterling game for the home side scoring the only goal of the game in the first half. With no managers or coaches pitchside in those days it was the duty of the captain of the team to instigate any changes on the field, and late in the second period captain George Kitchen gave directions for Randall and Watson to switch positions which did make an improvement, but it was too little, too late.

George Kitchen

On the following Monday West Ham entertained Crystal Palace in a Western League fixture and with this competition it was no surprise that the outcome was another defeat (1-2). It meant six games in this league, one draw, and five defeats.

Both Watson and Lindsay were left out of the Southern League line-up against Brentford. Watson in particular, was really struggling with his form so far, and Kemp came in for him alongside

Blackburn. Tommy Randall switched over to Lindsay's position on the wing, and Grassam came in after injury. Harry Stapley scored a brace in a 4-1 victory that put the Hammers into 6th position in the table.

Randall, despite being criticized for hanging on to the ball for too long, also scored his first goal for the club. The rapidly balding Tommy, still only twenty-one years of age, was to be a successful wing half within another year, but currently when picked, was in the forward line. He was barracked on occasions at this time for his slow, thoughtful approach to the game, and was nicknamed 'Old Mother Randall' but gradually over time, it would be forgotten.

The Western League competition was now becoming a nightmare. Due to poor results from the first few matches, the Hammers' executive, along with Syd King, did not always choose to put out the strongest eleven, which was a Western League requirement, but with injuries and loss of form it was not easy to prove that the club had acted otherwise. This of course appears hypocritical, considering their concern just two seasons earlier when they wrote an official letter to all clubs in the competition expressing their concern over the Western league becoming a league for reserve teams. For the visit to the Boleyn enclosure by 'Spurs, the home side had a forward line that read Featherstone, Randall, Watson, Kemp and Lee, hardly an explosive unit. With interest waning, home attendances were well down for this league, and it was no surprise when 'Spurs went away with both points in a 3-1 victory for them. By the end of the campaign the Hammers had managed just one victory, and with a final record of one win, one draw, and ten defeats, there is nothing more to add!

Frank Piercy was obliged to play at left back in the away fixture at Bristol Rovers due to Archie Taylor picking up an injury against Brentford, and Bill Wildman being out with a long-term injury (which ended his career). Jimmy Gault was Piercy's defensive partner at right back, but just before the break Jimmy was also injured and unable to take any further part. Robert Young fell back to take Gault's place and this unusual pairing did their best to keep the Rovers at bay. Having only ten men for half the game was a struggle against a decent side, and George Kitchen added another penalty kick save to his record, but Rovers eventually scored to take the points.

A home defeat by local rivals Leyton by two goals was an even bigger disappointment. Kitchen, although his all-round performance was good, was at fault for the visitor's first goal, but the forwards were distinctly off colour, with Bill Brown, given a rare outing, and Tommy Randall, particularly poor. The result was Leyton's first away win of the season, and they would go on to add just one other before the campaign's end, and finish one from bottom in the Southern League.

The Irons gave the left back spot to Alf Harwood for the visit to Reading. He had been signed as a centre-forward from Leeds City where he had scored 40 goals for their reserve side, but he had now been converted into a full-back. He made a valuable contribution to the East Ender's 1-0 victory. This was a milestone in Reading v West Ham matches at Elm Park in the Southern League, as it was the first time that the Hammers had triumphed there in eight outings, (six of those being defeats).

For the visit of Watford, it was good for the home crowd to see the original five forwards Lindsay, Grassam, Stapley, Watson and Blackburn, who had performed so well in 1906/07, playing together again, (as they had done at Reading.) Watson and Stapley were the scorers in a 2-0 win over a Watford side that included former Hammers' goalie William Biggar, who played 8 games during the Memorial Grounds days in 1902/03, and Alf Hitch, who played for Thames Ironworks FC in 1898/99 before the club became West Ham United in 1900.

Alf Harwood

In December 1907 came three consecutive drawn matches: Norwich 1-1 away, Northampton 1-1 home, and Southampton 0-0 away. Harry Stapley was unable to play in the Norwich fixture, as he was picked for the England amateur side to play against Ireland, and he scored three of England's six goals. Into the West Ham team came 20-year-old Danny Shea to make his debut. As an amateur he had been banging in the goals for local side Manor Park Albion in the South Essex League, but he was to become, without doubt, West Ham United's greatest legend in this pre-World War One period, and for some years afterwards. The fact that he played for Blackburn Rovers in the Football League from January 1913 to the end of 1914/15 did not diminish that adulation whatsoever.

Over the Christmas period the Hammers were lucky to have no less than three fixtures all at home. New Brompton on Christmas Day, QPR on Boxing Day and Plymouth Argyle on the 28th December. What could be expected? Any result, if you know the East End club. In true Hammers' fashion a defeat came against bottom club New Brompton (1-2), a victory was won against eventual champions QPR (3-0), and a draw resulted against high riding Plymouth (1-1).

Stanley Bourne

There was a crowd of 17,000 for the visit of QPR. Four forced changes were made as the injury list had grown. Those replacements that came in certainly made their mark, and it was significant that they were all local men. Stanley Bourne, an amateur, the only West Ham player to have played in spectacles, came in for his first appearance of the season at left back. Stan was on the club's books from 1906 to 1911, and made just 13 Southern League and 3 FA Cup appearances in 5 seasons! George Horn came in at right half, Arthur 'Moppy' Featherstone took the right wing position and scored into the bargain, and Danny Shea also took the field after missing two matches.

It was appropriate that the match was on Boxing Day, as it was more akin to a bout of fisticuffs than a football match. Both sides lost their heads, and the game was continually stopped for players to receive treatment or as one correspondent put it:- *'the players received first aid from......the gentleman who runs out from the pavilion with a Gladstone bag.'* Dick Jarvis had to leave the field with an injured leg, but fortunately there were no other serious injuries. There was criticism of the players' idea of what constituted a 'fair charge', with some being described as *'below the belt.'*

A fair charge should have been 'shoulder to shoulder', but many players at the time got away with challenges that were far more violent. There was one humorous incident to lighten the proceedings when a visiting player's shorts were ripped from knee to waist, and he rose to retire to the dressing rooms holding the two ends together. However, as far as the home crowd was concerned it was the result that counted, and that was that QPR were defeated by three clear goals.

For the encounter with Plymouth, Dan Woodards replaced Dick Jarvis at left half, which meant that along with Harry Stapley there were six locals in the team for the 1-1 draw, and Danny Shea scored his first ever goal after beating two defenders. It was described as an 'absolute beauty.' There was no doubt at all that one of the virtues of the West Ham club was their nurturing of local talent, something that has become an East End tradition, right up to modern times. Over this early 20th Century period, the directors might well have preferred to pick the team, but it was Syd King and men like Charlie Paynter who discovered the local talent.

The first fixture of the New Year was at White Hart Lane where the Hammers reverted to the line-up that defeated QPR, which meant that Jarvis was back in the side. With Tottenham 3-0 up at the break it looked like a disaster, but with Stapley grabbing two goals back in the second period it seemed as if a point might be gained, but it was not to be, and 'Spurs took both points.

West Ham were drawn against Rotherham Town in the first round of the FA Cup. The Yorkshire club was not in the Football League at the time but were members of the Midland League, and had won their way through six qualifying rounds to get to this stage. In those ties they had scored 17 goals to just one conceded, so they would be no pushover.

The game was a typical cup-tie, where the side from a lower league, with no reputation to uphold, gave a fearless, positive display. The home side were on the defensive more often than not, and Kitchen and his two backs, Gault and Hammond (who had come in for Bourne) had a busy time defending their goal. The Hammers had their share of possession which was to be expected, and it was Blackburn and Shea who were the most impressive. The latter had several tremendous shots at goal, and it was a deflection from one of those efforts that fell to Blackburn who merely had the easy task of tapping the ball home. Rotherham spent the last 15 minutes on the attack, but the score remained at 1-0. When the draw was made for the next round West Ham found themselves having to make the long journey to Football League giants Newcastle United.

When the Hammers visited Crystal Palace at Sydenham, the side had a more familiar look about it as Allison, Lindsay, Watson and Archie Taylor returned and took their part in a somewhat easy 3-1 victory that was hampered by fog in the second half.

The following week Tom Robinson took the players to Leigh-on Sea for special training preparations for the cup-tie at Newcastle, but they returned to the Boleyn ground for the visit of Luton Town. During this time the club signed Jimmy Frost from Chelsea, and he made his debut against the 'Hatters'. He combined well with Danny Shea on the right flank, but overall it was a difficult match as the tight 1-0 scoreline suggests. The Hammers had a couple of goals disallowed, one of which the crowd had difficulty in understanding, for the ball was netted by Shea after Blackburn had sent over a corner, but the referee explained later that the ball had floated out of play on its way from the corner kick.

Tommy Allison

George Kitchen on his selection for the International trial, was unable to keep a clean sheet when he appeared for the South against the North at Hyde Road Manchester, where the score was a draw of four goals each. One London newspaper was extremely critical of George, highlighting his errors and concluding that *'Kitchen failed to prove that he is as good a goalkeeper as he is.'* West Ham fans knew differently as he had already proved himself time after time in League and Cup matches.

A future 'all-time great' at Upton Park was now playing in the London Schoolboys Corinthian Shield semi-final match for West Ham Boys against South London Boys. The 12-year-old boy's name was Syd Puddefoot from Park School, West Ham (which created a production line of exceptional players) and he would become a big favourite with all Hammers' fans between 1913 and 1922. In this particular match he had the misfortune to fall heavily after a tackle, and sustain a broken arm, which happily set well and healed quickly. So well was he considered that there were offers to postpone Park's matches in the schools intermediate league (which the school were heading at the time) until he was fit to play.

On February 1st 1908 West Ham met Newcastle United at St James' Park in the FA Cup. The journalist who criticized George Kitchen would have his comments 'rammed down his throat' after the goalkeeper's display in this cup-tie, as from the start it became Newcastle v Kitchen. The Hammers' favourite saved everything that was thrown at him, and with excellent support from the defence, especially Gault and Taylor, kept a clean sheet for the first half. It was much the same after the interval, but after about 15 minutes Kitchen received a serious foot injury, and had to leave the field. Piercy went into goal, but against ten men the inevitable came and the home side ran out winners by two goals to nil. When the team arrived at King's Cross station on the Sunday night Kitchen was put in a wheelchair to enter the Great Northern Hotel. His injury was so bad that he did not play again until the following season.

On a lighter note, a black and tan pup joined the club group at Newcastle the day they arrived, and followed them onto the train to Tynemouth and stayed with team. Archie Taylor claimed the dog for his own, bought a licence for him and was to be seen with him at the Boleyn enclosure. As the Premiership stars of today turn up in the car park in their Ferraris and Porches, Archie walked to the ground with a dog on a lead.

Dave Clark came into the side for Kitchen, and with both Shea and Stapley going down with 'flu, Watson and Billy Brown took their places against Portsmouth at Upton Park. Frost, scored his first goal and Watson hit the target in a 2-1 victory. This was followed by a solid performance at Bradford Park Avenue where Watson scored the only goal of the game. It meant that Lionel had scored in four consecutive League matches, and he was back to his form of the previous campaign.

David Clark

There was the usual anticipation mixed with intimidation and suspense around the Boleyn ground when Millwall paid their visit. Despite the persistent drizzle, a downpour towards the end, and a very strong wind, there was a crowd of 12,000 around the enclosure. With these types of weather conditions, and a muddy pitch, the visitors chose to use the 'long ball' game, whilst the Hammers persisted in short passing methods that were entirely inappropriate. As a consequence, and in a nutshell, Millwall ran out winners by two clear goals. As Stapley was on amateur international duty for England against Wales, Shea was back in the side, but he received no assistance from his partner Frost, and the forward line had a poor game. The halves were therefore under constant pressure, and possibly because of this, Frank Piercy was sent off near the end of the game for a heavy charge on Millwall's Comrie who fell very heavily to the ground, and was carried off in an unconscious state to the dressing room where it took him some time to recover. After the match Comrie said *'It was a pure accident. We were both going for the ball, when I slipped, and Piercy's knee caught me just below the heart. Had I not slipped, nothing would have happened'.* The referee refused to comment after the game, and Frank was later suspended.

On the same Saturday West Ham Schools met Walthamstow Schools in the final of the Corinthian Shield at the Spotted Dog, winning by four goals to one. This time the spotlight fell, not on Syd Puddefoot, for he was forced to watch from the sidelines, but on another future West Ham player, Albert Denyer. He had already starred in the final of the 1906/07 English Schools Shield, but he showed his class and potential in this game by scoring the first goal, laying on the second, and being responsible for a penalty for the young Hammers, which was converted. The result was all the more remarkable for the fact that a West Ham lad by the name of Douglas suffered a broken arm (seems a habit!) in a collision with the opponent's 'keeper within 5 minutes of the start, which meant 85 minutes with ten players!

West Ham Schools now had the remarkable record of holding three major trophies at one time. The English Schools Shield for 1906/07, held until the next final was settled, and which currently adorned the walls of Park School, the Dewar Shield, which was the individual London Schools championship won by Godwin Road School, and now the Corinthian Shield.

The defeat by Millwall deflated the Irons somewhat, but on their visit to Brentford, there was very little to choose between the teams right through to the mid point of the second half, when within 5 minutes the home side banged in three quick goals in succession, and went on eventually to win by four clear goals distorting what was, possession wise, a very even match. Freddie Corbett, the former Thames Ironworks and West Ham forward, was prominent for the Bees.

With just a point won in a 0-0 draw at home to Bristol Rovers any chance of finishing in the top four was now quickly disappearing, but a more light-hearted event took place during the week when a number of the West Ham team, along with Syd King the manager, engaged in a billiard match at the Denmark Arms, East Ham. This is a scene that could be imagined today, as this particular pub has altered little over the last one hundred years, and the snooker tables are still there. The smoky atmosphere and men in their caps and mufflers would be missing of course, along with the present day players, too 'busy' in the night clubs and bars. The players of the day were opposed by a group of local lads lead by a Mr Martin Lewis. Frank Piercy captained the Hammers, but they were beaten by 74 points losing six games out of ten. Frank then challenged the winners to a 'blow ball' match, and a comical game was witnessed:- *'An egg was blown, and at each end of a billiard table two glasses were placed a couple of feet or so apart, and these took the part of goalposts. Between the sticks was Kitchen, defending for the footballers, and Mr Martin Lewis for his side. It was very amusing to see the opponents each endeavouring to blow the balls into the opposite goals, and loud was the laughter which greeted their efforts. In the end the footballers won by three goals to two.'*

For the visit to local side Leyton, the Hammers were expected to gain revenge for the defeat at Upton Park, but the team were without both Stapley and Shea, which reduced the fire-power up front. Billy Grassam came into the line and Robert Young, who had twice filled in at no.9 in the Western League switched to that position. It was Bill Brown however, who scored his first goals for the club in an unsatisfactory 2-2 draw against a side that were languishing in the bottom two of the table.

There was a much better display when Reading came to town. Watson came in for Young, and scored, and Lee took Blackburn's place. The Hammers won 2-1 in what was Piercy's last game before a three-match suspension.

Robert Young

As the return fixture with Brighton took place in mid-week at the Goldstone Ground, it meant a miserable turnout of no more than 1,500 spectators. The result was even more miserable for the Irons as the home side were 3-1 victors. It should come as no surprise to know that the Sussex club were third from bottom at the time.

It was typical of course, for the Boleyn lads to follow up with a victory at Watford by 3 goals to 2. With the scorers being Frost, Jarvis and Stapley, the match turned out to be Harry Stapley's last in West Ham colours as he signed for Second Division side Glossop for 1908/09 after he had appeared for England against Denmark in the Olympic Games final. It seems that there was very little comment or fuss about his departure considering he had served the club so well and had been top scorer for three seasons. Being an amateur of course, he was not duty bound to stay at the club, and he maintained his amateur status at Glossop.

The chance of a top four finish were greatly increased with a 3-0 home success over Norwich City, where Robert Young, now in at centre half for Piercy, had a storming game in defence and also scored a 'screamer' of a goal in the first half. Just before the interval there was a violent thunderstorm, which made the pitch a quagmire in the second half. Dick Jarvis, being in his element in such muddy conditions, had an excellent game at half-back, tackling and then supplying his forwards with a number of effective passes.

With the campaign's end fast approaching, there were five matches yet to be decided with four of those on opponents' territory. The Hammers had achieved a reasonable away record so far, but that was blown apart when all the remaining four resulted in defeat. There were some excuses for the first at Northampton where poor Frank Piercy, back in the side after suspension, collided with a home forward and was knocked out in the first couple of minutes, and due to a head injury took no further part in the subsequent 0-4 defeat.

On Good Friday there were no excuses whatsoever on the visit to New Brompton. The Kent club were bottom of the table and trounced West Ham by three clear goals. Naturally.

Southampton came to the Boleyn ground for the final home game of the season on the following day and the Hammers won by 4-2, but this was just a respite, as the last two matches saw defeats at new champions QPR (0-4), whose supporters were positively ecstatic throughout the game, and at Plymouth by 0-2.

It was an awful end to a campaign that resulted in a finish of 10th place, and something clearly needed to be done in the close season with some new faces in and several out.

Back: S Hammond, W Wildman, D Clark, G Kitchen, C Simmonds, A Taylor, J Gault. Centre: T Robinson (trainer), D Woodards, T Allison, F Piercy, ES King (secretary), L Jarvis, R Young, G Horn, C Paynter. Front, seated: D Lindsay, T Randall, W Brown, A Reed, W Grassam, H Stapley, A Harewood, L Watson, F Blackburn, T Lee. On Ground: A Featherstone, F Kemp. The Western League trophy was won in 1906/07.

1907/08

10th in Southern League Division One

League matches

No		Date	Opponent	Score	Scorers	Att
1	Sep	2	SWINDON TOWN	1-2	Grassam	8000
2		7	TOTTENHAM HOTSPUR	1-1	Blackburn	13000
3		14	Swindon Town	1-1	Grassam	5000
4		21	CRYSTAL PALACE	1-0	Grassam	8000
5		28	Luton Town	3-0	Stapley 2, Grassam	7000
6	Oct	5	BRIGHTON & HOVE ALB.	0-0		7000
7		12	Portsmouth	2-0	Blackburn, Watson	12000
8		19	BRADFORD PARK AVE.	0-0		12000
9		26	Millwall	0-1		13000
10	Nov	2	BRENTFORD	4-1	Stapley 2, Grassam, Randall	6000
11		9	Bristol Rovers	0-1		10000
12		16	LEYTON	0-2		8000
13		23	Reading	1-0	Watson	6000
14		30	WATFORD	2-0	Stapley, Watson	6000
15	Dec	7	Norwich City	1-1	Grassam	4500
16		14	NORTHAMPTON T	1-1	Stapley	4000
17		21	Southampton	0-0		6000
18		25	NEW BROMPTON	1-2	Floyd (og)	10000
19		26	QUEEN'S PARK RANGERS	3-0	Grassam 2, Featherstone	17000
20		28	PLYMOUTH ARGYLE	1-1	Shea	10000
21	Jan	4	Tottenham Hotspur	2-3	Stapley 2	12000
22		18	Crystal Palace	3-1	Shea, Stapley, Watson	8000
23		25	LUTON TOWN	1-0	Watson	8000
24	Feb	8	PORTSMOUTH	2-1	Frost, Watson	10000
25		15	Bradford Park Avenue	1-0	Watson	9000
26		22	MILLWALL	0-2		12000
27		29	Brentford	0-4		4000
28	Mar	7	BRISTOL ROVERS	0-0		6000
29		14	Leyton	2-2	Brown 2	11000
30		21	READING	2-1	Grassam, Watson	6000
31		25	Brighton & Hove Albion	1-3	Jarvis	1500
32		28	Watford	3-2	Frost, Jarvis, Stapley	3000
33	Apr	4	NORWICH CITY	3-0	Blackburn, Frost, Young	6000
34		11	Northampton Town	0-4		6000
35		17	New Brompton	0-3		6000
36		18	SOUTHAMPTON	4-2	Brown 2, Blackburn, Shea	8000
37		20	Queen's Park Rangers	0-4		11000
38		25	Plymouth Argyle	0-2		4000

Appearances and Goals

Player	Apps	Goals
Allison T	29	
Blackburn F	36	4
Bourne S	3	
Brown W	18	4
Clarke D	15	
Featherstone A	5	1
Frost J	13	3
Gault I	34	
Grassam W	32	9
Hammond S	2	
Harwood A	3	
Horn G	4	
Jarvis L	29	2
Kemp F	2	
Kitchen G	23	
Lee T	6	
Lindsay D	14	
Piercy F	23	
Randall T	7	1
Robertson	1	
Shea D	13	3
Stapley H	23	10
Taylor A	25	
Watson L	22	8
Wildman W	2	
Woodards D	1	
Young R	33	1

One own goal

F.A. Cup

Round		Date	Opponent	Score	Scorers	Att
R1	Jan	11	ROTHERHAM TOWN	1-0	Blackburn	9500
R2	Feb	1	Newcastle United	0-2		47000

F.A. Cup line-ups (by shirt number):
- R1: Blackburn 11, Frost 7, Gault 2, Grassam 10, Hammond 3, Horn 4, Lindsay 1, Piercy 5, Stapley 8, Taylor 9, Young 6
- R2: Blackburn 11, Frost 7, Gault 2, Grassam 10, Kitchen 6, Lindsay 1, Piercy 5, Stapley 8, Taylor 9, Watson 3, Young 4

England's amateurs won the gold medal for football at the 1908 Olympic Games. Harry Stapley of West Ham is second from the left on the front row.

Southern League Division One — Final Table

		P	W	D	L	F	A	W	D	L	F	A	Pts
1	Queen's Park Rangers	38	12	4	3	46	26	9	5	5	36	31	51
2	Plymouth Argyle	38	13	5	1	33	13	6	6	7	17	18	49
3	Millwall	38	11	5	3	25	9	8	3	8	24	23	46
4	Crystal Palace	38	10	4	5	35	28	7	6	6	19	23	44
5	Swindon Town	38	12	6	1	41	12	4	4	11	14	28	42
6	Bristol Rovers	38	11	5	3	36	19	5	5	9	23	37	42
7	Tottenham Hotspur	38	11	2	6	33	18	6	5	8	26	30	41
8	Northampton Town	38	9	6	4	30	17	6	5	8	20	24	41
9	Portsmouth	38	14	1	4	43	19	3	5	11	21	33	40
10	WEST HAM UNITED	38	9	6	4	27	16	6	4	9	20	32	40
11	Southampton	38	11	5	3	32	21	5	1	13	19	39	38
12	Reading	38	12	1	6	38	18	3	5	11	17	32	36
13	Bradford PA	38	6	7	6	30	27	6	5	8	23	37	36
14	Watford	38	9	4	6	31	22	3	6	10	16	37	34
15	Norwich City	38	10	4	5	31	16	2	5	12	15	33	33
16	Brentford	38	13	3	3	38	15	1	2	16	11	38	33
17	Brighton & Hove Alb.	38	9	6	4	29	19	3	2	14	17	40	32
18	Luton Town	38	9	4	6	21	13	3	2	14	12	39	30
19	Leyton	38	6	6	7	30	31	2	5	12	22	43	27
20	New Brompton	38	7	3	9	24	29	2	4	13	20	46	25

1908/09 AN UNENVIABLE CLUB RECORD

The club was in need of new faces, but there were some players who were released or moved on. David Lindsay, Arthur Featherstone and Fred Kemp were those released whilst Tommy Lee went to Coventry City and Lionel Watson joined Manchester City. Those arriving at the club did not include any players of real note who were likely to make a significant improvement to the previous season's position, but should those players blend into a real team then perhaps a modicum of success would be on the cards. Two experienced forwards were signed, 33 year old Jack Burton from Blackburn Rovers who had also played for Derby County as long ago as 1897/98, and ex-Sunderland player Jack Foster who was coming up for his 32nd year. Three other forwards joined the club—David Waggott from West Stanley, Walter Miller from Sheffield Wednesday, and right-winger Herbert Ashton from Accrington. The latter was to become a great favourite with the Boleyn crowd over the years, and create a club Southern League appearance record. Also acquired were James Dyer, a utility player from Manchester United, half-back Pat Tirrell from Northampton, full-back Fred Shreeve from Millwall, and a player well known to Hammers' fans –Bill Yenson. Bill had begun his career with Thames Ironworks and stayed with the club

The centre pages of the WHU v Portsmouth match programme, October 10 1908

as it became West Ham United, before joining Bolton Wanderers in 1903. Although primarily a half-back he played at centre-forward in the 1904 FA Cup final for Bolton, and then went on to play for Queens Park Rangers. He was captain of the team that won the Southern League championship in 1907/08.

The campaign began on September 1st, which was a Tuesday, with a late afternoon kick off. It was an attractive opening fixture against the reigning champions QPR. The West London club had put themselves in a very awkward position during the close season as they had resigned from the Southern League in anticipation of joining the Second Division of the Football League. Tottenham Hotspur, who had finished 7th in the table were elected instead, and QPR had to go back 'cap in hand' to the Southern League Committee to rejoin. Constitution and fixtures had already been arranged without them, but the club were allowed back providing they played all their games in mid-week, other than in special circumstances.

The Hammers made a great start to the season by beating the current champions by 2-0. Bill Yenson came in at right half against his old club, but it was the forward line that had a 'new look' about it. Ashton and Dyer were the right wing pair with Jack Foster in the centre. Partnering 'old boy' Blackburn on the left was Jack Burton. Foster scored with a cracking solo goal, and the second goal was set up buy Ashton, who sent the ball over and Foster hit the goalkeeper with his shot, but Blackburn put in the rebound. Bill Yenson stood out with his tackling, especially against former Hammers' favourite Billy Barnes who was kept quiet the whole game.

Supporters who travelled down to the South Coast to the match at Brighton were hoping that that the reasonably good away form of 1907/08 (with the exception of the final four matches) would at least be maintained, but defeat by the odd goal in five gave it a bad start, although new boys Burton and Foster both scored for the Irons.

On the Monday following, the club opened their Western League season at home to Millwall. The team line-up was Clark, Shreeve, Taylor, Yenson, Young, Jarvis, Ashton, Shea, Foster, Brown and Blackburn. In front of a crowd of 4,000 the 'Dockers' won 3-1, with Shea scoring the Hammers' goal. Would this be another poor Western League campaign?

When Crystal Palace came across the river from South London the match should have been billed as West Ham United v Johnson, as the Palace 'keeper saved shot after shot in defence of his goal, but even so the visitors still found time to nip to the other end, and with a forward unmarked, drive the ball into the net.

Archie Taylor

The return Western League fixture with Millwall took place at Greenwich. With several changes to the side, would there be an improvement? No is the answer. Two-nil to Millwall.

The visit to Griffin Park to play Brentford was very much like the encounter with Palace in reverse as George Kitchen was at his absolute best, making save after save from the home forwards, and he was ably assisted by Archie Taylor at full-back who was playing against his old team. Unfortunately there was a different outcome for it was not the Hammers then went down and 'nicked' the winner, but the home side who eventually squeezed the ball past Kitchen to take both points.

Both teams met one another again on the Monday in the Western League, but the line-ups were distinctly different. There was only a small crowd in attendance at the Boleyn ground. Those that stayed away were obviously already fed up with the earlier performances of the club, whatever league it was, but at least those that were there witnessed a victory. James Dyer opened his account for the club in a single goal victory. Walter Miller played his first game at centre-forward, but did not impress.

One of the West Ham supporters in front of the grandstand did not exactly impress the referee either, as the game was stopped for the official to rebuke the man who had been making insulting remarks regarding some of the 'man in the middle's' decisions.

The Southern League fixture with Luton Town was significant in that the directors of the club, perhaps with the team's poor start in mind, gave Syd King entire responsibility for team selection, something that the Board, with minor occasional input from the manager, had previously undertaken themselves. Although such a statement was made at the time, it must be taken 'with a pinch of salt' as

James Gault

Syd King certainly did not always have full responsibility. Often it was joint, and on some occasions he had no input at all. It was not until Charlie Paynter became first team trainer in 1912 that the two together had some influence on team selection. It is not generally realised that all football managers of the period were managers or secretaries in the sense of the 'day to day' running of the club, and all that was involved on the commercial side of the business. There were exceptions, but they were very few, with the great Herbert Chapman coming to mind, who at the time was having a great influence managing (in the modern sense) Northampton Town.

In the Luton match, those players that were picked certainly gave an all-round display. Ashton was responsible for the first two goals with an excellent cross for the opener, converted by Foster, and another cross direct to Blackburn, who in turn found Piercy who banged the ball into the net, much to the crowd's joy. Ashton scored the third himself. All three goals came in the first half, and virtually sunk the visitors. Foster scored his second after the interval for a 4-0 victory.

With just a couple of changes to the side, the Irons were on the road for their next two fixtures, but both were lost, 1-2 at Watford and by three clear goals at Swindon. Whoever had taken the responsibility for team selection had not yet found the right blend.

When Plymouth came to town for a Western League match it must have been difficult for the 2,000 hardy souls present to drum up any enthusiasm for this competition, especially as the Argyle went away with both points after Alf Harwood had a 'misunderstanding' with 'keeper Clark, which led to a really soft goal for the opposition.

Memories were stirred up at the club regarding the case of Peter Kyle back in the season of 1901/02. This was the player, it will be remembered, that despite possessing undoubted ability, was averse to training, and the club were obliged to dispense with his services. Now the club were faced with a similar problem. Jimmy Gault, the Scottish full-back signed for 1906/07 was failing to turn up for training. In the West Ham United club programme for the match against Portsmouth the following diatribe appeared:-

'About a fortnight ago, a hint was thrown out that if an alteration was not made the Directors would have to take drastic measures. I am sorry to say that the Directors on Monday were obliged to suspend Gault for one month for breaches of the training regulations which order that a player should keep himself fit. A months loss of wages is a severe punishment, but Gault has no one to blame but himself, for he has refused to take heed of more than one admonition. The old Aberdeen player during the present season has never given any such display as he did last year, when he was looked upon as one of the best backs in the South. Possibly when he comes back in November he will have learnt his lesson, and will again thrill us all with more dashing displays.'

Without Ashton in the side the writer went on to remark on another player:-
'He (Ashton) can badly be spared just now, as Frost is far from being a success. The latter gives one the idea that he has never forgotten his accident—at Newcastle, was it not? (in 1906/07) for at times there is an absence of thrustfulness in his work.'

The official club programme at the time never did 'beat about the bush'. There was nothing patronising in its approach. Should the writer wish to criticize a certain player or even a poor team display he never failed to do so, and it was refreshingly honest. Reading a copy, without all the nonsensical features that are included in all the modern top league issues today, is a joy.

Pat Tirrell

In the absence of Ashton, out through injury, the right wing spot was given to Harry Eastwood, a young Clapton amateur, who although capable gave a nervous start when Portsmouth were the visitors. Despite some good defensive play, especially from Archie Taylor who was outstanding, it looked like another Southern League defeat with Pompey one goal up with just ten minutes left for play. Foster then amazingly hit a hat-trick before the final whistle which gave the score a lopsided look, as a fairer result would have been a draw.

Danny Shea then added to his Western League total when he scored the winner against Brentford to give the Hammers the double over the West London side in this competition, but it was not a lot to get excited about as the opposition were heading for the 'wooden spoon' anyway.

There were enforced changes for the visit to QPR when both Foster and Piercy picked up injuries, and Miller and Young deputised. With Jack Burton coming in for Bill Brown the team had an unfamiliar look about it, and it showed when Rangers gained an easy 3-0 triumph.

The season was definitely becoming a 'win at home, lose away' campaign as the Hammers defeated Northampton Town at the Boleyn ground by two goals to one. Billy Grassam came into the side for his first game of the season after a long illness and played his usual unselfish game. Freddy Blackburn, now in his fourth campaign for West Ham received some rough treatment from the 'Cobblers' right back Brittan who sent Freddy crashing against the side fencing without receiving a caution from the referee. Both Hammers' goals were scored by players not usually on the score sheet. Pat Tirrell scored against his old club, and Fred Shreeve hit home from the penalty spot after Brittan handled in the area. Justice, considering the full-back's previous demeanours.

True to form, the visit to Kent to meet New Brompton, ended in defeat. West Ham's efforts were not helped when Shreeve was injured in the first half and he left the field, returning but only as a passenger in the second. Miller opened his account for the club, but the 1-2 final score meant that, in the Southern League, the Irons had played six games away from home and lost the lot.

After missing the previous game through injury, Foster returned up front in place of Miller, and scored the only goal of the match against Millwall. In front of a crowd of 14,000, the best of the season so far, West Ham had just the edge, and it was the first time that the team had beaten the 'Dockers' in the Southern League since 1905/06.

The Hammers paid their first ever visit to Roots Hall, Southend, for the club's next away fixture. Southend United had been formed as recently as 1906, but won the 2nd Division of the Southern League in 1907/08 and were promoted. Would the East End club finally gain their first away win in this competition? A draw was the next best thing, and it was a 0-0 draw at that. It was a fair result, but Foster came close with a couple of well directed shots which Charlie Cotton the ex-West Ham 'keeper confidently saved. It was good to see Ashton back after injury, performing well on the right flank, and proving himself to be a great signing.

Coventry City was another club new to the division, and the Irons met the Midland side for the first time at the Boleyn ground. City were struggling in their first season and West Ham, with the same line-up that played at Southend, won quite comfortably by two goals to nil.

It was fortunate that those two points were picked up, because there were three consecutive away matches to follow. No upturn on the club's travels arrived:- Bristol Rovers 1 WHU 0, Plymouth Argyle 2 WHU 0, and Norwich City 6 WHU 3. In the latter game the Hammers were 3-1 up at half time, but fell to pieces in the second half. After these results the club stood 5th from bottom of the table.

Tommy Allison was now in his 6th season with the club, and he became the first West Ham player to be granted a benefit match. The occasion chosen was a Western League fixture against Portsmouth at the Boleyn ground, but sadly this was a most unfortunate choice. The team's performances in this league were even worse than those in the Southern, which did not give supporters much of an incentive to attend, although had the weather been better it might have improved the size of the crowd. Unfortunately it was a wet and miserable Monday afternoon in mid December, and less than 2,000 hardy souls turned up. It was rumoured that the club were to approach the FA to allow them to make a grant to Allison for the player's loyalty. As a postscript, the result was as gloomy as the day - 4-2 to Pompey.

It was at this time that Middlesbrough came in for Robert Young. Since his acquisition from St Mirren he had proved himself to be an accomplished defender playing both in the full-back and half-back positions, and it was a great pity the club accepted Middlesbrough's offer. He went on to make 34 appearances for the North East club before he joined Everton for a £1,200 fee, which was a substantial amount at the time. After 38 starts there, he went on to Wolves where he appeared on 67 occasions.

With Young off to pastures new, Tommy Allison came back into the side for his first Southern League outing of the season. Shea, who had missed the two away matches at Plymouth and Norwich was also back on duty. With such an appalling record 'on the road' (one draw and nine defeats), it was essential that games at the Boleyn ground had to be won to keep the club away from the very bottom of the table.

So it was that Reading were defeated 2-1, but the cards were shuffled again on Christmas Day with Allison excluded in favour of Bill Yenson, and a debut was given to an amateur centre-half signed from Custom House FC, by the name of George Chalkley. The switches paid off as the Hammers won by a single goal scored by Fred Blackburn.

Before a huge crowd of 20,000 at Leyton on Boxing Day however, the team continued their miserable away record in the Southern League with another defeat, although the vital goal came inside the final 5 minutes.

A 4-0 home triumph in the match against Plymouth Argyle, with Danny Shea scoring all four, was overshadowed by some extraordinary events at the Boleyn enclosure on the holiday Monday. The original referee Mr Peers, of Liverpool, was unable to fulfil his engagement, and a Mr E.J. Cooke, one of the linesmen, took his place. With the encounter only five minutes old, the new referee awarded a penalty to West Ham for hands against an Argyle defender. With the visiting players surrounding the referee, arguing fiercely against the decision, the 'discussion' went on for three or four minutes. Then the Plymouth captain called up George Kitchen, the West Ham captain, who was obviously in agreement with his counterpart, and with the referee's permission left the field to consult the officials of the club. Meanwhile Horne, the visiting goalkeeper, and a West Ham player practised penalty kicks, which amused the crowd. Kitchen and Clark returned, obviously with instructions to 'get on with it', and the ball was placed on the spot. The West Ham captain turned to Foster, with an apparent remark, gave him the ball to take the kick. His shot along the ground, which went past the post, was more like a deliberate pass. And everyone thought that was it.

But there was more to come. A few minutes later a Plymouth player had an argument with the deputy linesman over a decision, during which the linesman dropped his flag, and was pushed over by the same player, but the referee appeared to take no action. That was not all. West Ham's Waggott, in the side in place of Burton, was kicked by an opponent. His retaliation was a 'straight arm' response. In the ensuing confrontation a spectator jumped over the fence and tried to join in, but some home players forced him back into the crowd. At half time two FA Councillors who happened to be present, were invited by club officials into the referee's dressing room. Serious allegations were made by some Argyle players, but the referee demanded an apology, which was forthcoming.

In the second half, the players, with the knowledge that the FA Councillors were still in the stand, were on their best behaviour. It did not hide the fact that the 'man in the middle' was weak and had no control at all over the incidents in the first half, even cautioning one player twice when the first offence was worthy of a dismissal.

Contrary to what some believe, players of this period did not always take kindly to the authority and decisions of the match officials. It is not difficult to imagine similar scenes in the modern game, although the award of a penalty would have been gratefully accepted these days, with the chance to take the lead not deliberately thrown away. The referee, of course, would be brandishing red cards into the bargain, whether he was 'weak' or not.

It was a pity that Danny Shea's four goals were overshadowed in the Plymouth fiasco, as the Hammers scraped just a draw in the last minute when Brighton & Hove Albion were the visitors. The second away point of the season followed at Crystal Palace when the teams shared four goals.

All the West Ham faithful were looking forward to the excitement of the first round proper of the FA Cup, and the visit to Queens Park Rangers at their Park Royal ground. The Great Western Railway had made special arrangements for their trains to run from both Bishopsgate and Aldgate, and changing at Praed Street or Westbourne Park for Park Royal station. The fare was to be 7d return. 'Specials' were also running from Paddington. On the day, the travelling fans, and there were several thousand of them, could be seen all around the ground and in the stands. (No segregation in those days). There were groups together of 30 or 40 sporting the colours of claret and blue, (described at the time as 'the red, white and blue) creating not only a vocal noise, but there were muffin bells, burglar alarms (!) and musical instruments, creating a continuous din along with cries of 'Come on you Irons'. These were the early days of the motorbus, and a party of supporters from the Boleyn Castle Social Club took that mode of transport to the game.

As for the match itself, it was a very even and exciting encounter with both teams having a number of chances, but it finished scoreless, which meant a replay at Upton Park. In defence Shreeve had an excellent game, and the half-back line of Yenson, Chalkley and Tirrell were outstanding, with Yenson, against his old team, consistently breaking up QPR's left wing of Drake and former Hammer Billy Barnes. Although Danny Shea did not score, he was now showing in his all round play what a magnificent prospect he was becoming. His shooting and goalscoring ability, and his undoubted skills on the ball were never in question, but he was now adding an understanding of the advantages of teamwork to his repertoire, something that had been lacking in his general play.

Being a midweek reply the attendance did not reach that of the previous Saturday (17,000), but for an afternoon kick off in January it was respectable enough at 11,400. Another very even game followed, but Shea nipped in for the winner after 15 minutes, and so it remained with George Kitchen pulling off some important saves in the second half, putting West Ham through to the next round.

The good home record of nine wins and two draws from eleven matches in the Southern League continued with a comfortable 3-0 victory over a poor Brentford side that would eventually finish in bottom position. Miller scored the first with a superb twenty-yard strike, Waggott notched the second with a strong header from a cross by Frost, and Frost himself from close in.

Also in January, the club held their half-yearly shareholders meeting at East Ham Town Hall. Mr Grisdale the club's chairman, pointed out that gate receipts for the half year had averaged £250 compared with £245 for the same period last season, and the reserve team gates had risen to £38 from £21. The total receipts had amounted to £3981. As for expenses, he stated that wages had shown an increase of £600.

Walter Miller

The statement made earlier in the season that Syd King would have full control of team selection was brought into doubt after some lengthy discussion (for it was obvious that he did not) and there were also questions over the training of players. Some shareholders were keen to move the club forward, and the Board were questioned over what the policy was regarding the possibility of the formation of a third division of the Football League. It was something some members felt strongly about.

When the Hammers visited Luton and were on the end of a 0-1 reverse their minds may well have been on the forthcoming cup-tie against Leeds City at Elland Road. For those supporters that travelled it was a four-hour journey to a Yorkshire town that was full of excitement at the prospect of the North/South clash. It was the London lads who fairly stormed into the first half, and were good value for their 1-0 lead at the interval from a shot from Miller, who put the ball well out of the reach of Naisby in the Leeds goal. Anxious to equalise, it was all Leeds in the second period, but the defence, particularly Archie Taylor and the half-backs, kept Kitchen's goal well guarded. The 'keeper also played his part, and when the home side were awarded a penalty, Kitchen threw his cap into the corner of the goal, and kept the taker waiting whilst he rolled up his sleeves. This Edwardian form of 'gamesmanship' paid off as Gemmell struck the bar with the spot kick. George also made two good saves, but was beaten with just three minutes left, for Leeds to force a replay.

For the subsequent replay there was an attendance of 13,000 at the Boleyn ground. Once again, as in the previous game, it turned out to be an encounter where both sides had their dominating period. With the visitors it was the first half, as they took the lead as early as the second minute. Applying steady pressure, it appeared that Leeds were intent on settling the game as early as possible, but once the Hammers survived that spell they opened out the play, and took it to their opponents. Nevertheless, it was the Northern side that looked the most dangerous in their attacks, and Kitchen, on one occasion, shook Tirrell's hand vigorously after the left half had cleared the ball off the line.

It was West Ham's turn to press after the interval as they tried manfully for the equaliser, which came after the Leeds 'keeper had saved Blackburn's shot and Shea hit in the rebound. Both teams then went for it from then on, but extra-time was needed. There were just three minutes left when Danny Shea got the winner. Contrary to what is often thought about goal celebrations of many years ago being made with 'a shake of the hand' this was not always the case, especially in cup matches. Danny was said to have been *'almost hugged to death'* by his colleagues. This triumph put the club into the 3rd round (now the 5th) for the very first time, and when the draw was made Newcastle United were to be the club's opponents, as they had been in the 2nd round the previous season.

On the same evening, both teams visited the East Ham Palace, which was situated adjacent to East Ham station, where pictures of the match were shown on the bioscope screen. An early form of 'Match of the Day'.

Perhaps the exertions of the replay affected the team's performance for the visit to the South Coast to play Portsmouth. Ashton returned on the right wing after his long injury, and Jarvis took the centre half spot from George Chalkley, but it was the same old story away from home, Pompey running out easy winners by 4-1.

Despite the West Ham directors doubling the cost of admission to the ground for the cup-tie visit of Newcastle United, a crowd of 17,000 assembled at the Boleyn ground. Whether this increase was a wise move is debatable, as crowds for league matches that followed appear to have been adversely affected, but that could have been due to the relatively poor league season the club were experiencing. The cup match was a vigorous affair, with the visitors not producing the quality of football expected of a

Football League First Division side. Maybe this was due to Newcastle not being allowed any time on the ball whatsoever and this surprised them, and it was in this first period that the home side should have capitalised in front of goal, but good chances were not taken and Miller was the main culprit. Mention must be made of Archie Taylor at full-back, for he played probably his best game in West Ham's colours. Always calm and collected, his tackling, passing and covering of his colleagues was first class, especially as the visitors had their fair share of chances late on. As it was, the game finished in a goalless draw, which meant a replay.

So it was on to St James' Park, where the Hammers lost the toss and the game began with a very strong wind blowing against them. Combined with an onslaught by the home side, this meant a gruelling first half for the defence, with the forwards not getting over the halfway line more than half a dozen times. When Newcastle's Veitch missed a penalty just before the break, there was a sigh of relief from the small band of Hammers' supporters. But the second half proved to be a big disappointment. Not from a performance angle, as the team now had the benefit of the gale force wind with the 'Geordies' forced back on the defensive. West Ham's downfall came about through two controversial refereeing decisions. The first occurred after a long clearance downfield by the Newcastle defence. Shreeve's reaction was to head the ball across to his totally unmarked colleague Taylor, who controlled the ball on his chest with a view to passing the ball forward. Much to everyone's surprise, friend and foe alike, the referee awarded a penalty for handball to the home side and Shepherd converted.

The decision spurred the visitors on, and Danny Shea equalised just three minutes later. With the Hammers now on top further attacks were made, but Newcastle broke away and an enormous cross-field pass found Anderson, who was clearly yards offside when the pass was made. Left on his own Anderson duly scored. Despite protests the goal stood, and the Hammers were out of the cup.

The party of West Ham officials dined out at the Metropole Hotel in Newcastle that evening, and revived their 'spirits' after the disappointment of the afternoon.

Three days later several changes were made for the trip to high-riding Northampton Town, a team heading for the Southern League championship come the end of the season. The Hammers were overrun to the tune of 6-0, and it could have been more. David Clark in goal, Gault and Harwood the full-backs, did not play in the first eleven again. Gault, since his earlier club suspension, had been in and out of the side.

The large number of changes to the eleven throughout the season had certainly affected the form of the team, and although injuries were a factor it has to be said that not all changes were enforced.

With George Kitchen still unavailable due to an injury, a local lad from Barking by the name of Dawson was brought in to keep goal, and after recently swapping Jack Foster for Frank Costello of Southampton, the ex-Saints man was included in the side against New Brompton. Frank had previously score 13 goals in 48 matches for the South Coast side. The appalling ground conditions on the day were not conducive to any player trying to impress on his debut, and the small crowd of 3,000 enjoyed the mudlarking on the quagmire of a pitch more than anything else. Either side could have gained the points, but it was the Kent side that were victorious by a single goal. The Hammers were both literally and metaphorically slipping and sliding towards the bottom of the division.

The team redeemed themselves on the Monday following against a good Swindon side. Shea and new boy Costello worked well together and between them they were responsible for all the Hammers' goals in a welcome 4-2 victory. Shea scored two penalties, one awarded for a foul on Costello, and then completed his hat-trick with a solo goal. When Costello scored it was as a result of a perfect cross from Shea. Making a welcome return to the team was Frank Piercy, who had been out of action for 16 league and cup games with torn leg sinews that necessitated the wearing of a plaster cast to help heal the problem.

The visit to Greenwich to meet local rivals Millwall resulted in a 0-3 reverse, but the Lions were flattered by the scoreline. Sadly, it meant a fourth from bottom placing, and the club's awful away record stood at two draws and 14 defeats in sixteen games.

Syd King gave a young player from the Birmingham area by the name of Atkins a run-out at centre-forward against Southend United at the Boleyn ground. The crowd had no knowledge of his identity at the time as he was marked in the programme as 'A.Centre' Although he scored a goal from a 'tap in', his display was less than average and it is a puzzle as to why this position could not have been filled from the existing players at the club. George Kitchen returned from injury for this game, but he was not as busy as his counterpart in the 'Shrimpers' goal ex-Hammer Charlie Cotton. Frank Piercy headed a rare goal from a corner, and Shea and Costello scored the others in a 4-0 victory.

After a defeat at Coventry by 3 goals to one, with Atkins making a really anonymous contribution, Sid King turned to the club's reserve side, which had an important fixture in the South Eastern League against Fulham. The Hammers stood proudly at the top of the table, but needed a victory to be certain of the title. The game finished in a 2-2 draw, but King could not have failed to notice the performance of George Webb, a young local lad at centre-forward. He scored West Ham's first goal, and his general all-round display of speed and skill, combined with a powerful physique, fairly frightened the life out of the opposition.

The manager, however, tried Walter Miller as the main striker once more for the visit of Exeter City, and he scored twice in a 4-1 victory. This was the third home match in succession that the Hammers had scored four goals. Why could the team not reach this standard on their travels?

Miller however, missed several opportunities to score when Bristol Rovers visited, and the West Country side scored twice and went away with both points. Whilst West Ham had such a poor away record such home defeats were a disaster, and with another two fixtures at Upton Park, King, with the agreement of his directors, gave the centre-forward spot to George Webb.

The first of these encounters was on Good Friday against local rivals Leyton, and George did not disappoint. When Whitbourne, the Leyton 'keeper was not quick enough to clear a ball from a shot, George, with his hefty frame, charged him, ball and all, into the net for the only goal of the game. On the following day, Easter Saturday, with only one change of Yenson for Piercy, the Hammers entertained Watford, and with all the forward line combining well, came out on top by three goals to one, with Danny Shea scoring another two.

A 2-2 draw at the Dell against Southampton meant an unbeaten Easter period. The highlight of the game was a run from the halfway line by George Webb past several of the opposition players, and a shot into the corner of the net for West Ham's second goal. George obviously had a good footballing future.

By the time that the Hammers met Norwich City for the last home game of the season Coventry City were at the bottom of the table with 30 points, Norwich and Brentford both had 31, Watford had 33 and there were no less than five teams on 34 points including West Ham. However, there was no threat of relegation for all those clubs this year, as promotion and relegation had been carried out on something of an irregular basis up until then. It was not until 1909/10 onwards that the bottom two would be automatically relegated. So it was then, that with West Ham in their current position 5th from the bottom, finishing out of the bottom few was really a matter of pride. Unfortunately, in the Norwich fixture both teams played out the game in an 'end of season' mood. The scoreline ended in favour the Hammers favour by 2-1.

There was obviously no sense of pride in the final two matches, which were both away from home. Both were lost, which meant three draws and seventeen defeats from 20 away games. History now has it that from the club's humble beginnings as Thames Ironworks in 1895, 1908/09 has been the only season that the club failed to win an away match in their major league competition. Fortunately that is a record that has not been equalled since.

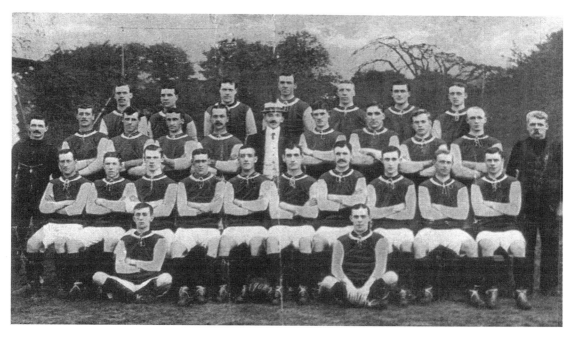

Back: F Shreeve, J Gault, D Clark, G Kitchen, A Taylor, S Bourne, A Harwood. Middle: G Chalkley, W Yenson, T Allison, F Piercy, E S King (secretary/manager), R Young, L Jarvis, P Tirrell, T Randall. Seated: J Frost, D Shea, W Brown, J Dyer, J Foster, W Miller, W Grassam, J Burton, D Waggott, F Blackburn. On the ground: H Ashton, T Lee

1908/09

17th in Southern League Division One

No	Date	Opponent	Score	Scorers	Att	Allison T	Ashton H	Atkins C	Blackburn F	Bourne S	Burton J	Chalkley G	Costello F	Dawson C	Eastwood H	Foster J	Frost J	Gault J	Grassam W	Harwood A	Jarvis L	Kitchen G	Miller W	Piercy F	Randall T	Shea D	Shreeve F	Taylor A	Tirrell P	Waggott D	Webb G	Yenson W	Young R
1	Sep 1	QUEEN'S PARK RANGERS	2-0	Blackburn, Foster	7000		7		11		10					9		2			6	1		5				3				4	
2	5	Brighton & Hove Albion	2-3	Burton, Foster	6000		7		11		10					9		2			6	1		5				3				4	
3	12	CRYSTAL PALACE	0-1		10000				11							9	7	2			6	1		5	8			3	4			9	6
4	19	Brentford	0-1		6000				11								7	2				1		5	8			3	4			9	6
5	26	LUTON TOWN	4-0	Foster 2, Ashton, Piercy	3000		7		11		10					9				3		1		5	8			2	6			4	
6	30	Watford	1-2	Shea	3000		7		11		10					9		3				1		5	8			2				4	
7	Oct 3	Swindon Town	0-3		6000		7		11		10					9		3			6	1		5	8			2				4	
8	10	PORTSMOUTH	3-1	Foster 3	8000				11						7	9				3	6	1		5	8			2	4				
9	17	Queen's Park Rangers	0-3		6000				11		10				7				9	3	6	1			8			2	4			5	
10	24	NORTHAMPTON T	2-1	Shreeve, Tirrell	9000				11						7	9			8		6	1		5		10	2	3	4				
11	31	Gillingham	1-2	Miller	6000				11						7							1	9	5	8	10	2	3	4				6
12	Nov 7	MILLWALL	1-0	Foster	14000				11						7	9		2	10		6	1		5	8			3					
13	14	Southend United	0-0		6000		7		11							9		2			6	1		5	8	10		3					
14	21	COVENTRY CITY	2-0	Foster, Randall	6000		7		11							9		2			6	1		5	8	10		3					
15	28	Bristol Rovers	0-1		8000		7		11							9		2	10		6	1		5	8			3					
16	Dec 5	Plymouth Argyle	0-2		7000		7		11		10								8		6	1	9	5			2	3					
17	12	Norwich City	3-6	Burton 2, Grassam	4500		7		11		10					9		2	8		6	1		5				3					
18	19	READING	2-1	Blackburn, Grassam	5000	4	7		11		10								8	3	6	1		5		9	2						
19	25	SOUTHAMPTON	1-0	Blackburn	15000				11	5	10			7					8	3	6	1				9	2						
20	26	Leyton	0-1		20000		7		11	5	10								8	3	6	1				9	2						
21	28	PLYMOUTH ARGYLE	4-0	Shea 4	10000				11	5						9	7	2				1				8		3	6	10		4	
22	Jan 2	BRIGHTON & HOVE ALB.	1-1	Waggott	5000				11	5						9	7	2				1				8		3	6	10		4	
23	9	Crystal Palace	2-2	Shea 2	5000				11	5							7			2		1	9			8		3	6	10		4	
24	23	BRENTFORD	3-0	Frost, Miller, Waggott	7000				11	5							7					1	9			8		3	6	10		4	
25	30	Luton Town	0-1		3000				11	5							7					1	9			8		3	6	10		4	
26	Feb 13	Portsmouth	1-4	Miller	5000		7		11													1	9	5		8		3	6	10		4	
27	27	Northampton Town	0-6		5000		7		11		10							2		3	4		9		6	8						5	
28	Mar 6	GILLINGHAM	0-1		3000		7		11	2			10	1					4				9		6	8		3					
29	8	SWINDON TOWN	4-2	Shea 3, Costello	4000		7		11			9	10						4		2		6			8		3					
30	13	Millwall	0-3		9000		7		11		10	9							4			1	6			8	2	3					
31	20	SOUTHEND UNITED	4-0	Atkins, Costello, Piercy, Shea	9000		7	9	11				10									1	5	6		8	2	3					
32	27	Coventry City	1-3	Shea	7000		7	9	11				10									1	5	6		8	2	3					
33	Apr 1	EXETER CITY	4-1	Blackburn 2, Miller 2	4000	4	7		11				10									1	9	5	6	8	2	3					
34	3	BRISTOL ROVERS	0-2		7000	4	7		11				10									1	9	5	6	8	2	3					
35	9	LEYTON	1-0	Webb	13000	4	7		11				10									1		5	6	8	2	3			9		
36	10	WATFORD	3-1	Shea 2, Costello	7000	4	7		11				10									1			6	8	2	3			9	5	
37	12	Southampton	2-2	Shea, Webb	7500		7		11				10									1	5		6	8	2	3			9	4	
38	17	NORWICH CITY	2-1	Blackburn, Shea	5000		7		11	3			10									1	5		6	8	2				9	4	
39	21	Exeter City	0-1		7000		7		11		8		10	1									5		6	9	2	3				4	
40	24	Reading	0-1		2500		7		11										5	1						8	2				6	9	
		Apps				5	27	2	40	3	15	7	12	4	6	15	7	13	8	9	23	35	11	26	17	35	19	35	13	8	4	26	9
		Goals					1	1	6		3		3			9	1		2				5	2	1	16	1		1	2	2		

D Clarke played at 1 in game 27
W Brown played at 10 in games 8 and 42
J Dyer played in games 1 and 2 at 8 and game 4 at 10

F.A. Cup

No	Date	Opponent	Score	Scorers	Att	Allison T	Ashton H	Atkins C	Blackburn F	Bourne S	Burton J	Chalkley G	Costello F	Dawson C	Eastwood H	Foster J	Frost J	Gault J	Grassam W	Harwood A	Jarvis L	Kitchen G	Miller W	Piercy F	Randall T	Shea D	Shreeve F	Taylor A	Tirrell P	Waggott D	Webb G	Yenson W	Young R
R1	Jan 16	Queen's Park Rangers	0-0		17000				11	5	10								7			1	9			8	2	3	6			4	
rep	20	QUEEN'S PARK RANGERS	1-0	Shea	11400				11	5									7			1	9			8	2	3	6	10		4	
R2	Feb 6	Leeds City	1-1	Miller	31500				11	5	10								7			1	9			8	2	3	6			4	
rep	11	LEEDS CITY	2-1	Shea 2	13000				11	5	10								7			1	9			8	2	3	6			4	
R3	20	NEWCASTLE UNITED	0-0		17000		7		11	6							10		4			1	9			8	2	3				5	
rep	24	Newcastle United	1-2	Shea	36500		7		11	6	10								4			1	9			8	2	3				5	

	P	W	D	L	F	A	W	D	L	F	A	Pts
1 Northampton Town	40	15	3	2	55	14	10	2	8	35	31	55
2 Swindon Town	40	18	0	2	68	15	4	5	11	28	40	49
3 Southampton	40	13	4	3	44	26	6	6	8	23	32	48
4 Portsmouth	40	13	5	2	42	17	5	5	10	26	43	46
5 Bristol Rovers	40	13	5	2	39	20	4	4	12	21	43	43
6 Exeter City	40	13	2	5	37	28	5	4	11	19	37	42
7 New Brompton	40	12	2	6	30	22	5	5	10	18	37	41
8 Reading	40	7	9	4	33	19	4	9	7	27	38	40
9 Luton Town	40	16	1	3	45	15	1	5	14	14	45	40
10 Plymouth Argyle	40	9	6	5	28	16	6	4	10	18	31	40
11 Millwall	40	14	3	3	38	17	2	3	15	21	44	38
12 Southend United	40	12	6	2	33	14	2	4	14	19	40	38
13 Leyton	40	13	3	4	35	12	2	5	13	17	43	38
14 Watford	40	12	7	1	37	16	2	2	16	14	48	37
15 Queen's Park Rgrs	40	12	6	4	41	24	2	6	12	11	26	36
16 Crystal Palace	40	10	4	6	42	23	2	8	10	20	39	36
17 WEST HAM UNITED	40	16	1	3	43	13	0	3	17	13	47	36
18 Brighton & Hove Alb.	40	11	4	5	46	20	3	1	14	14	41	35
19 Norwich City	40	11	8	1	44	18	1	3	16	15	57	35
20 Coventry City	40	10	4	6	44	37	5	0	15	20	54	34
21 Brentford	40	10	5	5	40	26	3	2	15	19	48	33

1909/10   A SETTLED SIDE

After such a poor campaign in 1908/09, West Ham needed to bring some new blood into the club in the close season, but not without releasing or transferring several others. One move was forced upon the directors when Archie Taylor joined Dundee after being in dispute with the club over wages. This was something of a setback as Taylor had been a valuable asset to the side, but the maximum wage existed in England, and this was not enough for Archie who joined Dundee, as Scottish clubs were not governed by English rules regarding players' wages. The most serious problem concerned Danny Shea who originally refused terms with the East End club, but the matter was thankfully resolved later in the close season. Bill Yenson and Jack Frost both left to join Croydon Common. The South London club had been accepted into the Southern League First Division, which would now consist of 22 clubs.

It was also goodbye to Tommy Allison who retired, and Len 'Dick' Jarvis who joined Bury in the First Division of the Football League where he was to make 55 appearances over the next three seasons. It meant the definite end of what had been the most regular half-back line in the history of the club at the time, although the 'old war horse' Frank Piercy would still be around for another three campaigns as a player. Since 1904/05 the Allison, Piercy, Jarvis combination had played together in that formation no less than 66 times in the Southern League.

Of the others, Jack Burton went to Birmingham, Alf Harwood to Spennymoor, Frank Costello to Bolton and Walter Miller to Blackpool, where he had a good ratio of goals to games of 15 in 37 appearances. Not retained were Pat Tirrell, James Gault and 'old stager' Billy Grassam, who left later in the season.

Those that came in were left winger Tommy Caldwell, signed from Southend United, Vincent Haynes, a six-foot centre-forward from Crewe Alexandra, Robert Fairman, an experienced full-back from Birmingham, and three players from Norwich City, Robert Whiteman, a half-back who was to prove an excellent acquisition, George Wagstaffe and William Silor.

Fred Shreeve

West Ham's opening game was at home to Exeter City on Thursday September 2nd 1909 with a late afternoon kick off. The team included four of the new men, Fairman, Whiteman, Haynes and Caldwell. The latter player took his place at outside left, with old favourite Fred Blackburn moving into the inside position. Freddie was now beginning his fifth consecutive season with the club.

In a 2-1 victory Ashton and Shea were the pick of the side, whilst the 'new boys' were bedding themselves in. Shea, already in a goalscoring mood hit both goals, one of them a penalty.

One redeeming feature of 1908/09, had been that the reserve team had won the London League title, but when they opened the new season's South Eastern League programme at Tottenham they were defeated by 7-3, but it was significant that the amateur George Webb scored all West Ham's goals.

The name of West Ham United came up the same week at East Ham Police Court when a Mr Webster, described as an advertisement contractor, was charged on remand with obtaining money by false pretences. The allegation was that the accused had visited various tradesmen in the district informing them that he was canvassing for West Ham United for advertisements in the club's official fixture list. He received orders and money from some, but when the official list came out none of their names appeared on it. In defence he stated that the list had not yet gone to the printers, as he had not decided which one to have. All the witnesses stated that Mr Webster told them that he was canvassing on behalf of West Ham United. Syd King, the Hammers' manager and secretary, said that the accused was a complete stranger to him, and he had no authority to canvass on behalf of the club. The accused was sent for trial at the Central Criminal Court.

After suffering the whole season of 1908/09 without an away win in the Southern League the team won their initial encounter 'on the road' at Norwich City by 3 goals to one. Once again Ashton and Shea shone in attack, along with Blackburn. Both Shreeve and Fairman were solid in defence. Shreeve had formed a good full-back partnership with Archie Taylor the previous season, and it is appropriate to examine the role of the last two defenders in the team. Full-backs were more exposed than they are now, as there was no 'stopper' centre half (let alone being part of a back four), to aid them. They did have the more stringent offside law to assist them, and the help of their halves, providing the latter were not too involved in attack. They had a duty to cover their 'keeper and give him space, with the obvious defensive role of tackling and clearing to their halves if possible, or longer to a forward if they were under pressure. They were not to be found wandering upfield, much the same as forwards were discouraged from defending.

The opening period of the first half in the home fixture with Brentford had the West Ham faithful believing in a hatful of goals after Shea had headed home and caused the visitor's Stewart to deflect a shot from the same player into the net for a two goal lead. The West London side had other ideas and scored two headed goals in two minutes before the half was over. With the 'Bees' using their obvious weight advantage – they were considered as perhaps the biggest in the South – the lighter Hammers' forwards found headway difficult, but when Caldwell found Ashton, his shot could not be held by Ling, the visiting 'keeper, and Shea with his quickness of thought had the ball in the net in a flash. Result 3-2, and top of the table.

Portsmouth came to the Boleyn enclosure and put a dent in the Hammers' good start, winning by two clear goals, which were both scored by ex-West Ham man Bill Kirby. This was the first and only time that Pompey would defeat the East London club at the Boleyn ground (or the Memorial Grounds) in the Southern League. Bizarrely the South Coast club had lost only one of six away matches at West Ham in the Western League.

With regard to the Western League competition, all the professional clubs who had been existing members resigned en bloc at the end of the previous season (1908/09), and clubs at a lower level that were more suited geographically to the West of England took their places. The benefits of the change were financial as attendances had fallen considerably, and any income was outweighed by the cost of travelling to places such as Plymouth, Portsmouth and Bristol. In addition players were at further risk from injury in what had gradually become an unimportant competition.

When West Ham visited Coventry City, a very even contest resulted in a 2-2 draw, but Vincent Haynes, already with a goal to his credit, could have won it in the very last minute when his shot scraped a post.

Ex-Hammers' goalkeeper Bill Biggar was the Watford player who stood between West Ham and a cricket score, keeping the score down to 2-0 as the home lads were all on song. Caldwell and Blackburn were now making a great left wing pairing to equal that of the two on the right, Ashton and Shea. George Webb, in now for his first appearance of the season, led the line confidently. Tommy

Tommy Randall

Randall, who scored with a tremendous 25-yard shot, had by now established himself at left half after sporadic appearances over the last two campaigns as a forward. He had become somewhat a butt of the crowd who nicknamed him 'Old Mother Randall' because of his slow and thoughtful approach to the game. As soon as he was converted to a half-back in the second half of the 1908/09 season, he found his true position and became a firm favourite with the fans whilst continuing to give sound performances up to and including 1914/15.

Betting on football, illegal at the time, was highlighted just before the above match when a Mr Alfred Burley was arrested outside the Boleyn ground for handing out notices to people going into the match. These notices invited individuals to bet on football results with a Mr C. E. Jones, a 'turf and football accountant' whose address was given as Flushing, Holland. When the defendant was summoned at East Ham Police Court he answered:-

'I am out of work, and a man asked me if I wanted to earn a couple of bob by giving bills out. I don't know his name, but he lives in New Kent Road.' When asked *'What number?'* he replied *'I don't know, he was a stranger.'* The defendant was found guilty and was fined £10 with costs.

What would have been the odds on West Ham still being unbeaten away from home after another two matches? The first was a 1-1 draw at Portsmouth, and the Hammers kept that going with a splendid 3-0 victory at Reading. The home side were having a very poor time of it, both at home and away, and this was evident in the showing of their weak forward line, whereas West Ham were strong in attack with George Webb scoring his first of the season, and Danny Shea (who else?) scoring the other two. 10 goals in 9 matches for him.

Due to the 42 match programme which was limited to a strict period of 8 months (beginning of September to end of April) several matches had to be completed in midweek, and as floodlights did not exist in those days, an afternoon kick off had to apply. It was a pity then, that for the visit of Bristol Rovers there were no more than 4,000 present on the Monday, as the Hammers fairly demolished their visitors by five goals to nil, with Tommy Caldwell, from the wing, grabbing a hat-trick.

With this in mind, it was something of a disappointment, in front of a crowd of 11,000, that the visit of Southend United resulted in a scoreless draw, with both defences on top. George Kitchen and his opposing counterpart ex-Hammer Charlie Cotton both having outstanding games.

A first round victory had already been achieved against Millwall by 1-0 in the London Challenge Cup and West Ham then faced Arsenal in round two. A similar score put the Hammers through, but talk was not so much about the result as to the amazing incident that took place on the field. Thompson, the Arsenal centre half, obviously mistaking the referee for a West Ham player, charged the 'man in the middle' to remove him out of his way. The referee, Mr Rowbotham, was dazed and astonished as both rebounded off one another. Quickly recovering, each then went for the other with all the force they had. It appeared that both were acting in what they thought was self defence, and as a result of the second

Dan Shea

collision both fell to the ground. The game was stopped whilst Mr Rowbotham received attention to a cut over his eye, and as the match was very near to the end, he carried on despite the sticking plaster covering his wound. The crowd, of course, thought it was a huge joke. It was considered a sheer accident, and the referee does not appear to have taken any disciplinary action, which was fortunate for Thompson.

The Hammers remained unbeaten away from home after taking both points against a good Leyton side. The Boleyn boys certainly did not have it all their own way, as the home side played some really clever stuff, but they were far more dangerous around the goal in contrast to Leyton who were cleverer in midfield. There were no goals until 15 minutes from time when Caldwell scored off a rebound and then eight minutes later Webb, at last shaking off the shackles that Hunt had gripped him with, went through the whole defence and scored a brilliant goal, before Leyton pulled one back on the stroke of full time. Big, bustling centre-forwards with an eye for goal were well in demand, and George was just that type. They were also admired for their ability to knock goalkeepers into the net, ball and all, and that action had been the result of his first goal in 1908/09 on his initial first team appearance, strangely enough also against Leyton.

On the following Wednesday evening the Boleyn Castle Social Club held a club supper in connection with West Ham United FC. The directors of the football club were present along with Syd King, manager/secretary, and most of the players. After an excellent meal, the Chairman proposed the 'King' which was loyally honoured. Then:-

'The toast 'the West Ham FC and the Boleyn Club' was next proposed by the Chairman...... He extended a very hearty welcome to the footballers, and he could assure them that amongst the members of the club they had nothing but well-wishers, and they had no more ardent supporters throughout the whole of West Ham and East Ham. He was very pleased at the success which had attended the efforts of the football club so far this season. (Hear, hear.) Their position in the Southern League was a very hopeful one, and the directors were to be congratulated on having such a splendid team, and he was hoping to see them winners of the League. (Applause) He was delighted to see so many directors present for it was a good sign when the 'heads' mixed with the 'workmen' (!!)

As regards the billiard match, of which that supper was the outcome, nineteen games of 100 up were played and the Boleyn Club won by 267. No doubt they caught the players 'offside' that evening. (Laughter) ......

The toast was received with enthusiasm, and Mr Cearns in reply, said he much appreciated the remarks which had fallen from the Chairman. In many respects the two clubs were identical. They were identical as in the past both had had many difficulties to contend with, and now they were both reaping the reward that was due to them. West Ham this year had a most loyal lot of players and good feeling existed between them and the directors. (Hear, hear) There was one thing the players appreciated, and that was the support they received from the 'blokes for women'....

('Blokes for women' was support for the suffragette movement)

Mr Hemmings said as Chairman of the (Boleyn) Club he was proud of its position. They had been established three years, and he well remembered the time when he thought they would have to close their doors. But they had now turned the corner, and, like the football club, they were now enjoying brighter and better days. He thanked Billy Grassam, who was one of the originators of the pleasant evenings with the players of the football club, for what he had done. (Applause)

(It is interesting to note that Tommy Robinson, the club's trainer, was involved in the musical programme that followed. A man of many talents).

A good performance against Plymouth at the Boleyn ground when a 4-1 hiding was given out to the Argyle, saw the Hammers on top of the table on points along with Crystal Palace, although Palace had the better goal average. The Hammers' forward line was quite breathtaking with Shea and Webb each scoring twice, but on the day, there was quality right throughout the side.

A hiccup came when the Hammers lost their first match away from home, when Bristol Rovers gained the points by a single goal, but it was a poor game by both sides. Without a doubt, West Ham missed Danny Shea who had been picked for a London representative eleven against Birmingham. Danny was on the losing side, but he was much praised by the reporter of the 'Morning Leader' who wrote:-

'It will be generally admitted that the young West Ham forward, born at Wapping, was one of the best forwards on the ground. He was certainly the best of the London forwards, alive and eager from end to end, and when during the second half, Woodward got into his International stride, these two men played delightful football. It was the combined work of this pair—a pretty bit of passing and repassing—that culminated in the London goal about midway through the closing stage, and Shea was

unlucky not to have a couple more points to his personal credit. He is the best and quickest shot I have seen this year.'

Danny was back in the side again for the trip to Southampton and proved what a fine player he was when he opened the scoring for the Hammers, and then laid on the second for Haynes to put them two goals up at the break. Unfortunately the 'Saints' piled on the pressure in the second half and pulled both goals back, but for the London side it was a useful point gained against one of the better sides in the division.

Tommy Caldwell

On the following Monday the London FA Charity match was played against Leyton which was a one-off match with all proceeds going to charity. The previous year the Hammers had defeated Millwall and members of the winning team were awarded medals. Much was made of these prizes as they were said to be 'the best given in any competition.' The medals were 18ct gold and guaranteed to be worth 50s.each. Those that had not been in the side the previous season were especially keen to acquire this reward and the team treated the game seriously. The proceeds to charity were £146, from an attendance of 5,000, and the crowd were not disappointed in the Hammers' performance. The forwards were nothing short of outstanding, even though both Shea and Webb were carrying injuries, with the latter having to leave the field in the latter stages. Caldwell scored the first from Ashton's pass, Webb laid on Shea's goal and then scored himself in a 3-0 victory.

Croydon Common made their first ever visit to the Boleyn enclosure on November 6th 1909. The club had been formed in 1897, but did not turn professional until 1907/08 when they were accepted into the Southern League Division Two, where they won promotion in the following season.

The visitors were finding the better class very difficult to handle and were struggling at the time. The Hammers had no problems at all in overwhelming the South London club and rattled in five goals, missing several more in the process. George Kitchen had very little to do, except pick the ball out of the net on one occasion. Two of West Ham's goals were penalties, both converted by Shea.

There was no doubt at this stage, with 16 league matches having been played, that the benefit of an unchanged team was paying dividends. Without the encumbrance of the Western League matches, with the possibilities of injuries sustained, it had led to consistent team selection. Up until the Croydon game no less than nine players had played in every match.

West Ham's involvement in the London Challenge Cup however, was ended at neutral White Hart Lane in the semi-final stage when Fulham, now members of the Second Division of the Football League, won through to the final by two goals to one.

As usual the local derby with Millwall was a hard fought affair, and although there was the inevitable quota of fouls, the referee kept the players in check and the crowd at North Greenwich saw an excellent encounter. Acting by now as an unofficial West Ham United Supporters Club, the Boleyn Social and Sports Club, as they did against QPR in the previous season's FA Cup, hired a specially chartered motor bus for the game. In a match that had Millwall using the 'long ball' method, whilst the Hammers kept the ball along the ground, there was a strong contrast of styles, but considering it was a goalless draw it was a magnificent game played at a cracking pace.

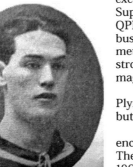

George Webb

Despite another game where neither side find the net (away to Plymouth), the East London club were still in second place in the table, but this was soon to change, and not for the better.

In the third consecutive league match away from the Boleyn enclosure, the Hammers met the current champions Northampton Town. The two previous visits had resulted in two resounding defeats, 0-6 in 1908/09 and 0-4 in the season before, and although West Ham at least scored, the final result was a defeat by 3 goals to 1. Maybe it would have been a different story if at 0-1 down Kitchen had not needed to leave the field after a collision. In his absence the 'Cobblers' scored when Shreeve had gone into goal, and completely misjudged a shot from Whittaker, one which Kitchen would have had covered. George did return in goal, and Webb pulled one back for the Hammers before half time. After the break the referee consulted his linesmen on two occasions when the light got so bad it was difficult to see the movement of players, but the game went on and it was the home side that added another just before time.

To get back near to the top for the visit of QPR, it was essential that two points be picked up, as it was now three games without a win. There was certainly no lack of effort by everyone in the side, and if had not been for Shaw, in the Rangers goal, being on top form it would have been two points. There was also the matter of a penalty in the first half, one that Shea was usually so accurate with, but which he blasted wide of the goal. After the break the play was of a more even nature and because of the heavy pitch the players appeared to have lost a lot of pace. West Ham should have scored on one occasion when the home forwards crowded round the goal, and shot after shot was being banged in, but more by luck than judgement the ball was kept out. When George Webb was pulled down however, a penalty resulted. This time Shreeve took the kick and scored. Victory was now on the cards, but it was former Hammer Billy Barnes, who had renewed acquaintance with old friends before the game, who had other ideas and netted for QPR, and to add insult to injury Hartwell hooked in another from a corner near the end, and Hammers were pointless again.

Worse was to follow. At Luton the Hammers, due to injuries, were forced to play Lavery in place of Shreeve and Wagstaffe for Piercy. This had an adverse effect on the defence, and the home side were three goals up before Ashton reduced the arrears in the second half. Tommy Randall was forced to retire, and Luton finally won by 4 goals to 2

Shreeve and Piercy resumed for the visit of Swindon Town, but Bourne came in for one of his rare games in place of Fairman, and Fred Massey, recently signed from 'Spurs and who was previously with Leyton as an inside forward, came in for the injured Tommy Randall. The Hammers were determined to end their poor run and attacked the 'Railwaymen' from the start. Ashton struck a shot against the post, and Shea hit the bar, but amazingly Swindon's England international Harold Fleming, made his way past three defenders and scored. In the second half it was more of the same, but Kitchen was badly caught out from a not especially strong shot from twenty yards, and it was two goals down. To their credit the home forwards continued to press, and they were rewarded with a goal courtesy of Fred Blackburn, but there were just seven minutes remaining. With a number of people leaving and another two points seemingly lost, Shea was bowled over in the area with seconds to go, and Shreeve stepped up and converted, and a point was saved.

Fred Massey

Brighton & Hove Albion proved a handful on Christmas Day at the Boleyn ground and were much the better side in a 1-1 draw, both sides meeting in the return at the Goldstone ground on Boxing Day.

Half an hour before the start of the game at the Goldstone, which lay in a hollow, the ground was covered in a dense fog, and it seemed likely that the match would be postponed. The gates were not opened until a quarter of an hour before kick off, and then the crowd broke open the main gates and tore down a portion of the fencing at the south east end of the ground. For some time the police were powerless to intervene and hundreds poured in without paying. For long periods in the second half the light was very bad, but the referee was adamant that the game would be completed, perhaps fearful of the consequences with the home side three goals to the good, but for the Hammers it was another two points that had disappeared.

The West Ham directors allocated all the proceeds of the Southern League match against New Brompton to 'old stalwart' Frank Piercy, who was now in his sixth full season with the club, since he came down from his native North East. With a 7,000 attendance he must have been pleasantly pleased, taking the financial circumstances of professional players into consideration at that time. Also a good local cricketer and first class golfer, he was later expected to become involved in the pro' golf circuit on retirement, but he stayed with the club in a coaching capacity until his untimely death at the age of 51 in 1931. He was awarded a posthumous benefit match in 1931/32.

(Mention of the 'Grim Reaper', former West Ham goalkeeper Charlie Cotton died during this month of Bright's Disease. He was just 32 years of age.)

As for the match itself, Jack Geggus, a local lad from Custom House FC came in for George Kitchen, who had a troublesome knee injury, and Frank Cannon the ex-QPR forward came in at No. 9.

Caldwell was the star of the attack, scoring the first goal and setting up the second for Shea, and the general performance of the team in the first half gave hope of a first win in nine league matches. The quality deteriorated after the break and New Brompton hit back with a goal. Cannon was not a success, his slowness causing lost opportunities up front, and Massey at half-back, had a poor second half. At the 89 minute mark the Hammers still led by 2-1, and then disastrously Geggus failed to clear and the visitors equalised in the 90th minute.

Victory came at last when Norwich were the visitors. Once the opening ten minutes or so had passed the Boleyn lads got into their stride and the Norfolk side, who were one of the biggest in the league, were outplayed by the smaller, but far nippier, London team. The final score of 5-0 should have actually been greater as the more skilful West Ham forwards overdid some their approach play in front of goal.

The Hammers' fans were hoping for a good run in the FA Cup comparable to that which the club had experienced in the previous campaign, and when the draw was announced expectations were high for a good start for the first round pairing with Carlisle United. The North Western club were members of the Lancashire Combination, and all connected with West Ham were confident of a reasonably easy afternoon.

Trouble was, they were too confident, especially after taking a lead as early as the seventh minute, and then failing to convert chances after having the majority of the attacking in the first half. This continued for a short while after the break, but surprisingly as the game wore on their opponents appeared to be very much fitter, and they began to get on top. Due to injuries, Bourne and Lavery had been drafted into the Hammers' defence, and it was fortunate that both players had excellent games as the visitors went forward. Carlisle however eventually equalised when they were awarded a penalty that was converted, and the match ended in a draw. Fortunately the directors of Carlisle, realising the financial aspect of another good crowd, waived their club's right to play the replay on their own ground, and on the following Thursday the teams met again at the Boleyn ground. On this occasion the Hammers did convert their chances and ran out easy winners by five clear goals.

Goals were hard to come by for both sides for the visit to Brentford as the result was a not very inspiring goalless draw, although former Thames Ironworks player George Reid twice went close for the West London club.

An inspired performance against Coventry City, who had celebrated an FA Cup upset by defeating First Division Preston North End, pleased the 6,000 home fans, especially as it was achieved with only ten men for the majority of the match, as Bourne received a bad knee injury in the first half. Shea was at his absolute best, and was ably assisted by Ashton and Haynes, and all three players scored in a 3-2 triumph.

In the next round of the FA Cup West Ham certainly made a name for themselves with a sensational victory over Football League Second Division Wolverhampton Wanderers by 5-1, and it took place on Wolves own territory at Molineux. The victory was no fluke with the visitors scoring inside five minutes when Webb turned the ball into the net after a shot from Caldwell was partially saved. In the home side's efforts to equalise Shreeve was particularly prominent with his defending, and then Webb banged in another goal from a cross from Shea, followed by the latter scoring himself, and amazingly the visitors were three up at the interval. The second half began in unbelievable fashion. With just two minutes gone, Webb, after cleverly tricking Jones, hit an unstoppable shot past Lunn, the Wolverhampton 'keeper, and five minutes later Shea put away another fine effort, and the Hammers were five goals up!! Mission accomplished, West Ham 'shut up shop', and with Wolves scoring just a consolation goal, it was back to the East End to celebrate.

It often happens in football, that an outstanding display is followed by a poor one. When Reading came to Upton Park, the visitors were bottom of the table and in financial trouble, and the Hammers were expected to romp home, but were surprised when the 'Biscuitmen' took the lead in the first half. West Ham had the chance to go level with a penalty, but Shreeve's shot struck a post. In the second half another was awarded, but the Reading 'keeper saved it. The referee, however, decided that the goalkeeper had moved off his line, and ordered it to be retaken. This time Shreeve made no mistake. Bedford, of Reading, obviously incensed, was then ordered off for something he said to the referee. At this, the Reading players gathered together with a view to walking off, but after some persuasion on the part of the Hammers' team carried on, and the game fizzled out to a 1-1 draw.

Excitement was intense for the 3rd Round match (equivalent to the 5th today) of the FA Cup at the Park Royal ground of Queens Park Rangers. Many West Ham diehards made the journey and the Boleyn Sports and Social Club once again had a large organised contingent travelling by chartered motor buses. There was much noise and commotion in the streets surrounding the ground, with the shouts of 'one, two, three, four, five' rending the air, together with a constant ringing of bells. (The chant of one, two, etc was a theme that would be heard in the run-up to the FA Cup Final at Wembley in 1923). Overall it was a fairly even game, but once again Shaw, the QPR goalkeeper, who always seemed to be at his best against the Hammers, made some outstanding saves. When West Ham eventually scored, it began with a pass from Webb to Shea. His shot was saved by Shaw, but the goalkeeper was unable to hold it, and Webb knocked in the rebound. The away support went wild with excitement, and hats flew in the air, all to be retrieved, as everyone wore one. Unfortunately, Rangers equalised which meant a replay during the following week.

On the Sunday an event was organised by the 'Brotherhood' a local religious organisation at the Central Hall, East Ham. Invitations were made to the Directors and players of West Ham United and several of the team arrived and were accorded an enthusiastic reception. Mr John Lewis, the well-known referee, was the main speaker and he stated that '......*Sport, and especially football, was for the benefit of the church and the nation as a whole. When playing football they must always play the game, as it should be played. The man playing the game could not afford to lead a bad life, but he must lead an honourable and true life, and then he would derive some benefit from the game. He was glad to be associated with the game because it was a counter attraction to the public houses, and if for no other reason it was worthy of the support of the churches. Dealing with professionalism, Mr Lewis said he did not believe in a man giving his whole time to the game. If he could find some light work to do it would be of greater benefit to him, and would keep him away from the temptations which existed in the dressing rooms. Referring to the gambling that takes place at matches, the speaker said it was high time the legislature took some steps to stop the distribution of coupons etc. They did not want the grand old game to come under the heel of the bookmaker the same as horse racing had done, but they wanted the game to be pure. The FA had done all they could to put a stop to this course. In conclusion he said football was worthy of the support of all well thinking people.'*

William Silor

There is no record of what the players who were present thought of the remarks that Mr Lewis made. It was typical of the times regarding drinking and gambling, but it would have been interesting to have heard their reactions to the phrase ' temptations which existed in the dressing rooms.'

That which existed in the dressing rooms after the replay against QPR, was just an air of disappointment as the Hammers were knocked out of the FA Cup after extra time, and in the last minute at that. It was a typical cup-tie but the honours went to the defence, especially Shreeve and Fairman at the back, and Whiteman, Piercy and Randall in midfield, but all the forwards were sadly 'off song' on the day.

Possibly feeling the effects of the cup-tie and the extra time involved just two days before, West Ham shared the points with Leyton at the Boleyn ground before a crowd of 10,000. It could have been won just two minutes from the end, but Shreeve had his spot-kick saved. In midweek both points were lost at Watford where young George Butcher, signed from nearby St Albans City, made his debut and scored in a 1-2 defeat in front of a measly 1,000 spectators.

There was a continued slide down the top half of the table after defeat at Exeter City by a single goal. The visitors had to make a number of changes. George Kitchen, who was suffering from rheumatism, was replaced by Dawson. Silor signed from Norwich City earlier in the season, came in at centre-forward, and Dan Woodards played at half-back for his first game for over two years. None of these players let the side down, for it was a fairly even and vigorous contest, but the 'old war horse' Frank Piercy had to be carried from the field, late in the second half, with a fractured rib, which was to keep him out of the side for the remainder of the season.

When Southampton came to Upton Park they always looked the likelier side to score even though the home side did most of the attacking, and that proved to be the case when the Saints opened the scoring in the first half. Just before half time West Ham were awarded a penalty when Webb was pulled back in the area. Kitchen, the captain, called upon Webb himself and then Randall to take the kick but both men refused. Shreeve took the responsibility, and missed his second spot kick in succession. The Hammers never gave up the ghost in the second period and were rewarded with just two minutes left when Blackburn scored to level it up.

If West Ham had any aspirations regarding a place in the top three of the table the team really should have been beating the likes of Croydon Common who would eventually finish second from bottom. As it was both teams took a point in a 1-1 draw at Croydon.

On Good Friday it was a different story when Crystal Palace came to the East End. The Hammers put on a good display of football as it should be played - 'all along the ground', with the half-backs joining up with the forwards in a number of triangular passing moves which were pleasing to the eye. Unfortunately it did not pay off in the first half as Palace broke away and scored. The stylish football however, was rewarded after the break. Ironically it came after a strong shot from Massey, now chosen at centre half, that was deflected by Bulcock, a visiting defender, into the opposition's net. The ever-reliable Danny Shea then pitched in with two more conventional goals, to give a scoreline that reflected the play.

Albert Scanes

A very good gate of 15,000 saw the Palace game, and for the Millwall fixture at the Boleyn ground on the following day the attendance was 12,000. Disappointingly for the home crowd it was the supporters of the visiting side who went home the happiest when the Hammers lost 1-2, but the team were undoubtedly handicapped by the loss of Webb through injury in the second half.

Making the trip across to South London for the return match with Crystal Palace on Easter Monday brought another bonanza attendance of 20,000. Financially it meant a profitable few days for the East End club. And it was a success on the field into the bargain as West Ham went into a 3-0 half time lead, with young Barking lad Albert Scanes, deputising for George Webb grabbing two. It ended 4-2 with Ashton and Shea also on the score sheet.

Very much is made in today's game regarding the amount of matches played by the more successful clubs, but with the season compressed into a strict September to April timescale in the period before the First World War, it was a matter of playing some fixtures over a tight schedule. So it was when the Hammers had to rearrange their visit to Southend United, due to a postponement on the original date when West Ham were involved in the FA Cup. The rearranged date came the day after the Palace game which meant that the club were playing their fourth match in five days, with no less than 9 players playing in all four!! Victory by a single goal at Roots Hall also meant six points from a possible eight over that period, and with five games remaining a similar run could mean a third or fourth place in the final table.

There was a relatively small financial disadvantage regarding the Southend fixture. Because it had to take place in midweek with an afternoon kick off the attendance was only 1,200. As the rearrangement was not, in this case, Southend's fault they were due compensation from West Ham. With only £58 taken at the gate the Hammers had to pay the 'Shrimpers' another £36.

Possibly there was an element of fatigue to be considered for the encounter at New Brompton, but it was not especially apparent as the team, with the only change being new boy Fred Curtis for Albert Scanes, fought back well after conceding a goal in the first half, but the breakthrough did not come and two points were lost.

Strangely enough it was the following match at home against Northampton where signs of a 'nothing to play for' attitude set in, with both teams seemingly 'going through the motions'. This appeared to not only affect the players, but one of the linesmen who carried out his duties near the halfway line seldom moving more than a yard or two from there! Scanes coming in for Curtis scored, giving the Hammers both points.

Having been knocked out of the FA Cup by QPR, and having lost to the West London side at the Boleyn ground in the league, there were thoughts of revenge for the trip to the Park Royal ground. Rarely do such statistics affect the players. It seems more a matter of pride for those that support a team, especially against local rivals.

Those that travelled with the club were for some time during the game quite delighted with the Hammers' performance and more importantly the score. Dave Waggott who had not appeared in the side all season, came in at outside left, and it was his cross that Shea headed home before half time. Waggott, after the break, beat man after man before hitting the second, which went in off a post. Curtis, back in again for Scanes, netted the third, and it looked all over at 3-0. Then, with twenty minutes left Barnes pulled one back for Rangers, and the West Ham defence amazingly fell apart to concede two more.

A third or fourth place finish was out of the question when Luton ran out winners by two goals to one in the Hammers' final home game, and the last match of the campaign saw Swindon demolish West Ham to the tune of 5-0, the club's biggest defeat of the season. What's more it meant a drop down to a finish of ninth place in the Southern League.

The club's final league position should have been much higher considering there was a settled side for the majority of the league fixtures. With a programme of 42 matches there were no less than eight players who made 35 appearances or more. Not only that, there was undoubted quality in the forward ranks, and there were few teams in the Southern League that could normally boast a forward line with such ability that consisted of Ashton, Shea, Webb, Blackburn and Caldwell.

Back: S Hammond, F Shreeve, C Dawson, G Kitchen, R Fairman, HS Bourne. Centre: C Paynter (assistant trainer), R Whiteman, R Stanley, W Lavery, D Woodards, ES King (secretary-manager), E Wagstaff, F Piercy, T Randall, F Rist, T Robinson (trainer). Front: H Armstrong, H Ashton, D Shea, F Cannon, GW Webb, WF White (chairman), V Haynes, C Carvossa, D Waggott, F Blackburn, T Caldwell, W Silor.

9th in Southern League Division One

#		Date	Opponent	Result	Scorers	Att	Ashton H	Blackburn F	Bourne S	Butcher G	Caldwell T	Cannon F	Curtis F	Dawson C	Fairman R	Geggus J	Haynes V	Kitchen G	Lavery W	Massey F	Piercy F	Randall T	Scanes A	Shea D	Shreeve F	Silor W	Waggott D	Wagstaffe G	Webb G	Whiteman R	Woodards D
1	Sep	2	EXETER CITY	2-1	Shea 2	5000	7	10			11				3		9	1			5	6		8	2					4	
2		4	Norwich City	3-1	Blackburn, Haynes, Shea	7000	7	10			11				3		9	1			5	6		8	2					4	
3		11	BRENTFORD	3-2	Shea 3	10000	7	10			11				3		9	1			5	6		8	2					4	
4		13	PORTSMOUTH	0-2		6000	7	10			11				3		9	1			5	6		8	2					4	
6		18	Coventry City	2-2	Haynes, Shea	8000	7	10			11				3		9	1			5	6		8	2					4	
7		25	WATFORD	2-0	Randall, Shea	10000	7	10			11				3			1			5	6		8	2					4	
8		29	Portsmouth	1-1	Haynes	2000	7	10			11				3		9	1			5	6		8	2				9	4	
9	Oct	2	Reading	3-0	Shea 2, Webb	3000	7	10			11				3		9	1			5	6		8	2					4	
10		4	BRISTOL ROVERS	5-0	Caldwell 3, Shea, Webb	4000	7	10			11				3			1			5	6		8	2				9	4	
11		9	SOUTHEND UNITED	0-0		10000	7	10			11				3			1			5	6		8	2				9	4	
12		16	Leyton	2-1	Caldwell, Webb	13000	7	10			11				3			1			5	6		8	2				9	4	
13		23	PLYMOUTH ARGYLE	4-1	Shea 2, Webb 2	10000	7	10			11				3			1			5	6		8	2				9	4	
14		25	Bristol Rovers	0-1		2000	7	10			11				3		9	1			5	6			2				8	4	
15		30	Southampton	2-2	Haynes, Shea	7000	7	10			11				3		9	1			5	6		8	2					4	
16	Nov	6	CROYDON COMMON	5-1	Shea 2, Ashton, Caldwell, Whiteman	10000	7	10			11				3		9	1			5	6		8	2					4	
17		13	Millwall	0-0		10000	7	10			11				3			1			5	6		8	2				9	4	
18		20	Plymouth Argyle	0-0		8000	7	10			11			1	3			1			5	6		8	2					4	
19		27	Northampton Town	1-3	Webb	7000	7	10			11				3		9	1			5	6		8	2					4	
20	Dec	4	QUEEN'S PARK RANGERS	1-2	Shreeve	12000	7	10			11				3			1			5	6		8	2				9	4	
5		11	Luton Town	2-4	Ashton, Shea	3000	7	10			11				3			1			5	6		8	2				9	4	
21		18	SWINDON TOWN	2-2	Blackburn, Shreeve	10000	7	10	3		11							1	2			6		8				5	9	4	
22		25	BRIGHTON & HOVE ALB.	1-1	Shea	15000	7	10	3		11							1		6	5			8	2				9	4	
23		27	Brighton & Hove Albion	0-3		10000	7	10			11							1		6	5			8	2				9	4	
24	Jan	1	NEW BROMPTON	2-2	Caldwell, Shea	7000	7	10			11	9			3	1				4	5	6		8	2					4	
25		8	NORWICH CITY	5-0	Caldwell 2, Shea 2, Cannon	6000	7	10	2		11	9						1		4	5	6		8	3						
26		22	Brentford	0-0		4000	7	10	2		11	9						1	3	4	5	6		8	2						
27		29	COVENTRY CITY	3-2	Ashton, Haynes, Shea	6000	7	10	3		11						9	1		4	5	6		8	2						
28	Feb	12	READING	1-1	Shreeve	8000	7	10			11				3			1		5		6		8	2				9	4	
29		26	LEYTON	0-0		10000	7	10			11				3		9	1		4	5	6		8	2						
30	Mar	2	Watford	1-2	Butcher	1000	7	10		8	11				3		9	1		4	5	6			2						
31		5	Exeter City	0-1		6500	7	10			11			1	3						5	6		8	2	9					4
32		12	SOUTHAMPTON	1-1	Blackburn	4000	7	10			11				3			1		4		6		8	2			5	9		
33		19	Croydon Common	1-1	Webb	6000	7	10		8					3	1				4		6		8	2	11		5	9		
34		25	CRYSTAL PALACE	3-1	Shea 2, Bulcock (og)	15000	7	10							3			1			5	6		8	2	11		5	9	4	
35		26	Millwall	1-2	Shea	12000	7	10							3			1			5	6		8	2	11			9	4	
36		28	Crystal Palace	4-2	Scanes 2, Ashton, Shea	20000	7	10							3			1			5	6	9	8	2					4	
37		29	Southend United	1-0	Shea	1200	7	10							3			1			5	6	9	8	2	11				4	
38	Apr	2	New Brompton	0-1		5000	7	10				9			3			1			5	6		8	2	11				4	
39		9	NORTHAMPTON T	1-0	Scanes	10000	7	10			11				3			1			5	6	9	8	2	11				4	
40		16	Queen's Park Rangers	3-3	Curtis, Shea, Waggott	7000	7	10				9			3			1			5	6	9	8	2		11			4	
41		23	LUTON TOWN	1-2	Curtis	4000	7	10			11	9			3	1					5	6		8	2		11			4	
42		30	Swindon Town	0-5		4000	7	10		8					3	1	9			4					2		11			6	5

	Ashton H	Blackburn F	Bourne S	Butcher G	Caldwell T	Cannon F	Curtis F	Dawson C	Fairman R	Geggus J	Haynes V	Kitchen G	Lavery W	Massey F	Piercy F	Randall T	Scanes A	Shea D	Shreeve F	Silor W	Waggott D	Wagstaffe G	Webb G	Whiteman R	Woodards D
Apps	42	42	4	3	35	3	3	2	37	4	15	36	2	20	29	39	3	38	41	6	2	3	18	33	2
Goals	4	3		1	8	1	2				5					1	3	28	3				7	1	

One own goal

F.A. Cup

		Date	Opponent	Result	Scorers	Att	Ashton H	Blackburn F	Bourne S	Butcher G	Caldwell T	Cannon F	Curtis F	Dawson C	Fairman R	Geggus J	Haynes V	Kitchen G	Lavery W	Massey F	Piercy F	Randall T	Scanes A	Shea D	Shreeve F	Silor W	Waggott D	Wagstaffe G	Webb G	Whiteman R	Woodards D
R1	Jan	15	CARLISLE UNITED	1-1	Blackburn	11000	7	10	3		11	9						1	2		5	6		8						4	
rep		20	CARLISLE UNITED	5-0	Blackburn 2, Randall, Shea, Webb	7000	7	10			11							1	3	4	5	6		8	2				9		
R2	Feb	5	Wolverhampton Wan.	5-1	Webb 3, Shea 2	17000	7	10			11							1		4	5	6		8	2				9		
R3		19	Queen's Park Rangers	1-1	Webb	31000	7	10			11				3			1		4	5	6		8	2				9		
rep		24	QUEEN'S PARK RANGERS	0-1		18000	7	10			11				3			1			5	6		8	2				9	4	

	Team	P	W	D	L	F	A	W	D	L	F	A	Pts
1	Brighton & Hove Alb.	42	18	2	1	50	11	5	11	5	19	17	59
2	Swindon Town	42	15	3	3	63	20	7	7	7	29	26	54
3	Queen's Park Rangers	42	12	5	4	41	28	7	8	6	15	19	51
4	Northampton Town	42	16	3	2	66	11	6	1	14	24	33	48
5	Southampton	42	11	7	3	39	25	5	9	7	25	30	48
6	Portsmouth	42	13	5	3	43	17	7	2	12	27	46	47
7	Crystal Palace	42	13	3	5	48	20	7	3	11	21	30	46
8	Coventry City	42	11	6	4	50	24	8	2	11	21	36	46
9	WEST HAM UNITED	42	10	7	4	43	23	5	8	8	26	33	45
10	Leyton	42	11	4	6	45	22	5	7	9	15	24	43
11	Plymouth Argyle	42	14	5	2	40	8	2	6	13	21	46	43
12	New Brompton	42	16	5	3	52	21	3	3	15	24	53	43
13	Bristol Rovers	42	13	5	3	25	8	3	5	13	12	40	42
14	Brentford	42	13	5	3	33	13	3	4	14	17	45	41
15	Luton Town	42	10	7	4	45	34	5	4	12	27	58	41
16	Millwall	42	9	6	6	24	17	6	1	14	21	42	37
17	Norwich City	42	11	5	5	42	26	2	4	15	17	52	35
18	Exeter City	42	12	4	5	45	22	2	2	17	15	47	34
19	Watford	42	8	8	5	32	24	2	5	14	19	52	33
20	Southend United	42	10	4	7	26	17	2	5	14	25	73	33
21	Croydon Common	42	8	2	11	29	38	5	3	13	23	58	31
22	Reading	42	7	6	8	27	25	0	4	17	11	48	24

CUP MAGIC

Despite 'fizzling out' at the end of the previous campaign there was no doubt that it had been an entertaining one. The position of 9th place was something of an underachievement as there were some very good players at the club who knew that, as a team, they could, and definitely should have been in the top three.

George Kitchen, still one of the best in the Southern League was about to begin his sixth consecutive season with 160 league appearances to his credit at this point. Now in his 35th year he could be compared to a 'keeper that graced Upton Park in the latter part of the 20th Century – Phil Parkes.

Frank Piercy, the 'old war horse', fit again now after his fractured rib injury, was on his seventh season in succession with the club, now turned thirty and still 'raring to go.' Tommy Randall, who initially had something of a rough time as a forward was now becoming the complete half-back, and would later receive representative honours before his career was over. Outside right Herbert 'Tiddler' Ashton, and Fred Blackburn, a player who could operate at both inside and outside left, had already given excellent service and would continue to do so. With Danny Shea and George Webb up front, the Hammers had the basis of not just a good side, but an exceptional one.

It was a pity then at this point that the directors of the club did not broaden and fortify the squad, or at least engage players for one or two positions that were currently just that bit lacking in class, in order to progress further.

OCTOBER 8TH, 1910.   LOTINGA'S WEEKLY.   657

The Southern League Competition.

Some striking scenes taken during the course of the match between West Ham United v. Queen's Park Rangers, known respectively as "The Hammers" and "The Rangers," at Upton Park, in which the former team outplayed and quite heavily defeated the men of Park Royal.

EXCLUSIVE PICTURES BY OUR OWN PHOTOGRAPHERS

1. An attack on the Rangers' goal from the left wing. The full back impedes the forward and gives his goalkeeper an opportunity of clearing.
2. Clearing the Rangers' lines from a dropping centre across the field.
3. Shaw, the active little Rangers' goalie, who was in the picture of the play nearly all the time.
4. A portrayal of the enthusiasm of the crowd at the scoring of the Hammers' first goal—a storm of cheering, hat-waving, and general gratification at the home team's success. We have ringed out two heads, the proprietors of which qualify for one guinea each on application at our offices.
5. A back-header to a lofting drive from the Hammers' rearguard.
6. The Rangers' goalkeeper deftly catches and punts the ball up the field. Note how the photographer has caught him high in the air with both feet off the ground.

The club's overdraft had by now been eliminated, but due to a threatened nationwide professional players' strike in 1909, the maximum wage was to be increased within 2 years to £5 per week, along with a system of bonus payments. Perhaps with this in mind the directors were more in favour of gradually improving the ground facilities for the spectators before adding to the playing staff. Some said the club lacked ambition when William White, a barge builder by trade, was elected to be the new club chairman, but the directorate remembered the early days and were not inclined 'to push the boat out too far'.

As it was, at the beginning of the season, the club brought in three players only, and none made an early debut. Bill Kennedy who was an amateur centre-forward and a schoolteacher by trade, who had played for Grays, and latterly Kent side Northfleet. He did not appear in the first team in a Southern League match until November. Jim Rothwell, a full-back from the Liverpool area, in December, and Joe Miellear, who had played for amateur club Bromley, made a solitary appearance at outside right in March 1911. Their delayed appearances confirmed that they were not exactly breathtaking additions to the squad.

Before the season began the team played the usual game against the Manor Park Constitutional Cricket Club at Rectory field. The players showed their ability at the summer game with a victory, scoring 142 runs against Manor Park's 78. On the batting side Bill Lavery was top scorer for the Hammers with a score of 37, but Dave Waggott received more praise for an unbeaten 30 after going in at tenth man. Fred Shreeve was the bowling star taking six wickets for 24 runs.

Dave Waggott

Tom Robinson took charge of the usual pre-season training mixed in with a quiet game of bowls in Central Park, East Ham, and it was said that some of the team were becoming as proficient as they were with their cricketing skills.

In the close season some further alterations had been made to the ground. Looking at the earliest photograph of the Boleyn ground in 1904, the dressing rooms and offices are shown at the South Bank end, and these had been removed giving additional accommodation of 3,000 in that area by means of extra banking. The dressing rooms had been moved to a vacant space at the north end of the grandstand enclosure. The offices were moved to a new position over the entrance to the grandstand where the turnstiles and gates were, with room for the spectators to pass underneath. These alterations meant that ground capacity would now be 27,000. The cost of the operation came to a figure between £700 and £800.

The attendance for the opening Southern League fixture was 15,000, but there were no new faces in the team for the crowd to scrutinize. This was no hardship for the first 45 minutes as West Ham totally outplayed Southend United. Webb, Ashton and Blackburn scored, and the home side were three goals up in just twelve minutes play, and a 'cricket score' looked to be on the cards, even though the visitors pulled one back through a penalty just before half-time. Thinking they were on to a comfortable ride in the second half the Hammers became casual and negligent, and once Southend notched a second, pluck and energy drew them level after Massey and Kitchen between them made a complete hash of a back pass. In the end West Ham could even have lost both points but it finished all square at 3-3.

At Coventry, the team could certainly not be accused of lack of effort, but the home defence were in top form and the game remained scoreless at the break. On the resumption George Kitchen was kept very busy and coped well, but on one of his runs well out of goal, which had always been a characteristic of his play, he was badly caught out and Coventry opened the scoring, and were finally victorious by three clear goals. No win, and six goals conceded was not a good start to the campaign.

It was something of a pleasant surprise then that West Ham defeated Queens Park Rangers at Park Royal on the following Monday. After an even first half, the Hammers changed their tactics somewhat by spreading out their play, and when Caldwell crossed from the right wing Danny Shea netted with a strong header. The second was scored by the same player by dint of his sheer speed and intuition, stepping between dithering full-backs and getting to the ball before Shaw, the Rangers' goalkeeper and scoring.

A creditable performance at home to New Brompton resulted in a 2-0 victory, but the crowd became incensed when Nobbs, of the Kent side, badly fouled Ashton. There was much abuse and shouting which led to the referee stopping the play and administering a caution to several spectators, something that would be considered extraordinary today. Shea and Webb were the West Ham scorers.

As the London Challenge Cup tie against Leyton had a midweek late afternoon kick off, the referee decided to start the game well before time. Some spectators missed two very early goals for the home side through Caldwell and Curtis, but overall Kitchen was the star of the side in a 3-2 victory.

On the visit to Millwall a milestone was reached at last when the Hammers beat the 'Dockers' by 2-0, for it was the club's first-ever success on their opponents ground in the Southern League. The team's 'dodgy' start to the campaign was already fading into the background. This resulted in a 20,000 crowd for the return game with QPR at the Boleyn ground, and the West Ham team did not disappoint with a strong attacking display. Curtis came in at centre-forward and had a fine game, scoring twice in the first half. When Rangers did manage to get through the defence, Lavery, at full-back, was finally difficult to get past, and his current form was keeping Shreeve out of the side. With the exception of former Hammer Billy Barnes, who gave yet another good display against his former club, it was mostly the home side who were dominant and Shea scored a third goal before the finish. This latest victory saw West Ham now in second place in the table.

An unexpected setback at Norwich followed, but overall it was an even encounter with the home side not taking the lead until well into the second half, but unfortunately the Hammers' efforts to equalise were very much thwarted by an injury to Piercy, and only one minute later by another to Curtis, leaving the side with just nine men. With backs to the wall, it enabled Norwich to add a second goal near the end.

In the next round of the London Challenge Cup at Bromley, Bill Kennedy showed some promise in a mixed first team and reserve side when he scored one of the goals in a 5-0 drubbing of the Kent amateur side. Danny Shea scored a hat-trick and Blackburn notched the other.

For the trip to Luton Dan Woodards came in for his first Southern League match of the season for Frank Piercy at centre half, and George Webb also returned at centre-forward. It was a tough match with the Hammers taking the lead in the second half when a centre from Caldwell was completely misjudged by the Luton 'keeper and Shea had the simple job of putting the ball in the empty net. The home side equalised late in the half.

Portsmouth came to East London, and had it not been for Cope in goal, would have been swamped by more than the score of 3-1 to West Ham, although there were no goals scored until the second period. Shea got the first, which was probably the best seen at the ground during the current season at the time, when he crashed in a shot from fully thirty yards. George Kitchen, who had not taken a penalty for some time past, scored from the spot, but only on the rebound after Cope had saved the original shot. When a second was awarded later, George stepped up again, but Cope saved and held on. Shortly afterwards Pompey scored in a surprise breakaway, but Ashton made the score look more respectable with a drop shot in the final minute, sending the home crowd happy.

For additional entertainment the locals now had the opportunity on a Saturday evening after the match, to visit the newly opened Boleyn Electric Theatre, situated next to the Boleyn Tavern on the corner of Barking Road and Green Street. It was opened by the Mayor on October 20th 1910, and built on a site that had been for many years a source of annoyance, with the Council having received many complaints with regard to roundabouts and swings and noise in general. The theatre itself had seating accommodation for 700 people, and there would be an afternoon and evening performance daily, including Sundays. Films would be shown along with still picture shows, with various stage effects, and there was to be a complete change of programme twice weekly. There had been complaints from a number of church ministers regarding the opening of such places on the Sabbath, but the Mayor stated that he could see no more harm in people visiting those places than going to the museums and picture galleries on Sundays and all he could say was 'Evil be to them who evil think.'

George Butcher

Coincidently there was another opening on the same day of an Electric Theatre directly opposite the East Ham Palace (and East Ham station) in High Street North by Lady Bethell wife of Sir John Bethell MP, who was also the architect of the new building. The seated accommodation here was for 600, with 'tip-up cushioned chairs.'

So the supporters of the football club and many locals in general had another form of entertainment to turn to when they felt so inclined.

George Butcher came in for Fred Blackburn when the Hammers travelled to Northampton, but did not impress in a game where the home side gained both points by two goals to nil.

Fred Blackburn returned and Bill Kennedy came in for his first game in the Southern League for the unavailable George Webb, when the current champions, and leaders, Brighton & Hove Albion came to Upton Park. Frank Piercy also made a welcome return in place of Woodards. It was the visitors who did most of the early pressing, but when Caldwell placed the ball into the Brighton goalmouth, Piercy headed neatly on to Kennedy, who put the ball into the net. After the interval the game took the same shape and when George Kitchen converted a penalty, which was awarded for handball, he had to take a bombardment himself from the visiting forwards, but came through with flying colours although he was very ably assisted by Lavery at full-back. Shea then scored from close range, but the South Coast club did find the net just before time. West Ham's victory now saw them in fourth place in the table.

After a 0-0 draw at Exeter City in a game that was more exciting than the score suggests, the Boleyn lads now received a visit from the new leaders Swindon Town. This turned out to be the Hammers' best performance of the season up to this point because the 'Railwaymen' were undoubtedly at the top on merit. The first half of the game was very close, but attacks on the home goal were kept at bay by Geggus, in goal for Kitchen, who was suffering from lumbago, and Lavery and Fairman who both stood firm. Ashton and Shea were no slouches up front, but the home forwards were hampered by the loss of Fred Blackburn who had to leave the field due to a bad leg injury, which would turn out to be a long term one. Down to ten men in the second half they were greatly handicapped, but withstood the visitors' pressure, Piercy and Randall both getting in some splendid work. Wheatcroft, of Swindon, then received an injury and the game became more even, but West Ham never gave up and Shea netted the winner after hitting a post.

Crystal Palace became the new leaders, and the Hammers were equal second with Swindon and Brighton, but gaining just one point at Bristol Rovers pushed them down to fourth.

Those who were present at the Boleyn enclosure for the match against Crystal Palace saw a real stunner of an encounter. The visitors were now top of the table and it was admitted that they played football worthy of their position. George Butcher kept his place in the inside left position, and due to Blackburn's long term injury would stay in that role for the rest of the campaign. George Webb was back in the centre and George Kitchen returned in goal. Palace tried to dictate the play, but the Hammers were more than equal to it, although the team had to thank Kitchen for his heroic display between the sticks. The match was something of a ding-dong struggle with both sides having the upper hand in turn, but when a strong shot from Webb was punched out by the Palace 'keeper to Ashton, the ball was thumped back, and was fumbled after saving, and like lightning, quicksilver Danny Shea had it in the net. The South London side fought fiercely for the equaliser but Kitchen was in top form, ably assisted by Fairman at full-back. In the second half play became a lot more vigorous especially from the visitors. It was the Hammers who were penalised however, when two Palace forwards tangled with two home defenders. All went down in a heap in the penalty area, and the referee awarded a penalty against Lavery, much to everyone's surprise. Once again Kitchen was the hero as he saved the kick, and dived at the taker's feet after an attempt to net the rebound. Unfortunately the visitors did equalise just two minutes later, and from then it was a battle for the winner, but the score remained at one goal each.

On the same day West Ham reserves met Barking at Vicarage Field in a London League Premier Division fixture. Representing Barking were two ex-Hammers', Syd Hammond and 'Moppy' Featherstone, who were both regulars in the Barking side. The West Ham eleven were:- Geggus, Shreeve and Rothwell, Redward, Woodards and Massey, Miellear, Curtis, Kennedy, Waggott and Morrison. Every player in the team had, or would have, experience in the Hammers' first team. For the record the 'stiffs' won 3-0, with goals from Curtis, Miellear and Morrison.

After such a battling performance against Crystal Palace it was a big disappointment to come away from Griffin Park pointless after a 0-3 defeat against Brentford. The scoreline did not really reflect the play, but against this type of opposition West Ham should have been gaining valuable points in their pursuit of the Southern League title. The thorn in their side in this encounter had been George Reid, who had played for Thames Ironworks in their first season in the Southern League in 1898/99, and was now a top scorer for the West London club. He netted two goals in this particular game and provided the other.

An improved display against a rather disappointing Leyton side saw the Hammers home quite comfortably by three clear goals before they faced a gruelling three game in four days over the Christmas period. The point of interest here is that Leyton fielded 19 year old Charlie Buchan, the future England international who was a great servant to both Sunderland and Arsenal before he retired in 1928, and whose fame continued through his production of 'Charlie Buchan's Football Monthly' which was first published in 1951.

On Christmas Eve, before a measly crowd of just 2,000 at Cassio Road the Hammers defeated Watford by 3-1 after being a goal down at half time. The star of the visiting side was the indomitable Danny Shea. He equalised after the break when Beaumont of Watford passed back to his goalkeeper and Danny nipped in and got there first, rounding Webster and netting. His second goal showed another side of his play when he scored after a magnificent run over half the length of the field. Sandwiched between Shea's goals, Frank Piercy converted a penalty.

On Boxing Day before a 14,000 crowd West Ham overcame the Plymouth side by four clear goals, and although the team played very well there were mitigating circumstances. Sutcliffe the Argyle's regular 'keeper had to be confined to bed with an illness, and Horne, the reserve, (and twelfth man) was suddenly taken ill himself with a feverish chill, so they took the field with only ten men, with the right back Butler, keeping goal. By the half time break the Hammers were already three goals to the good, from Webb (2) and Shea, but the visitors were allowed to include their trainer in the team after the break and conceded just the one goal, a penalty by Rothwell. Although frequently under pressure, Plymouth gained their revenge the next day at Home Park by a single goal.

Ten of the West Ham team attempted to net balls of a different kind just prior to the holiday fixtures, when they were entertained by the Plashet Liberal Club at Plashet Grove to a billiards match. The Hammers lost by 6 matches to 4, with their four winning players being Ashton, Shreeve, Waggott and Lavery.

It was also at this time that a West Ham supporter and boxer by the name of Dick Knock, fought a bout against Liverpool's Jim Holland at Liverpool Arena. This was scheduled as a twenty round fight, which came to a conclusion in the sixteenth round when Holland received a blow to the chin that put him on the canvas. When he fell he struck his head on the boards, became unconscious and did not recover, dying in the Royal Infirmary. Dick Knock was upset, more so because it was not the force of his punch, but the violent contact with the boards when his opponent fell which caused the fatality. The day after Knock was charged with causing grievous bodily harm, and when he was in the dock he requested bail, stating that he had fought over 300 fights in the previous seven or eight years and this had never occurred before. Bail was refused, and when Knock left the hearing he was in tears.

Bill Kennedy

The Hammers' next game was a visit to Southend at Roots Hall, and it turned out to be something of a sensation. The team had four changes with both full-backs Shreeve and Lavery appearing, Woodards coming in at number five, and Bill Kennedy at centre-forward. The Southend eleven included George Chalkley who had appeared for the Hammers in 1908/09, and Frank Curtis who had only recently been transferred from West Ham. With Southend being very much in the ascendancy in the first half there was little to suggest a heavy defeat for the home side, but losing Evans to injury just before the break did them no favours. The home side still went forward in the second half, but they were certainly to rue a couple of near misses later. In the 60th minute West Ham went ahead through Shea, and by the 80th minute it was 6-0!! Danny Shea, now called 'The Wapping Pet' by the press, had scored four, with the others coming via Kennedy and Caldwell. It was somewhat ironic that the fog was so bad at half time, the referee considered abandoning the match.

The proceeds for the game against Coventry City were set aside as a joint Benefit Match for George Kitchen and Fred Blackburn. From an attendance of 11,000 there were gate receipts of £252, which together with the monies from the benefit concert would probably have amounted to something in the region of £400 to be divided between the two players. Blackburn was of course still out injured, but Kitchen took up his usual position in goal. It was a pity for both players that a victory could not be recorded and a 1-1 draw kept the team in fourth place in the table.

All excitement now focused on the FA Cup with a 1st Round tie against First Division Nottingham Forest at Upton Park. Unfortunately the game turned out to be something of a farce as 'King Fog' took over from the start, and very little could be seen by spectators in all parts unless the action was close by. Play appears to have been very even in the first half, but at the break there was a consultation between the referee, captains of both sides and Directors regarding the conditions, and it was decided to carry on. The interval was dispensed with, and play recommenced immediately.

West Ham went on the attack and Tommy Randall took the ball from the halfway line, ran right through, drew the defence and passed to Shea who scored with a great shot. Within ten minutes or so the fog lifted somewhat and play was easier to see. Forest were playing some attractive stuff, but Ashton and Shea were on top form and most of the home attacks originated from this pair, but it was from a Caldwell cross on the left that Shea ran the ball into the net for the second. The opposition were shaken by this, and picked up to attack but the Hammers' defence held on well. Finally Forest did pull one back, but it was far too late and to the crowd's great delight West Ham were victorious by 2-1.

Bill Lavery

The Nottingham club lodged a protest to the Football Association on the grounds that the fog was so dense as to render play impracticable, and should not have been played, but this was rejected. (Why do clubs only protest when they lose?)

The Hammers fought out another 1-1 draw at New Brompton with George Kitchen saving a penalty in the first half, and when Millwall made the short journey to the Boleyn ground a third consecutive draw in the League resulted. The home side held the initiative in the opening half, and opened the scoring when Shea worked the ball smartly to put Webb clean through and he almost walked the ball into the net. Millwall were later awarded a doubtful penalty which was converted, but Randall surprised everybody, himself included, when he hit a very long shot into the top of the net. When the second half began there was a situation similar to the Forest game with fog descending rapidly. Very little was seen and incidents were interpreted by the shouts of the sections of the crowd nearest to the play. One further goal was scored, which went to Millwall, for a final score of 2-2. Towards the end of the game the fog became thicker and play continued practically in the dark, but the referee let it continue.

It was FA Cup time and the Hammers were drawn at home again for the visit of First Division Preston North End in the second round. This turned out to be a first rate performance, and it was a pity that the directorate of the club decided to greatly increase the prices for admission, because those that could not afford to be present missed an enjoyable afternoon. As it was, the attendance was not above 12,000, which was a pity, for West Ham outplayed their lofty opponents from start to finish. Whereas George Kitchen had played his part in many encounters, he experienced a lonely ninety minutes, for he was only tested seriously on one occasion, and he came out with flying colours. McBride, the Preston 'keeper, on the other hand was the busiest player on the field, fielding and saving numerous shots and headers behind a beleaguered defence.

The Hammers took the game to their Northern opponents right from the start, interrupted by one or two brief sorties initiated by a familiar face from the past – Arthur Winterhalder, who had gone on to Everton in 1907 and from there to fellow Lancashire club Preston a year later. There was not a weak spot in the home side, but it was George Webb who took most of the accolades with a hat-trick. His first came just before half time after a cross from Ashton, and a pass from Butcher that George converted. West Ham continued in the same vein after the interval, but there was just 10 minutes remaining when Webb added another, quickly followed by a third, and it was all over.

It was back to League fare when Norwich came to the East End, and the Hammers maintained momentum with a 2-1 victory, after being a goal down. Webb equalised and Rothwell put them ahead with a penalty.

Luton Town were to receive the same fate when they came to the Boleyn ground for West Ham's second home league game in succession. George Webb was on amateur international duty with England, and Danny Shea was not available, which meant starts for Bill Kennedy and A. Frost, recently acquired from Southend United. Kennedy duly obliged by opening the scoring, and Frank Piercy netted a rare goal when his shot went in off a post for a two-goal victory which kept the club in fourth position in the table.

The Hammers were fortunate enough to be drawn at home again in the third round of the FA Cup when their opponents would be none other than Manchester United, who had won the trophy only two seasons previously, and were now battling it out for the First Division title, which they would eventually win come the end of the current season. The West Ham directors decided once again that the basic admission charge would be one shilling, whilst reserved seats in the stand would be three and four shillings according to position. This was a match, that despite the increase, could not be missed, and the club had a record attendance of 27,000. When the draw was made an official of the Manchester club suggested the availability of playing the tie at Stamford Bridge, which was quickly rejected.

The game turned out to be a classic cup-tie. West Ham fielded their best side with Webb and Shea returning. Manchester United were captained by Charlie Roberts, one of the best centre halves of the time, and had the famous Welsh international Billy Meredith on the wing, but they were also strong in all positions. It was full credit to the home side that they were not overawed at the prospect of playing against them. The northern club had the best of the opening chances, but it was Webb who eventually neatly tricked his way through the opposing defence to pass to Shea, who promptly put the ball in the net. It was said that the resulting cheer from the home supporters must have been heard several miles away. Sadly the lead was short lived as Manchester forced a corner, which was headed home. Webb broke away and his shot hit the upright, and seconds after Shea clattered the ball against the bar. Butcher then headed the ball and it stopped dead on the line with the 'keeper falling on it. All heart-stopping moments, but it remained all-square at the interval.

The second half saw the Hammers keep up an unrelenting pace, and United started to throw their weight about in frustration, but two of their own players, Hulse and Turnbull, collided with one another to add to their woes. The contest became somewhat scrappy and looking like a traditional cup-tie, but when Meredith did make one of his typical runs he was stopped short by Tommy Randall. United's Charlie Roberts was imperious in their defence, but they were kicking out towards the end as the tie looked likely to go to a replay. Just three minutes from time, however, Ashton sent the ball over after a throw-in and Caldwell got to it and scored with a first time shot. United tried desperately in the last ninety seconds, but to no avail, and the Hammers were through to the Quarter Finals for the first time.

Pandemonium broke out at the final whistle as thousands ran across the pitch to get a 'touch' of their favourites, and several of the Hammers' players were carried shoulder high to the pavilion. Spare a thought for the opposition supporters. To avoid a crush, hundreds of them left the ground five minutes from the end to catch their train back to Manchester, keenly anticipating a replay at Old Trafford. When they arrived at Manchester station they were dumbfounded to hear that their team had been defeated.

With much good fortune West Ham were drawn at home yet again for their 4th Round (Quarter Final) match against Blackburn Rovers. Drawn at home or not, the team had had to meet First Division opposition in every round, and with the resulting headlines had put themselves in the eye of the sporting public.

Perhaps with the prospect of another important encounter in view, Syd King and the directors put out a much-changed side for the visit of Northampton Town to Upton Park. Piercy, Randall, Ashton, Shea and Webb stood down, and it showed as the 'Cobblers' came away with two points. The 1-2 scoreline meant it was the Hammers' first defeat on their own ground in 1910/11. Few teams go a whole season without one.

At East Ham Police Court there was a post-script to the West Ham United/ Manchester United cup-tie when a tram conductor, Henry Bonham, was summoned for allowing more than a specified number of passengers to travel inside a tramcar. A Police Sergeant Haywood said that when he boarded the car it was proceeding along Barking Road and although it was licensed to carry 22 passengers there were 32 passengers inside the car. There had been complaints about excessive overcrowding because it was exceedingly unpleasant to those who were inside. He admitted that there had been a big football match, and that there had been an exceptionally large crowd at the game.

For the defence, Chief Inspector Somerville, of the West Ham Tramways, said he was on special duty in the neighbourhood of the football ground. They had twenty special cars out waiting to take the people away in addition to the usual service, which had been augmented for the occasion. The crowd clambered on the cars from all positions, climbed over the gate and through the stair rails. Every car that went away was absolutely packed. The police and tramway officials did all in their power to prevent overcrowding, but they were unable to do so.

A number of other witnesses were called, who gave evidence as to the great crowd present at the match, and that the police were helpless in coping with them. It was impossible for the conductors to keep the people off the cars.

The Stipendiary stated that an Act of Parliament was passed in 1842 at a time when there were no trams, not even horse trams, and it was obvious that this Act had reference to smaller vehicles drawn by horses. When the District railway was electrified the legislature allowed them to provide facilities for passengers to stand up. Everything possible was done to cope with the crowd, and yet there was overcrowding. He thought it extremely hard on the part of the police to have selected this particular day in order to watch and see whether there was over crowding on the cars. His case was that the conductor was overwhelmed.

He stated further that it was a difficult case to decide. It was a very great nuisance for ordinary passengers in these cars to be crowded out of existence, but it seemed to him that what occurred on this occasion was that the tramway officials and police were overwhelmed by this crowd, and although he quite believed the evidence of the police, it seemed unfair to visit on the officials of the tramways what the crowd was really responsible for. The summons was dismissed on payment of costs.

Not only was there great excitement at the prospect of the forthcoming FA Cup tie with Blackburn Rovers, but it was an honour for the club that George Webb had so impressed the 'powers that be' in the Football Association that was chosen to represent the full England team against Wales and France, making him the first West Ham player to receive the honour.

George Kitchen was also chosen to keep goal for the Southern League in a representative match against the Irish League.

The club were now, of course on a 'high', but they were taken to task by the Southern League at the same time, for their decision to field five reserves in the match against Northampton, as the result could have had a bearing on the league positions near the top of the table. The club pleaded guilty and were fined £10.

The attendance for the Blackburn cup-tie was 20,000. Not so large as for the previous round, but it was another exciting contest. West Ham did not seem to have the pace that they possessed in the Manchester United encounter, but overall it was a good performance despite the disappointing outcome. It was very much even for most of the first half, but the visitors opened the scoring when Kitchen could only push out a terrific cross shot from the wing and Latheron, running up, put the ball in the net. The Hammers' equaliser came when Ashton put in a centre which Butcher met full on giving Ashcroft, the Rovers' 'keeper no chance. With much excitement on the terraces, the Rovers defence then had a harrowing time for a period before half time.

After the interval Blackburn took the lead again when the home defence panicked somewhat after a free kick had been awarded on the edge of the area. With the ball rebounding here and there, Simpson hit the ball home via an upright. Despite having the 'wind taken out of their sails' for a while West Ham came back into it, and Webb made a incisive run before releasing the ball to Butcher who scored with a hook shot. Play now became intense, and the Hammers began to tire more than their opponents, but the goal that decided it came in a most unsatisfactory manner. After Kitchen had fallen whilst partially clearing, there was a melee in front of the goal, and with West Ham defenders falling to the ground, the visitors' Davies got to the ball first and scored the deciding goal.

So ended the club's interest in the FA Cup. It was disappointing to go out at this stage of the competition with an appearance in their first semi-final being denied them. On the credit side, it was the third season running that the East End club had performed well in the competition, and the resultant publicity would do the club no harm at all, especially in any later attempts to gain entry into the Football League.

It was back to Southern League competition the following week with a home match against Exeter City. Incredibly, including cup-ties, this was the EIGHTH consecutive Saturday (from Jan. 28th to March 11th inclusive) that the Hammers had a first team home fixture, and it is still a club record. How this affected the pockets of the faithful fans that attended them all is not known!

At this stage there was still a good chance of gaining that elusive Southern League title and with that in mind Exeter were given a real drubbing by 4 goals to one. The result was never in doubt even though it stood at 1-0 at the break. The forwards were on top form especially George Webb who scored a hat-trick, and Danny Shea, who notched the other. West Ham was the only club in the top five to win on the day, but still remained in fourth place with 36 points. Crystal Palace and Swindon were joint top of the table with 39 points.

On the Monday following, the representative match between the Southern League and the Irish League took place at the Boleyn ground. West Ham had three players in the Southern League side – Kitchen, Webb and Shea. Kitchen was outstanding, making almost impossible saves at times, but unfortunately both Webb and Shea did not impress with their displays at all. What was worse, Webb was badly injured in the second half, which meant he would be unavailable for the forthcoming clash at top of the table Swindon Town.

With George Kitchen and his excellent goalkeeping displays, it must be pointed out that there was another 'keeper in the district who is worthy of mention here. This was Tommy Robinson, son of none other than the long-standing West Ham United trainer Tom Robinson. Young Tommy was an amateur who had been on West Ham's books, but did not appear at all, which was a pity given his subsequent displays. He served Plashet, Leytonstone and at this time Barking, who were playing in the London League Premier Division, the same competition in which West Ham reserves were members.

For all the teams he represented he constantly received rave reviews, and it is something of a mystery why he was not considered by the club where his father gave such long service, although this may have been due to the fact that he was only 5ft 6 inches in height and of very light frame, a build that was not considered strong enough for the professional game.

To indicate the reputation that he had earned for himself, a description of one of his displays from the local press is worthy of mention here. Leyton Reserves v Barking:
(Barking).. were beaten by 3-1 in spite of a marvellous display of goalkeeping by that little wonder, Tommy Robinson. If ever you want to see Tommy at his best, give him something hard to do, and plenty of it, and he is pretty certain to rise to the occasion and give of his very best. The fifteen hundred spectators looked on in speechless amazement while the redoubtable Tommy was saving shot after shot, and all agreed that it was by far the best display of goalkeeping that had ever been seen on the Leyton ground, even in Southern League matches and English cup-ties. It simply did not matter how the shots came in, as they all went the same way, and the three scoring shots would have beaten anybody, as they were all well away from him......It looked any odds on a big score during the second half, but little Tommy stood in the breach and proved impassable –
> *'Wingers to the right of him,*
> *Wingers to the left of him,*
> *Centres in front of him,*
> *Volleyed and thundered!'*

But they could not beat him again......Tommy was as cool as the proverbial cucumber and although he only stands about five feet six inches, he appeared to the attacking forwards as if he stood seven feet eight, and possessed arms that covered the whole eight yards of space when they were outstretched.......Barking......were beaten as stated with two goals to spare. Had it not been for Robinson it might have been twenty. Bravo Tommy!

It is appropriate here to mention that two important rule changes were to be made in 1912 regarding goalkeepers. First, the rule that allowed 'keepers to use their hands in their own half (but not carry), was to be amended to their own penalty area only. As it stood, it still had a throwback to the early days of a type of 'quasi Rugby' that was played. A goalkeeper after all, was supposed to be the last line of defence, not another aid to attack. Second, goalkeepers had always worn identical shirts to those of their outfield colleagues, but due to the increasing problems that referees were having with identification this was to be altered, so that goalkeepers would be obliged to wear a different top or jersey. This would make life easier for the poor beleaguered referee, who must have had the difficulty of distinguishing whether it was the goalkeeper or another player who had used his hands in a goalmouth melee. Perhaps a goalkeeper could be recognized by his cap, should it remain on his head in a scramble! As for the numbering of shirts, this did not arrive nationally until just before the Second World War.

With George Kitchen unavailable for the visit to Swindon, perhaps the Hammers could have done with Tommy Robinson in goal, but to be fair, Jack Geggus was only at fault for just one of the home side's four goals, whilst West Ham scored just once, but were not helped by having to make four changes in all on a pitch that was covered by snow from the start. The result did nothing for the club's league ambitions as both Swindon and Crystal Palace also won and were now five points ahead, and West Ham were down to fifth place.

The prospect of league honours dropped considerably with a poor display against Portsmouth at Fratton Park. The South Coast side were at the bottom of the table, and something much better than a scoreless draw should have resulted. The forwards, who were still without Webb, quite frankly failed to do their job.

George Webb had by now been honoured as an England Amateur International on six occasions, which left the club short of his valuable services for league matches. He was not in the side for the visit of Bristol Rovers, but his absence this time gave great pride to the club for George had been selected to play for the full England side against Scotland at Liverpool, making him the first West Ham player to pull on a full England shirt.

The Bristol game turned out to be a scrappy affair as the West Country side were hanging around the bottom of the table. The crowd were pleased to see Freddie Blackburn back for the first time since mid November, and he was included as a half-back for the first time. With no goals at the break the visitors took the lead when Rothwell pulled down Peplow in the area, and the penalty was converted. Shortly after, Rovers went further ahead, which shook the Hammers up, and strenuous efforts were made to get back into the game. On a quick breakaway by the visitors however, Shreeve badly fouled Peplow and was sent off. As so often happens the team did better with ten men than with eleven, and from a centre from Whiteman, Caldwell scored. Shea scored the equaliser in the very last minute to give the Hammers a point they did not really deserve.

Fred Harrison

A thumping 1-4 defeat at Crystal Palace effectively meant goodbye to the Southern League title (now eight points adrift of Swindon, and six of Palace), although it was still quite possible that the Irons could finish in second place if the team had a good final run in.

Fred Harrison had recently been signed from Fulham, and was in the side to meet Southampton on Good Friday. Fred had previously had a good career at the Dell, and was a member of the Saints side that won the Southern League title in 1903 and 1904. He was a different type of centre-forward to the more bustling style of George Webb, and did not take long to fit in well with his forward colleagues. He had excellent control and was 'deft of touch'. The overall display of the team was in stark contrast to that at Palace, and Harrison headed the first goal from a corner from Ashton. Continuing to play well all afternoon the Hammers ran out winners by 4-1.

On the Saturday, Brentford came to the East End and were beaten by two clear goals. There was very little to choose between the teams as the Bees had just as many chances to score, but found Jack Geggus in top form in the Hammers' goal.

West Ham's visit to the Dell on Easter Monday resulted in another victory, which meant maximum points over the holiday period. Although the victory was just by one goal the visitors were far superior to Southampton, who were having a miserable season struggling towards their worst finish in the league to date. Ironically it was ex-Southampton star Harrison who scored the goal, which came in the very first minute when Glover, Saints full-back, gave a very weak back pass that was intercepted and rushed in by the new West Ham man.

There were three games remaining. All needed to be won for the club to be runners-up, but it was probably too much to expect. An uninspiring performance at near neighbours Leyton resulted in a 0-3 defeat. This was followed by a visit to the Goldstone Ground, a venue where the Hammers had never won, to meet Brighton & Hove Albion. The Albion were looking to establish the runners-up spot themselves, and gave Hammers a three goal pasting. The final game was now just a formality and the season limped to a finish, as West Ham shared the points with Watford in a 1-1 draw. The only interesting feature of this game was an outstanding performance from a 17-year-old Watford player, having only his second game in the half-back line, by the name of Arthur Grimsdell, who would be snapped up by Spurs and make 324 appearances for them and win six England caps.

Overall it had been a good season, but really it could have been even better. Points were dropped unnecessarily on a number of occasions. In the opening fixture against Southend, a 3-0 lead was cancelled out by the visitors. At Bristol Rovers, who had a relatively poor home record, and in three home draws with Coventry City, Millwall and Bristol Rovers, all teams in the lower half of the league, plus the away draw with bottom club Portsmouth, which should have been another victory. So at least six extra points were lost giving a final total of 51 points, which would have meant a runners-up position. The high spot of the season, of course, was the exciting cup run against four First Division sides, and a quarter final finish which brought the club to the attention of the football public in general.

"Critic" had this view of Syd King's office after the 1910/11 FA Cup run. The caption read:

A King was in his parlour, counting up his money, When up came a Black....... And chipped off his record.

1910/11

5th in Southern League Division One

#	Date	Opponent	Score	Scorers	Att	Ashton H	Blackburn F	Bourne S	Butcher G	Caldwell T	Curtis F	Fairman R	Frost A	Geggus J	Harrison F	Kennedy W	Kitchen G	Lavery W	Massey F	Miellear J	Piercy F	Randall T	Redward F	Rothwell J	Shea D	Shreeve F	Webb G	Whiteman R	Woodards D
1	Sep 3	SOUTHEND UNITED	3-3	Ashton, Blackburn, Webb	15000	7	10			11		3					1		4		5	6			8	2	9		
2	10	Coventry City	0-3		6000	7	10			11		3					1	2	4		5	6			8		9		
3	12	Queen's Park Rangers	2-0	Shea 2	7000	7	10			11		3					1	2	4		5	6			8		9		
4	17	GILLINGHAM	2-0	Shea, Webb	12000	7	10			11	9	3					1	2	4		5	6			8				
5	24	Millwall	2-0	Blackburn, Shea	10000	7	10	3		11							1	2	4		5	6			8		9		
6	Oct 1	QUEEN'S PARK RANGERS	3-0	Curtis 2, Shea	20000	7	10			11	9	3					1	2	4		5	6			8				
7	8	Norwich City	0-2		8000	7	10			11	9	3					1	2	4		5	6			8				
8	15	Luton Town	1-1	Shea	8000	7	10			11		3					1	2	4		5	6			8				
9	22	PORTSMOUTH	3-1	Ashton, Kitchen, Shea	10000	7	10			11		3					1	2				6			8		9	4	5
10	29	Northampton Town	0-2		6000	7			10	11		3					1	2				6			8		9	4	5
11	Nov 5	BRIGHTON & HOVE ALB.	3-1	Kennedy, Kitchen, Shea	14000	7	10			11		3				9	1	2			5	6			8			4	
12	12	Exeter City	0-0		6000	7	10			11		3				9	1	2			5	6			8			4	
13	19	SWINDON TOWN	1-0	Shea	12000	7	10			11		3				9		2			5	6			8			4	
14	26	Bristol Rovers	1-1	Shea	6000	7			10	11		3		1		9		2			5	6			8			4	
15	Dec 3	CRYSTAL PALACE	1-1	Shea	10000	7			10	11		3		1		9		2			5	6			8			4	
16	10	Brentford	0-3		5000	7			10	11		3		1							5	6			8		9	4	
17	17	LEYTON	3-0	Ashton 2, Shea	7000	7			10	11		3		1							5	6		2	8		9	4	
18	24	Watford	3-1	Shea 2, Piercy	2000	7			10	11		3		1					4		5	6		2	8		9		
19	26	PLYMOUTH ARGYLE	4-0	Webb 2, Rothwell, Shea	14000	7			10	11		3		1					4		5	6		2	8		9		
20	27	Plymouth Argyle	0-1		8000	7			10	11		3		1					4			6		2	8		9		
21	31	Southend United	6-0	Shea 4, Caldwell, Kennedy	3000	7			10	11				1		9		2				6		2	8	3		4	5
22	Jan 7	COVENTRY CITY	1-1	Webb	11000	7			10	11		3					1				5	6		2	8		9	4	
23	21	Gillingham	1-1	Ashton	5000	7			10	11		3					1				5	6		2	8		9	4	
24	28	MILLWALL	2-2	Randall, Webb	8000	7			10	11		3					1				5	6		2	8		9	4	
25	Feb 11	NORWICH CITY	2-1	Rothwell, Webb	12000	7			10	11		3					1				5			2	8		9	4	
26	18	LUTON TOWN	2-0	Kennedy, Piercy	8000	7			10	11		3					1	6			5			2	8			4	
27	Mar 4	NORTHAMPTON T	1-2	Butcher	10000				10	11		3	8			9	1				5			2				4	5
28	18	EXETER CITY	4-1	Webb 3, Shea	8000				10	11		3	8			9	1	6	7					2				4	5
29	25	Swindon Town	1-4	Kennedy	6000	7			10	11					1	9					5	6	4	2	8	3			
30	29	Portsmouth	0-0		2000	7			10	11					1	9					5	6		2	8	3			
31	Apr 1	BRISTOL ROVERS	2-2	Caldwell, Shea	5000	7	6		10	11					1	9					5			2	8	3	4		
32	8	Crystal Palace	1-4	Shea	10000	7			10	11					1	9					5			2	8	3	4		
33	14	SOUTHAMPTON	4-1	Ashton, Caldwell, Harrison, Shea	12000	7	6		10	11		3		1	9						5	6		2	8		9	4	
34	15	BRENTFORD	2-0	Butcher, Shea	8000	7			10	11		3		1	9						5			2	8			4	
35	17	Southampton	1-0	Harrison	8000	7			10	11		3		1	9						5	6		2	8			4	
36	22	Leyton	0-3		10000	7			10	11		3		1	9						5	6		2	8			4	
37	26	Brighton & Hove Albion	0-3		4000	7	8		10	11		3		1	9						5	6		2				4	
38	29	WATFORD	1-1	Shea	5000	7	8		10	11		3					1				5	6		2	9			4	
		Apps				37	16	1	26	38	3	33	2	14	5	10	24	15	13	1	32	34	1	22	35	5	19	27	5
		Goals				6	2		2	3	2				2	4	2				2	1		2	25		10		

F.A. Cup

	Date	Opponent	Score	Scorers	Att	Ashton H	Butcher G	Caldwell T	Fairman R	Kitchen G	Piercy F	Randall T	Rothwell J	Shea D	Webb G	Whiteman R
R1	Jan 14	NOTTM. FOREST	2-1	Shea 2	12000	7	10	11	3	1	5	6	2	8	9	4
R2	Feb 4	PRESTON NORTH END	3-0	Webb 3	12000	7	10	11	3	1	5	6	2	8	9	4
R3	25	MANCHESTER UNITED	2-1	Caldwell, Shea	27000	7	10	11	3	1	5	6	2	8	9	4
R4	Mar 11	BLACKBURN ROVERS	2-3	Butcher 2	20000	7	10	11	3	1	5	6	2	8	9	4

The England squad for the game against Scotland. George Webb is the tallest player, at the centre of the back row.

		P	W	D	L	F	A	W	D	L	F	A	Pts
1	Swindon Town	38	16	2	1	54	9	8	3	8	26	22	53
2	Northampton Town	38	14	3	2	39	7	4	9	6	15	20	48
3	Brighton & Hove Alb.	38	15	2	2	41	12	5	6	8	17	24	48
4	Crystal Palace	38	11	5	3	35	23	6	8	5	20	25	47
5	WEST HAM UNITED	38	12	6	1	44	17	5	5	9	19	29	45
6	Queen's Park Rangers	38	11	6	2	37	16	2	8	9	15	25	40
7	Leyton	38	13	3	3	37	15	3	5	11	20	37	40
8	Plymouth Argyle	38	10	6	3	37	14	5	3	11	17	41	39
9	Luton Town	38	13	4	2	42	18	2	4	13	25	45	38
10	Norwich City	38	12	5	2	31	13	3	3	13	15	35	38
11	Coventry City	38	12	4	3	47	21	4	2	13	18	47	38
12	Brentford	38	12	5	2	32	13	2	4	13	9	29	37
13	Exeter City	38	8	5	6	31	28	6	4	9	20	25	37
14	Watford	38	10	5	4	32	23	3	4	12	17	39	35
15	Millwall	38	8	3	8	21	20	3	6	10	21	34	31
16	Bristol Rovers	38	6	6	7	24	23	4	4	11	18	32	30
17	Southampton	38	8	3	8	25	28	3	5	11	17	39	30
18	New Brompton	38	10	5	4	19	15	1	3	15	15	50	30
19	Southend United	38	7	4	8	28	26	3	5	11	19	38	29
20	Portsmouth	38	6	10	3	21	15	2	1	16	13	38	27

MANY GOALS, FEW POINTS

With basically the same squad of players, and just several on the fringe, there was no doubt that West Ham had underachieved in 1909/10 and missed out on the Southern League title in 1910/11. Would there be any improvements or additions to the team in order bring some silverware to the Boleyn club? The answer was 'very little.'

With Bill Lavery being released at full-back, there was only one significant signing, that being Horace Glover, an experienced defender from Southampton who had been with the club since 1906/07, later becoming captain of the Saints. He would prove to be strong competition for both Fairman and Rothwell. Surprisingly and unfortunately, George Kitchen was allowed to go in the opposite direction. Although now 35 years of age George was still a top-notch goalkeeper, and he appeared for Southampton in 39 Southern League and cup matches before retiring in 1914 to take up his first love of professional golf. His leaving West Ham would mean a 50% increase in goals conceded in the forthcoming season.

The regular pre-season game of cricket was played at the Rectory Field, Little Ilford against Manor Park Constitutional Club in front of around 1,000 interested onlookers. The West Ham players led again by Frank Piercy, put on a creditable performance, and it was notable that almost four innings overall were played. The Hammers' totals were 121 in the first innings, with the top scorer being George Redwood with a useful 37. He had joined West Ham from Fulham along with Fred Harrison at the back end of 1910/11. The 'Consti's' hit 90 in reply, with Dan Woodards claiming 5 wickets. The second innings saw West Ham notch 142 for 8 wickets declared with Frank Piercy hitting 36. Their opponents second innings could not be completed at 147 for 6 wickets, Bob Fairman taking three wickets.

The footballers were commended for their fielding with Ashton and Blackburn taking part in a spectacular 'run out', but the 'hottest' moment of the match came shortly after the start. With the contest taking place on a boiling hot day, the dry grass caught fire and some of the players were jumping around stamping out the flames! Two firemen finally arrived with 'hastily improvised' fire appliances to extinguish the fire!

On to the serious business of the opening league game, the Hammers travelled to South London to meet Crystal Palace on an equally hot day. The East End lads did most of the attacking, but just before the break Geggus, now the first choice 'keeper, was pulled up for carrying the ball. From the resultant free kick, two Palace players stepped over the ball, deceiving the 'keeper, and the third hit the ball into the net. West Ham began the second half on the attack again, but the heat appeared to affect them more than the home eleven, and they eventually tired, losing by that first half goal.

Whilst the first team were on their travels the reserve eleven were entertaining their Woolwich Arsenal counterparts at Upton Park. The spectators who frequented the North Bank must have been pleased when they entered the ground to see that terracing had been laid down, and a concrete wall had been erected at that end. According to the club programme *'Considerable expense has been incurred ... the public will have a splendid uninterrupted view of the game from that end of the field.'* Slowly but surely the club were making gradual improvements, and moving forward off the field. To those who said once more that the club lacked ambition, the directors could point to the steadily improving situation off the field, with the assets now exceeding liabilities for the first time in the club's history. Any significant success on the field would remain to be seen.

Robert Whiteman

As for the game, there was controversy with some of the referee's decisions. He frequently overruled his linesmen, on occasions incorrectly, and was inclined to listen to protests of the players instead of sticking to his decisions, correct or otherwise. In one incident, the Woolwich men thought they had scored, but the referee decided it was offside. The visiting players then walked up to the centre circle and declined to carry on, unless the referee spoke to the linesman about the decision. Whilst he did so the Arsenal captain spoke to his men, and although the offside was confirmed, the players resumed. Just for the record the Hammers' 'stiffs' won 2-0.

On the Monday following, West Ham met Fulham at home in a friendly game that was arranged as part of the transfer agreement which had brought Harrison and Redwood to the club. The visitors of course, were now a Football League side but they were swept aside by five goals to one, the scorers being Rothwell (pen), Kennedy, Harrison and Shea (2).

Considering the West Ham side was pretty much the same as the previous campaign, the players' teamwork was poor for the most part of the contest against Southampton. The visitors by contrast, had several new men but looked the better combination. For the Hammers, only Ashton, Whiteman and Randall played anything like their usual game, whilst Jack Geggus in goal, had a nightmare, being responsible for both the Saints' goals. The first was bizarre to say the least. When an opponent hit a hard shot along the ground Geggus fell on the ball, and lay on it.

Rules being what they were at the time, the Saints' forwards harassed him, and Jack in an attempt to get it clear, mistakenly threw it into his own net. His second error came when he ran out to clear and collided with Piercy, and Southampton's Brown headed the ball into the empty net. West Ham roused themselves late in the second half, and pressed forward. Harrison scored and Kennedy equalised in the very last minute to gain a somewhat lucky point.

When the Hammers travelled to Plymouth they dropped Tommy Caldwell in favour of J Morrison, a young local amateur lad. He performed well and put in some good crosses for the forwards, but unfortunately no goals were scored. At least the team came away with one point.

West Ham played Fulham in the first round of the London Challenge Cup at the Boleyn enclosure, and a 2-2 draw resulted, with Shea and Butcher the scorers. The London FA's rule was for extra time to be played, but Fulham refused, asking to see the order. The rule also stated that the referee had to be notified before the match began. This had not been carried out, so the match went to a replay. Played later in the season, Fulham ran out winners.

Bob Fairman

Bob Fairman broke his finger in the Fulham game, which meant a debut for Horace Glover, the club's close season signing, for the home fixture against Reading.

On the day before the match the West Ham players enjoyed a boat trip on the Thames on the steam launch 'Mirry', which was kindly lent out for the occasion by a Mr W Lotings, a club supporter. Possibly the unusual day out benefited the players the next day as they at last found their form, particularly the forwards, with the Hammers' first goal coming after Webb had been bowled over in the area. Rothwell duly converted the penalty. Goals followed from Piercy, Whiteman and Webb, but the fifth and best came late in second half when the ball quickly went from Piercy to Webb and then on to Shea, who raced around a defender, before beating the opposing 'keeper.

It is well here to consider the responsibilities of the forwards at this time. They were a 'forward line', and to all intents and purposes they played as a line. The wingers were to get round the back of the defence and deliver crosses, whilst the two inside men and the centre-forward, who was the leader, were there to score goals. Basically there were no deep-lying inside forwards doing a foraging and supplying task, that was the duty of the half-backs. Inside forwards were expected to pitch in with as many goals as the centre-forward, whilst the wingers, apart from their supplying role, were also expected to claim their share too. Forwards were certainly not expected to help out in defence, that was the duty of the half-backs when necessary. Studying goalscoring over this period also shows that goals from positions other than the forwards were very few and far between. Of the goals scored in the previous three league campaigns, 7 were scored by halves and full-backs out of a total of 56 scored in 1908/09, 5 from 69 in 1909/10, and 7 from 63 in 1910/11 (and 2 of those were from Kitchen's penalties), emphasising the forward line's responsibilities.

Both Fairman and Glover were unavailable for the trip to Watford, so Piercy went to full-back, and with the first appearance of Fred Blackburn in his new position in the half-back line as cover for Tommy Randall, the half-back line had an odd look about it with Dan Woodards taking over Frank Piercy's position. The Hammers, maybe due to the strange line-up, took the unusual step of playing the offside game which did them no favours, and Watford went on to score in the first half. Later in the second period Whiteman was injured, and with ten men West Ham played the one back game, which made the offsides even more frequent, and the home side scored again to complete a 2-0 win.

The reason for Tommy Randall's absence in the above game was due to his selection to represent the Southern League against the Football League at Stoke. He received generous plaudits for his performance in that game, but could not motivate his forwards to score in the meeting with New Brompton at Upton Park. Given so much freedom to score they failed miserably in a scoreless draw.

Shooting boots were found at last on the visit to Devon to meet Exeter City. The Hammers had more than their fair share of the play and were 2-1 up at the break. They had survived a penalty kick awarded against Fairman (in the side for the injured Rothwell), but after the interval the home side converted their second which was given for handball. At 2-2 West Ham still pushed for the winner and thought they had it after Shea, directly from a corner kick, hit the ball on the volley into the net. But annoyingly, Exeter got the equaliser right on the stroke of full time.

Those that witnessed the encounter with Brentford saw a most astonishing and extraordinary event. It was not the quality of the play that caught the eye, but the number of goals that were scored, and the mistakes that were made in abundance. Much of the high scoring can be put down to errors made by both goalkeepers. There was some excuse for Ling, the Brentford man who had injured his arm the previous week and had been receiving further treatment. Jack Geggus, for some unknown reason, was a bag of nerves.

The goalscoring feast began in the tenth minute when Rippon, the ex-Bristol City and Woolwich Arsenal forward, headed in for the Bees. This was equalised by Shea, scoring off a defender's legs. Ling's first mistake came when he could not hold a shot from Harrison, and Kennedy put the Hammers ahead (2-1). Danny Shea raced away on his own and netted (3-1). Shea scored again after Ling had mishandled Danny's first shot (4-1). Jack Geggus mirrored Ling's error by fumbling Anderson's shot and Rippon scored (4-2). Kennedy ran the ball in which Ling could have saved (5-2), right on half time.

Some way into the second half Fairman handled in the penalty area. Everyone stopped playing except Brentford's Hendren who hit the ball from 25 yards, which Geggus allowed to fly into the net. Big mistake. (5-3). Kennedy quickly made it 6-3 after a centre from Harrison, and then Harrison himself from Ashton's cross (7-3). Rippon pulled one back from the tamest of shots at Geggus. Final score 7-4! Equally amazing was the fact that three players had the honour of scoring hat-tricks. Shea and Kennedy for the Irons, and Rippon for Brentford. Kennedy was, of course, deputising for George Webb, who was on duty for the England amateur eleven against Denmark on this particular day. Would George have scored as many, or more than Bill Kennedy? It is an interesting thought.

The above number of goals was, of course, not a regular occurrence, but there is no doubt that the majority of matches were fought out with the positive attitude of obtaining a victory. It must be remembered that it was just two points for a win, which could have meant that teams away from home might have gone out with the object of settling for a draw from the start, but in general it was not the case. In the modern professional game, especially at top level, there is too much at stake, creating a state of fear, and very often the main object is just 'not to lose', and a defensive system is employed from the first whistle.

After the Brentford game, West Ham came down to earth when visiting QPR at Park Royal. Rangers were riding high at the top of the league and would be a difficult side to beat, and so it proved as the home side were victorious by four goals to one. The Hammers actually had an equal portion of the play, and territorially they were not disgraced.

The annual London FA Charity match took place at Upton Park and West Ham beat Leyton by 4 goals to two with Danny Shea scoring all four. One of Leyton's goals came about from a bad mistake by Geggus who saved a long shot, but let the ball slip through his fingers. As a consequence of Jack's recent errors and the number of goals conceded he was dropped from the side, along with Bob Fairman who was in poor form, and was responsible for three penalties in recent matches.

Edward Leahy, who was the young understudy to Geggus had been playing for the reserves, but although quite competent he was sometimes quite nervy and lacking in confidence. He never made the first team until 1915/16 during the First World War, when he played in over 60 matches in the London Combination. He later appeared for Southend United, and in 1921 joined Aberdare Athletic in the Third Division South.

Another young 'keeper by the name of Joe Hughes, who had been with the South Weald club was given a trial, and put in the side against Millwall which was really something of a baptism of fire. He

Joe Hughes

did not disappoint, and was to become the first team choice until regular league competition ceased at the end of 1914/15 due to the 'Great War', as it was called at the time. Joe showed good judgement in what was the usual fierce battle against old rivals. The attendance was 23,000, which was the highest Southern League gate at the Boleyn ground at the time. Such was the excitement just before the interval that the crowd swayed forward and broke through the fencing, causing spectators to spill out on the pitch. By a miracle there was only one injury reported, and that was not a serious one.

As for the game itself the Hammers were victorious by 2-1. Millwall drew first blood, ironically from the boot of W. Davis who was the son of the West Ham Deputy Mayor. The Boleyn lads fought back in the second half with Tommy Randall playing one of the games of his life, prompting his forwards on. Fred Harrison equalised, and from a fine cross from Shea grabbed the winner. Shea himself almost made it three with one of his hook shots, which missed by inches. Overall it was a well-deserved victory.

Despite West Ham's official colours being claret and blue, the team were still described as the 'red, white and blues' in the local press over this period. It was indeed a fact that when the club employed a band to play at matches the theme tune was 'Three cheers for the red, white and blue'. As for the nickname, 'Come on you Irons' could still be heard at matches (as it still is today) more so than the reference to the 'Hammers' as it was in the national press.

The second home match in succession resulted in another conquest as Luton Town were beaten by three clear goals. It was a good display as Luton's goalkeeper stood between the Hammers and an even bigger margin. George Webb was injured early on in the encounter, forcing him to leave the field for ten minutes or so, but he was still in considerable pain when he returned, and indeed for the remainder of the game. Despite this, he scored one of the best goals of the season so far. Taking the ball at the halfway line he moved forward and hit a tremendous shot from fully twenty-five yards into the top corner of the net. Harrison scored the second, but later in the match darkness began to fall, and Luton protested at the bad light, but after the referee had consulted a linesman play continued. Shea rounded it off with a goal from a hard drive for the third goal.

An important but sad event took place in November 1911 when the great Thames Ironworks and Shipbuilding Company went into receivership. This would affect the future well being of between three to four thousand workers at the yard, quite a number of whom had been supporters of the old Thames Ironworks FC, and who had continued to support the club under its new name of West Ham United. In 1910 the company had a contract from the British Government to build the 'Thunderer', which at 22,500 tons was the Navy's largest dreadnought when it was launched in February 1911. It was originally thought that this contract would be followed by others, but the costs incurred were considered too great for the Admiralty to bear, even though the work was completed on time, and without any strikes to hinder it. Time would tell whether the company had any chance of continuing. (There is a very brief history of the Company and its successes in the book on Thames Ironworks FC entitled 'Iron in the Blood'.)

It is interesting to note that whilst West Ham United were earning a hard grafted point at Bristol against the Rovers in a 1-1 draw, the old amateur Thames Ironworks eleven were playing East Ham Avenue at the Memorial Grounds in the second round of the East Ham Hospital Cup, the Avenue winning by a single goal.

Swindon Town, the current champions came next to Upton Park with a record at the Hammers' ground that was not that special. However, lady luck seemed to favour the visitors in a contest that saw them take both points by two clear goals. West Ham were certainly on top for most of the opening half with Shea, Webb and Harrison all going close. The game was then turned when both Glover and Piercy together brought down Swindon's Fleming in the area and the kick was converted. The Hammers appeared to lose heart afterwards, but picked up again after half time. The same pattern of play continued, but the home forwards anxiety at not scoring grew greater, and Swindon broke away and scored a second.

Northampton's fortunes had been turned around with Herbert Chapman as manager. He was to become one of the Football League's most accomplished managers in the 1920s and 1930s when he took Huddersfield to two, and Arsenal to three consecutive league titles. In 1907 he had taken on the job at Northampton when the 'Cobblers' had finished bottom of the Southern League. In the following campaigns the club had finished in 8th, 1st, 4th, and 2nd positions after Chapman had persuaded his board to put in some money and help him make, what turned out to be, some very astute signings, and it is clear that he had responsibility for team selection.

Over the previous four seasons West Ham had lost convincingly on each visit to the County Ground, but on this meeting were two goals to the good. Before the interval Frank Piercy broke a rib in a collision and took no further part. This, without doubt altered the scheme of things completely, and the home side pulled one goal back before the break. Even after Northampton drew level, the Hammers might still have won, for late on they were awarded a penalty, but Rothwell kicked it wide of the goal, and just five minutes from time the 'Cobblers' scored the winner. Some games are just not meant to be won.

When West Ham beat Brighton & Hove at home, it was the South Coast side that considered they were hard done by. After Shea had netted by means of a 'right old scramble' in the goalmouth, the visiting side complained bitterly about 'unseen demeanours'. This proved to be the only goal of the game, but Brighton also appealed to the referee that Joe Hughes had carried the ball over his goal line late in the game, but the official once again, refused their appeals.

The Hammers had next to make the long journey up country to meet Stoke City. Like the Bradford Park Avenue club that had entered the Southern League in 1907/08 (albeit for one season), the 'Potters' could hardly be described as a club that was located in the South of the country. They had been one of the original twelve members of the Football League in 1888/89, but resigned from the Second Division in 1907/08 due to financial reasons. The club applied to join the Southern League in 1909/10 and were accepted, but had to be content with the second tier until they were promoted in 1910/11.

West Ham made a great start on their first visit to the Victoria Ground and were ahead by two goals early on in the first half, through Kennedy and Randall. Stoke replied and then the visitors lost Randall with a bad ankle injury, which altered the flow of the Hammers' game. The 'Potters' subsequently took control with the advantage of the extra man, and banged in another three before Kennedy, after good work by Shea, got his second and West Ham's third.

Another disappointing result followed when Coventry came to Upton Park. The visitors scored in the first half, and Harrison missed a penalty for the Hammers in the second.

The left wing pairing of Harrison and Morrison was dropped, and Butcher and Caldwell came in when local rivals Leyton made the short journey to West Ham on Christmas Day. The home side redeemed themselves somewhat with a 2-0 victory, but the display was far from satisfactory. Amateur George Webb actually objected to being picked to play on this holiday morning, and his subsequent performance confirmed his reluctance to appear, although Dan Woodards also had a poor game in the half-back line.

At least the Leyton game resulted in two points, for disaster followed when Crystal Palace arrived for the Hammers' third consecutive home fixture. Towards the end of the first half with the visitors ahead by 2-1, Tommy Caldwell missed an open goal. Had the ball gone in, there may have been a different story, as West Ham were having the best of the attacking play from the start of the second period. When Palace broke away and scored again, the Hammers fell to pieces and the visitors ran in another three goals for a 6-1 victory! This was to be the worst defeat at home in the whole of the 1900 to 1915 period.

For the trip to Southampton Rothwell lost his place to Fairman at full-back, Fred Massey came in for Redward at centre half and Caldwell lost his place, with Harrison moving to outside left and Butcher coming inside. These changes certainly worked as the forwards gave a fine display, whilst Glover, playing against his old team, was the best of the defenders. The 2-1 victory was the Hammers' first away win of the season.

There was always excitement at the prospect of a good run in the FA Cup, and West Ham were drawn against Gainsborough Trinity at the Boleyn ground in the first round. The visitors were in the Second Division of the Football League at the time, and had been members since 1895/96. The club was struggling at the foot of the table, and were to finish there at the end of the campaign, and would not be re-elected. Due to the Lincolnshire club's poor season, West Ham were favourites to win which they did, but not without a struggle, as the visitors had the knack and enthusiasm to play above their form before succumbing by the narrow margin of 2-1, with Webb and Harrison scoring the Hammers' goals. This would prove to be George Webb's final goal for the club.

There was further news at this time with respect to the Thames Ironworks & Shipbuilding Company's proposed tendering for the building of two new cruisers at the yard. This was despite the Company having been put into receivership in mid November. Whilst the northern shipyards had been consistently undercutting Thames with lower costs, especially labour costs, the Company had been struggling to win the larger contracts that would maintain their survival. This could only now be achieved by Thames cutting the wages of those men who had recently received an increase. A ballot was taken (1) to increase the hours to 53 a week from 48, which received just 5% of the votes and (2) to work for the rates of pay paid prior to November 11th 1911, which received 50.5% approval. The Company would still seek Admiralty approval claiming *'that the absence of a substantial order from the government from the 1912 naval programme will create poverty to thousands of workers who are anxiously waiting for the Admiralty's decision and the consequent increase of poor law relief with its costly administration.'*

Two weeks later the workmen put forward a resolution declaring their willingness to revert to the wage rate that applied in the Works before November 1911, provided that the proposal would enable the Admiralty to place the order for the two cruisers, and that the reduction in the wage rate would not exceed one half of the advance granted in November. Arnold Hills came to the meeting in his invalid chair, thanking the men for their sacrifice. If the Admiralty accepted, the orders would come to the Thames shipyard and Hills would be able to secure the capital necessary for the discharge of the receiver, and for placing the Thames on a sound financial basis once again.

Unfortunately this did not sway the Admiralty and the orders for the two cruisers went elsewhere. All that the Thames shipyard received by way of orders in 1912 were from Turkey for three 500 ton passenger steamers, with the inevitable results, as we shall see.

Back on the playing field West Ham received Plymouth Argyle before an attendance of 10,000. The fixture was allocated as Tommy Randall's benefit match, and with a reasonably good crowd he received a healthy sum. Both Tommy and Frank Piercy had returned after injury, but poor Frank was crocked again. He did not leave the field, but this proved to be his last ever game after 214 Southern League appearances over eight seasons for the Hammers. Tommy Randall himself was also injured and limped around the field, and with two injuries in vital positions the prospects of a win against a really good side were remote. So it proved, as Argyle won by two clear goals. Their first however, was controversial. When Boden, of Plymouth struck a thunderbolt at the Hammers' goal, the ball appeared to strike the boards behind the goal and bounce straight out. It was quite obvious that Hughes, in goal, did not see the ball enter the goal and neither did any of the players. The referee after consulting the linesman, pointed to the centre spot, much to the anger of the home crowd.

A 1-3 defeat at Reading meant that in the last ten league games the Hammers had won three and lost seven, and were floundering around in the bottom half of the table.

There was no doubt however, that over the last three seasons West Ham were gaining something of a reputation for their cup exploits, and the forthcoming encounter with Football League First Division side Middlesbrough was keenly anticipated, despite the Hammers' indifferent league form. A change of scenery and rest at Matlock in Derbyshire a few days before the match in the North East must have been beneficial as the encounter at Ayresome Park was an exciting one, with the Hammers giving as good as they got. Syd King, the manager, tried the switch of playing George Webb on the left flank with Harrison at number nine. The idea paid off, with George providing a number of crosses from his unaccustomed position, and Harrison scoring just before half time with an unstoppable drive. The first half had been a very even contest, and continued to be so after the break. After Harrison hit the 'Boro bar, the home side went straight to the other end, where Glover's handball resulted in a penalty. The kick was taken by Williamson, the home 'keeper, but he ballooned the ball over the bar. Play continued end to end, but with just three minutes remaining Middlesbrough grabbed an equaliser, which meant a replay at Upton Park.

With George Webb unavailable to appear in the replay, Tommy Caldwell came in at outside left, and Frank Redward came into the half-back line in place of Whiteman. The admission prices were doubled again for this cup-tie but 12,000 still came through the gates. Considering it took place in midweek with an afternoon kick off, it was a good attendance. Again it was a 'ding-dong' battle but the Hammers were considerably handicapped by a knee injury to Bill Kennedy after just ten minutes. Despite this the home side did practically all the attacking in the first half and were rewarded when Harrison scored after Williamson had let the ball through his legs.

Frank Redward

In second half, the heavy pitch began to take its toll on ten-men Hammers, and it was 'Boro's turn to attack, forcing corner after corner. Joe Hughes in goal, despite injuring his wrist in a fall, and the full-backs, Fairman and Glover kept them at bay. Finally the visitors did equalise after a scramble, and were jubilant, but they did not count on West Ham's resilience. Within a minute, Ashton raced down the wing and crossed for the unmarked Caldwell who put the ball in the net. Further 'Boro pressure came to nothing and the Hammers had won a great victory.

Bill Kennedy's injury was worse than at first thought. The dislocation to his knee caused further complications, and he never played first class football again. This was something of a double disaster, as the club did not realise at the time that George Webb had already played his last game for the Hammers. Being an amateur and heavily involved in his business as a toy manufacturer, George was not always available for selection. Add on his appearances for the England Amateur eleven, (and, of course, two for the full England side) and absences for injuries, he was not in the West Ham side as much as Syd King and the directors would have liked. In the latter part of the 1911/12 season he did not play due to illness, and joined Manchester City in July 1912, later to leave in controversial circumstances, as we shall see. George's record for the Hammers was 32 league and cup goals in 62 appearances, a very impressive ratio.

Two days after the club's cup exploits, several changes were made for the trip to Kent to face New Brompton. The team did remarkably well considering the home side had most of the play, but with Jack Geggus making his first appearance in goal since October, and keeping a clean sheet, West Ham won by three clear goals.

When Exeter City came to Upton Park the Devon side shook the home crowd by scoring two goals in the first fifteen minutes, but as Danny Shea was in top form scoring two (to add to the brace he scored the previous week), the game was turned round and Harrison also scored for a 3-2 victory.

In both the above games neither away side came to 'shut up shop', it was simply a case of going out to win. Football has gradually gone from 2-3-5, right through to 4-2-4, 4-3-3, 4-4-2 and now the negative 4-5-1. What next 5-5-0?

A 20,000 crowd was present when Swindon Town came to the East End for the FA Cup 3rd Round (now the 5th). The visitors brought a large number of fans with them and the atmosphere was electric. West Ham had their strongest available side out, and took the lead inside 6 minutes when Tommy Caldwell took the ball down the left, passed on to Ashton, who in turn found Butcher who scored, and the home crowd roared themselves hoarse, *'a long drawn out yell, its echo to be heard a mile off.'* Swindon, who were the current Southern League champions, and no mean side, equalised in the 31st minute, and forced three corners just before the break. The second half was fought out evenly, which meant a replay at the County Ground.

Due to the absence of Kennedy and Webb, and without Harrison, who was injured, West Ham were really short in attack, and gave a run out at centre-forward to Joe Miellear. Joe was essentially a flank man and it showed. Swindon scored twice in the first twenty-five minutes, and the visitors were pretty much demoralised thereafter. Both goals came about through mistakes made by the usually reliable Glover at left back. The first came after a Swindon cross that Glover headed on to the back of Joe Hughes, the ball bouncing off to Wheatcroft who ran it in. The second goal came when Glover headed into his own net.

George Walden

Within two days, it was back to Southern League fare for the fixture with QPR. The Rangers came across London sweeping all before them at the top of the table. The visitors showed their superiority in all departments except scoring, but with just fifteen minutes remaining it still seemed just a matter of time before they did. Then came a remarkable twelve minute period when they were completely 'run off their legs' as the Hammers scored no less than three times through Ashton, Caldwell and Shea.

Disappointment at elimination from the FA Cup, was now tempered by the fact that the Boleyn lads had won three consecutive league matches, and a respectable position was a possibility. But the faithful did not hold their breath. This *was* West Ham after all, and any possibility flew out of the window at the Den, on the visit to Millwall, as the home side were victorious by no less than 5-1. Just to rub it in, the West Ham deputy Mayor's son, W. Davis scored a hat-trick. The attendance for this local derby was an amazing 28,500!

Another setback followed at the Boleyn ground when Watford were the visitors. The Hammers included Morrison at outside left, and a young Clapton amateur by the name of George Walden, making his first appearance on the opposite flank. Although West Ham had most of the possession, the forwards were accused of too much interpassing, whereas the visitors more direct methods on the break took the points. The Hammers' only goal was a penalty by Rothwell in a 1-3 reverse.

The signing of former Everton and Blackpool left winger Harold Dawson from Croydon Common, saw him drafted into the team for the visit to Kenilworth Road, Luton. He did well, providing dangerous centres, but overall this was a poor performance against a team battling against relegation (a battle they finally lost), and after Harrison had put Hammers in the lead in the first half, Luton replied twice after the interval.

The miserable weather and the in-and-out performance of the side brought an attendance of just 4,000 to Upton Park for the Bristol Rovers encounter. Those that stayed away however, missed a goal treat. Young local lad, Frank Burrill, who had made his debut at centre-forward in the recent QPR game, was included at inside right, and had a good game up until the interval when the pace became too much for him. It was Frank who was responsible for the cross that provided the opening goal for Woodards in the very first minute, and it was not long before Dawson notched the second. Shea scored the third before the Rovers replied for 3-1 at the break. It was a similar score in the second half, providing a 6-2 victory. It was certainly a day for quick moving forwards, as defenders found it difficult to turn on the wet surface. All in all, the number of goals sent the small crowd home in a happy mood.

Tommy Randall returned after two months out for the trip to Brentford. The victory against the Bees was obtained more through the atrocious shooting of the home forwards than anything else, and one of the Hammers' goals was an own goal. Harrison scored the other in a 2-1 win. The pairing of Burrill with George Walden on the right was not a success, and the latter would not appear again, although he would go on to gain an FA Amateur Cup Final winners medal in 1915 with Clapton.

Frank Burrill

On Good Friday Norwich City were the visitors and went home pointless after the Hammers secured a 4-0 victory. Harrison had scored in the first half, and it looked to be staying that way until the final twenty minutes, when Dawson showed his skill by providing the crosses to Danny Shea who gratefully put no less than three of them into the back of the net.

On the following day, Easter Saturday, another good crowd turned out for the visit of Northampton Town. There was no doubt that when Harrison was unavailable Syd King and the directors were struggling to find a suitable replacement for the centre-forward position. On this occasion, George Bell, a young Barking amateur, was thrown in at the deep end. One of the reasons why the team was not showing the consistency of the previous season was the constant changing of the forward line. A settled side will always bring its rewards, but football, being what it is, is always subject to change with injuries, suspensions, drops in confidence and loss of form all being factors in a lack of success.

Northampton were a team that showed cohesion and understanding in their game and ran out more comfortable winners than the two goal scoreline suggests. One aspect of the game that was disturbing was the constant barracking of Walter Tull. Walter was the first professional black *outfield* player in Britain. He began his career at Tottenham and then went on to Northampton Town. He was subjected to verbal abuse at most away matches, much to the disgust of the more far-sighted individuals in the crowd. This type of behaviour must be taken in the context of the times of course, when the 'man in the street' was not aware that this kind of prejudice was unacceptable, and was totally ignorant of the hurt it caused. Sadly, even in modern times there is still work to be done to eradicate such moronic conduct, but slowly and surely we are getting there.

Walter Tull's life was a short but admirable one. When the Great War (later known as the First World War) commenced in 1914 he was still playing for Northampton Town, but in 1915 he enlisted, along with a number of other professional footballers, in the 17th (1st Football) Battalion of the Middlesex Regiment, and by 1915 he was made a sergeant. He took part in the first battle of the Somme, but before the end of 1916 he was invalided home with trench fever. Upon recovery he went to officer cadet training school in Scotland and was recommended for a commission by his superior officers, something unheard of as 'Negroes' were technically barred from taking command. On the Italian front in 1917 as a second lieutenant in the 23rd (2nd Football) Battalion of the Middlesex Regiment he was mentioned in dispatches. In 1918 he returned to France and fought in the second battle of the Somme. On the 25th March 1918, with less than 9 months of the war remaining, he was killed in no-man's land near Favreuil. His commanding officer remarked *'how popular he was throughout the battalion. He was brave and conscientious......the company have lost a faithful officer......'*. Due to research and publicity by Paul Vasili, a social science lecturer for the Open University in 1996, a belated tribute in the form of the Walter Tull Memorial Garden was opened next to Northampton Town's Sixfields Community Stadium in 1997.

Following the Northampton defeat the Hammers dropped both full-backs for the journey to Norwich. In general Fairman and Glover had both been accused of poor distribution when clearing, with the former criticised for dribbling with the ball in the area, much to the agitation of the supporters on the terraces. With West Ham twice surrendering the lead in the opening half after Shea and then Woodards (with a tremendous 30-yard strike) had scored, the game finished all square at 2-2. Woodards' goal was one of those rare goals from a centre half. That position was not one of a bulky and strong defensive centre back as it is today, but one that had a roving commission between defence and the link to attack. A perfect example of a centre half at the time was Billy Wedlock, of Bristol City. He appeared for England on 26 occasions between 1907 and 1914. He was just 5ft 4in and weighed 10st 7lb.

A visit to Leyton meant that over Easter there had been no less than four games in five days, and it was beginning to show, with defeat coming as no real surprise to those supporters who travelled the short distance to their nearest rivals. Being on the Tuesday directly after Easter, there was a crowd of just 3,000 present, but the Hammers' supporters must have very disgruntled at the team's performance against a club that was bottom of the table, for they took their frustration out on their own 'keeper Jack Geggus. With the score at 2-1 in favour of the home side, Jack was directly at fault for Leyton's third, and the travelling support 'let him have it' in terms of verbal abuse. Geggus wasted no time in leaving his goal and attempting to scamper to the dressing rooms, but his colleagues quickly surrounded him and persuaded him back on the pitch. Had he not returned he would have been severely punished, not only by the club, but by the F. A. as well.

The third consecutive away match resulted in another defeat, this time against Brighton by two clear goals. Of more interest was the reserve game against the same club back at the Boleyn ground. The Brighton second string were fighting neck and neck with Chelsea reserves for the title in the South Eastern League, with 'fighting' being the operative word. As the Hammers led by the odd goal in three, the Brighton players were dishing it out, more with their fists than with their football, and all control was lost to such an extent that a large number of fans invaded the pitch. Order was eventually restored and the score stayed the same. There is no record of any further action having been taken.

West Ham's final home game was a disappointing 0-0 draw, and there was criticism of the club's continuing selection of Danny Shea in an unfamiliar inside left position. Danny had been far more valuable to the side with his right wing partnership with 'Tiddler' Ashton. As it was Ashton himself was unavailable (something of a rarity) for this game, and Syd King rather surprisingly included an amateur from the Stockton on Tees area by the name of T. Bradford. This lad had been in the Stockton side that had played Royal Engineers in the semi-final of the FA Amateur cup at Spotted Dog a month previously. Apart from his speed he was not a success.

The final two matches of the campaign were both away from home to Swindon Town and Coventry City and both were defeats (1-3 and 0-2).

On the 14th April 1912 the Titanic disaster took place in the Atlantic, and at the Coventry game a collection was made on behalf of the Titanic Fund. Whilst players and officials of both clubs gathered in the centre of the field, the band played 'Nearer my God to Thee'. Tommy Randall was selected to represent London against Kent in a Titanic Fund match at New Cross on 1st May, but West Ham United were criticised for not arranging a similar match, even more so, considering the club's strong shipbuilding connections.

And so a quite miserable season ended with team finishing in 13th place. The local press put the blame soundly on the shoulders of the directors and manager. We must not forget that the situation between players, the club manager and directors was quite different to that which exists today. Match tactics that are much the responsibility of the team manager today, can be amended by him and his coaching staff according to circumstances during the game. Formations were far more rigid over the period in question, with directors being involved in selection, as well as the manager, and once that team selection was made it was generally down to the team captain to make any onfield adjustments if necessary. The local correspondent let his views be known at the end of the season thus:-

......the directors must realise that it is bad management that has led to this present lowly position. What can one expect when players are not allowed to use their judgement how to play on the field, but instead are told by officials just before they go out what they are to do? Is it surprising that the team has lost matches? How can you follow a settled plan of campaign successfully unless you know what the other side are going to do? Captains must be allowed free hands from the time the game starts. If your captain has not got the brains necessary to direct, then let the directors get one, but for goodness sake don't let them try to hamper the team with amateurish advice.'

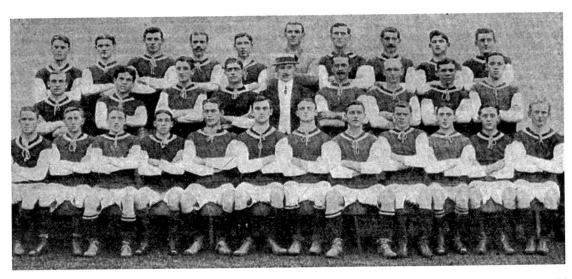

Back: A Hutchinson, F Warrick, J Rothwell, F Shreeve, C Dawson, G Kitchen (capt.), J Geggus, R Fairman, W Lavery, HS Bourne. Centre: R Whiteman, T Mason, F Massey, D Woodards, Mr ES King (Sec. Manager), F Piercy, T Randall, W Trueman, D Mooney. Front: J Miellear, H Ashton, D Shea, G Butcher, GW Webb, W Kennedy, F Curtis, A Scanes, F Blackburn, J Mackesy, T Caldwell, D Waggott.

1911/12

13th in Southern League Division One

#	Date		Opponent	Score	Scorers	Att
1	Sep	2	Crystal Palace	0-1		14000
2		9	SOUTHAMPTON	2-2	Harrison, Kennedy	8000
3		16	Plymouth Argyle	0-0		9000
4		23	READING	5-0	Piercy, Rothwell, Shea, Webb, Whiteman	10000
5		30	Watford	0-2		6000
6	Oct	7	NEW BROMPTON	0-0		5000
7		14	Exeter City	3-3	Shea 2, Webb	8000
8		21	BRENTFORD	7-4	Kennedy 3, Shea 3, Harrison	10000
9		28	Queen's Park Rangers	1-4	Webb	16000
10	Nov	4	MILLWALL	2-1	Harrison 2	23000
11		11	LUTON TOWN	3-0	Harrison, Shea, Webb	9000
12		18	Bristol Rovers	1-1	Shea	7000
13		28	SWINDON TOWN	0-2		11000
14	Dec	2	Northampton Town	2-3	Harrison, Morrison	6000
15		9	BRIGHTON & HOVE ALB.	1-0	Shea	7000
16		16	Stoke	3-4	Kennedy 2, Randall	8000
17		23	COVENTRY CITY	0-1		7000
18		25	LEYTON	2-0	Ashton, Butcher	17000
19		30	CRYSTAL PALACE	1-6	Shea	8000
20	Jan	6	Southampton	2-1	Shea 2	3000
21		20	PLYMOUTH ARGYLE	0-2		10000
22		27	Reading	1-3	Ashton	4000
23	Feb	10	New Brompton	3-0	Shea 2, Butcher	5000
24		17	EXETER CITY	3-2	Shea 2, Harrison	10000
25	Mar	2	QUEEN'S PARK RANGERS	3-0	Ashton, Caldwell, Shea	10000
26		9	Millwall	1-5	Harrison	28400
27		11	WATFORD	1-3	Rothwell	4000
28		16	Luton Town	1-2	Harrison	6000
29		23	BRISTOL ROVERS	6-2	Harrison 2, Shea 2, Dawson, Woodards	4000
30		27	Brentford	2-1	Harrison, Spratt (og)	4000
31	Apr	5	NORWICH CITY	4-0	Shea 3, Harrison	10000
32		6	NORTHAMPTON T	0-2		10000
33		8	Norwich City	2-2	Shea, Woodards	12000
34		9	Leyton	1-3	Shea	3000
35		13	Brighton & Hove Albion	0-2		5000
36		20	STOKE	0-0		8000
37		22	Swindon Town	1-3	Mackesy	2000
38		27	Coventry City	0-2		5000

Played in one game: S Bourne (33, at 3), T Bradford (36, 7), J Mackesy (37, at 10, one goal)
G Bell played in games 32 and 37 at 9

Player appearances (shirt numbers):

Player	Apps	Goals
Ashton H	33	3
Blackburn F	22	
Burrill F	7	
Butcher G	16	2
Caldwell T	11	1
Dawson H	10	1
Fairman R	21	
Frost A	2	
Geggus J	13	
Glover V	29	
Harrison F	30	13
Hughes J	25	
Kennedy W	11	6
Massey F	5	
Miellear J	2	
Morrison J	15	1
Piercy F	10	1
Randall T	23	1
Redward F	6	
Redwood G	3	
Rothwell J	23	2
Shea D	36	24
Walden G	2	
Webb G	11	4
Whiteman R	27	1
Woodards D	20	2

One own goal

F.A. Cup

	Date		Opponent	Score	Scorers	Att
R1	Jan	13	GAINSBOROUGH TRIN.	2-1	Harrison, Webb	14400
R2	Feb	3	Middlesbrough	1-1	Harrison	12300
rep		8	MIDDLESBROUGH	2-1	Ashton, Harrison	10000
R3		24	SWINDON TOWN	1-1	Butcher	20000
rep		28	Swindon Town	0-4		13328

		P	W	D	L	F	A	W	D	L	F	A	Pts
1	Queen's Park Rangers	38	12	5	2	36	14	9	6	4	23	21	53
2	Plymouth Argyle	38	16	2	1	42	7	7	4	8	21	24	52
3	Northampton Town	38	16	2	1	57	15	6	5	8	25	26	51
4	Swindon Town	38	14	3	2	52	19	7	3	9	30	31	48
5	Brighton & Hove Alb.	38	15	2	2	54	12	4	7	8	19	23	47
6	Coventry City	38	14	3	2	46	15	3	5	11	20	39	42
7	Crystal Palace	38	11	5	3	43	14	4	5	10	27	32	40
8	Millwall	38	11	6	2	43	19	4	4	11	17	38	40
9	Watford	38	10	5	4	35	20	3	5	11	21	48	36
10	Stoke	38	11	4	4	35	25	2	6	11	16	38	36
11	Reading	38	10	7	2	35	14	1	7	11	8	45	36
12	Norwich City	38	8	10	1	27	17	2	4	13	13	43	34
13	WEST HAM UNITED	38	10	3	6	40	27	3	4	12	24	42	33
14	Brentford	38	10	5	4	43	18	2	4	13	17	47	33
15	Exeter City	38	8	6	5	30	22	3	5	11	18	40	33
16	Southampton	38	9	3	7	29	27	1	8	10	17	36	31
17	Bristol Rovers	38	7	8	4	24	18	2	5	12	17	44	31
18	New Brompton	38	7	6	6	23	23	4	3	12	12	49	31
19	Luton Town	38	7	5	7	33	28	2	5	12	16	33	28
20	Leyton	38	6	8	5	15	19	1	3	15	12	43	25

1912/13   THE BEST SO FAR

It was announced that the club was now in a situation where it was enjoying an operating profit, and had been since 1905. Possibly stung by outside criticism regarding the lack of real achievement on the playing side, the directors released around nine players and took on a similar number that they hoped, with the right blend, would bring a degree of success.

In addition to the playing staff, the decision was taken to retire long-term trainer Tommy Robinson, and to promote reserve team trainer Charlie Paynter in his place. Charlie's position was to go to Frank Piercy, now retired from playing. This, it was said, came as something of a shock to Tommy, but he took the disappointment in the right spirit, for he was the type of individual with a genial and good-hearted disposition. He was to be awarded a benefit match against QPR in October when the club hoped for a good attendance to enable Tommy to set up the small business he had set his heart on when he retired.

Now at the age of 62, he had been a trainer for over forty years. At the old Prince of Wales ground in Bow in 1873, and later at the renowned Lillie Bridge grounds, he trained athletes, both amateur and professional, for sprints, middle distance and long distance races, at major running and walking competitions. Tommy trained many who became champions and record holders at their respective events. Not only did he act as trainer to several City Business Houses, but his expertise was instrumental in the success of well known cyclists and boxers of the day.

Charles Paynter

He will always have a place in the early football history of West Ham, as he was trainer to the local Old St Lukes and Castle Swifts clubs that played a part in the formation of the Thames Ironworks FC, the forerunner of West Ham United. His final tenure lasted from 1904/05 until 1911/12.

Those players that were released were Jack Geggus, Horace Glover, Joe Miellear and George Redwood. Bob Fairman joined Birmingham City, Tommy Caldwell went to Gillingham, Jack Morrison left for Brentford, A.Frost returned to Southend United and Fred Massey joined Belfast Celtic.

Probably the club's worst decision of the close season was to allow the transfer of George Webb to Manchester City in July although he was, as an amateur, free to go. As he had not played due to illness since the previous December, it was perhaps thought that the club could survive just as well without him. Sadly there was to be some recriminations and misunderstandings regarding the club's refusal to allow George to train at Upton Park. This was something that the national press latched on to without knowing the real circumstances. (Nothing unusual, even in those days). According to those journalists, Webb aired his grievances, but in truth, he remained diplomatically quiet about it. The reasons for West Ham's stance would be revealed at the half yearly shareholders' meeting in January 1913.

For the pre-season practice match, those of the Upton Park faithful who were in the habit of frequenting the South Bank, were delighted to find that the end had been completely terraced with a retaining wall erected behind the goal line. Now the terracing at both ends was of a good standard. 5,000 turned up for the game and all those players that were retained plus those that were new to the club, with one exception, fought out the usual 'Probables v Possibles' pipe opener. The receipts for the game as usual went to various charities and from a total of £79 10s 3d, the West Ham Hospital received £26 10s 3d. One of the adverts in the club programme publicized the 'Greengate Electric Theatre - The Latest and Most Popular Picture Show - Selected Cowboy and Indian & Sensational Dramas' 3d, 6d and 9d.

West Ham's opening Southern League fixture was a home meeting with Exeter City. There were four of the 'new men' in the side, a full-back partnership of George Irvine signed from Barrow, and Harry Forster from Sunderland, where the burly 29 year old had made 101 First Division appearances in various defensive positions. At centre half was Leslie (Billy) Askew ex-Aston Villa and Norwich. He would fill the boots of Frank Piercy on a permanent basis. At centre-forward was the young amateur from Ilford, Albert Denyer.

The Hammers opened the scoring after 15 minutes when Denyer lobbed a first time pass to Ashton who sent on to Shea. Pym, in the Exeter goal, had no chance with the shot that went in off the crossbar. The crowd were pleased to see the normally successful right wing partnership of Ashton and Shea together again following half a

Harry Forster

dozen matches at the back end of the previous campaign when Shea went to inside left. The second goal came about through Ashton's slipping past a defender and dropping the ball on Harrison's toe, and it was in the net in a flash. Left-winger Dawson hit the third just on half time. Just six minutes were taken for the interval as it was an extremely dark afternoon with a kick off at 5.20. Shea, who was in tremendous form, scored the fourth within three minutes of the restart, and a complete rout was on the cards. Twenty minutes from the end however, the buoyant mood of the crowd was almost stifled when the referee stopped the game owing to the increasing darkness, but after consulting his linesmen it was agreed to continue. This resulted in the correct decision as the storm cloud that had hovered over the ground, almost as if under instruction, miraculously disappeared. A fifth goal was nearly added, when a huge punt from the halfway line by Forster shot its way towards goal. When someone in the crowd called 'Let it go!' the defenders duly obliged, and with Pym beaten, the ball hit the post.

It had been a very confident start to the campaign. The two new full-backs had performed well, and Askew was cool and confident. As for the 19-year-old Denyer, his display was up to the standard of the other forwards. His only possible drawback was his light frame and lack of inches, but there was time for him to 'fill out'. 'Bert' would actually have not been in the team, had it not been for an ankle injury George Hilsdon picked up in training. 'Gatling Gun', as George had become known, was back at West Ham after an absence of six complete seasons with Chelsea. His record there had been phenomenal with 98 goals in 150 Football League appearances, and 13 goals in just eight England games. He had fallen out with the West London club who were not at all satisfied with his latest form, which they attributed to his private lifestyle. As far as the Hammers were concerned he was a good acquisition. At 27 years old, almost to the day he signed, he had plenty of skill and experience to benefit the club in future.

With Hilsdon still unfit the same team was fielded for the visit of Coventry City to the Boleyn enclosure. Without knowing it at the time, the result of this game and that against Merthyr later in the campaign, would affect the final outcome of the club's standing in the Southern League. It is pure conjecture, but those results may possibly have also affected their whole future.

It was said that two decisions by the referee had a direct influence on the result. There was no doubt either that the home forwards had themselves to blame for some glaring misses when well placed. The visitors, it had to be admitted, put up a tremendous defensive performance into the bargain. With regard to the referee, (who like Coventry City originated from Warwickshire), awarded a penalty against Tommy Randall who ran across goal and cleared a high ball with an overhead kick. As Tommy fell back the ball touched his fingertips. This action had the effect of knocking the ball towards the goal, hardly a deliberate attempt to handle! Not so, according to the 'man in the middle'. With score 1-1 at the time, the visitors hit home the resultant penalty. The second debatable decision came later when Ashton had hit the ball towards goal and Coventry's Feebery handled in the area. To everyone's surprise the referee awarded a corner as the ball went out of play. Two points down the drain.

For the visit to Watford, young Albert Denyer was replaced by the legendary George Hilsdon, but George failed to shine on his initial reappearance for the club. The plaudits fell to Danny Shea who scored from a volley, and Fred Harrison who got on the scoresheet when he latched onto a loose ball and fired it into the net. According to the West Ham programme the following week, Harrison's goal *was met with the 'terrific silence' which is usual on provincial grounds when the home team is losing.'* Both goals came in the first half, but after the interval, with the home side desperate to get back into the game, play became rough and ragged. The final whistle brought relief from the poor quality, but it meant that the Hammers had made a winning start to their matches 'on the road'.

On the Tuesday following, the players had an unusual but enjoyable break in their training routine when they spent the day in Epping Forest. It was said that *'the long walk through the forest gave them an excellent appetite for the lunch provided by host John Jelly at the 'Blacksmiths Arms', and the afternoon was spent in gathering blackberries.'*

George Hilsdon

Weather conditions were perfect when Merthyr Town made their way from the Welsh valleys for their first ever visit to Upton Park. The club had been promoted from the second division of the Southern League, where that section was expressing a distinctly Welsh flavour in 1912/13 with ten of the thirteen clubs originating from the province. The band played 'Men of Harlech' when the Merthyr players ran on to the pitch, but ironically there was not one man in the team who was Welsh! One of those was former Hammer Charlie Craig, who had originally come down from his native Scotland in 1897 to work at Tates Sugar Refinery at Silvertown, and thence to Thames Ironworks where he was employed as a marine engine fitter, before playing as a professional with the Southern League side in 1899.

Captain Tommy Randall won the toss, and the visitors kicked off defending the North Bank end. Tommy was to receive a full-blown strike of the ball from a very short distance, and in a 'very low place', which left him squirming in agony. Unsurprisingly, he did not perform to his usual ability for some while. The interval arrived with a blank scoresheet, but only a minute after the restart Merthyr scored. Harrison later hit a post, and Randall, despite his discomfort, hit the bar from thirty yards out. With twelve minutes remaining a lovely move brought the equaliser. The ball went from Ashton to Harrison, and then on to Hilsdon who touched it on to Shea, and Danny made no mistake. Further pressure was unproductive and the match ended in a 1-1 draw.

With such tremendous fire-power in the front line, with Harrison in the centre and Hilsdon and Shea alongside, the Hammers should really have been scoring more goals, but this did shortly materialize when Millwall made the short journey to the Boleyn ground for the London FA Cup first round contest. No less than a crowd of 8,000 turned up for a late Monday afternoon kick off, so great was the rivalry for a competition that was not of such great importance other than one of pride. West Ham were behind at 0-1 and 1-2, but fought back to win by no less than 6-2, with Shea grabbing a hat trick, and Harrison, Hilsdon and Ashton providing the others. Proof that, on their day, the front line could deliver.

On the visit to New Cross during the previous season for a Southern league fixture, Millwall had been victorious by 5 goals to one. The 'Dockers' followers delighted in a refrain of 1,-2,-3,-4,-5. Now it was revenge time and pleasing to the ears as Hammers' fans chanted 1,2,3, – 4,5,6!!

West Ham reserves had made a very good start to their South Eastern League campaign. With victories against Brentford, Arsenal and Portsmouth under their belt the 'Stiffs' faced equally high-riding Chelsea at Upton Park. The West London club, even in those days, were recognised as a 'moneybags' concern as the West Ham programme for the day pointed out. *'You will witness a rousing game today for the visiting team will have all the talent (and money)......'.* This was also echoed in the local press, with the comments – *'Many first division southern teams cost less for wages than this 'reserve' lot of Chelsea......'.* That may well have been the case as the visitors gained the points in a 2-1 win.

On the same day the first team were visiting Crystal Palace at Sydenham. The contest was fairly even throughout as the 1-1 score suggests. There was a contrast regarding the respective goalkeeping displays. Joe Hughes was in top form for the Hammers, making several vital saves, whereas Johnson of Palace, despite being beaten only once had an uncertain game, taking risks with some very poor punching. West Ham's goal came from a penalty for hands which was hotly disputed. Hilsdon did the necessary, but at the final whistle a posse of police were called to protect the referee against, it was said, *'a hundred or so well-dressed hooligans.'* (One West Ham season ticket holder who made the trip to South London did not have a profitable day out, falling victim to a pickpocket inside the Palace ground).

When the Hammers played Queens Park Rangers at Park Royal in a benefit match for ex-West Ham player Billy Barnes, Harry Forster strained his knee which was to keep him sidelined for a couple of weeks. Benefit matches have their place, but players are often reluctant to appear for fear of unnecessary injuries.

It was around this time, with Thames Ironworks & Shipbuilding Company still in serious financial difficulties, that Clement Mackrow, one of the 'leading lights' in the company, was tragically killed at the level crossing at the works. Due to a possible misunderstanding at the crossing gates manned by a young attendant, Mr Mackrow was under the impression that the railway line was clear, and he drove across in his motor vehicle. A freight-train engine, apparently out of his vision when he set off, struck the car and killed Mr Mackrow instantly. Clement Mackrow who was 56, was the manager of the shipbuilding and Naval architect department, and had worked for the company for many years. There were several members and ex-members of the West Ham United directorate who knew Mackrow well through the club's connections to the Ironworks and were shocked and saddened at his untimely death.

Albert Denyer

Young Frank Burton made his debut at full-back in place of the injured Harry Forster for the visit of a first-rate Plymouth side that promised a good battle, but the Hammers were outstanding on the day, with all the front men's combination play bearing fruit. Ashton in his usual position on the right was responsible for the making of all three goals. In the first half his dropping pass enabled Hilsdon to hit the ball first time into the net, and Dawson scored with a stinging shot, again from Ashton's cross. After the break, Horne in the Plymouth goal punched away Ashton's shot, but Shea, manoeuvring the ball to his advantage, hit it home. Plymouth replied late on after Rothwell had given away a free kick.

An unchanged team collected another two points on the visit to the Dell to play Southampton. After Hilsdon had scored from the penalty spot, the Hammers' excellent forward play was a joy to watch as Shea scored with a half-backward kick over the heads of the opposing defenders (a speciality of his, that did not always come off) which left the goalkeeper helpless. Harrison and Hilsdon sprayed the ball about with 'mathematical precision' before Shea scored the third, and the Saints got a consolation goal for a final score of 3-1. It was acknowledged by the opposition that West Ham were the best team to visit the Dell so far.

The reserves were still doing well with Frank Piercy responsible for picking his fair share of local players in all matches, and in the latest triumph young Albert Denyer scored both goals in a 2-0 victory over Spurs reserves.

Tommy Robinson's benefit match took place on the following Monday against QPR. This was a friendly fixture that unfortunately only attracted a crowd of 2,000, but was entertaining enough, despite some whistling of 'Dear old Pals'. Although there was no hint of 'rough stuff', the oddest feature of the game was the fact that West Ham were awarded three penalties, with George Hilsdon scoring all three, in a 3-2 victory.

The Hammers received a setback to their progress when Reading were the visitors. The 'Biscuitmen' played very much what we would now call a 'closing down game', which was unusual at the time, and it threw West Ham out of gear, and an injury to Woodards certainly did not help the cause. Once the visitors got two goals ahead it was all over, despite Hilsdon scoring yet again from the penalty spot.

On the same day, there were interesting West Ham connections at Bingley Road, Custom House where the locals were playing Barking in a South Essex League match. (The Custom House ground would later become transformed into the West Ham Stadium with a capacity of 80,000 and where the West Ham Speedway team would make its home). The Custom House team had Dan Bailey at inside right. Dan was to make his debut for the Hammers later in the season. In the Barking side was Arthur Featherstone ex- West Ham United (1905-1908) and Jack Tresadern, a future star at the Boleyn ground.

To move forward in the London FA Cup a victory was needed against QPR, which was gained after a continuous bombardment on the visitors' goal, where Shaw was outstanding for Rangers. Much more pressure brought its reward when Shaw punched the ball into his own net, and then Ashton scored a second before the finish. At Norwich, rain came down in torrents after early fog, but the home side were dominant from the start. With the absence of Woodards, Forster was moved to right half from left back, which was not a success, and with Randall having an unusually poor game the Norwich forwards ran the game. This gave Joe Hughes in goal, the chance to shine and he proved to be the Hammers' best player. Another injury, this time to Hilsdon, who left the field with half an hour to go, was an additional blow, and the Norfolk side ran out winners by two goals to nil.

A long journey to Devon in midweek saw a disappointing display in front of a poor attendance of 2,000 against Exeter City, although a point was gained in a 0-0 draw.

When Gillingham (ex-New Brompton) came up from Kent to the Boleyn enclosure the Hammers had Jack Casey, signed from Bromley, in the team at outside left, for his first game, and young 'Bert' Denyer at centre-forward. Hilsdon was back in, and the forward line had some real goalscoring potential. After twenty minutes of attacking play, George Hilsdon put away yet another penalty, after a defender had handled. With only another five minutes gone Hilsdon hit home a left foot drive, and West Ham were well in command. The third home goal followed on the half hour mark when Bert Denyer, who was brought down in the act of shooting, got straight up, and hit the ball into the top of the net. Perhaps the referee felt sorry for 'The Gills', for with fourteen minutes of the half still to go, he blew up for half time, much to the amusement of the crowd. Realising his mistake, the game continued. The Hammers added just one more goal after the break, when neat work involving Shea and Hilsdon enabled Denyer to score from close range.

Jack Casey

The result meant a rise to a respectable position in the table and sent the home crowd away in a happy mood. Some may have spent their Saturday evening at the East Ham Electric Theatre (opposite East Ham Station), where the film 'Queen Bess' starring Sarah Bernhardt was being shown, in what was billed as 'The greatest historical film ever produced.'

On the following Monday, those with the means to do so, made their way to Upton Park to see a friendly game against Manchester City. It was said that the match was arranged as part of the transfer deal regarding George Webb's move to the northern club. George actually made only two starts for City, before injury kept him out, but there were repercussions about the whole affair later, as will be seen.

As for the game itself it was very much something of an exhibition match. With the visitors going in front, Shea equalised before half time, when instead of retiring to the dressing rooms, Oxo was served out to the players on the pitch. The final result was a 4-2 win for the First Division side, with Shea also scoring Hammers' second.

Even with Hilsdon out with a groin strain West Ham were still on the 'goal trail' at Northampton when the team scored three. Burrill, Casey and Shea all found the net. Sadly, the home side scored four. Despite the result, it was a cracking game, even for the band of supporters who made the journey by excursion train from St Pancras for a return fare of 4 shillings and three pence.

Still in a scoring mood, the Hammers met Chelsea at the 'Den' in midweek in the semi-final of the London FA Cup. The First Division side presumed that they would more or less just need to turn up to face a team that they described as 'containing a forward line consisting of diddling schoolboys and an old crock.' Hilsdon was out for revenge, and he hit two goals, with Shea and Askew scoring the others in a 4-0 humiliation of the West London side.

The proceeds of the benefit match for Tom Robinson were announced, and the old trainer was said to be happy with his lot. In the West Ham match programme it stated that '£75.10s was the amount raised for Tommy Robinson's benefit and on Monday his smiling face was seen in the London and Provincial Bank.'

Queens Park Rangers came to Upton Park as Southern League champions and were riding high in the league again. The teams had already met three times, in the LFA Cup and in two benefit matches, but the league game was much more important. It was a compelling contest, but the Hammers excelled themselves with some great attacking play. The visitors did not have a shot at goal until the 25th minute and that was wide of the mark. In fact Joe Hughes did not handle the ball until the 35th minute. Rangers had more of the game after the interval, but the Hammers were still on top with the Ashton/Shea partnership, assisted very ably by Whiteman at right half, making some delightful attacking triangular movements. The only goal of the encounter came when Ashton lobbed into the opposition area. Hilsdon bobbed down for Denyer to head past Shaw. Hilsdon, in his excitement, grabbed the lightweight Denyer, lifted him up, and carried him several yards in celebration. Who said players of many years past did not show their excitement and satisfaction at a job well done?

After the good form, and goals, of recent matches, it was pure West Ham for the visit to Griffin Park to meet Brentford. The 'Bees' were in a sorry state close to bottom and playing poorly. For the Boleyn lads, it was a case of 'the poorer the opposition, the poorer the display.'

The home crowd were expecting another defeat for their favourites, but it was said that the Hammers were shaping up 'like the song of the Boer War period "Don't be in a hurry boys, wait a week or two."' The Brentford supporters were already barracking their own team when Sibbald struck a shot from fully thirty yards past Joe Hughes, and it stayed that way till half time. For the first half, and at the beginning of the second, the target for the crowd's abuse was the 'Bees' centre-forward Chapple. The expression is often used 'football is a funny old game', and so it proved as throughout the course of the final 40 minutes the same player scored a hat-trick, and Brentford eventually won by 5-1. It was pure hypocrisy when the home crowd gave him a standing ovation at the finish.

With Millwall as the visitors a 16,000 crowd was present for the usual local derby. The game was played at a fast and furious pace, which was normal for this fixture, but the Hammers had a slight edge throughout. It was Hilsdon who opened the scoring with a strong oblique shot, something which he almost repeated before the break. Tension was always evident between the teams, but the referee, a Mr Sant, took the sting out of several incidents. One example came when Askew lunged unfairly at Vincent, and the 'man in the middle' with a smile, cuddled the two players round the neck and 'literally rushed them into good humour.' The game was essentially one with defences on top, but the visitors did equalise much to the home crowd's disappointment.

West Ham had not beaten Bristol Rovers at Eastville since the opening day of the 1901/02 season, and despite a dazzling display of pure football, they could not turn their superior play into goals, except the lone tally from Denyer in a 1-2 defeat. Shea and Hilsdon had great performances in all but

Dan Woodards

scoring, and Casey showed his phenomenal speed on the left wing. He was responsible for supplying the Hammers' goal when, it was reported, 'he got away from Phillips like a racer from a dray-horse.' The visitors' best player was the balding Tommy Randall, showing his old form with 'his shining cranium bobbing up at every turn.'

At the 'Den' on the Monday following, the Final of the London FA Cup took place before a 9,000 crowd against Crystal Palace. A scoreless draw was finally a fair result with the replay to come at White Hart Lane.

The Hammers, with their fine football of recent games, deserved a positive victory, and it came against Swindon at Upton Park. With a solid display at the back with Irvine and Rothwell in fine form, as was the half-back line of Woodards, Askew and Randall, the Railwaymen had little chance to shine. Bert Denyer, slight of frame, but with brilliant skills, was now fitting in perfectly with the pace and trickery of Shea and the experience of Hilsdon. Add the outstanding wing play of 'Tiddler' Ashton and now the speed of Casey on the opposite flank, the forward line was potentially lethal.

Arguably, these five forwards were the best line to appear, as a forward unit over the whole 1900-1915 period. It is a great pity that these five did not appear together more than the 8 occasions that they actually did.

Bearing this in mind West Ham finished 4-1 winners and every one of their goals was a gem. The first came after only three minutes. Hilsdon had the ball at his feet at about twenty yards out. With defenders closing down he feinted to pass out to Casey, but changed feet to pass to Denyer, who had the ball in the net directly. After 22 minutes Denyer tried a long shot, but Hilsdon, already in the penalty area, brought the ball down, turned quickly and hit the ball into the net. When Randall stopped the ball from going out, he passed directly to Hilsdon who left-footed number three. Denyer immediately hugged George round the neck and '*kissed him affectionately.*' (!) With fifteen minutes to go Shea dribbled past three players, and slipped the ball to Ashton. He, in turn, centred high to Denyer who headed home the fourth.

The Hammers' display contrasted with that of the replay of the LFA Cup Final at White Hart Lane, which Crystal Palace won by the only goal in a distinctly moderate encounter.

As mentioned previously the Thames Ironworks, Shipbuilding & Engineering Company went into receivership in November 1911. Because the Company had only received orders from Turkey for three steamers during 1912, and the Admiralty's orders went to the Northern Shipyards, the Receiver finally wound up the business resulting in the loss of 3,000 local jobs. A notice was placed on the gates, of the Thames Ironworks Company signed by the Receiver, Mr F Smart:-

'*I regret to state that I am instructed to close these works on this day, Saturday December 21st 1912. All workmen can claim their back pay on Tuesday December 24th.*'

In January Arnold Hills took the case of closure to the Court of Appeal pleading that he might be given liberty to borrow a further sum of £50,000 to carry on the business, in addition to £35,000 already borrowed. He also wrote to four local councils, West Ham, East Ham, Poplar and Greenwich for some financial assistance. Although they supported in principle his proposals for the reconstruction the Thames Ironworks, they could not help. As it was, the Court of Appeal, after all the facts had been taken into consideration, dismissed the appeal. The bond and close association with West Ham United was over in one sense, but historically and spiritually it would never be broken.

The Hammers gave their fans a pre-Christmas present when the club visited Fratton Park to play Portsmouth, coming away with both points after a solid performance. Harry Forster, coming in for George Irvine at left back, was the only change. The indomitable pairing of Ashton and Shea saw them scoring the goals in a 2-1 victory, which moved the team up to seventh place in the table.

Drizzling rain greeted those keen to see West Ham meet Stoke City at Upton Park on Christmas morning with a kick off at 11.00am, and in the uncovered areas a sea of umbrellas was on display. The 'Potters' were languishing at the bottom of the league, but would poor opposition provide one of those poor displays by the Hammers? Not so, as Ashton scored an early goal, and on twenty minutes Denyer added another. Askew hit the third just two minutes later. The game was virtually over before half time when Shea, after a mazy run, passed to Ashton. His cross fell straight on to Danny's head and he made it 4-0.

In the muddy conditions the Stoke City players could not keep their feet, but after the break it was the turn of West Ham to slip and slide. This did not stop an excellent move involving Casey, Hilsdon and Denyer, finishing in Shea scoring the fifth. Any further incentive then fell away, and the visitors got into the game without scoring. Right at the finish, Hilsdon failed to convert an easy opening. He could hardly be blamed - he was literally covered in mud from head to toe. Heading was particularly a problem for players in such conditions, with a heavy ball and its deadly injurious lace-up made even heavier from the clinging mud.

Those that saw the match from the covered terrace opposite the stand (i.e. the 'chicken run') now had the benefit of a rear-centre exit gate, recently installed to relieve congestion. Yet another improvement to the ground as a whole.

The return game with Stoke City on Boxing Day resulted in a 1-0 victory, which meant a fourth consecutive win, and a climb to fourth position in the table.

At Coventry City the run came to an end. Fred Blackburn, still with the club, and helping the young players in the reserves, came in to the left half position for the injured Tommy Randall. Coventry were becoming something of a bogy team as their victory over the Hammers was their fourth 'on the trot' against the Boleyn boys, and although the Midland side deserved their win, an injury to George Hilsdon in the first half, and his non-appearance in the second, had a distinct influence on the final margin of 4 goals to 1.

The result of the contest against Watford at the Boleyn ground was of little significance compared to the news that the incomparable Danny Shea would be making his final appearance for West Ham United in the Southern League. Blackburn Rovers had obtained his signature and he would be playing regular First Division football. Not only had he been the leading Southern League scorer in 1909/10 and 1910/11, he hit 111 goals in 179 Southern League matches for the Hammers, an unbelievable scoring rate. It was a wonder that he had not been lured away much sooner than he had. Whilst he was with the Lancashire club he scored 61 goals in 97 matches and helped Rovers to the First Division title in 1913/14, also gaining two England caps whilst there. During the First World War, with the Football

League competition suspended, he played 73 matches for the Hammers in the London Combination as a guest player scoring 64 goals, albeit that the competition was not at the highest level. After leaving Blackburn he returned to Upton Park in 1920, but played just 16 games before leaving for Fulham. He later appeared for Coventry, Clapton Orient and Sheppey United. During the Southern League period he was probably the most revered player of that era at West Ham United, and will always be part of the folklore at the club. Shea had many attributes. Like many exceptional forward players, he had a low centre of gravity at 5ft 6in, and with his chunky build he had perfect balance. He had speed, trickery and a tremendous shot. He was versatile, combined well with colleagues and was a strong header of the ball. Above all he was a goalgetter, from all angles and at any distance. He was a big loss to the East End club.

In Shea's final game it was appropriate that he would score in the 2-0 victory over Watford, although his last goal was a penalty. Off the field there was, naturally, much discourse and disappointment over the loss of Danny, even to the point of some of the supporters boycotting the club. It is always sickening for supporters when a star player leaves to join another side, but sadly for the smaller clubs this is just a fact of life in the football business. Most transfers result in a favourable financial return for the player concerned, and even at this time the maximum wage, which was now pitched at £5 per week, depending on certain conditions, was not always paid to professionals, especially by the poorer clubs. Players could however, gain by agreeing a reasonable cut of the transfer fee, and in Shea's case he took 35% of the fee of £2,000 (a record at the time) which amounted to £700, an awful lot of money in 1913.

It was generally considered, that without Shea, West Ham would suffer at the hands of First Division West Bromwich Albion when the clubs met at the Hawthorns in the first round of the FA Cup. The Albion had been FA Cup runners up in the previous season, but reputation counted for nothing as the Hammers more than held their own and gained a draw, with the replay just three days later.

15,000 witnessed the replay at Upton Park, and by half time the tie already seemed to have been settled with West Brom two goals ahead. When Askew was injured and limping throughout the second half things could not have been worse, but the Hammers found something extra 'in the locker' and when Hilsdon scored, the visitors faltered and Ashton supplied Hilsdon with equaliser with 18 minutes remaining. Extra time brought no further score and a second replay was required.

Before West Ham returned to the Hawthorns to continue the cup saga, a Southern League fixture had to be completed in far away Wales against Merthyr Town. Syd King and the directors made no less than seven changes to the team that fought out the cup-tie. Considering the circumstances at the time this was probably the most practical decision to make. The team had put all their strength into the West Bromwich game just two days

before, and there was still the prospect of causing an upset. Making further progress was perhaps considered more important than possibly conceding league points, especially from a financial viewpoint. Nevertheless even one point here would have made a difference to their final league position.

At one point in the clash in the Welsh Valleys the Hammers were 2-1 up, but they fell away disastrously in the second half, and suffered a defeat by no less than six goals to two. Along with the loss at Brentford this was the worst defeat of the season.

Maybe the West Bromwich Albion side thought that West Ham's result against Merthyr would pave the way for an easy victory in the second replay, but they were in for a nasty shock. In the absence of Askew, Harrison switched from centre-forward to centre half, and was a qualified success. George Butcher was at inside right in a forward line shuffle. Wasting no time in attacking, the game was only seven minutes old when Denyer struck the first goal. Given heart the Hammers dominated from then on and Hilsdon scored before the break. When the same player netted within seven minutes of the second, it was all over apart for some late West Brom pressure, which was easily dealt with. Unbelievably, 3-0 to the Hammers!

At the half yearly meeting of the shareholders, Mr White, the vice chairman stated that ' *the gate receipts had gone up all round, with the expenses diminished. Total receipts up to December 31*st *were £5,088 and expenditure £3,653. The average Southern League gate was £365 as against £297 the previous year. South Eastern League gates were £56 as against £40, and London League gates £27 against £19.*'

After attacking the press for what they had printed regarding both George Webb and Danny Shea, the vice chairman first dealt with the case of George Webb. He stated that '*...... the club did not receive a halfpenny for his transfer. George Webb knew all about the friendly match* (with Manchester City) *and as far as the Board were concerned, they had clean hands. They were acting within the law......*' He then went on to deal with the question of the amateur's training on the West Ham ground. He stated that '*George Webb had been at liberty to train on the Boleyn ground, but there was a rule that only players who had signed some League form for the club were allowed to train there. Any old player signing South Eastern League forms could have the liberty of training on the ground. Manchester City were informed of this, and they could have told George Webb.*'

There are a number of unanswered questions regarding George Webb's transfer. After making just two starts for City, and after receiving an injury in the second, he remained on the injury list until he discovered that a fee was accepted for his transfer. He immediately resigned from the club. If this was indeed the case why did the West Ham board deny that any fee was received? If George was aware of the friendly match, there is also the question of the destination of the receipts for the match. With respect to the liberty to train at the Boleyn ground, surely the West Ham board could equally have informed George of the conditions?

With regard to the case of Danny Shea it was stated that '*they had the liberty under the rules to make any arrangements, and what they had done they had done in the interests of three parties – Shea, the Blackburn Rovers, and West Ham. Shea asked to be put on the transfer list, knowing that he was entitled to a proportion of any fee received. With regard to Shea's promised benefit, the £200 guaranteed was the player's own figure, as was every other arrangement in his agreement, and they as a board had carried them out. Shea......was supposed to have said in an interview that he was dissatisfied with the way he had been treated.*'

Harold Caton

This was repudiated, and in a letter received from Shea, and read out at the meeting, the gist of it was that he thanked the directors for the way he had been treated.

West Ham had been drawn away to Aston Villa in the second round of the FA Cup, but before that game they had an important meeting with high-flying Crystal Palace at Upton Park. The Hammers were well on top before the break when only Johnson in the visitors' goal kept them out. Forster received a foot injury on half time and did not appear for the second half, which changed the game in Palace's favour, even though George Butcher scored in the first minute on their return to the field. Then, under pressure due to being down to ten men, a blunder in the defence led to the visitors equalising.

The much-anticipated 2nd Round FA Cup match at Villa Park, proved to be great disappointment to everyone connected with the club. Aston Villa opened the scoring very early on, forcing the Hammers on the back foot straight away. Faced by a very clever and skilful side, they were overwhelmed and by the 60th minute the score was 5-0. In the remaining half an hour West Ham had eleven men behind the ball just to keep the score down. It was scant consolation that Villa would eventually go on to lift the trophy after a 1-0 victory over Sunderland in the final at the Crystal Palace.

When the Hammers visited Plymouth Argyle, the club were in equal fourth place in the Southern League alongside Millwall and Exeter. At the top were QPR, followed by Reading in second and Crystal Palace in third. Argyle were in eighth place seven points behind the leaders, but their position by the end of the season would change dramatically.

West Ham opened their account when Dan Woodards scored direct from a free kick after Butcher had been fouled. This kind of goal was most unusual for West Ham at the time, but was very welcome. Plymouth attacked, but Henry Carter who had come into the side, showed a very safe and clean pair of hands between the sticks. After the interval Hilsdon was playing particularly well, distributing like a half-back, but very dangerous in front of goal, and combining well with Bert Denyer. It was the latter who wrapped the game with a goal after a pass from Caton.

With Southampton having a poor season by their standards, it was frustrating that a point was dropped at home in a 1-1 draw. Harrison, still playing in his temporary role at centre half due to Askew's injury, scored first when a speculative lob from distance dropped over ex-Hammer George Kitchen. George had received a great ovation when he took the field on his first appearance at the Boleyn since he left the club. Henry Carter, on the other hand, had the bad luck to be flattened after going up for a cross, and with the ball running loose Saint's Kimpson run the ball into an empty net. The rules did not extend towards protection for goalkeepers in such an instance.

Following the club's statement regarding their relationship with Danny Shea, West Ham confirmed their appreciation and their amicable understanding with the player when it was stated in the club programme that:-

'Our Chairman and Vice Chairman paid a visit last night to the Salisbury Hotel where the Rovers are staying the weekend, and presented Danny with a gold watch on which was the following inscription:-

Presented to Danny Shea by the Directors of the West Ham United Football Co. Ltd, after five years service. With best wishes for his future welfare.'

The expression 'The King is dead! Long live the King!' is appropriate at this point. After the final salutations to Danny Shea, enter Syd Puddefoot. Syd was a local boy born in Bow, and a pupil at Park School, well-known as the prolific producer of good class players to West Ham United. Playing in local football, the eighteen year old came to the notice of Syd King, the West Ham manager, who signed him. He came into the reserve team at the Boleyn and played in the both competitions of the South Eastern League and the London League, and immediately made an impact as an exceptional marksman from day one. Making his reserve debut at Watford he scored two goals in a 4-3 victory. That was just the start. In six competitive matches, 'Puddy', as he became known, scored 15 goals, including 6 against Waltham in the London League and a hat-trick against Reading in the South Eastern League. Quite a phenomenal beginning.

With this in mind he was given a chance in the first eleven against Norwich at Upton Park. The senior league was a different 'kettle of fish', but it would give Syd a taste of a higher grade and an idea of what to expect. As it was, he was well held by the Norwich defenders in a game that the Hammers won without being too convincing in a 2-1 victory. Going behind in the first half, a bizarre incident gave them an equaliser. Mellor, the visitors' 'keeper, fielded a long shot just in front of his left hand post with Puddefoot rushing in. He then held the ball over his head rather dramatically, and with the forward just a yard away gently lobbed it to a defender standing close by. The latter, seemingly confused, caught it, and a penalty was given. Hilsdon thankfully converted.

At Gillingham a better performance should have led to both points, but a 2-2 draw was the final outcome with Casey scoring both goals.

Another youngster, nineteen year old Dan Bailey, and one who also had an eye for goal, had been persuaded to join the club from Custom House FC in January. On the day that the first team were in Kent, Dan appeared for the reserves at the Boleyn against Croydon Common in the South Eastern League. The 'stiffs' won 5-0, and Bailey scored all five!

Syd King, after resting Bert Denyer, immediately brought Bailey into the side for the home game against Northampton. Now, along with Puddefoot, both high scoring youngsters were in the forward line, but everyone drew a blank in a 0-0 draw, despite Forster, captain for the day in the absence of Randall, changing things around in the second half.

Dan Bailey

Although a point was picked up against Brighton at the Boleyn enclosure on Good Friday, it should have been a victory. When Brighton's Booth was injured with two colleagues helping him to his feet, the West Ham players stopped, and the opposition went on and scored, emphasising the advice 'Play to the whistle!' This occurred just two minutes from the end. Askew, at centre half, was criticised for 'hampering the backs' instead of feeding his forwards, and Casey, on the wing with his turn of speed, for 'falling back and helping the defence'! *'Backs worth their salt prefer to be unhampered by zealous forwards and halves, and, when they break up an attack, like to see their own attacking force in readiness to receive the wing punt.'* Thus wrote the local scribe. This criticism at the time, shows how much the game has altered over the last 100 years or so.

The 1-1 result meant the third consecutive draw, and the chance of lifting the Southern League title which was there for the taking, was becoming more confused. No less than *eight* teams were involved. Crystal Palace led on 38 points, and West Ham, QPR, and Millwall in 6th, 7th, and 8th respectively, all had 35.

His short run of experience over, Puddefoot was replaced by Denyer, and it was he who scored the vital winner at Park Royal against close rival Queens Park Rangers, on Easter Saturday. Every one of the Hammers' team could be congratulated on their display on a pitch that was like a lake, but Forster's play at full-back was exceptional. Joe Hughes, in goal, was also at his best. The difference between football then and the modern game was emphasised again when Joe, on one occasion fell with the ball under him and several Rangers' players were attempting to kick it from him, without the referee taking any action. Joe held on and kicked clear.

The return encounter with Brighton & Hove Albion came on Easter Monday. The Hammers had an absolutely appalling record at the Goldstone Ground having drawn one and lost eight over the last nine seasons. Still a victory eluded them but a 0-0 draw broke a run of six consecutive defeats at Brighton. A draw was a fair result with both team's defences being impassable, and Forster, once again being the best defender on the field.

With a home fixture against a Brentford side that were heading for relegation, and with the memory of a 1-5 defeat earlier in the season, there was enough incentive to go for an impressive victory. There was still the prospect of a Southern League title as the team were just 3 points behind the leaders (now Exeter City). The end result was indeed a victory, but by the narrow margin of 2-1. The main talking point was the switching of Ashton over to the left wing, with Caton coming in on the right. In addition, Harrison came in at right half, an unaccustomed position for him. Forster was also out with a knee injury, so Frank Burton came in at left back. Apart from the changes, the players surprisingly just went 'through the motions', and the visitors in all honesty were unlucky to lose.

Playing with what was considered the usual line-up, there was definitely a different spirit in the side for the short trip to Millwall. This proved to be a good performance especially playing into a strong wind in the first half, when Dan Bailey ran close in to beat the offside trap and scored. Millwall were demoralised for a while in the second half as Ashton scored inside two minutes. Randall, just 4 minutes later, right on the wing and the halfway line, took a kick that was carried by the strong wind towards goal. Spendiff, the Millwall goalkeeper reached up, caught the ball and let it slip through his hands. 3-0 to the Hammers. The home side pulled one back, but it was a very important two points. West Ham were now just two points behind Swindon at the top of the table.

To keep up the pressure, a victory against Bristol Rovers was needed and the Hammers duly obliged. Randall opened the scoring with a left foot drive inside five minutes. It was one-way traffic from then on with just about everyone in the side having a 'pop' at goal, without adding to the score. When Woodards retired with a cut head before half time, it could have altered the game, but after the break Askew increased the lead with a swerving shot from fully thirty yards out. Woodards then returned, but strangely enough Rovers pulled one back from a shot that Carter should have saved. Further pressure from West Ham however saw Hilsdon head home from Ashton's free kick.

Mention must be made here of Dan Woodards, who had been a loyal servant to the Irons since 1906/07 when he first made his debut. Including that campaign and the following four consecutive seasons his first team appearances read 2, 1, 0 (he appeared for Hastings during that campaign), 2, and 5. From 1911/12 to 1914/15 he was to make a further total of 99 Southern League appearances. Truly, the perfect example of a loyal player biding his time until he made a position in the team his own! Nicknamed both 'Dapper Dan' and 'Beau Brummel' due to his smart turn-out and appearance, he went on to play during the Great War in the London Combination. When the club were admitted to the Football League Second Division he played in 16 matches over two seasons, and later assisted the reserves, eventually becoming club groundsman. Dan was the only person at the Boleyn enclosure in August 1944, when a German V1 'Doodlebug' landed on the ground and destroyed part of the South Bank. Dan was a 'bit worse for wear' but was more concerned about the state of the pitch!

Before the vital clash with Swindon, the Wiltshire club had played one other game in midweek and drawn. This meant that Swindon had 47 points with Plymouth Argyle and West Ham on 44, Crystal Palace on 43, and QPR, Millwall and Exeter on 42. Tight, to say the least.

The home club had assigned this fixture as a benefit for their English International Harold Fleming, which was commendable, as all the receipts from the game would go to the player. Fleming was a prolific goalscorer for Swindon and before the First World War he made eleven appearances for the England side.

Ten minutes before the start a hailstorm caused a large portion of the crowd to dash for cover, and even the band took shelter whilst continuing to play. When the hail ceased, there was a strong wind blowing down the pitch, not the most ideal conditions to play under. Fleming himself scored for the home side inside the first twenty five minutes, when the 'Railwaymen' were on top, but after that opening period, it was all West Ham, and Denyer made a brilliant run, poking the ball home as the opposing 'keeper came out. Despite not adding to their score the Hammers' effort and skill could not be faulted, but the game ended in a 1-1 draw. A similar score at Reading meant that any hope of taking the Southern League title was over as an amazing winning run of five matches by Plymouth Argyle, put the Devon side on top with a superior goal average and a game in hand.

For the final match of the season Portsmouth were the visitors. They brought a raucous crowd of soldiers and sailors to give them support, with one sporting a megaphone. He did not have much to shout about when the Pompey 'keeper carried the ball outside the area and the referee awarded a free kick. Hilsdon shaped to take the kick, but Ashton nipped in to score, with the opposing defenders looking at one another. The Hammers went down to ten men just before the interval when Casey had his foot trodden on. Pompey took advantage of the extra man and scored, and when they nearly repeated that, a spectator fell over the barrier on to the pitch in his excitement. Play became quite vicious at times, but it was not helped by some strange decisions from the referee. West Ham managed to wrap the game up in the 25th minute of the half when Denyer hit the crossbar, and Bailey scored from the rebound. Despite being a man short, there were a number of near misses and the Hammers finished the campaign on a winning note.

Plymouth won the title with 50 points, Swindon followed with 48 and West Ham finished also on 48, but were third due to their inferior goal average.

Season 1912/13 had been the club's best campaign so far, but for the sake of just three points it would have meant the Southern League title coming to the Boleyn. The loss of Danny Shea in mid season was quite significant, although very strangely the team, immediately after he left, went on an unbeaten run of 15 games right to the end of the season. Three matches stand out for the loss of those three vital points: (1) Coventry City at home, where the referee gave two vital decisions which cost at least a point; (2) The decision, which was understandable at the time due to the FA Cup commitments, to field six reserves for the game at Merthyr, where a 2-1 half time lead turned into a 2-6 defeat; and (3) the dropping of a home point against an average Northampton side.

Had West Ham United have won the title, the directors may have sought permission to join the Football League, and it is likely that they would have been accepted. How would the club's history have altered? Football, of course, is full of 'shoulds' and 'might-have-beens' and 'ifs' and 'buts'.

The campaign must also be remembered for the performances of the reserve eleven as a whole and a number of its unsung individuals. There were two leagues that were competed for — the South Eastern League and the London League. The Hammers won the latter and finished runners-up in the former, just two points behind Chelsea, who had players in their second eleven on the full first team maximum wage of £4 per week at the time.

The players that were more or less regulars in the reserve side, were full-back Frank Burton, half-backs Frank Redward, Bob Whiteman and Fred Blackburn who was captain, and forwards George Butcher, Dan Bailey, Jack Mackesy, Frank Burrill, Harold Caton and Harold Dawson. Others that gave good displays on a number of occasions were Henry Carter in goal, George Irvine, Reynolds, Fred Harrison, Syd Puddefoot, Morfee, Stan Bourne (in a rare appearance at outside left), George Walden, Pedley, Chapman, Rodgers, W. Bourne (signed late on from Crystal Palace), and a player for the future; Jack Tresadern.

West Ham,
Ashton Shea Askew Dawson Rothwell Hilsdon Burton Hughes Harrison Woodards Randall

1912/13

13th in Southern League Division One

#		Date	Opponent	Score	Scorers	Att	Ashton H	Askew W	Bailey D	Blackburn F	Burrill F	Burton F	Butcher G	Carter H	Casey J	Caton H	Dawson H	Denyer A	Forster H	Harrison F	Hilsdon G	Hughes J	Irvine G	Mackesy J	Puddefoot S	Randall T	Rothwell J	Shea D	Whiteman R	Woodards D
1	Sep	2	EXETER CITY	4-0	Shea 2, Dawson, Harrison	9000	7	5									11	9	3	10		1	2			6		8		4
2		7	COVENTRY CITY	1-2	Ashton	12000	7	5									11	9	3	10		1	2			6		8		4
3		14	Watford	2-0	Harrison, Shea	5000	7	5									11	9	3	10		1	2			6		8		4
4		21	MERTHYR TOWN	1-1	Shea	7000	7	5									11		3	10	9	1	2			6		8		4
5		28	Crystal Palace	1-1	Hilsdon	15000	7	5									11		3	10	9	1	2			6		8		4
6	Oct	5	PLYMOUTH ARGYLE	3-1	Dawson, Hilsdon, Shea	8000	7	5				3					11			9	10	1				6	2	8		4
7		12	Southampton	3-1	Shea 2, Hilsdon	9000	7	5				3					11			9	10	1				6	2	8		4
8		19	READING	1-2	Hilsdon	15000	7	5									11			9	10	1				6	2	8		4
9		26	Norwich City	0-2		7000	7	5									11		3	9	10	1				6	2	8		
10		30	Exeter City	0-0		2000	7	5			10							9		11		1	3			6	2	8		
11	Nov	2	GILLINGHAM	4-0	Denyer 2, Hilsdon 2	10000	7	5							11			9			10	1	3			6	2	8	4	
12		9	Northampton Town	3-4	Burrill, Casey, Shea	6000	7	5			10				11			9				1	3			6	2	8	4	
13		16	QUEEN'S PARK RANGERS	1-0	Denyer	14000	7	5							11			9		10		1	3			6	2	8	4	
14		23	Brentford	1-5	Shea	7000	7	5							11			9		10		1	3			6	2	8	4	
15		30	MILLWALL	1-1	Hilsdon	16000	7	5							11			9		10		1	3			6	2	8	4	
16	Dec	7	Bristol Rovers	1-2	Ashton	8000	7								11			9		10		1	3			6	2	8		4
17		14	SWINDON TOWN	4-1	Denyer 2, Hilsdon 2	14000	7	5					5		11			10		9		1	3			6	2	8		4
18		21	Portsmouth	2-1	Ashton, Shea	10000	7	5							11			9		10		1	3			6	2	8		4
19		25	STOKE	5-0	Shea 2, Ashton, Askew, Denyer	8000	7	5							11			9	3	10		1				6	2	8		4
20		26	Stoke	1-0	Shea	5000	7	5							11			9	3	10		1				6	2	8		4
21		28	Coventry City	1-4	Shea	7000	7	5		6					11			9	3	10		1					2	8		4
22	Jan	4	WATFORD	2-0	Harrison, Shea	10000	7	5							11			10		9		1	3			6	2	8		4
23		18	Merthyr Town	2-6	Butcher 2	4000			6				8		7	11		9		5		1	3	10			2		4	
24		25	CRYSTAL PALACE	1-1	Butcher	14000	7						8		11			9	3	5	10	1				6	2		4	
25	Feb	8	Plymouth Argyle	2-0	Denyer, Woodards	8000							8	1	11	7		9	3	5	10					6	2			4
26		15	SOUTHAMPTON	1-1	Harrison	5000	7						2	8	1	11		9	3	5	10					6				4
27	Mar	1	NORWICH CITY	2-1	Hilsdon 2	8000	7								11			8	3	5	10	1				6	2			4
28		8	Gillingham	2-2	Casey 2	5000	7								11			8	3	5	10	1		9		6	2			4
29		15	NORTHAMPTON T	0-0		9000	7		8						11				3	5	10	1		9		6	2			4
30		21	BRIGHTON & HOVE ALB.	1-1	Puddefoot	15000	7	5	8						11				3		10	1		9			2		6	4
31		22	Queen's Park Rangers	1-0	Denyer	10000	7	5	8						11			9	3		10	1		9		6	2			4
32		24	Brighton & Hove Albion	0-0		11000	7	5	8						11			9	3		10	1				6	2			4
33		29	BRENTFORD	2-1	Denyer, Hilsdon	7000	11	5	8			3		1		7		9		4	10					6	2			4
34	Apr	5	Millwall	3-1	Ashton, Bailey, Randall	24000	7	5	8					1	11			9	3		10					6	2			4
35		12	BRISTOL ROVERS	3-1	Askew, Hilsdon, Randall	8000	7	5	8					1	11			9	3		10					6	2			4
36		19	Swindon Town	1-1	Denyer	9000	7	5	8					1	11			9	3		10					6	2			4
37		23	Reading	1-1	Denyer	2000	7	5	8					1	11			9	3		10					6	2			4
38		26	PORTSMOUTH	2-1	Ashton, Bailey	8000	7	5	8					1	11			9	3		10					6	2			4
			Apps				36	30	10	2	2	5	4	9	24	3	12	29	25	19	32	29	16	1	4	35	32	22	8	29
			Goals				5	2	2		1		3		3		2	12		4	13				1	2		15		1

F.A. Cup

		Date	Opponent	Score	Scorers	Att	Ashton H	Askew W	Carter H	Casey J	Dawson H	Denyer A	Forster H	Harrison F	Hilsdon G	Hughes J	Randall T	Rothwell J	Woodards D
R1	Jan	13	West Bromwich Albion	1-1	Harrison	20000	7	5		11		8	3	9	10	1	6	2	4
rep		16	WEST BROMWICH ALB.	2-2	(aet) Hilsdon 2	15000	7	5		11		8	3	9	10	1	6	2	4
rep2		22	West Bromwich Albion	3-0	Hilsdon 2, Denyer	27075	7		8	11		9	3	5	10	1	6	2	4
R2	Feb	1	Aston Villa	0-5		50000	7		8	11		9	3	5	10	1	6	2	4

R1 replay 2 at Stamford Bridge

West Ham defend an Albion attack in the second replay at Stamford Bridge, January 1913

		P	W	D	L	F	A	W	D	L	F	A	Pts
1	Plymouth Argyle	38	15	2	2	47	9	7	4	8	30	27	50
2	Swindon Town	38	13	5	1	44	16	7	3	9	22	25	48
3	WEST HAM UNITED	38	11	6	2	39	15	7	6	6	27	31	48
4	Queen's Park Rangers	38	14	4	1	33	10	4	6	9	13	26	46
5	Crystal Palace	38	13	3	3	38	13	4	8	7	17	23	45
6	Millwall	38	14	0	5	36	17	5	7	7	26	26	45
7	Exeter City	38	13	3	3	29	16	5	5	9	19	28	44
8	Reading	38	12	3	4	34	20	5	5	9	25	35	42
9	Brighton & Hove Alb.	38	12	5	2	39	19	1	7	11	9	28	38
10	Northampton Town	38	11	4	4	42	17	1	8	10	19	31	36
11	Portsmouth	38	11	5	3	28	15	3	3	13	13	34	36
12	Merthyr Town	38	9	8	2	27	17	3	4	12	16	43	36
13	Coventry City	38	9	6	4	42	27	4	4	11	11	32	34
14	Watford	38	8	5	6	28	24	4	5	10	15	26	34
15	Gillingham	38	7	7	5	19	21	5	3	11	17	32	34
16	Bristol Rovers	38	9	6	4	37	23	3	3	13	18	41	33
17	Southampton	38	7	7	5	28	25	3	4	12	12	47	31
18	Norwich City	38	8	7	4	26	17	2	2	15	13	33	29
19	Brentford	38	10	3	6	27	17	1	2	16	15	38	27
20	Stoke	38	8	3	8	21	17	2	1	16	18	58	24

1913/14   A NEW GRANDSTAND

Although West Ham United had not won the Southern League title, the club was now in a financially sound position, and with relatively strong personnel all round, it might have been hoped or even expected that those in control would have made an application to join the Football League. After all, other London clubs - Arsenal, Chelsea, Fulham and Tottenham, were already members and pitting their wits on a wider scene against the Northern and Midland clubs.

Perhaps the directors had a more parochial attitude, preferring to be safe in the knowledge that the club was now in a financially stable position, and taking risks on a bigger outlay for better players might undermine their current financial position, which had taken many years to put 'in the black'. There were shareholders involved, although these were few in number, and the club had to be run at a profit, and there was not one person on the board who was able to give support to the club out of his own pocket. A decision was made however, to advance the club further, not on the field of play, which is a risky venture at any time, but on the investment in bricks and mortar. Providing better facilities for those that came to watch and hopefully continue to support the club would pay off any initial expenditure in the long term.

With this in mind it was agreed that a new stand would be built to replace the one that had been erected in 1904. At 300ft in length and 20ft in depth it was estimated to hold around 7,000, all under cover. There was to be a terraced enclosure 320ft long and 25ft deep in front of the stand. The stand would be divided into five bays A, B, C, D, E. C bay in the centre would be for reserved seat holders. A and E would be for spectators who pay a shilling and prefer to sit rather than stand on the terrace, and B and D would be reserved at an extra charge. A main staircase would lead up to the distributing area, leading up to five staircases to the various blocks. Those finding blocks A and E full would be able to descend another staircase at the far end of the stand down to the terracing. Under the structure were to be the offices, dressing rooms and other facilities, with a passage leading out on to the pitch for the players and referee to enter the playing field.

It was a tribute to the club, and the construction company, that all the work was 'done and dusted' during the close season. Built of course, by Cearns & Co.

Alf 'Dick' Leafe

With the first team performing so well in 1912/13, it was considered that the side needed just a little fine-tuning, and there were few new recruits to add to the existing squad of players. Tommy Brandon, a 20-year-old full-back was signed from Blackburn, along with 22-year-old Alf (Dick) Leafe who had scored a very creditable 15 goals in 28 outings with First Division Sheffield United. Alf Tirrell, after his good display against West Ham reserves in the previous season, joined the club from Peterborough City.

Just two players left. Fred Harrison signed for Bristol City, and Harold Dawson went back to his first love, Croydon Common. Goalkeeper Henry Carter was released later in the season and signed for Workington.

The campaign opened against arch-rivals Millwall at Cold Blow Lane. This first match was scheduled for September 1st, which was a Monday, with a kick off at 5.30, and as it was a dark and overcast day, the closing stages were fought out in semi-darkness, and it was 'touch and go' whether the referee would abandon the game. It would appear to have been common sense to open the season on the previous Saturday (August 30th), but it was deemed that the Southern League campaign should begin no earlier than the first day of September, and every season in this period from 1900/01 to 1914/15 this rule applied. As for the match itself, it was fought out in the usual fast and vigorous manner. The new signing Alf Leafe had injured his foot in training and was unable to participate, so Bert Denyer, who looked to be the player who might have to give way, took his place. There had been some rain during the day which made the ball greasy, and this caused Joe Hughes to let the ball slip through his hands and into the net after Millwall's Noble hit a slanting shot, on the twenty minute mark. Denyer was hurt later on, and Hilsdon moved into the centre, and it was he who crashed the ball home to equalise. A point at Millwall was a satisfactory start.

Alf Leafe made his first appearance when Swindon came to Upton Park, and fairly delighted the crowd with a real centre-forward display scoring two goals into the bargain, but for all the Hammers' pressure, the 'Railwaymen' scored three to take the points. Although the first half was reasonably quiet, all hell broke loose in the second. Fought out like a cup-tie, things were happening 'off the ball' as well as on it, and the crowd became enraged with the referee and some of his decisions. At last he gave a penalty for handball which appeased the home support, but the usually reliable Hilsdon shot wide. The Hammers then fairly blitzed the visitors' goal, but the equaliser unfortunately never came.

There was some criticism of the cramped position of spectators passing one another along the seating in the new grandstand, but full marks to Syd King, this was subsequently very quickly rectified.

The initial victory of the season was achieved at Bristol Rovers by 2 goals to one. Historically this was long overdue as the last time that the Hammers had won at Eastville in the Southern League was in the 1901/02 season. The Rovers took the lead in the first half in a game which both sides missed easy chances, but Denyer equalised shortly after the break, and Leafe scored the winner late on.

Merthyr had won their two opening fixtures and looked a good footballing side when they

visited the Boleyn enclosure. Despite their clever footwork, it was West Ham that took the lead through Casey from Denyer's cross, but the Welsh club levelled after scoring from a deflection. A period of each side giving the other too much respect was ended when Casey, now well renowned for his lightning speed, gave Leafe the pass to head home. There was no holding Hammers after this, and Ashton put the result beyond doubt for the third goal.

Ex-Hammer Danny Shea was already showing his skills at Blackburn Rovers, having scored four in his last match, and he was selected for the Football League representative side to meet the Irish League along with his wing partner John Simpson.

West Ham were now seemingly settling down, securing a 2-2 draw at Loftus Road against QPR, but came a 'cropper' at Plymouth where they were beaten by the current champions by three clear goals. There had been no sign of this when Hammers were playing well, but they then adopted to play the 'one back' game, which Argyle were caught out by. As the home side got the better of it, the game changed, but once

Herbert Ashton

again an opposition side scored from a sharp deflection. Ashton had bad luck when his shot struck a post, but in the second half it was more a case of 'hanging on' until Plymouth scored twice more before the end.

With Randall away on representative duty for the Southern League, Frank Burton took his place and George Hilsdon was made captain for the day, when Southampton came to town. The Saints had conceded just five goals in their opening seven matches, so it came as something of a shock that the Hammers hit home another five in this one game. The team were in blistering form from the start and Hilsdon (2), Ashton, Casey and Burton notched the goals.

There had been a large contingent of Southampton supporters present, but even in defeat, like all fans, they made their presence felt. One lot of Saints' supporters wore red and white caps and sported a red and white umbrella with a figure of a jester on top carrying a harp, and underneath were the words 'Yi, Yi, Yi!' (whatever that meant). After the match this group were to be seen marching up Green Street to Upton Park station ringing a big bell and singing 'Are we downhearted?'

After such a good victory, it was disappointing then to lose at Reading in a very close game, where either side could have won, but Joe Hughes was at fault for the first of two goals when he dropped a high shot, from which Reading's Brown scored. Following this, the club acquired the signature of Tommy Lonsdale from Grimsby Town. Tommy was an experienced 'keeper, said to be quick, cool and agile, and also something of joker, according to he ex-team mates. Grimsby let him go in order to finance the purchase of Willis Rippon, a centre-forward.

Tommy came in straight away for the visit of Crystal Palace, but despite most of the play the whole team had an off day with the exception of Ashton, who was just as nimble and tricky as he always was, providing a number of crosses which were wasted by others. Casey scored in a 1-2 defeat.

In what was described as 'a rattling good game', West Ham went to Coventry City and beat them by 4 goals to two, after twice being behind. Ashton, just recently married, was on his honeymoon, so was replaced by Harold Caton, and Frank Burrill came in for Hilsdon. The Hammers played some terrific football throughout the game, so it was a surprise when the home side opened their account, although it was Randall who headed into his own net for them to score. Leafe soon equalised before the break. After 'lemon time' Coventry took the lead again when Brandon and Forster let Davison nip in to score. Nothing daunted, the Hammers continued with some good interplay and Leafe, with a shot from fully thirty yards equalised. The same player got his hat-trick for the third, and Denyer added the fourth from Casey's centre.

The same eleven, with exception of Hughes in for the injured Lonsdale, was expected to deliver the same result against Watford, but had to be satisfied with a 1-1 draw.

When West Ham visited Norwich, the Norfolk side had recorded a recent run of five consecutive draws. There was something inevitable about the outcome of this statistic – Norwich won by 1-0. Joe Hughes, in for the still injured Lonsdale, was at fault with the goal. Potter, of

Syd Puddefoot

Norwich, seeing Joe yards off his goal line, lobbed the ball over him, and in the scramble back, a shot from Ingham went in off the Hammers' goalkeeper.

The match against Gillingham was set to kick off at 2.45 pm but it was decided to kick off some three minutes earlier due to the darkness of the day. Hilsdon, playing poorly at Norwich was replaced by the 'up and coming' Syd Puddefoot, and Carter, getting what was to be his one and only appearance, replacing Hughes in goal. An improved display saw Puddefoot justify his inclusion with a goal, and further goals were added by Leafe and Burrill, in a 3-1 victory in which the visitors' goal was scored by ex-Hammer Tommy Caldwell.

Tommy Lonsdale returned in goal, and was outstanding in a scoreless draw at Northampton, in which defences dominated. Another game without scoring followed when Southend United were the visitors. Both points were dropped however in a 0-1 defeat, and the season was turning out to be one that could not measure up to 1912/13, and with roughly the same personnel this was a big disappointment.

It was typical of West Ham of course, to then go to Brighton and grab a win against a side that had not tasted defeat on their own ground this campaign. Much of this was due to the goalkeeping of Lonsdale, who not only did some remarkable shot stopping but also ran out to break up a number of promising attacks, ably assisted by both Irvine and Brandon, the full-backs. Mention of Brandon - at this time the English League Board imposed a fine on West Ham for signing on Tom Brandon from Blackburn Rovers without first negotiating his transfer. The fine amounted to two guineas.

Tommy Brandon

The busy Christmas period was coming up, with five games in eight days, but on the Thursday before their next match Herbert 'Tiddler' Ashton's benefit concert took place at East Ham Town Hall. The players and West Ham Directors were all in attendance, and the musical evening was a great success with almost 700 people present. The event proved to be a nice little sum of money for him to add to the receipts of his forthcoming benefit match against Bristol Rovers in January.

Portsmouth were the visitors for the first of the five fixtures, and after the Hammers had taken the game to Pompey from the start, the home crowd were stunned when the visitors went down and scored in their first attack. When Puddefoot then hit the angle of the post and crossbar, the Portsmouth forwards immediately added insult to injury by combining for a second goal. West Ham then went to pieces for a long period, but got back in when a visiting defender casually facing his own goal was robbed by Hilsdon, who tapped the ball to Puddefoot for him to score. In the second half, the Hammers swapped the forward line around, but Portsmouth stayed in control quite comfortably. They were to regret their overconfident attitude however, when a penalty was awarded late on, and Leafe equalised. Ashton, Puddefoot and Denyer then combined, and with the very last kick of the game the latter scored the winner, amidst great excitement in the crowd.

Those Southern League officials who arranged the holiday fixtures certainly did not possess any Christmas spirit or give any thought to the players' families when they decided that West Ham and

Exeter would meet one another home and away on Christmas Day and Boxing Day. At the Boleyn ground the result was a 1-1 draw, with Lonsdale in brilliant form, and Brandon proving what a good full-back he was, especially with his remarkable quickness in recovery.

The long journey to Devon resulted in another 1-1 scoreline, with Pym, the Exeter goalkeeper, showing his skills for the home side. Dick Pym was to join Bolton Wanderers in 1920, and would appear as their 'keeper in the 1923 FA Cup final against West Ham United.

As Boxing Day fell on a Friday, it meant three fixtures in three days when the Hammers had to return from their far off visit to Exeter and make the journey to Swindon the following day. Another fine piece of logistical scheduling!

Three changes were made for the game, one of which was at left back, where J. Goddard came into the side. He had come from Exeter and had been swapped for F. Goodwin, a left winger who had been a regular in the reserve team. Strangely enough Goddard did not appear again in the Hammers' first eleven, but Goodwin made 40 appearances for the Devon side over the next one and a half seasons.

The Swindon encounter resulted in a 1-4 defeat, although the overall performance did not reflect the score. (Brandon was sent off in this game, which meant he would be suspended for the FA Cup tie in January). In comparison to West Ham's travels, Swindon had two home fixtures over the holiday and made the short trip to Bristol to meet the

Les Askew

Rovers. West Ham could have been scheduled to meet Millwall, Crystal Palace or QPR., with Southend and Watford within a reasonable distance. It was not logical planning by the Southern League Committee at all.

Ample amends were made to the above result when Bristol Rovers came to the East End. This was the fixture chosen by the club's directors as Ashton's benefit match. With a reasonable attendance of 14,000 it was a profitable game for Ashton financially, and for the side pointswise, as a 6-1 victory was chalked up, with Syd Puddefoot scoring his first Southern League hat-trick. The other goals came from Bailey, Casey and Leafe, although the half-back line of Woodards, Askew and Burton played a big part in the team's success.

It was now the fateful year of 1914 and it is worth mentioning here that the Thames Ironworks, Shipbuilding & Engineering Co. was now officially closed, with no apparent chance of a re-opening or rebirth. This had been an absolute tragedy for employment in the West Ham and surrounding area, because the build up of armaments in Germany had prompted Winston Churchill to make an announcement that our dockyards would now turn out a large armoured unit every 45 days for the following eighteen months. At the beginning of the year, of course, nobody in Government or elsewhere was aware that 'the Great War', as it would be known, would materialise in August 1914, but Germany in particular, would find the appropriate excuse when it came, and the country had to be prepared.

It was particularly galling to discover that the Navy League demanded that nine ships were to be built at once, and that Vickers Ltd., Armstrong Whitworth & Co., and Cammell, Laird & Co., amongst others, would be carrying out the construction. Many of those who would otherwise have been employed at Canning Town would perish on the fields of France.

January meant FA Cup time again and the Hammers were drawn against Chesterfield FC, a Midland League club that previously had been in the Football League Division Two from 1899/1900 to 1908/09. All fears of an upset were quickly dispelled when Dan Bailey scored in the opening minute and

others quickly followed, as the visitors' half-backs were running around 'like headless chickens'. It was 5-0 by the break, with Ashton, Leafe and Puddefoot (2), adding to Bailey's opener. 19-year -old Syd Puddefoot hit a second half hat-trick to bring his tally to five. Young Puddy certainly hit the headlines, but once again Ashton was the main supplier, and 'Tiddler's' goal was greeted with as much enthusiasm as any. Chesterfield scored on the final whistle for a final score of 8-1. Joe Hughes had returned in goal, as Tommy Lonsdale had blotted his copybook, and gone 'absent without leave'. Tommy was fined a week's wages by the club and was relegated to the reserves.

Back to the Southern League and a victory was obtained in Wales against Merthyr Town by two goals to one, after a fine display of attacking football when the margin of goals should have been far greater. In fact Merthyr were outclassed in every department with Brandon and Rothwell at full-back especially in fine form.

The half yearly results of the club were announced at the shareholders' meeting, and receipts were up again. Gross receipts were

Frank Burton

£5,748 compared to £5,088. Southern League gate receipts averaged £372 against £365 the previous year, South Eastern League £99 against £56, and the London League average was £34 as against £27. There had been an increase in expenditure, chiefly due to increased wages (£280) and transfer fees (£400). Total wages paid were £2,260.

The team's good form continued when Queens Park Rangers came to Upton Park, although the visitors played some really good stuff and should have been in front, being let down by some awful shooting. The Hammers took advantage of this before half time as Casey headed on to Leafe, who headed into the net, and Bailey's goal after Puddefoot's pass. After the break Casey scored the goal of the match, racing down the left wing, leaving two opponents standing and scoring from an oblique angle. Leafe added another, before QPR got their only goal. 4-1 to the Hammers.

As they had done for the preparations for the Chesterfield match, the team, with trainer Charlie Paynter, went to Southend, and took to the salt baths there, combining that with light training for the next round of the FA Cup.

Crystal Palace were having a good season and were in contention for the Southern League title when they came to the Boleyn ground for the 2nd Round of the FA Cup. Both team's official colours were claret and blue, so it was the visitors who changed into an outfit of white shirts and black shorts.

As a spectacle the contest was somewhat disappointing from a neutral's point of view as it consisted of a lot of scrambling play, but that is often the case in cup-ties. West Ham were always on top and had most of the attacking play. The first goal came after a superb run by Casey from the half-way line to the penalty area. His pass went to Leafe, whose fierce shot was saved by Johnson, in the Palace goal, but as the 'keeper failed to hold it, Bailey came rushing in to bang it into the net. To further dispel the myth that players of that time showed little emotion on scoring, Bailey was fairly mobbed by his colleagues in celebration, and when he scored again to seal the game late in the second half, he was almost mauled to annihilation in the excitement.

It was back to the 'bread and butter' of the league when current champions Plymouth were the visitors. This was a splendid match, but the Hammers were now in a rich vein of form and were the better side, despite the Argyle taking an early lead. Heavy pressure saw Horne, in the Plymouth goal repulsing the Hammers' efforts, but it brought about an equaliser just before half-time when Ashton supplied the cross for Puddefoot to score, and just one minute after the interval, Leafe headed home Ashton's corner to make the score 2-1. It stayed that way, although the visitors did their best to equalise without success.

With this fourth league victory in succession it meant a climb to fourth position in the table, and the next fixture was a visit to the South Coast to meet Southampton. It was an interesting fact that the Saints had failed to beat West Ham at the Dell since 1905/06, and when the home side went into a two goal lead that little run appeared to have ended. The Hammers were down to ten men at the time of the second goal when Rothwell had to leave the field due to an injury. Just before half time with Ashton and Casey on the wings beginning to cause problems, a penalty was awarded when a Saint's defender handled. Burton duly converted. In the second period it was Casey's speed that provided a centre for

Jim Rothwell

Bailey to score. With the score now at 2-2, Rothwell returned and needed to be there as Southampton attacked. On the break Hammers attacked swiftly and Leafe put the team in front. It was then 'nip and tuck', but finally it was another victory to enjoy. Everyone was now looking forward to the visit of Liverpool in the third round of the FA Cup.

The club's record in the FA Cup had been a reasonably good one. Several First Division teams had been beaten over the years, and it was hoped that the club could go one round further than the Quarter Final, which was reached in 1910/11. Rain greeted the players as they entered the pitch, and the ground became muddy and pondlike in places. From the outset it could be seen that the visitors were not a side that could easily be thrown off their usual game, despite the cup-tie atmosphere. Whilst the West Ham forwards had their moments, there was always the feeling that Liverpool were holding something in reserve, and most of the time they appeared to be in command. When the Hammers, in a bustling style, did break through, Campbell, in the visitors' goal was always sound. The First Division club showed their pedigree in attack, with some fine football, but the Hammers' defence especially Brandon, kept them out.

After half time Liverpool did eventually score, but thought the game was won until Puddefoot, from an Askew pass, levelled the score, and for a while this set up the Hammers for further pressure. The visitors survived, and often showed their class until the end of the game with some of their midfield tactics, passing in one particular area, and then switching the play to a colleague who was virtually unmarked. There was a feeling amongst the home support that the replay might be a formality if Liverpool opened up and played at their best. Sadly this was the case, as the Merseyside men, in the replay just four days later gave the Hammers a 5-1 drubbing.

At the Essex referees meeting at the 'Earl of Essex' pub in Manor Park, the main speaker was a Mr Sidney Goodger, a Clapton Orient director, who gave an address entitled 'The Trinity of Power - the Referee and Linesmen'. The 'man in the middle' at the time was just as important a part of the game as he is today.

'Referees...... require a keen sense of justice. They must be absolutely fair, and unbiased, and it was also essential that they kept calm. It was a lie when it was said referees were paid extra to favour a team...... Referees must possess self control and resourcefulness and speak to the players as man to man. They should be men capable of instant decision, and wherever possible men of personality - possessing personal magnetism, that valuable asset to all men. The referee...... should never be too big to consult his linesmen whenever he was in doubt, and the referee and linesmen together could form a power strong enough to control the twenty two players...... (he) should also possess enthusiasm. Mr Goodger continued that he 'liked to see an enthusiastic referee and enthusiastic linesmen, men full of energy and who were not slovenly...

A top referee by the name of Mr Child pointed out 'how the linesmen could assist the referee in cases where players waited until the referee's back was turned before committing an offence......an incident that occurred in a game between Brighton and Southampton. One player repeatedly fouled an opponent, and a friend afterwards remarked upon it to the player. 'Yes,' said the player, 'I did let him have one didn't I?' 'But,' replied the friend, 'If the referee had seen you I know he would have sent you off for it.' ' Oh, I know,' came the player's response, 'I knew, and I watched when he wasn't looking.' Referees could not control that sort of thing...... but linesmen could stop it.'

Mr Chalkley, a local referee, told a good story of an incident that happened when he refereed a match at Clapton. "I gave a penalty against the Orient, and the Orient were a goal down at the interval. At half-time, down came the directors to tell me it ought not to have been a penalty. 'It was *quite a fair charge,' said one, and another had not seen a fairer charge in his life etc, etc. 'Neither have I' I replied ... it was a most palpable case of hands which made me give the penalty."*

Pity the poor ref. He's always to blame.

West Ham had now to concentrate on their league position. Despite the cup disappointment they had won five consecutive league matches, and were in fourth place in the table. Crystal Palace were the current leaders and were the next opponents on the road. Tommy Lonsdale was back in side and Alf Tirrell, signed in close season, came in for his first game at left back. Mackesy came in for Casey at outside left. The Hammers were on the receiving end of Palace's attacks in the first half, but the home forwards missed a number of easy chances. The second half saw Woodards, Askew and Randall take charge of the middle of the field, and through their superiority Dan Bailey opened the scoring. An injury to Tirrell saw Randall go to full-back, with Makesy taking his place, and strangely enough West Ham improved their game. Ashton scored after a pass from Puddefoot, and it was not until close to the final whistle that Palace pulled one back, but it was a creditable and important victory for the Boleyn lads.

Coventry City were at the foot of the table when they came to Upton Park, but their position in the table looked quite false as the game was evenly fought out in the first half. The visitors' display was even better after the break, and for the West Ham supporters it was annoying that their team put on an indifferent performance after the club's winning run in the league. Those that left before the end might not have been surprised to hear however, that in the very last minute the Hammers grabbed the only goal of the game, when Leafe shot through a crowd of players for the winner. The victory, unconvincing as it was, put the club up to third in the league.

A journey to Watford turned out to be a waste of time, as the match against the Hertfordshire club had to be aban-doned due to weather conditions, with West Ham one goal to the good after Leafe

Action from the West Ham v Reading match, March 1914

had netted. Considering the result of the rescheduled match it was a pity it was abandoned, but the worst aspect was that Syd Puddefoot received a bad ankle injury that was to keep him out of the side for seven matches. Syd had been the subject of an offer from Sunderland during January, and with West Ham considering the form of an amateur by the name of Arthur Stallard, who had been scoring regularly at Chatham, the club were tempted to let Puddefoot go, but thankfully they did not. The Hammers had the best of both by signing Stallard on professional forms and holding on to Puddefoot.

The run of seven consecutive victories came to an end when Norwich came to Upton Park, a 1-1 draw being the result. This was a game where each team distinctly dominated one half. West Ham the first, and Norwich the second. There had been heavy rain and the pitch was like a quagmire. With the very heavy ball that was in use in those days collecting a coating of mud, some players who were frequently heading the ball had to take vital seconds to recover from the blows to the head, and there were also stoppages for incidents in the mud where players on both sides were losing their tempers.

Two days later the Hammers had a late Monday afternoon fixture against Reading. Alf Leafe was injured in the Norwich game, which meant that with Casey and Puddefoot also out, the forward line read, Ashton, Butcher, Denyer, Bailey and W. Bourne (coming in for his one and only first team game). Considering the outcome was a 0-0 draw it was an exciting match; the home stars were Brandon and Burton, the full-backs, who had their work cut out against a forward line that were fast, but consistently caught out for offside.

The visit to Gillingham resulted in the Hammers' first league defeat since late December. Although the home side gave the West Ham defence something of a roasting in the first half, it was surprising that the Kent side had scored just once during that time. Any chance of getting something from the game was diminished after the break when Bailey failed to take the field, due to a knock, and to make matters worse Brandon received a foot injury which left him limping throughout the remainder of the game. Although the Hammers did score through Randall, the score at the final whistle was 3-1 to the home side.

The result of the rearranged fixture with Watford made any hopes of the title appear lost, as the worst defeat of the season saw the home side bang in six goals without reply. There is certainly some excuse for this result as Brandon, Bailey and Casey were all out injured, with Tommy Randall taking the latter's place at outside left. Coming into Tommy's place was a star of the future at West Ham, young Jack Tresadern. On top of the enforced changes to the side, Butcher received a dislocated ankle in the second half of the game.

Jack Tresadern

Northampton were still in the running for the title when they came to the Boleyn ground. Casey returned to the side after injury and George Hilsdon was also recalled. The final result of 1-1 was a deceptive one, as the Hammers produced so many chances in the first half it should have been over at half time. After the break both sides missed a penalty, and then the visitors took the lead when a free kick by Walter Tull was converted, but Leafe did eventually score to equalise. Both Swindon Town and Crystal Palace had won their previous two fixtures, which left any chance of the title for the Hammers exceedingly remote.

With three matches over the Easter period, the situation could change of course, but those who arranged the Southern League fixtures did West Ham no favours again over the holiday period, as the club had to travel to Cardiff for the Good Friday match and then travel straight back to visit Southend United on Easter Saturday.

The long journey produced nothing in the way of points as the Welsh side won 2-0. It was not for want of good football that defeat came, it was once again a tale of missed chances, and the home side took two of theirs.

For the visit to Southend, the home side were battling against relegation, and played as if their lives depended upon it and hustled and bustled the Hammers' defence. As at Cardiff, both Bert Denyer and his brother Frank played. Frank had played at full-back in his debut game, but in this fixture he was at right half, and he was as busy as Askew and Randall who had their work cut out to keep the opposition at bay. There was no scoring in the first period, but Southend scored first from a penalty before Bailey equalised. By a strange coincidence none of the top six teams gained any advantage in the table as they all drew. For the return match with Cardiff City, it was good to see Syd Puddefoot return to the team; the 1-1 draw was a fair result. The Hammers led through Leafe before Cardiff equalised from a penalty.

Young Arthur Stallard was given his debut against Millwall in midweek in place of Puddefoot, and George Hilsdon came into the side again. By now there was no chance of the title, but fixtures against the old rivals had never been anything but exciting, sometimes for the wrong reasons, but it was a fixture that was always looked forward to. West Ham took the lead in the first half when Hilsdon scored with a neat header, before Millwall missed a penalty. In the second half Stallard justified his upgrade from the reserves by scoring from the rebound after Casey had hit the bar, and then Hilsdon hit the third with a tremendous drive. At 3-0 it looked all over but Millwall then converted their second penalty, and then added another, which made the closing stages frantic to say the least, but the score remained at 3-2.

The final home game of the season came against Brighton & Hove, and it was a typical 'end of season' game, although it was interesting to see how Jack Tresadern and Arthur Stallard would progress in the team. Jack showed quick powers of recovery, and his tackling was good against what might be called 'hefty opponents, but Stallard definitely required more experience. The match finished at 1-1.

The campaign ended with a trip to Portsmouth, and the home side made the Hammers look second rate throughout. Robert Beale played his solitary game in goal, but it was not his fault that Pompey knocked in the goals in a 1-5 defeat. A disappointing end to what could have been a season of triumph. Just one victory in the final eleven games says it all.

The consolation of the 1913/14 campaign was the form of the reserve team as they went one better than their runners-up spot of the previous year by winning the South Eastern League championship, topping highly rated Fulham and Chelsea into the bargain. Those players who deserved credit for that achievement by making the majority of appearances were Carter, Irvine, Tirrell, Redward, Whiteman, Caton, Burrill, Bert Denyer, Goddard, Rothwell, Butcher, W. Bourne and Mackesy. They were ably assisted by Hilsdon and Puddefoot on several occasions.

Back: T Brandon, G Irvine, J Rothwell, J Hughes, H Carter, F Burton, A Tirrell, H Forster. Next to back (committee men): J Johnson, A Smith, T Williamson, G Fundell, ES King (secretary-manager), G Davis, T Taylorson, H Iggulden, H Sutton. Standing: C Paynter, A Cox, F Redward, D Woodards, L Askew, F Harrison, R Chapman, T Randall, G Hillsdon, J Tresadern, H Bourse, F Piercy (assistant trainer). Seated: H Ashton, H Caton, D Bailey, A Denyer, A Leafe, S Puddefoot. On ground: G Walden, G Butcher, R Whiteman, J Macksey.

131

1913/14

6th in Southern League Division One

#	Date		Opponent	Result / Scorers	Att	Ashton H	Askew W	Bailey D	Brandon T	Burrill F	Burton F	Butcher G	Casey J	Caton H	Denyer A	Denyer F	Forster H	Goddard J	Hilsdon G	Hughes J	Irvine G	Leafe A	Lonsdale T	Mackesy J	Puddefoot S	Randall T	Rothwell J	Stallard A	Tirrell A	Tresadern J	Whiteman R	Woodards D
1	Sep	1	Millwall	1-1 Hilsdon	12000	7	5	8					11		9		3		10	1						6	2					4
2		6	SWINDON TOWN	2-3 Leafe 2	25000	7	5	8					11				3		10	1		9				6	2					4
3		13	Bristol Rovers	2-1 Denyer, Leafe	10000	7	5		2				11		8		3		10	1		9				6						4
4		20	MERTHYR TOWN	3-1 Ashton, Casey, Leafe	15000	7	5		2				11		8		3		10	1		9				6						4
5		27	Queen's Park Rangers	2-2 Denyer, Leafe	12000	7	5		2				11		8		3		10	1		9				6						4
6	Oct	4	Plymouth Argyle	0-3	10000	7	5		2				11		8		3		10	1		9				6						4
7		11	SOUTHAMPTON	5-1 Hilsdon 2, Ashton, Burton, Casey	6000	7	5				6		11		10		3		8	1		9					2				4	
8		18	Reading	0-2	8000	7	5						11		10		3		8	1		9				6	2				4	
9		25	CRYSTAL PALACE	1-2 Casey	13000	7	5						11		10		3		8			9	1			6	2					4
10	Nov	1	Coventry City	4-2 Leafe 3, Denyer	7000		5		2	8			11	7	9		3					10	1			6						4
11		8	WATFORD	1-1 Denyer	10000		5		2	8			11	7	9		3				1	10				6						4
12		15	Norwich City	0-1	7000	7	5		2	8			11				3		9	1		10				6						4
13		22	GILLINGHAM	3-1 Burrill, Leafe, Puddefoot	10000	7	5		2	8			11				3					10	1		9	6						4
14		29	Northampton Town	0-0	5000	7	5		2	8			11				3					10	1		9	6						4
15	Dec	6	SOUTHEND UNITED	0-1	10000	7	5		2	8			11				3					10	1		9	6						4
16		13	Brighton & Hove Albion	1-0 Leafe	6000	11	5		2						7				8		3	10	1		9	6						4
17		20	PORTSMOUTH	3-2 Denyer, Leafe, Puddefoot	9000	11	5		2						7				8		3	10	1		9	6						4
18		25	EXETER CITY	1-1 Puddefoot	18000	7	5	8	2				11	10							3		1		9	6						4
19		26	Exeter City	1-1 Leafe	7000	7	5		2				11				10				3	8	1		9	6						4
20		27	Swindon Town	1-4 Puddefoot	8000	7	5	8	2				11					3				10	1		9							4
21	Jan	3	BRISTOL ROVERS	6-1 Puddefoot 3, Bailey, Casey, Leafe	14000	7	5	8	2	6			11									10	1		9			3				4
22		17	Merthyr Town	2-1 Casey, Puddefoot	8000	7	5	8	2	6			11								1	10			9					3		4
23		24	QUEEN'S PARK RANGERS	4-1 Casey 2, Bailey, Leafe	11000		5	8	2	6			11	7							1	10			9					3		4
24	Feb	7	PLYMOUTH ARGYLE	2-1 Leafe, Puddefoot	8000	7	5	8	2	6			11								1	10			9					3		4
25		14	Southampton	3-2 Bailey, Burton, Leafe	7000	7	5	8	2		6		11		9						1	10								3		4
26		28	Crystal Palace	2-1 Ashton, Bailey	12000	7	5	8	2													10	1	11	9	6			3			4
27	Mar	7	COVENTRY CITY	1-0 Leafe	14000	7	5		2	3											8	10	1	11	9	6						4
28		21	NORWICH CITY	1-1 Leafe	6000	7	5	8	2	3					9							10	1	11		6						4
29		23	READING	0-0	5000	7	5	10	2	3	8				9								1			6						4
30		28	Gillingham	1-3 Randall	7000	7	5	9	2	3	8	11										10	1			6						4
31	Apr	1	Watford	0-6	4000	7	5		9	3	8						2					10	1			11					6	4
32		4	NORTHAMPTON T	1-1 Leafe	10000	7	5		2	8			11						9	1		10				6						4
33		10	Cardiff City	0-2	12000	7	5	8			3		11		9	2						10	1			6					4	
34		11	Southend United	1-1 Bailey	7000	7	5	8	2		3		11		9	4						10	1			6						
35		13	CARDIFF CITY	1-1 Leafe	15000	7	5	8	2		3		11									10	1		9	6						4
36		14	Millwall	3-2 Hilsdon 2, Stallard	15000	7	5	8	2		3		11						10				1					9			6	4
37		18	BRIGHTON & HOVE ALB.	1-1 Hilsdon	10000	7	5	8	2		3		11						10				1					9			6	4
38		25	Portsmouth	1-5 Bailey	8000	7	5	8	2		3		11									10			9						6	4
				Apps		35	38	19	31	8	19	4	31	3	17	2	15	1	17	15	5	33	21	3	16	28	10	2	1	4	7	30
				Goals		3		6		1	2		7		5				6			20			9	1		1				

Played in one game: R Beale (38, at 1), W Bourne (29, 11), H Carter (13, at 1)

F.A. Cup

	Date		Opponent	Result / Scorers	Att	Ashton H	Askew W	Bailey D	Brandon T	Burrill F	Burton F	Butcher G	Casey J	Caton H	Denyer A	Denyer F	Forster H	Goddard J	Hilsdon G	Hughes J	Irvine G	Leafe A	Lonsdale T	Mackesy J	Puddefoot S	Randall T	Rothwell J	Stallard A	Tirrell A	Tresadern J	Whiteman R	Woodards D
R1	Jan	10	CHESTERFIELD	8-1 Puddefoot 5, Ashton, Bailey, Leafe	16000	7	5	8			3		11								1	10			9	6	2					4
R2		31	CRYSTAL PALACE	2-0 Bailey 2	18000	7	5	8	2		6		11								1	10			9			3				4
R3	Feb	21	LIVERPOOL	1-1 Puddefoot	16000	7	5	8	2		3		11								1	10			9	6						4
rep		25	Liverpool	1-5 Puddefoot	45000	7	5	8	2		6										1	10			9	11		3				4

		P	W	D	L	F	A	W	D	L	F	A	Pts
1	Swindon Town	38	14	3	2	57	11	7	5	7	24	30	50
2	Crystal Palace	38	12	5	2	41	13	5	11	3	19	19	50
3	Northampton Town	38	11	8	0	31	11	3	11	5	19	26	47
4	Reading	38	14	4	1	32	12	3	6	10	11	24	44
5	Plymouth Argyle	38	11	6	2	25	12	4	7	8	21	30	43
6	WEST HAM UNITED	38	9	7	3	39	22	6	5	8	22	38	42
7	Brighton & Hove Alb.	38	12	5	2	30	16	3	7	9	13	29	42
8	Queen's Park Rangers	38	10	6	3	28	14	6	3	10	17	29	41
9	Portsmouth	38	10	7	2	31	13	4	5	10	26	35	40
10	Cardiff City	38	10	6	3	27	11	3	6	10	19	31	38
11	Southampton	38	11	2	6	36	23	4	5	10	19	31	37
12	Exeter City	38	7	8	4	21	11	3	8	8	18	27	36
13	Gillingham	38	10	6	3	35	15	3	3	13	13	34	35
14	Norwich City	38	7	10	2	34	19	2	7	10	15	32	35
15	Millwall	38	10	6	3	34	20	1	6	12	17	36	34
16	Southend United	38	7	7	5	29	28	3	5	11	12	38	32
17	Bristol Rovers	38	10	5	4	32	25	0	6	13	14	42	31
18	Watford	38	9	4	6	37	20	1	5	13	13	36	29
19	Merthyr Town	38	7	7	5	23	18	2	3	14	15	43	28
20	Coventry City	38	4	8	7	28	28	2	6	11	15	40	26

Whilst the club were making the usual preparations for the new season, events took place that were to lead to a war that was to become the greatest bloodbath in European history. The entry of Great Britain into the Great War (years later to be known as World War One) began on August 4th 1914, and was to have the utmost effect on millions of people, not only in this country but worldwide.

Both committees of the Football League and the Southern League, obviously without any idea to what extent and how long the conflict would last, decided to continue with the usual league and cup programmes. Many considered, as they were to do many years later in September 1939, that as far as the war was concerned, 'it will all be over by Christmas.'

The West Ham club's AGM in June 1914 saw the largest attendance of shareholders, and with the club now in good shape financially there was a proposal to make further improvements to the ground, as the building of the main stand in 1913 with the extra income it provided had proved to be a success. The Board's decision showed their commitment to the club, but any further improvements had to be put on hold when war broke out. With many men enlisting in the army, and with the general situation on the home front, attendances dropped alarmingly and economy measures were put in place in May 1915. By that time, the decision had been taken by all the football authorities that the normal league programmes would be suspended, and that it would be a sensible conclusion to introduce regional leagues.

During the close season the club released full-backs Harry Forster and Jim Rothwell, and another full-back, George Irvine, returned to Barrow. Goalkeeper Tommy Lonsdale joined Southend United, as did Frank Burrill, who would go on to score 10 goals for them in 24 matches. After the war he played for Wolves, Charlton and Walsall. Bert Denyer was signed by Swindon Town, and he stayed with the Wiltshire club until 1929.

Those players that joined the Hammers were Joe Webster, the experienced Watford goalkeeper, who had been the regular first team choice for the Hertfordshire club for the past three seasons, 27 year old Bill Cope, a chunky, tough tackling full-back of 5ft 8ins and 12 stone with vast experience at Burslem Port Vale, Stoke City and latterly, Oldham Athletic, and another full-back, George Speak from Gainsborough Trinity. From Hull City came Alf Fenwick. He had scored 7 goals in 17 appearances for them, although he might be described as a utility player, capable of playing well in several positions. Always known as Alf, his real first names were the rather upmarket handles of Austin Randolph, ones that were certainly unfamiliar with the East End of London. Also signed were two outside lefts, Percy Wright from Sheffield Wednesday (6 goals from 20 games) and Jimmy Carr, a 19 year old from Watford.

Before the season actually kicked off, the Great War had already broken out in early August, and there were many strange instructions, reports, stories, rumours and unusual sights in the local district. On the evening of August 4th, on the corner of Barking Road and Green Street outside the Boleyn pub, familiar of course to all West Ham United fanatics, was a scene described in the local press:-

'*The Boleyn corner on Tuesday night was busier than it has been for some time. There were tears and goodbyes mixed up with general rejoicing, and many pathetic incidents as big men in military attire took little babies in their arms for a goodbye kiss. The scene was one long to be remembered and lasted long after 11 o'clock.*'

Along a route on the Barking Road that has been taken by many Hammers' supporters on their way to the match over the last one hundred years or so, another unusual sight was witnessed around this time and was also reported:- '*East Ham had a visit last week from several Highlanders, whose attire made picturesque novelty for the children, and quite a crowd followed them along the Barking Road between the Denmark (Arms) and the Boleyn (Tavern). They were only here a couple of days, and came to see some friends at Manor Park before going to the front.*'

The above examples show that regular soldiers were on their way to carry out a job that they always knew they could become involved in, i.e. active service in wartime. Such was the mood in the country at the time, that there was a strong call for all men to leave their civilian jobs and volunteer for the armed forces.

Mr E. Hart of the Essex Society of Association Referees wrote to the press thus:- '*(the) Society are sending circulars to members expressing the hope that they will uphold the prestige of footballers and sportsmen generally by doing their share in the war and joining where at all possible, one of the several bodies now forming, in answer to the appeal of the King and Country. ......Be sure and do something for the sake and honour of England.*'

Another article appeared entitled 'A look around Football and War.', as follows:- *It was almost unavoidable that a difference of opinion should arise as to the wisdom of playing football matches during war. Once more I would assess that there is no harm whatever in the act of playing football during the coming weeks. As a matter of fact some of our brave soldiers indulged to pass the time and keep fit whilst at Boulogne prior to the march to Mons......Is it credible that A or B would allow the fact of playing to deter him from volunteering for service? I have a far better opinion of the British to think so badly of him'.* This would not be the last to be said about the matter before the year was out.

After the pre-season practice matches West Ham United stated that the £143 receipts had been released for allocation to various charities, and that £60 of the total would go to the Prince of Wales Relief Fund (the War Fund). The players themselves had decided to send donations every week to the War Fund, and in their spare time they would be putting in a few hours rifle practice in the Boleyn Social Club grounds next door.

The opening fixture of the season was a home game against Gillingham, and it was easy to see what effect the war would have on attendances when a crowd of just 5,000 came through the gates. Five of the new men were included – Joe Webster in goal, Cope and Speak in the full-back positions, Fenwick at right half and Wright at outside left. The team took quite some while to settle down, and the light ball did not tend to produce quality football, and it was the visitors who scored first. The two new backs were shaky for a while, but Fenwick showed that he could be a capable addition to the club. Puddefoot equalised before half time, and from a cross from Percy Wright scored a real beauty to give a first day win of 2-1.

At Exeter the Hammers were holding their own quite well, and Ashton went off on one of his lightning runs and with just Pym, in goal, to beat he tapped the ball to Puddefoot who opened the scoring, and both wings troubled the home defence consistently. Amazingly, Exeter started a run of scoring that left West Ham reeling. With just a few minutes remaining of the first half, F. Goodwin, who had been swapped for Goddard during the previous season, after performing well in the reserves, provided a cross for Exeter's Lovett to score easily. He then came through the centre and got round Speak, before beating Webster with an angled shot from close in. Without time to take breath, the home side scored a third to make the score 3-1 at half time. Ashton in particular, never stopped trying after the interval causing problems to the home defence, but Exeter were really robbed of another goal before the end, when Holt, on the wing, got clean away with only Webster to beat when he was recalled by the referee because a lost ball had been retrieved and thrown on to the field!

Just two weeks later it was reported that Goddard, the player the Hammers took in exchange for the above-mentioned Goodwin, was reported 'killed in action' at the front, whilst serving with his regiment, the R.F.A. In a bizarre twist, he was reported 'alive and well' in Norwich Barracks just a few days later.

Had Goodwin not signed for Exeter he would not have had the experience of playing in South America when the Devon club made a tour of Argentina in May 1914, just a few months before the Great War began. Swindon Town had carried out a similar tour in 1912, which was a success, but sadly, Exeter were to receive hostility from their hosts, due, it was said, to their inferior play, and the visitors could not wait to return home.

In the return game with Gillingham, Randall's place was taken by Burton. Tommy's leg injury was giving him constant problems and he needed to rest up. The home team gained revenge for their opening day defeat, being the faster side especially after half time. With the West Ham defence having a torrid time, the Kent side won by four clear goals.

At home to Luton Town, Hilsdon came into the side in place of Leafe, and George duly obliged with a goal. Mitchell, in the Luton goal, made several excellent saves in the first half, but with the Hammers showing the more aggressive tactics after the break, a 3-0 victory was the outcome. Puddefoot scored the other two, making his total 5 goals in four games. During the interval the band played 'It's a long way to Tipperary', and the crowd sang along heartily, and from this match onwards a sentry-box was stationed under the offices of the club, with a recruiting officer on hand to hopefully persuade men to enlist.

Recruitment was taking place in all the local districts, with some doing better than others. Patriotism was riding high, and at a recruitment meeting at Poplar Borough Council, a member was supplied with the following poem:

> *Kaiser Bill went up the hill,*
> *In search of blood and slaughter,*
> *But Bill fell down and lost his crown,*
> *And so we think he oughter.*

West Ham's miserable start on 'on the road' continued with another defeat, this time at Portsmouth. Early on, the home supporters showed some anxiety at the way the Hammers were performing, with Puddefoot, Ashton and Wright testing the home defence severely, but Pompey then slowly but surely got into their stride, and took the lead in 28 minutes, and scored again before half time. In the second half Pompey's Buddery caught Webster napping when he was attempting to clear, and the ball was rushed into the net. Towards the end Hilsdon grabbed a consolation goal.

A crowd of 11,000 witnessed the home match against Swindon, which was encouraging after attendances overall being low, but the game was not particularly exciting. Both Puddefoot and Hilsdon missed chances in the first half, but ex-Hammer Bert Denyer was involved when Fleming took the lead for Swindon in the second period. Bailey then hit the bar with a stinging shot, before 'Puddy' equalised with a header from an accurately placed centre from Ashton. The second half was an improvement entertainment wise and it was said that *'it was as well that there was something exciting to hold the spectators' attention, or they might have given up the whole of the afternoon to scanning the sky for aeroplanes. The one that did pass over the ground...... created a more lively interest and more excitement than the match did at any period.'*

There was relief after the visit to Southend United when the first away victory was claimed. Alf Leafe came in for Hilsdon and scored the only goal of the game.

The team was unchanged for the visit of QPR, and the match turned out to be an exciting 'ding dong' battle. Both the wingers Ashton and Carr gave excellent support to the centre where Leafe and Puddefoot were the scorers. The latter could well have added to his total when the Rangers 'keeper tripped him up on way to goal, but the referee insisted that 'Puddy' had fallen over the goalie's leg. The visitors also netted twice for a 2-2 draw. The result broke an amazing sequence of Southern League encounters between the two teams. In the previous fourteen seasons that the two clubs had met in the competition at both the Boleyn and Memorial grounds, there had not been one single draw, with West Ham winning no less than twelve of those fixtures against Rangers two. Visits to the East End club in the Western League from 1901/02 to 1905/06 also resulted in 5 straight victories for the Hammers. The West London club's home record against West Ham was not at all impressive either, so over this period QPR could complain that the Hammers were without doubt their bogy side.

Next up was the short trip to the Den for another local derby against Millwall. Although this fixture had always been an intense battle the Hammers did not have a good record on their opponents ground, and this contest went in Millwall's favour by two goals to one. It was a fine game nevertheless with West Ham taking the lead through Puddefoot, but the home side rallied round and scored twice to take the points. It was described as 'value for money' for the attendance of 15,000.

In the past five seasons against Bristol Rovers at home, four victories and one draw had resulted in West Ham rattling up a total of twenty-two goals overall, and another four were added in a 4-1 victory. It could have been a different story, as Rovers were denied a goal that the referee had given in the first minute of the game, only for a linesman to insist that the ball had not crossed the line, and the referee changed his mind. The Hammers did not really show their best until the second half, with Percy Wright, on the left wing, being one of the scorers in an isolated appearance, and Frank Burton scoring from the penalty spot. Bailey and Leafe scored the others.

At the Boleyn Social and Sports Club next door to the Boleyn ground, the West Ham players were still carrying out their rifle practice, and it was at this time that the club held another of its flying billiard handicaps of '25 up'. None other than Tommy Brandon, now out of favour and playing in the reserve side, who won the final. A '250' handicap was also held, and another of the Hammer's reserves, R. Appleby, put up a good display to finish runner-up. The game of billiards was very much a favourite of many footballers at the time, as we have seen.

A victory was expected for the visit to Croydon Common, now back in the first division of the Southern League after a spell of four seasons in the second. The South London club were finding it hard going having won just one match and drawn two from ten starts. The Hammers duly obliged with a victory by 2 goals to 1.

Most of the meetings with Reading over the years had produced good football, and the visit of the 'Biscuitmen' was no exception. From the spectators' viewpoint with its fast flowing football, it was the best game of the season so far. Casey, back in the side for the first time this season, supplied Bailey with the pass to open the scoring in the first half, but during the second period the visitors unbelievably scored twice inside one minute to go in front. The referee blew his whistle for a goal seconds before Alf Leafe put the ball into the net for the equaliser, which the Reading defenders complained distracted their attention, but the referee waived them away. The winning goal was a gem from Syd Puddefoot. Going through the visitors' defence, he feinted to pass the ball, dribbled round a defender and slid the ball past

Jack Macksey

the opposing 'keeper. 'Puddy' had now scored nine goals in twelve games, and was already proving a force to be reckoned with at the early age of twenty.

West Ham's record over the previous eight seasons against Southampton at the Dell had been quite phenomenal. They had recorded five victories and three draws over that period, winning the last four. All good things have to come to an end, and the Hammers were decisively beaten by 3 goals to one. After twenty-five minutes the 'Saints' opened the scoring from a penalty kick, and in the next minute went further ahead. It was the second match running that the Hammers had conceded two goals in very quick succession. A third was almost added before the break, but another did come in the second half when Webster was drawn out of his goal by the Saints' Dominy, who put the ball in the empty net. West Ham's forwards were poor on the day with the exception of Ashton, but Leafe scored before the end. Only Whiteman and Burton came away with any credit.

The reserve team were having another good season with Stallard, gaining in experience, hitting in the goals. Injuries had been hampering the side with Woodards, Wright and young Jack Tresadern being particularly affected. George Hilsdon, who had been 'nursing' forwards along in the second eleven, had also dislocated an elbow.

Club captain Tommy Randall had been out of action for eleven weeks, but had fought back bravely to be included in the team for the visit of Northampton Town. The 'Cobblers' had never been an easy side to play against, but on this occasion the visitors would have had a record beating, had it not been for the stubborn display of Thorpe in the visitors' goal, whereas it was 40 minutes into the game before Joe Webster had a shot to stop. Thorpe made no less than 14 saves in the first half and another 13 in the second!! There was sympathy for the 'keeper that despite this number of saves, it took just one goal, from Leafe after a pass from Butcher, to take both points.

Failure to score more than one in the above game saw three regulars rested for the fixture at Watford. Puddefoot, Casey and Leafe were left out, and replaced by Bailey, Carr and the ever-loyal Jack Mackesy, coming in for just his fifth appearance in the first team in three seasons. The changes worked well as the side put on a good forward display despite the rain and muddy conditions. There was just one goal that divided the teams, but it was another victory. Bailey scored just before the interval from a corner taken by Carr. The attendance at Cassio Road was just 2,000, a reflection of the reduced interest due to the War and the call to arms.

There had been much discussion and debate from early in the season as to whether professional football should continue under the current circumstances. The press had instituted a boycott of matches, but in an inconsistent manner. As the West Ham United programme pointed out, if business in general was to go on as usual, then reporting should go on just the same.

The Management Committee of the Football League met on November 30th 1914, and decided to re-affirm the decision to continue the game, and to send a copy of the resolution to the FA The same evening the representatives of the London professional clubs held a meeting and passed the following resolution:-

'Whilst strongly of opinion that the present agitation of a certain section of the daily London Press is unscrupulous, unwarrantable and undignified and an abuse of the liberty given to the Press, this meeting of representatives of London professional football clubs is, nevertheless, prepared to discontinue the game and close grounds simultaneously with the closing of racecourses, golf links, theatres, music halls and picture palaces and kindred entertainments. This resolution has reference to the decision of the London daily press not to publish reports of professional matches. The question that naturally intrudes itself is whether the abandoning of the game would have the desired effect of inducing the spectators of serviceable age to enlist. Undoubtedly the attendances at professional matches have suffered by the enlistment of football partisans, and this goes to show that the football public have not been backward in giving their services to the country; in fact, a comparison of the enlistments from the partisans of this sport and partisans of other sports would be interesting. With regard to the players themselves, they are a comparatively small body, but some interesting figures have come to hand with regard to professionals in London. At the beginning of the season out of a population of seven million in London there were 306 registered professionals, and of that number 56 are now serving with the forces. Of the 250 remaining, 156 are married leaving only 94 unmarried players, several of whom are responsible for the maintenance of homes. The record of the sport as regards assisting various war funds will bear inspection. That the professional, whether married or single, is doing his share towards relief is evidenced by the fact that the majority of them are making a weekly contribution from their wages. It does seem rather odd too, that the papers that have decided to discontinue the publishing of reports, should still publish the results of matches, and that some of them should even publish reports in their country editions.'

The Football League and the Southern League did not, of course, curtail their current league programmes, but from 1915/16 when the war intensified and Government restrictions were introduced, they were shut down, to be replaced with various regional competitions, until 1919/20.

Nobody realised it at the time but 'Tiddler' Ashton had played his last ever game in the Southern League at Watford, and due to illness he did not turn out for the match against Plymouth. Ashton had held the outside right position on a regular basis since 1908/09. Any player holding down such a position for so a long period must be a player of quality, and he can be rightly referred to as one of the West Ham 'all-time greats'. His appearances in the Southern League constitute a club record for that competition – 224 in total. When the wartime London Regional competition got under way he made another 81 appearances up to 1918/19, but he did not appear when West Ham took their first steps into the Football League.

Dan Bailey moved into Ashton's position and Puddefoot returned for the visit of Plymouth. The fixture turned out to be a very tense affair, and there were a number of incidents during the game that the referee had difficulty in controlling. It is strange that a number of fixtures between the two clubs had resulted in some extremely rough play. Injuries came as a result of some heavy tackling, and the Hammers were the first to suffer when Tommy Randall received a knock to his already suspect knee early in the game. Fortunately they were already a goal up at this stage after Bailey had supplied a pass from the right for Butcher to easily beat the advancing goalkeeper. Through some pretty rough play on both sides, Plymouth's Blott left the field with an injury, and Butcher received a nasty kick on the foot which meant his retirement, but he returned before half time. During that period, the four remaining forwards still played some clever football, and Puddefoot scored to increase the lead. The second half saw no let-up in dubious play, and unpleasant incidents were far too common. Inevitably each team lost another player, Wilcox of Plymouth and West Ham's Alf Tirrell, both with knee injuries. There was no further scoring despite the increased space with nine man teams.

Crystal Palace had always proved to be a tough nut to crack and had not been beaten at the Boleyn Castle since 1909/10. The visitors were to retain that run with a 2-1 victory. Once again the Hammers repeated the fault of conceding goals in quick succession when Palace scored twice in the first seven minutes of the match. Despite a continuous onslaught throughout the remaining 83 minutes, the opposition goal was only breached once when Mackesy score with a long shot with just 6 minutes left. The visitors' stubborn defence was almost all down to Johnson in goal. His numerous saves were lost count of, and so frequent were they made that he proved himself to be a goalkeeper of quality.

On the following Monday the club arranged a fixture between West Ham reserves and the 2nd East Anglian Territorial Artillery (Stratford) in aid of the War Fund. Despite the pros' obvious superiority the score was just 1-1 at the break, but the final score was 6-2 to the reserves. For the record Hilsdon scored three, with Appleby, Brandon and Price adding the others. The score of course, was irrelevant. The aim was to provide extra finances for the War Fund.

At this time there was still an ongoing campaign from a number of quarters for the banning of all professional footballers' contracts and the dissolution of the current league fixtures. There were several influential and high profile individuals involved in this campaign, as it was felt that the cancelling of football, involving those playing or those who were attending matches, prevented fit men from joining up when the regular Army was crying out for new recruits. We have already seen how the Football League Management Committee set out their objections to such proposals, but the pressure still continued. What was conveniently forgotten by this so-called 'stoppers campaign' was a number of important arguments. Many professional footballers had already joined up as individuals, and many clubs in Britain had opened up their grounds for recruiting, military training, war charity collections and (as the game above), special fixtures arranged to supplement the War Fund.

Matters were now coming to a head however, as one of the protagonists, Sir John Lonsdale, a Unionist MP, was ready to ask Prime Minister Asquith a question in Parliament that was intended to result in football being officially abandoned with immediate effect. What Lonsdale was not aware of was that Sir George McCrae, a former MP, had founded the 16th Royal Scots, a battalion formed in Edinburgh on 25th November 1914, and amongst the ranks were footballers from various Scottish clubs, with Heart of Midlothian providing a large number of players. This group was soon joined by men from many professions including almost 600 supporters of Hearts and 150 from Hibernian. McCrae made a successful approach to the War Office, which enabled him to gain some concessions for the footballers that had volunteered. Lord Kitchener gave an assurance that any professional footballer that joined the battalion would be allowed to complete any playing commitments for his club until the end of the season. The agreement helped satisfy directors of clubs who would otherwise be facing financial difficulties as time went on. Confirmation of the news of the battalion, and the agreement arrived at, reached Prime Minister Asquith just in time to nip Lonsdale's pernicious opinions in the bud, and helped to solve the problem, by persuading the 'stoppers' that numbers of professionals were willing to make their sacrifice, but the action taken would also stave off the demise of the professional game as a whole.

This had an almost immediate effect on professional players in England as more, from a number of clubs, joined individual units, though it was significant and disappointing that none of the clubs were from London. With this in mind a meeting was arranged for the 15th December 1914 at Fulham Town Hall, with various dignitaries and directors and officials from professional clubs present. The main purpose was to raise a Footballers' Battalion, which would be officially known as the 17th Service Battalion of the Middlesex Regiment. After a number of speeches the appeal went out to those players present to join the Footballers' Battalion. The first player to step on to the platform was the Clapton Orient outside right F.W. Parker, and after a while 35 players from a total of 500 who were present joined up, including ten players of the Clapton Orient club. Sadly of course, many professionals who did eventually 'go to war' were killed in action. It is not known how many West Ham men attended that meeting, but several current and ex-players played their part in the war in various armed services, some of whom sadly perished.

For the match at Norwich, Joe Hughes returned as Joe Webster had suffered an injury to his hand, and Dan Woodards came back into the side and remained there due to the continued absence of Tommy Randall, who was not to recover from his knee injury, and would retire from the game come the end of the season. Tommy, the bald headed genius, had been a great servant to the club, and had notched up 189 appearances in the Southern League, making the first of those as far back as the final game of the 1906/07 season.

Jimmy Carr was injured within 5 minutes of the match, when through an accidental clash his scalp was laid bare which was so bad he could not stand, so to gain a point with ten men for 85 minutes was admirable. The team were helped in their struggle, which finished scoreless and very even throughout, by the cheers and encouragement of hundreds of Army Territorials from Essex who were training in Norfolk at the time.

It must have been depressing for the team to journey down to Brighton on Christmas Day and play in front of the worst attendance of the season – just 1,000 souls – for another 0-0 draw. Those that stayed away had the right idea. In contrast there were 9,600 at the Boleyn ground for the return on Boxing Day when the Hammers won by 2-1 with Puddefoot, returning after a two game rest, scoring both of them. His second was 'a beauty'. Hilsdon was also back in the side and would play in the vast majority of the remaining games. The victory meant that the club were now in fourth place in the table.

Puddefoot was again at his best when Exeter came to Upton Park. Despite a surface that was extremely slippery due to the recent heavy rains, Syd controlled and passed the ball superbly, and after fourteen minutes he opened the scoring, and ten minutes later found the net again. In defence, the full-backs, Burton and Cope, played their part and were impassable. After the break Fenwick scored from a rebound, before Puddefoot claimed his hat-trick, after a pass from Hilsdon. The visitors got a consolation goal just before the end of the game.

January was a time when all Hammers' fans became excited at the prospect of facing Football League First Division opposition in the FA Cup. They had had the good fortune to be drawn at home to such clubs on several occasions in their fifteen-year spell in the Southern League, and 1914/15 was no exception. Newcastle United were the team's opponents for the third time in eight seasons, and it was at the Boleyn ground.

West Ham opened quite shakily against a swirling wind, and inside three minutes were a goal down when the visitors scored direct from a corner, which Hughes appeared to got a touch to the ball, but failed to divert. Some fine play by the Newcastle men had them on the attack, and ten minutes later when Burton missed his kick, Goodwill netted. This was a staggering blow to the Hammers—two goals down in thirteen minutes! The team pulled themselves together for the rest of the half, with Hilsdon once hitting a tremendous cross shot towards the goal, which was pushed round the post. West Ham appeared determined to get into the game in the second period, and continually attacked. Whether or not the visitors were just content to defend a two goal lead is pure conjecture, but the whole Newcastle defence had to work like Trojans to keep the Hammers out. With thirteen minutes left, Casey took a corner and Mellor, the 'keeper, missed it completely and Leafe headed home. Amidst great excitement in the crowd the pressure was maintained and eight minutes from the end the equaliser came. Leafe, from fully thirty yards out on the wing, hit a strong shot that firstly appeared to be going outside, but the wind caused the ball to swerve, and it hit the inside of the post and went in. Suitably hugged by his team mates, the same player, just before the final whistle, tried the same shot. The ball hit the post and agonizingly rolled along the line, before being kicked clear. It meant a replay at St James' Park.

Because of wartime restrictions, cup-tie replays were prohibited from being played in midweek and the match had to take place on the following Saturday. The team and officials caught the 2.30pm train from Kings Cross and stayed overnight at the Turks Head Hotel in Newcastle. During the week George Hilsdon was confined to bed with 'flu, and 'Tiddler' Ashton was recalled (for what turned out to be his final peace time competitive game) with Leafe moving inside to fill Hilsdon's position.

The replay was just as exciting as the first game. On this occasion it was the Hammers that took the lead early on, when Casey scored after 6 minutes. Newcastle's Pailor headed an equaliser after 30 minutes, and West Ham continued the recent bad habit of conceding two goals in quick succession when the same player hit home within another two minutes. The 'Magpies' got on top, and 15 minutes after the interval Hibbert scored their third, and it appeared all over, but Leafe scored with 17 minutes remaining, and from that point it was all-out attack from the Boleyn boys, and the home side had to desperately defend. They could consider themselves very fortunate late on when McCracken handled a shot from Puddefoot in the area, which the referee ignored. The general consensus of opinion was that a penalty should have been given. Casey, with his lightning speed, was the pick of the Hammers' side, and it was a pity that Ashton received a fractured jaw in the second half, to hinder the team's forward play, although Puddefoot and Fenwick were well held. The weak spots in the team were at full-back where Cope and Burton had, in modern parlance 'a bit of a 'mare.'

West Ham reserves, being the current holders of the South Eastern League championship, met a Rest of the League side at Boleyn Castle and won by a solitary goal, which was scored by full-back Tommy Brandon, who was playing very well, but for some reason could not get back into the first team.

The second eleven also entertained Boscombe in the South Eastern League. Those that were present welcomed 'old timer' George Kitchen, who by now was 39 years old. George was just as good as ever and conceded just the one goal in a 1-1 draw. The south coast side changed their name after the Great War to Bournemouth & Boscombe Athletic and entered the Southern League. In 1923 the club were accepted into the Football League Division Three (South).

There were further falls of snow on an already snowbound pitch when Portsmouth were the visitors. In modern times the game would have been postponed, and with players unable to pass the ball accurately and slipping over in the snow, the encounter was a very ragged one. West Ham were the most forceful and went two goals up before Pompey replied. The final score of 4-3 appears close, but the visitors never drew level and were always one goal behind. The Hammers' scorers were Burton (a penalty), Leafe (2) and Casey.

As a result of the poor conditions in the previous game, injuries were picked up and Askew, Burton and Leafe were all unable to make the trip to Wiltshire to meet Swindon Town. Butcher, Brandon and Carr came in as replacements, and overall the team could consider themselves unlucky not to take both points in a 1-1 draw. Both goalkeepers were busy, and Joe Hughes made one or two outstanding saves, one of which was from an effort from ex-Hammers' favourite Bert Denyer. The home side took the lead after half time, but both sides could have then scored, but for some erratic shooting. West Ham then had Hilsdon running through to feed Casey who netted the equaliser, and then Swindon were on the defensive, but there was no further score.

When Southend United came to Upton Park, they were struggling near the bottom of the table, but with their bustling play they obtained an early goal that shook the Hammers, and it looked likely that they might add to their lead. The game gradually turned after home side gradually got on top, and Marshall, under pressure in the visiting defence put through his own goal before the break. The Boleyn boys got into their stride in the second half and Leahy, the visiting goalkeeper who had been with West Ham as a reserve, showed his ability with several good saves. He could not however, prevent Leafe from heading home a cross from Casey with twenty minutes left, and Puddefoot scoring from a pass from Leafe for a 3-1 victory for the Hammers. Southend, throughout the campaign, had good service from ex-West Ham players Alf Frost and Frank Burrill, and the latter was to finish up their top scorer for the season.

At half time in the above game, the Parliamentary Recruiting Department of Westminster addressed the spectators, and it was also announced that since the season had started the West Ham players had contributed over £61 to the War Relief Fund.

For the journey to meet Queens Park Rangers, the Hammers had to travel to the Kensal Rise Athletic Ground, which had originally been the West London side's home from 1899 to 1901. This move back was due to the requirements of the Military and the 'Defence of the Realm Act', which meant that the club's HQ at their Park Royal Ground was to be used for Army purposes for the remainder of the war.

Although the weather was bad with gale force winds, and with the pitch in an awful state, the quality of football was good. West Ham's combination play was impressive but QPR had more of the attacking, and Joe Hughes brought off a number of good saves especially crosses from the wing. This enabled the Hammers to score later in the half when Macleod, in the Rangers' goal was penalised for 'carrying'. Casey took the kick across the goalmouth and Whiteman scored. An even second half saw the home side equalise, and Puddefoot strike a post, but it remained 1-1 at the end.

For the visit of Millwall the highest attendance of the season was realised when 17,000 came through the turnstiles. This was a very welcome addition to the club's finances, as gates right across the country for professional matches had been very low due to the war situation. The game was very fiercely contested throughout, and it was Puddefoot who opened the scoring with a delightful goal. Millwall had a chance to equalise when they were awarded a penalty, but the ball was put wide, much to the extreme delight of the Hammers' fans. The visitors did draw level before half time, but there was no further scoring.

The point gained meant that West Ham had now gone nine consecutive league games without defeat - four wins and five draws. More importantly they were lying in second spot in the table. Could they at last take the Southern League title?

The run had to come to an end of course, and it happened at Bristol Rovers, where in a very disappointing game, partly spoilt by a strong wind, the home side scored the only goal just before the break following a free kick. There was some ill-feeling throughout causing constant stoppages by the referee, and West Ham suffered through the loss of Whiteman due to an injury.

Young Arthur Stallard came into the side for his first game of the season after a good scoring record in the reserves. Croydon Common, really struggling against relegation, were the visitors, and on the play it should have been a 'cricket score' for the Hammers, but a mixture of really awful shooting by all the home forwards, and some outstanding goalkeeping by Williamson in the visiting goal, stopped that from happening. Croydon had their moments on a number of breakaways, and 'Bronco' Burton at full-back was found wanting on several occasions. With play being around the visitor's goal for 80% of the time, and with Williamson performing goalkeeping heroics, it was

Arthur Stallard

just three minutes from the end when Hilsdon finally got the ball in the net. West Ham got the points. Williamson got the sympathy.

It was now second place in the table again just two points behind Watford, and that was maintained with a good solid victory over Luton Town at Kenilworth Road. Dan Bailey came in for Hilsdon, and scored, with Leafe adding a second in a 2-1 victory.

Dan Woodards was unable to play at Reading, due to a thigh strain, and his place was taken by Fenwick. The home side were also in strong contention for the title, and had always been a difficult side to overcome at Elm Park. So it was to prove, when they triumphed by three goals to one. The Hammers had some excuse in that Stallard suffered a severe blow to his thigh, which rendered him useless for an hour, and Fenwick was handicapped throughout the match with a throat infection.

On the injury front Alf Tirrell was unlikely to play for the remainder of the season and Tommy Randall had an operation on his injured knee. Sadly for Tommy, and the club, it resulted in his retirement from the game altogether.

The club were back in contention for the title after they had 'seen off' Southampton at Upton Park. There were three changes to the team. Hilsdon came in for Bailey, Woodards returned in place of Fenwick, and George Speak was in at full-back for Burton. A 3-0 victory saw all the goals scored in the first half an hour. The first came after some excellent combination play. Casey crossed to Hilsdon who hit the bar with a rattling shot. From the rebound Stallard neatly passed to Leafe who netted. The second came from a penalty that Hilsdon converted, and the third came from a cross drive from Stallard.

The visit to Northampton saw an attendance of just 1,500 spectators. Previous away games had seen 2,000 at Gillingham, 2,000 at Watford, 1,000 at Brighton and 3,000 at Swindon Town. In retrospect, had it been prudent to continue with the normal league programme in time of war? From a financial viewpoint it certainly had not. Morally, and perhaps from a practical viewpoint, it was also questionable.

The lack of spectators did not detract from a from a stubbornly fought out contest at the County Ground, although West Ham threw away another point after dominating Northampton with their clever inter-passing game. Sadly, it was their finishing that let them down. The 'Cobblers' fought hard themselves and opened the scoring in the 17th minute. Stallard, who had been leading the line intelligently, was rewarded when his dropping shot hit the inside of the post and went in for the equaliser.

There were constant reminders of the war, and just before Easter West Ham United received a letter from British servicemen in France thanking the club for the donation of old footballs enabling the troops to have a game of football at the front.

On Good Friday Cardiff City came to the Boleyn ground still in with a chance of the Southern League title, as were West Ham. It was yet another story of the Hammers not taking their chances, especially as the visitors had ten men for most of the game. Stallard did find the net before half time, but in the second half an over zealous referee spoiled the flow of the game with continuous use of the whistle, but Stallard, who was having another fine game, notched a second goal before the Welsh side were awarded a penalty, which was converted. The decision was hotly disputed and led to the referee gathering the players together and giving them a lecture. The result left West Ham second in the table, nicely tucked in behind Watford, who were due at Upton Park the next day.

When West Ham United took the field, the players were wearing black armbands out of respect for the late George Webb, whose funeral had taken place in the morning. Never to be forgotten as the first West Ham United player to pull on an England shirt, George had not played at all for some time due to illness. He was just 28 years old when he died of consumption.

Dan Woodards was the only player in the current team to have played in the same eleven as Webb, and he was part of a half-back line, with Askew and Burton, who played a significant part by holding the Watford forwards in this important encounter. The Hammers' front line, led again superbly by Stallard, took the game to the visitors, and should have been in front by more than the goal scored by Puddefoot, who had converted a centre by Percy Wright. Williams, the Watford 'keeper, was the star of his team at this stage, but the visitors played much better after the break as the Hammers fell away, although Hilsdon added a second from the penalty spot after Stallard was blatantly pushed over in the area.

The result made the visit to Cardiff on Easter Monday crucial for both clubs. The Hammers immediately took the offensive, and it took some great defending by the home side to keep a clean sheet, but the game gradually turned Cardiff's way and they opened the scoring after 35 minutes. Following this, Billy Cope was spoken to by the referee, and was lucky not to be sent off for some dubious tackling. Cope had a tendency to overstep the mark on occasions, and tread a very fine line. In the second half, despite some near misses by

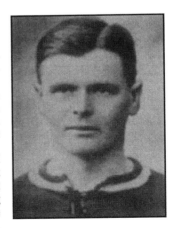

Billy Cope

Puddefoot, Hilsdon and Leafe, it was Cardiff who added their second goal with 25 minutes left for play. West Ham still pressed and Stallard eventually scored with a tremendous shot, but before the end were denied the chance of point from the game, when the referee turned down an appeal for a penalty against Cardiff's Brittan. It was a palpable case of handball, and the home side were fortunate to get away with it.

The Hammers were down to third and it would mean two wins from the final three fixtures, with the chasing teams all losing, for any remaining chance of the title.

It was not to be, and the season fizzled out like a damp squib. At Plymouth the home side won with a late goal, and a visit south of the river to meet Crystal Palace resulted in another defeat. The habitual malaise of conceding two goals in quick succession occurred again when Palace scored two goals inside the last five minutes of the first half. Stallard pulled a goal back just before the end.

Although it was not realised at the time, West Ham United's fifteen-year Southern League history ended with an unexciting 1-1 draw against Norwich City at the Boleyn ground. The club's progress on the field of play might be summed up in a little matrimonial ditty of the day, slightly altered to suit the subject:-

On the football parade
Our frustrating side
Always the bridesmaid
Never the bride

Back: H Sutton (Director), R Whiteman, R Beading, J Webster, J Hughes, F Burton, V Holliday, R Allen. Next to back: A Fenwick, W Cope, T Brandon, D Woodards, P Tirrell, W Askew, G Speak, H Tough, J Tresadern, T Randall. Centre: C Paynter, J Cearns (Director), T Taylorson (Director), G Fundell (Financial Secretary), ES King (Manager), J Grisdale (President), L Johnson (Vice-Chairman), G Davis (Director), A Smith, J Johnson, T Williamson (Ground Committee), J Holden (Director), G Handley (Director), F Piercy. Seated: H Caton, G Walden, H Ashton, D Bailey, R Appleby, A Stallard, W White (Chairman), A Leafe, J Macksey, G Hilsdon, L Young, J Casey, J Carr. On ground: R Thorndike, H Cordell, S Puddefoot, G Butcher, P Wright.

1914/15

4th in Southern League Division One

#		Date	Opponent	Score	Scorers	Att	Ashton H	Askew W	Bailey D	Brandon T	Burton F	Butcher G	Carr J	Casey J	Caton H	Cope W	Fenwick A	Hilsdon G	Hughes J	Leafe A	Mackesy J	Puddefoot S	Randall T	Speak G	Stallard A	Tirrell A	Tresadern J	Webster J	Whiteman R	Woodards D	Wright P
1	Sep	1	GILLINGHAM	2-1	Puddefoot 2	5000	7	5	8							2	4			10		9	6	3					1		11
2		5	Exeter City	1-3	Puddefoot	4000	7	5	8							2	4			10		9	6	3					1		11
3		9	Gillingham	0-4		2000	7	5	8		6					2				10		9		3					1	4	11
4		12	LUTON TOWN	3-0	Puddefoot 2, Hilsdon	5000	7	5	8							2	6	10				9		3					1	4	11
5		19	Portsmouth	1-3	Hilsdon	7000	7	5	8	2						3	6	10				9							1	4	11
6		26	SWINDON TOWN	1-1	Puddefoot	11000	7	5	8		3			11		2	6	10				9							1	4	
7	Oct	3	Southend United	1-0	Leafe	5000	7	5	8		3			11		2	6			10		9							1	4	
8		10	QUEEN'S PARK RANGERS	2-2	Leafe, Puddefoot	12000	7	5	8		3			11		2	6			10		9							1	4	
9		17	Millwall	1-2	Puddefoot	15000	7	5			3			11		2			8	10		9						6	1	4	
10		24	BRISTOL ROVERS	4-1	Bailey, Burton, Leafe, Wright	10000	7	5	8		3					2	6			10		9							1	4	11
11		31	Croydon Common	2-1	Bailey, Leafe	5000	7	5	8		2		11	7			6			10		9		3					1	4	
12	Nov	7	READING	3-2	Bailey, Leafe, Puddefoot	10000	7	5	8		2		11				6			10		9		3					1	4	
13		14	Southampton	1-3	Leafe	5000	7	5	8		2		11				6			10		9		3					1	4	
14		21	NORTHAMPTON T	1-0	Leafe	8000	7	5			2	8	11							10		9		3					1	4	
15		28	Watford	1-0	Bailey	2000	7	5	9		2	8	11								10		6	3					1	4	
16	Dec	5	PLYMOUTH ARGYLE	2-0	Butcher, Carr	6000		5	7		2	8	11								10	9	6	3					1	4	
17		12	CRYSTAL PALACE	1-2	Mackesy	5000		5	7		2	8	11								10	9		3				6	1	4	
18		19	Norwich City	0-0		4000		5	9		2	8	11			3		10	1	7									4	6	
19		25	Brighton & Hove Albion	0-0		1000		5	9		2	8	11			3		10	1	7									4	6	
20		26	BRIGHTON & HOVE ALB.	2-1	Puddefoot 2	9600		5			2	8	11			3	6	10	1	7		9							4		
21	Jan	2	EXETER CITY	4-1	Puddefoot 3, Fenwick	7000		5			2		11			3	10	8	1	7		9							4	6	
22		23	PORTSMOUTH	4-3	Leafe 2, Burton, Casey	3000		5			2		11			3	8	10	1	7		9							4	6	
23		30	Swindon Town	1-1	Casey	3000				2		8	7	11		3	5	10	1			9							4	6	
24	Feb	6	SOUTHEND UNITED	3-1	Puddefoot 2, Leafe	5000				2		8		11		3	5	10	1	7		9							4	6	
25		13	Queen's Park Rangers	1-1	Whiteman	5000		5			2			11	7	3		10	1	8		9							4	6	
26		20	MILLWALL	1-1	Puddefoot	17000		5			2			11	7	3		10	1	8		9							4	6	
27		27	Bristol Rovers	0-1		3000		5			2			11	7	3		10	1	8		9							4	6	
28	Mar	6	CROYDON COMMON	1-0	Hilsdon	5000		5			2			11		3		10	1	7		8			9				4	6	
29		10	Luton Town	2-1	Bailey, Leafe	7000		5	10		2			11		3			1	7		8			9				4	6	
30		13	Reading	1-3	Leafe	7000		5	10		2			11		3	6		1	7		8			9				4		
31		20	SOUTHAMPTON	3-0	Hilsdon, Leafe, Stallard	8000		5						11		2		10	1	7		8		3	9				4	6	
32		27	Northampton Town	1-1	Stallard	1500		5						11		2		10	1	7		8		3	9				4	6	
33	Apr	2	CARDIFF CITY	2-1	Stallard 2	13000		5								2		10	1	7		8		3	9				4	6	11
34		3	WATFORD	2-0	Hilsdon, Puddefoot	10000		5			4					2		10	1	7		8		3	9					6	11
35		5	Cardiff City	1-2	Stallard	10000		5								2		10	1	7		8		3	9				4	6	11
36		10	Plymouth Argyle	0-1		5000		5						11		2			1	7		8		3	9				4	6	10
37		17	Crystal Palace	1-2	Stallard	4000		5								2		10	1	7		8	11	3	9				4	6	
38		24	NORWICH CITY	1-1	Stallard	3000		5	7							2		10	1			8	11	3	9				4	6	
					Apps		14	36	20	2	26	9	9	19	4	31	19	20	21	30	5	35	5	13	11	6	2	17	34	20	10
					Goals			5			2	1	1	2			1	5		13	1	18			7				1		1

F.A. Cup

		Date	Opponent	Score	Scorers	Att	Ashton H	Askew W	Bailey D	Brandon T	Burton F	Butcher G	Carr J	Casey J	Caton H	Cope W	Fenwick A	Hilsdon G	Hughes J	Leafe A	Mackesy J	Puddefoot S	Randall T	Speak G	Stallard A	Tirrell A	Tresadern J	Webster J	Whiteman R	Woodards D	Wright P
R1	Jan	9	NEWCASTLE UNITED	2-2	Leafe 2	15000		5			2			11		3	10	8	1	7		9							4	6	
rep		16	Newcastle United	2-3	Casey, Leafe	28130	7	5			2			11		3	10		1	8		9							4	6	

Balls, boots and laces of the time …. though your publisher remembers playing with similar kit in the 1950s!

		P	W	D	L	F	A	W	D	L	F	A	Pts
1	Watford	38	12	4	3	37	15	10	4	5	31	31	52
2	Reading	38	12	4	3	37	16	9	3	7	31	27	49
3	Cardiff City	38	16	1	2	51	12	6	3	10	21	26	48
4	WEST HAM UNITED	38	14	4	1	42	18	4	5	10	16	29	45
5	Northampton Town	38	11	5	3	37	22	5	6	8	19	29	43
6	Southampton	38	14	3	2	56	28	5	2	12	22	46	43
7	Portsmouth	38	10	5	4	26	14	6	5	8	28	28	42
8	Millwall	38	9	4	6	28	23	7	6	6	22	28	42
9	Swindon Town	38	11	5	3	55	21	4	6	9	22	38	41
10	Brighton & Hove Alb.	38	11	5	3	29	16	5	2	12	17	31	39
11	Exeter City	38	10	3	6	32	16	5	5	9	18	25	38
12	Queen's Park Rangers	38	8	4	7	30	16	5	8	6	25	28	38
13	Norwich City	38	10	6	3	33	16	1	8	10	20	40	36
14	Luton Town	38	6	3	10	27	34	7	5	7	34	39	34
15	Crystal Palace	38	8	4	7	24	25	5	4	10	23	36	34
16	Bristol Rovers	38	12	2	5	42	28	2	1	16	11	47	31
17	Plymouth Argyle	38	8	7	4	34	25	0	7	12	17	36	30
18	Southend United	38	8	5	6	27	20	2	3	14	17	44	28
19	Croydon Common	38	7	6	6	28	18	2	3	14	19	45	27
20	Gillingham	38	6	7	6	32	29	0	1	18	11	54	20

EPILOGUE

The decision was made to bring the normal Football League and Southern League proceedings to a close due the continuing conflict in France and Belgium. The idea in August 1914 that 'the war will be over by Christmas' was shown to be a ludicrous and forlorn hope, and the country as a whole had no notion whatsoever of how long the hostilities would last. Top-flight football continued from 1915/16 to 1918/19 albeit on a regional basis, and many clubs struggled to survive, including West Ham United. Full credit must be given to Syd King, ably assisted by Charlie Paynter in their relentless efforts, not only to find the personnel and raise a regular team for the London Combination, but to create a very successful side for four consecutive seasons. This was difficult to achieve, as a number of players were not always available due to the part they played in the war effort by joining various service organisations, with some making the ultimate sacrifice.

Syd Puddefoot was one of those players fortunate enough to play for the club in the London Combination during the war, and he improved his reputation by scoring an amazing 98 goals in 126 appearances, including seven in an 11-0 victory over Crystal Palace in 1917/18. After the war his goalscoring record of 64 goals in 103 Football League brought him to the attention of a number of clubs, and having created the transfer record of £2,000 when Shea was sold to Blackburn in 1913, the club then broke that fee by selling Puddefoot to Scottish club Falkirk for the new record of £5,000 in February 1922, which caused consternation amongst the Irons' fans. After three years Syd moved on to Blackburn Rovers where he won an FA Cup winners medal in 1928 and obtained three England caps. He returned

Syd King in 1923

to the Boleyn towards the end of the 1931/32 season to assist West Ham in the club's unsuccessful attempt to avoid relegation. He moved on to coaching in Turkey in 1933 with Fenerbahce and then Galatasaray, but returned in 1935 to take the manager's post at Northampton Town.

For Syd King's part in the transfer of Puddefoot to Falkirk, the directors awarded him a bonus of £300, and until his eventual demise he was well respected in the club, operating between the players and the board within their financial restraints, but he was not a manager in the modern day sense with a lot of tactical 'nous'. Within his 31 year rule, as the board's ideal top employee, which included promotion from the Football League Second Division to the First Division and the Wembley Cup Final of 1923, he served safe in the knowledge that whatever the club's League position his job would not be in jeopardy. Financially, he was well rewarded by the directors by means of bonuses, and in 1920 he received a cheque for £1,000, a huge amount in those days. He was well-known in the local community, attending fetes, festivals and various openings, and was a well admired figure with his smart appearance and flamboyant personality. King's downfall however, was his liking for drink, which was to eventually lead to his dismissal and his death. In November 1932 he attended a board meeting where his drunkenness and insubordination to the directors led to a three-month suspension without salary, and in January 1933 he committed suicide by lacing an alcoholic drink with a corrosive liquid. It is pure irony of course, that Arnold Hills who was responsible for the founding of West Ham United, was a strict temperance man and an evangelist who campaigned against the evils of drink for many years.

The club's splendid playing record throughout the four seasons during the Great War, with Syd King at the helm however, undoubtedly had some influence over acceptance into the Football League when normal service was resumed in 1919. When the final vote count was made for the poll for membership, West Ham received 32 votes behind Coventry City (35), with Rotherham (28) and South Shields (28) all being voted into the new revised 22-club Second Division. Another new dawn beckoned.

WEST HAM UNITED SOUTHERN LEAGUE APPEARANCES AND GOALS 1900/01 to 1914/15

The year quoted is the first year of the season.

From	To		Apps	Gls
1900	1902	Allan, Robert **	52	1
1903	1908	Allison, Tommy	156	7
1901		Ambler, Charlie	1	0
1908	1914	Ashton, Herbert	224	22
1912	1914	Askew, William	104	2
1908		Atkins C	2	1
1912	1914	Bailey D *	49	13
1904		Bamlett, Herbert	18	0
1902	1903	Barnes, William	49	5
1913		Beale, Robert	1	0
1911		Bell, George	2	0
1900	1903	Bigden, James **	91	3
1902		Biggar, William	8	0
1903		Birnie, Alexander	1	0
1905	1912	Blackburn, Fred	218	24
1904		Blackwood, John	4	1
1902	1906	Blythe, Joe	55	0
1913		Bourne W	1	0
1906	1911	Bourne, Stanley	13	0
1911		Bradford T	1	0
1913	1914	Brandon, Thomas	33	0
1903	1905	Bridgeman, Billy	72	19
1907	1908	Brown, William	20	4
1904		Brunton, Fred	1	0
1911	1913	Burrill, Frank	17	2
1912	1914	Burton F *	50	4
1908		Burton, John	15	3
1902	1905	Bush, Robert	20	1
1903		Butchart J	3	0
1909	1914	Butcher G *	62	9
1909	1911	Caldwell, Thomas	84	12
1902		Campbell, John	18	1
1909		Cannon, Frank	3	1
1914		Carr J	9	1
1904		Carrick, Christopher	18	6
1912	1913	Carter H	10	0
1912	1914	Casey, Jack	74	12
1912	1914	Caton, Harry	10	0
1908		Chalkley, George	7	0
1903		Church, William	2	0
1906	1908	Clarke, David	17	0
1914		Cope W *	31	0
1900	1901	Corbett, Fred **	33	13
1908		Costello, Frank	12	3
1903	1905	Cotton, Charles	18	0
1900	1901	Craig, Charlie **	53	0
1909	1910	Curtis F	6	4
1902		Davidson, William	9	2
1908	1909	Dawson C	6	0
1911	1912	Dawson, Harold	22	3
1912	1913	Denyer, Albert	46	17
1913		Denyer, Frank	2	0
1900		Dove, Charles **	13	0
1902		Dow, James	13	0
1908		Dyer, James	3	0
1903		Earl	1	0
1908		Eastwood H	6	0
1902	1903	Eccles, George	59	0
1902		Evans	1	0
1902	1906	Fair, Aubrey	31	1
1909	1911	Fairman, Robert	91	0

From	To		Apps	Gls
1902		Farrell, John	20	3
1905	1907	Featherstone, Arthur	24	1
1900		Fenton, Fred	14	2
1914		Fenwick, Alfred	19	1
1904		Fletcher, Jack	25	7
1904		Flynn, Jack	20	3
1905		Ford, William	7	1
1912	1913	Forster, Harry	40	0
1908		Foster, Jack	15	9
1910	1911	Frost A	4	0
1907	1908	Frost, James	20	4
1904	1906	Gardner, Dave	77	0
1907	1908	Gault, James	47	0
1909	1911	Geggus, John	31	0
1911		Glover, Victor	29	0
1913		Goddard J	1	0
1900	1908	Grassam, Billy	169	65
1902	1903	Griffiths, Fred	48	0
1904		Hamilton	5	0
1904	1907	Hammond, Syd	32	0
1910	1912	Harrison, Fred	54	19
1907	1908	Harwood, Alf	12	0
1909		Haynes, Vincent	15	5
1904	1914	Hilsdon, George	85	31
1903		Hilsdon, Jack	1	0
1905		Hindle, Harry	3	0
1901		Hitchens J	1	0
1906	1907	Horn, George	8	0
1911	1914	Hughes, Joseph	90	0
1900	1901	Hunt, Fergus	42	9
1903		Ingham, William	2	0
1912	1913	Irvine, George	21	0
1905		Jackson, James	24	0
1903	1908	Jarvis, Len	133	5
1901		Jenkinson, William	19	2
1901		Jones, William	15	0
1900		Kaye, Albert	14	2
1900	1902	Kelly, William	33	0
1906	1907	Kemp, Fred	10	0
1910	1911	Kennedy, William	21	10
1900	1902	King, Syd **	59	0
1904		Kingsley, Matthew	29	0
1903		Kirby, William	33	10
1905	1910	Kitchen, George	184	5
1901		Kyle, Peter	1	0
1909	1910	Lavery, William	17	0
1913	1914	Leafe A *	63	33
1907		Lee, Tom	6	0
1906	1907	Lindsay, David	51	4
1901	1902	Linward, William	40	3
1913		Lonsdale, Thomas	21	0
1903		Lyon, Herbert	29	4
1911	1914	Mackesy J *	10	2
1905		Mackie, Charles	10	3
1903		Mapley, Percy	13	0
1909	1911	Massey, Frederick	38	0
1902		McAteer T	13	0
1905		McCartney, Alex	6	0
1904		McCartney, William	28	3
1901		McDonald, Alex	4	2
1900	1901	McEachrane, Rod **	53	5

From	To		Apps	Gls
1903		Mercer, Frederick	7	1
1902		Miecznikowski W	3	0
1910	1911	Miellear J	3	0
1908		Miller, Walter	11	5
1904		Milnes F	2	0
1900	1901	Monteith, Hugh	53	0
1900		Moore, Thomas **	4	0
1911		Morrison J	15	1
1900		Neil, George **	1	0
1903		Oakes, William	14	0
1902		Parkinson, Harry	2	0
1904	1911	Piercy, Frank	214	7
1900		Pinder	1	0
1900	1901	Pudan, Richard	7	0
1912	1914	Puddefoot S *	55	28
1900		Raisbeck. Len	2	0
1906	1914	Randall, Tom	189	9
1900	1901	Ratcliffe, George	41	14
1910	1911	Redward, Frank	7	0
1911		Redwood, George	3	0
1900		Reid, James **	13	5
1907		Robertson	1	0
1910	1913	Rothwell, James	87	4
1904		Russell, John	16	0
1903		Satterthwaite, Charlie	32	13
1909		Scanes, Albert	3	3
1907	1912	Shea, Daniel	179	111
1908	1910	Shreeve, Frederick	65	4
1909		Silor, William	6	0
1904		Simmons, Charles	34	8
1904		Smith, Sidney	2	1
1914		Speak, George	13	0
1913	1914	Stallard, Arthur	13	8
1905	1907	Stapley, Harry	71	39
1902		Sugden, Sidney	1	0
1907	1908	Taylor, Archie	60	0
1900		Taylor, Frank **	12	4
1906	1908	Taylor, William	4	0
1903		Thompson A	9	1
1913	1914	Tirrell A *	7	0
1908		Tirrell, Patrick	13	1
1900		Tranter, Walter **	4	0
1913	1914	Tresadern J *	6	0
1908	1909	Waggott, David	10	3
1909		Wagstaffe, George	3	0
1911		Walden, George	2	0
1900		Walker, Len **	1	0
1901	1902	Wallace L	17	3
1905	1907	Watson, Lionel	76	26
1903		Watts, Ernest	25	1
1908	1911	Webb, George	52	23
1914		Webster, Joseph	17	0
1909	1914	Whiteman, Robert	136	3
1906	1907	Wildman, William	39	0
1905		Wilkinson H	13	2
1905	1906	Winterhalder, Arthur	18	6
1905		Winterhalder, Herbert	4	0
1906	1914	Woodards D *	109	3
1914		Wright P	10	1
1901	1908	Yenson, William	50	0
1907	1908	Young, Robert	42	1

* Also played in the Football League.

** Also played in the Southern League for Thames Ironworks before 1900. Appearances and goals for the Ironworks are not included above.

WESTERN LEAGUE

Along with other Southern League clubs, West Ham were members of other League competitions from 1901/02 to 1908/09. The extra fixtures meant more gate money. Games were generally played mid-week. Reserve team players were sometimes used. West Ham's results were poor in the Western League, apart from 1906/07 when they were champions.

West Ham's scores are given first in the tables below.

1901/02 Division One

h	a		p	w	d	l	f	a	pts
2-4	2-3	Portsmouth	16	13	1	2	53	16	27
1-1	1-2	Tottenham Hotspur	16	11	3	2	42	17	25
1-1	0-2	Reading	16	7	3	6	29	22	17
0-1	0-1	Millwall Athletic	16	8	1	7	25	29	17
2-0	4-1	Bristol Rovers	16	8	0	8	25	31	16
1-0	1-2	Southampton	16	7	1	8	30	28	15
-	-	WEST HAM UNITED	16	6	2	8	30	20	14
0-1	4-1	Queen's Park Rangers	16	5	1	10	17	43	11
6-0	4-0	Swindon Town	16	0	2	14	8	53	2

1902/03 Division One

h	a		p	w	d	l	f	a	pts
0-2	0-2	Portsmouth	16	10	4	2	34	14	24
2-1	2-5	Bristol Rovers	16	9	2	5	36	22	20
1-1	0-4	Southampton	16	7	6	3	32	20	20
0-0	0-1	Tottenham Hotspur	16	6	7	3	20	14	19
2-2	1-2	Millwall Athletic	16	6	3	7	23	29	15
0-1	0-1	Reading	16	7	0	9	20	21	14
4-0	0-2	Queen's Park Rangers	16	6	2	8	18	31	14
2-4	3-6	Brentford	16	3	4	9	16	34	10
-	-	WEST HAM UNITED	16	2	4	10	15	29	8

1903/04 Division One

h	a		p	w	d	l	f	a	pts
0-1	1-4	Tottenham Hotspur	16	11	3	2	32	12	25
0-0	0-3	Southampton	16	9	3	4	30	18	21
0-1	2-3	Plymouth Argyle	16	8	4	4	22	18	20
0-1	0-3	Portsmouth	16	7	2	7	24	22	16
2-4	0-0	Brentford	16	6	4	6	19	23	16
2-1	1-3	Queen's Park Rangers	16	5	5	6	15	21	15
1-1	1-1	Reading	16	4	4	8	16	26	12
2-0	1-5	Bristol Rovers	16	4	3	9	29	29	11
-	-	WEST HAM UNITED	16	2	4	10	13	31	8

1904/05 Division One

h	a		p	w	d	l	f	a	pts
1-1	2-2	Plymouth Argyle	20	13	4	3	52	18	30
1-2	1-2	Brentford	20	11	6	3	30	22	28
1-0	0-8	Southampton	20	11	2	7	45	22	24
4-2	0-4	Portsmouth	20	10	3	7	29	30	23
-	-	WEST HAM UNITED	20	8	4	8	37	42	20
2-2	2-3	Fulham	20	7	3	10	29	32	17
4-3	0-4	Millwall	20	7	3	10	32	40	17
1-1	1-0	Tottenham Hotspur	20	5	6	9	20	28	16
3-0	0-2	Reading	20	6	3	11	27	37	15
6-0	1-5	Bristol Rovers	20	7	1	12	32	44	15
5-0	2-1	Queen's Park Rangers	20	6	3	11	27	45	15

1905/06 Division One

h	a		p	w	d	l	f	a	pts
3-0	2-4	Queen's Park Rangers	20	11	4	5	33	27	26
1-1	2-5	Southampton	20	10	5	5	41	35	25
3-2	2-3	Plymouth Argyle	20	8	8	4	34	23	24
4-1	0-1	Tottenham Hotspur	20	7	7	6	28	17	21
0-0	1-6	Bristol Rovers	20	8	3	9	34	34	19
1-2	0-0	Millwall	20	7	5	8	28	29	19
0-0	3-3	Portsmouth	20	6	7	7	26	29	19
-	-	WEST HAM UNITED	20	7	5	8	32	35	19
2-1	2-3	Reading	20	6	6	8	28	35	18
1-0	1-2	Fulham	20	5	5	10	23	32	15
2-1	2-0	Brentford	20	6	3	11	25	36	15

1906/07 Division 1(B)

h	a		p	w	d	l	f	a	pts
-	-	WEST HAM UNITED	10	7	1	2	25	14	15
6-2	0-3	Plymouth Argyle	10	5	1	4	17	12	11
3-3	3-2	Portsmouth	10	5	1	4	16	19	11
5-0	0-4	Tottenham Hotspur	10	4	1	5	13	15	9
3-0	1-0	Southampton	10	3	1	6	14	16	7
1-0	3-0	Millwall	10	2	3	5	7	16	7

Championship Decider
West Ham United beat Fulham 1-0 at Stamford Bridge on 15th April 1907, attendance 10,000

1907/08 Division 1(B)

h	a		p	w	d	l	f	a	pts
1-1	0-3	Millwall	12	9	2	1	31	13	20
1-3	1-2	Tottenham Hotspur	12	7	0	5	26	15	14
3-0	3-4	Bristol Rovers	12	6	2	4	22	29	14
1-2	0-1	Luton Town	12	4	4	4	16	21	12
2-3	2-4	Reading	12	4	3	5	20	25	11
1-2	1-2	Crystal Palace	12	3	4	5	16	17	10
-	-	WEST HAM UNITED	12	1	1	10	16	27	3

1908/09 Division 1(B)

h	a		p	w	d	l	f	a	pts
1-3	0-2	Millwall	12	8	2	2	24	11	18
3-4	1-2	Southampton	12	7	0	5	20	20	14
0-1	1-2	Plymouth Argyle	12	6	1	5	12	13	13
2-4	3-2	Portsmouth	12	5	2	5	21	21	12
-	-	WEST HAM UNITED	12	5	0	7	21	23	10
4-2	4-1	Bristol Rovers	12	4	1	7	16	23	9
1-0	1-0	Brentford	12	3	2	7	10	13	8

LONDON LEAGUE

West Ham's first team played for three seasons in the newly formed Premier Division of the London League. They were champions in 1901/02.

1901/02

h	a		p	w	d	l	f	a	pts
-	-	WEST HAM UNITED	8	5	1	2	18	9	11
3-1	2-2	Tottenham Hotspur	8	3	3	2	15	13	9
4-0	5-1	Millwall Athletic	8	2	4	2	9	13	8
2-1	1-2	Queen's Park Rangers	8	2	2	4	11	14	6
0-2	1-0	Woolwich Arsenal	8	2	2	4	9	13	6

1902/03

h	a		p	w	d	l	f	a	pts
0-0	0-4	Tottenham Hotspur	10	7	1	2	19	4	15
-	-	WEST HAM UNITED	10	5	3	2	15	13	13
1-3	1-0	Woolwich Arsenal	10	6	0	4	14	10	12
2-2	2-2	Millwall Athletic	10	3	4	3	18	14	10
1-0	2-0	Queen's Park Rangers	10	2	3	5	9	15	7
3-0	3-2	Brentford	10	1	1	8	9	28	3

1903/04

h	a		p	w	d	l	f	a	pts
0-3	0-4	Millwall	12	11	1	0	38	8	23
0-2	0-1	Tottenham Hptspur	12	7	1	4	23	14	15
2-4	1-4	Woolwich Arsenal	12	6	2	4	24	19	14
1-1	1-5	Queen's Park Rangers	12	5	2	5	18	23	12
2-3	2-2	Brentford	12	2	3	7	16	19	7
3-1	2-1	Fulham	12	3	1	8	13	29	7
-	-	WEST HAM UNITED	12	2	2	8	14	31	6

APPENDIX

On seven separate occasions West Ham United met teams from the First Division of the Football League in the FA Cup that would achieve either a Cup Final place or finish as champions during those respective seasons:

1900/01 Round 1 Liverpool	0-1	Liverpool Champions 1900/01
1906/07 Round 2 Everton	1-2	Everton FA Cup Runners up 1906/07
1907/08 Round 2 Newcastle Utd	0-2	Newcastle FA Cup Runners up 1907/08
1908/09 Round 3 Newcastle Utd	1-2	Newcastle Champions 1908/09
1910/11 Round 3 Manchester Utd	2-1	Manchester Utd Champions 1910/11
1912/13 Round 2 Aston Villa	0-5	Aston Villa FA Cup winners 1912/13
1913/14 Round 3 Liverpool	1-5	Liverpool FA Cup Runners up 1913/14

George Kitchen's remarkable record of penalty kicks saved and those scored is as follows:

	Southern	Western	FA Cup	Friendly	Total
Penalties saved	6	1		1	8
Penalties conceded	5		1		6
Penalties scored	5	2	1	1	9
Penalties missed	2	1			3

A fine record for a goalkeeper with a frame of 6ft 1in and 13st!

West Ham players who served in HM Forces in World War One:

Herbert Ashton (1908-15)	R F C (mechanic)
Dan Bailey (1912-21)	Army in Egypt
Frank Burton (1912-21)	Royal Fusiliers (received shrapnel wounds)
Frank Cannon (1909-10)	Killed in action Feb 1916
James Carr (1914-15)	Army service
Frank Costello (1908-09)	Killed in action 1915
Albert Denyer (1912-1914)	Served in Sportsman Battalion
Fred Griffiths (1901-03)	Sherwood Foresters. Killed in action October 1917
Fred Harrison (1910-13)	Suffered gas poisoning in France
George Hilsdon (1904-15)	Suffered gas poisoning in France
William Jones (1901-02)	Killed in action in Serbia May 1918
William Kennedy (1910-12)	Killed in action
William Kirby (1903-04)	Served with Royal Engineers
Arthur Stallard (1913-15)	Killed in action November 1917
Joe Webster (1914-20)	Served in Footballers Battalion

AFTERWORD

In June 1900, just a few days before West Ham United was born, but many years before "I'm Forever Blowing Bubbles" was sung on the terraces, the following article appeared in the local West Ham Guardian:

PREHISTORIC WEST HAM

Blowing bubbles was a common amusement, and the consequent demand for soap probably led to the foundation of the huge soap factories which exist in our midst, both in North West Ham and South. When each bubble was blown it was named after some political or social theory, or some fable, these theories or fables being only being only so much wind. It is true the people could have carried out many of their ideals if they had liked, instead of making soap bubbles of them, only somehow or other they didn't put enough energy behind their aspirations, and so things went on mostly in the old groove .... However the bubbles were really rather beautiful, and looking at them was an occupation which passed many a pleasant hour. All I say is that people ... liked to look at bubbles. So do I. When you think what a bubble is, in its scientific, mathematical, ethical, and aesthetic aspects, and how out of a puff of breath and a film of soapsuds you can evolve a phenomenon upon which many learned treatises have been written, in regard to the causes of its sphericity, the colouration and varying thickness and tension of the film etc, etc. I say, when you come to think of all this you will cease to wonder why one of the earliest diversions of our youth should continue to charm us in our maturity, whether we blow the bubbles ourselves or watch those that are blown by other people.

Therefore I don't want to be hard on the prehistoric gentleman who is the subject of our sketch, nor yet is it my intention to lead you to suppose that he was always engaged in the fascinating pursuit of bubble-blowing, or that he was the only person of public consequence who indulged in it. I suppose the sketch was preserved because this particular prehistoric person sometimes prided himself on his expertness in the art of dazzling the crowd with brilliant displays of an iridescent if transient nature.

'There you are, old dear,' he would observe, to anybody who happened to be looking on, 'did you ever see such a magnificent bubble as that? There's a whacker for you. Big as a balloon, isn't it?' 'Very fine indeed,'. the person addressed would reply. 'How do you manage to do it?' Then the expert would wink and say, 'Diplomacy, old dear. It wants a little diplomacy, you know, to produce things like that. Look at the splendid colours now ...' At this point the bubble would burst, but the expert, nothing daunted, would at once blow another, and dozens more for that matter. 'It was one down, another come on.'

BIBLIOGRAPHY

The Definitive West Ham United, John Northcutt, SoccerData, 2003
Iron in the Blood (Thames Ironworks), John Powles, SoccerData 2005
West Ham United, Charles Korr, Gerald Duckworth & Co. Ltd, 1986
Who's Who of West Ham United 1895-2005, Tony Hogg, Profile Sports Media, 2005
West Ham United, A Complete Record, Northcutt & Shoesmith, Breedon Books, 1993
Southern League Football, The First Fifty Years, Paul Harrison, 1989
The Southern League First Division 1894-1920 AFS Publications 1984
Football League Players' Records 1888-1939, Michael Joyce, SoccerData, 2002
Fulham Facts & Figures 1879-1998, Turner & White, Northdown Publishing, 1998
The Football Manager – A History, Neil Carter, Routledge, 2006
They Took The Lead, (Clapton Orient), Stephen Jenkins, DDP One Stop UK Ltd, 2005
The Story of Association Football, (Classic Reprint), Soccer Books Ltd, 2006
The Book of Football, Amalgamated Press 1906
Association Football & The Men Who Made It, Gibson & Pickford, 1905
The Leaguers, Matthew Taylor, Liverpool University Press, 2005
A History of the English Schools' FA 1904-2004 Colm Kerrigan EFSA:London 2004

Athletic News
East End News
East Ham Echo
Football Chat
Football News
Football Sun
Morning Leader
The Sportsman
Stratford Express
West Ham Guardian
The Footballer
Soccer History
Hammers Monthly 1982
West London Observer
Reading Observer
Southend Telegraph
Merthyr Express & Advertiser
Bristol Athletic News

West Ham United team group photographs and other material from the collections of Steve Marsh and Stuart Allen can be found on the web site at www.theyflysohigh.piczo.com

By the same author:

IRON IN THE BLOOD
ISBN 978-1-899468-22-5

The Thames Ironworks was a major employer in the Canning Town area of East London until 1912. Its products included ships for the Royal Navy, linings for the Blackwall Tunnel and iron bridges. Some of the employees, such as boilermakers and ship's platers, began to play organised football in the 1890s. As ambitions grew for the football club, professional players were employed. This eventually led to the Works withdrawing its support and the club we know today as West Ham United was then formed.

John Powles' book tells the story of these formative years. Full statistical details of the games played by Thames Ironworks are included, with pen pictures of the principal players. His account of the club is interwoven with events of the time in the Works and in East London generally.

Copies are available from Newham bookshops and by post from the publisher. If ordering by post, please send a cheque or postal order for £12 (which includes postage and packing) payable to Tony Brown to the address on the title page of this book.